PSYCHOLOGY AND THE BIBLE

PSYCHOLOGY AND THE BIBLE

A New Way to Read the Scriptures

VOLUME 4
From Christ to Jesus

Edited by
J. Harold Ellens and Wayne G. Rollins

Foreword by Donald Capps

PRAEGER PERSPECTIVES

Psychology, Religion, and Spirituality

Westport, Connecticut
London

Library of Congress Cataloging-in-Publication Data

Psychology and the Bible: a new way to read the Scriptures / edited by J. Harold Ellens
and Wayne G. Rollins; foreword by Donald Capps.
    p. cm.—(Psychology, religion, and spirituality, ISSN 1546–8070)
   Includes bibliographical references and index.
   Contents: v. 1. From Freud to Kohut—v. 2. From Genesis to apocalyptic vision—v. 3.
From Gospel to Gnostics—v. 4. From Christ to Jesus.
   ISBN 0-275-98347-1 (set : alk paper)—ISBN 0-275-98348-X (v. 1 : alk paper)—
ISBN 0-275-98349-8 (v. 2 : alk paper)—ISBN 0-275-98350-1 (v. 3 : alk paper)—
ISBN 0-275-98462-1 (v. 4 : alk paper)
   1. Bible—Psychology.   2. Psychoanalysis and religion.   I. Ellens, J. Harold, 1932–
II. Rollins, Wayne G.   III. Series.
BS645.P89 2004
220.6′01′9—dc22   2004050863

British Library Cataloguing in Publication Data is available.

Library of Congress Catalog Card Number: 2004050863

ISBN: 0–275–98347–1 (set)
       0–275–98348–X (vol. I)
       0–275–98349–8 (vol. II)
       0–275–98350–1 (vol. III)
       0–275–98462–1 (vol. IV)
ISSN: 1546-8070

First published in 2004

Praeger Publishers, 88 Post Road West, Westport, CT 06881
An imprint of Greenwood Publishing Group, Inc.
www.praeger.com

Printed in the United States of America

The paper used in this book complies with the
Permanent Paper Standard issued by the
National Information Standards Organization (Z39.48–1984).

10 9 8 7 6 5 4 3 2 1

Copyright Acknowledgment

Contents

Foreword

Donald Capps

I learned about the psychological study of the Bible as a PhD student, when, in a psychology of religion course taught by David Bakan, I was introduced to an essentially psychoanalytic approach to the Bible. Before that, despite two years of intensive graduate study, not one of my professors had ever breathed a word about the psychological study of the Bible. Even in Bakan's course, the idea that the Bible could be approached psychologically seemed idiosyncratic and odd, yet strangely compelling. At the time, Bakan was mostly interested in what he called the "infanticidal impulse," the desire of adults to kill children, and he viewed the story of Abraham and Isaac in Genesis 22 as illustrative not only of the infanticidal impulse itself but also of its displacement through animal sacrifice (see Bakan, 1968).

I might not have gotten hooked by this field of study had my introduction to it involved merely abstract theorizing, or had I not been introduced to it when young men were being sent by their political fathers to fight in a controversial war in Vietnam. In any case, I did get hooked, and the psychological study of the Bible has been the primary, perhaps the sole, means by which I have remained faithful to the religious legacy that was imparted to me as a child. I am sure that many others whose work is presented in these four volumes could make similar testimonies to the personal value and importance of the psychological study of the Bible and would subscribe to the view that the way to renewed faith and trust is not around but through psychology.

The field of the psychological study of the Bible has come a very long way since my introduction to it in the mid-1960s. As Wayne G. Rollins documents in *Soul and Psyche: The Bible in Psychological Perspective*, a "sheaf of articles and books in the late 1960s and early 1970s appeared from within the orbit of biblical scholarship," calling "for a fresh look at the contributions psychological and psychoanalytic research might bring to the task of biblical interpretation" (1999, 68). Many scholars both within biblical studies and in fields such as the psychology of religion, which had manifested considerable but erratic interest in the Bible in previous decades, responded to this call. Over the next two decades, so much interest had been generated that in 1991 the Society of Biblical Literature approved a proposal to establish a program unit on Psychology and Biblical Studies. This program unit would assess the significance of the approaches employed to date and would provide a forum for developing the future agenda of psychological criticism as a subdiscipline within biblical studies. The faithfulness with which these responsibilities have been carried out accounts to a large extent for the fact that, some thirteen years later, J. Harold Ellens and Wayne G. Rollins had little difficulty finding willing contributors to this four-volume collection titled *Psychology and the Bible*.

Both editors of these volumes have offered their own characterizations of the field. In a special issue on psychology and the Bible in *Pastoral Psychology*, a journal whose editor, Lewis R. Rambo, has been unusually receptive to psychological studies of biblical texts, J. Harold Ellens, who guest edited the issue, assessed the state of the field and clarified its focus. In his guest editorial, "Psychology and the Bible: The Interface of Corollary Disciplines" (1997a), he pointed out that, beginning in the early 1960s, a consciously crafted critique of the positivist assumptions of the Enlightenment had given rise to interest in interdisciplinary studies, and that one of the most significant of these was the application of interdisciplinary approaches using scientific models and methods for investigation of religious traditions, practices, and experiences. As one such scientific discipline, psychology has played an increasingly important role in these interdisciplinary approaches. As Ellens notes, "we found ourselves teaching courses and doing research in the sociology of religion, the psychology of religion, the Bible in Western literary traditions, psychotheology, psychospirituality, transcendental psychology, and the like. This undertaking was influenced, as well, by the birth of sturdy concerns to investigate the interface of many of the great religions of the world, particularly the encounter between Eastern and Western psychology and spirituality" (1997a, 159–160).

In his essay "The Bible and Psychology: An Interdisciplinary Pilgrimage" in the same issue of *Pastoral Psychology*, Ellens noted that one of the fruitful products of this new interest in interdisciplinary studies was the publication of many significant books and articles on the interface between the disciplines of psychology, theology, and biblical studies, and suggested that the focus of interdisciplinary work in psychology and biblical studies is that of bringing "the insights and models of psychology to bear upon a biblical text, assessing the nature and function of the author, of the implied or stated intended audience, of the real audiences in the church's history which interpreted the text, together with their interpretations, and thus assess the reasons, healthy or pathological, for the constructs that were expressed in the text and in subsequent uses of it" (1997b, 206). Note, here, the assumption that biblical texts have not only been used—misused—to legitimate pathological ideas and behaviors, but that the original texts themselves may also reflect pathological as well as healthy ways of thinking and behaving.

A very tangible reflection of this understanding of what psychology may contribute to biblical studies is the recent publication of four volumes titled *The Destructive Power of Religion: Violence in Judaism, Christianity, and Islam* (2004), edited by Ellens. One of the four volumes is devoted exclusively to sacred scriptures. In his own essay "Toxic Texts," Ellens notes that "sacred scriptures motivate ordinary people to amazing achievements in spirituality, religion, and cultural creativity." By the same token, "the inspiration of sacred scriptures can also be devastatingly destructive, spiritually, psychologically, and culturally" (2004, 3:1–2). To illustrate their destructive side, he explores the story in John 9 about Jesus' healing of a man who was born blind, noting that this text "is generally prized by Bible scholars and religious devotees," yet it "has a dangerous subtext or underside that has been ignored," a subtext that "can have a destructive effect on persons, communities, and cultures by the negative archetypes that it may generate at the unconscious psychological level" (2).

In "Rationale and Agenda for a Psychological-Critical Approach to the Bible and Its Interpretation, Biblical and Humane" (1996), published at nearly the same time as Ellens's two *Pastoral Psychology* articles, Wayne G. Rollins identified what he termed "a psychological-critical approach" to the Bible. The goal of this approach "is to examine texts (including their origination, authorship, and modes of expression, their construction, transmission, translation, reading, and interpretation, their transposition into kindred and alien art forms, and the history of their personal and cultural effect) as expressions of the structure, processes, and habits of the human psyche, both in individual and collective manifestations, past and present" (1996, 160). Key here is the understanding that the original texts, their transmission, and their transposition into other forms are all expressions of the human psyche, its cognitive and emotional structures and processes, its habits of mind and heart.

Three years later, in *Soul and Psyche*, which comprehensively reviews both past and present work in this burgeoning interdisciplinary field, Rollins cited a third effort to characterize the field and commended it for its accuracy and succinctness. This is Antoine Vergote's proposal that the purpose of psychological biblical criticism is "to understand the mental universe of the biblical tradition" (1999, 78). Building on the idea that the "mental universe" of the biblical tradition is its appropriate focus, Rollins went on to suggest that the fundamental premise that informs research in the field of psychological biblical criticism and that constitutes the insight that gave birth to the discipline can be stated as follows: "From a biblical-critical perspective, the Bible is to be seen as part and product, not only of a historical, literary, and socioanthropological process, but also of a psychological process. In this process, conscious and unconscious factors are at work in the biblical authors and their communities, in the texts they have produced, in readers and interpreters of these texts and in their communities, and in the individual, communal, and cultural effects of these interpretations" (1999, 92).

This premise not only includes the view that the Bible is part and product of "a psychological process" but also introduces the idea, emphasized by psychodynamic theorists such as Freud, Jung, and their followers, that both conscious and unconscious factors are at work in this process. Thus, one of the primary purposes of the "psychological-critical approach" is to make that which is unconscious conscious. Rollins goes on, however, to emphasize that what is especially under examination in a psychological-critical approach "is the *psychological context* and *psychological content* of the Bible and its interpretation" (1999, 93). Together, these two prongs of critical examination have the larger objective of enhancing the repertory of critical perspectives on the Bible (historical, literary, socioanthropological) "by adding to it a vision of the text as itself a psychic product, reality, symptom, and event, and as a source of commentary on the nature, life, habits, pathology, health, and purpose of the psyche/soul" (1999, 94). Thus, endorsing Ellens's view that a central focus of interdisciplinary work in psychology and biblical studies is to "assess the reasons, healthy or pathological, for the constructs that were expressed in the text and in subsequent uses of it," Rollins suggests that in addition to being "a source of commentary" on matters of pathology and health, the Bible, as itself a psychic product, may reveal both healthy and pathological mental and emotional structures and processes.

Because one of my own special interests is the pathogenic character-istic of some biblical texts, I am both impressed and encouraged by the fact that whether explicitly or implicitly, the essays included in these four volumes are concerned with the pathology and health of the psy-chological process at work in the biblical authors and their communi-ties and in their subsequent interpreters. For Rollins, as for Ellens, this concern is part of the second of two agendas in the psychological study of the Bible, the exegetical and the hermeneutical. In a section of his chapter "The Hermeneutical Agenda" in *Soul and Psyche*, bear-ing the heading "The History of Biblical Effects in Psychological Per-spective: Pathogenic and Therapeutic Effects," Rollins notes: "It is no longer a secret in scholarly and even ecclesiastical literature that the Bible and its interpretation can have pathogenic effects on individuals and cultures—an acknowledgment that has been both liberating and dismaying for those who treasure the text" (1999, 175).

By the same token, the very recognition of the pathogenic effects of the Bible and its interpretation has reawakened interest in its thera-peutic effects:

> Scholarly interest in the pathogenic aspects of the Bible has been matched at the end of the twentieth century with renewed interest in its therapeutic dimension. As much as the Bible provides evidence of patho-genic potential, even more does it provide evidence that it can transform consciousness, change behavior patterns, and open up a new cognition of reality in ways that have affected individuals and shaped entire cul-tures for generations. (Rollins, 1999, 177)

Rollins concludes that a major undertaking for psychological biblical criticism in the future

> will be to develop a critical method for identifying, measuring, and assessing the degree to which the text presents itself as the mediator of a therapeutic agenda, to come to an understanding of the strategies it recommends for achieving this agenda, to compare it with contempo-rary therapeutic models, and to consider what insight it can add to col-lective scholarship and thought on the *cura animarum* in our own time. (1999, 179)

   Although the psychological-critical approach to the Bible has much
in common with other critical approaches, these other approaches
are not as likely to give sustained or systematic attention to the
fact that the Bible has both pathogenic and therapeutic aspects. The
psychological-critical method bears a special responsibility for recognizing and pointing out the difference. Attempts throughout history to
make the case that certain biblical texts have priority over other biblical
texts because they are more central to the Bible's own intentionality—
the so-called canon within the canon—have been exposed as misleading and self-serving. However, those who endorse (as I myself do) the
view of the editors of these four volumes that the psychological study
of the Bible entails the assessment of the pathogenic and therapeutic
aspects of biblical texts may well accord the healing stories in the New
Testament Gospels a special status as a "source of commentary" on
matters of health and pathology, and thus as valuable in their own
right for assessing the healthy and pathological constructs in other
biblical texts and interpretations thereof. This means that it is not
merely a matter of bringing twenty-first-century understandings of
health and pathology to bear on biblical texts—after all, these understandings are implicated in the very constructs that they intend to
assess—but also of using the biblical tradition's own understandings
of what makes for health and pathology to assess its own psychological processes. Perhaps this is why Erik H. Erikson could both endorse
the spirit of Thomas Jefferson's attempt to provide Native Americans
an abridged version of "the philosophy of Jesus of Nazareth" extracted
from the four Gospels and critique his decision to eliminate "all references to Jesus' healing mission" (Erikson, 1974, 40–50).

   Finally, the very fact that the Bible continues to have an emotional
as well as intellectual attraction even for those of us who acknowledge
its pathogenic features is itself a question that invites and warrants
psychological examination and assessment. Three or four years before
I was introduced to the psychological study of the Bible, I read Erik H.
Erikson's *Young Man Luther: A Study in Psychoanalysis and History*
(1958). This book—which, with its advocacy of a psychohistorical
method attuned to religious themes, was itself an indirect contributor
to the development of the psychological study of the Bible field—
advances a psychological theory of the attraction that the Bible held
for Luther. I suggest that this theory may have wide application
and that it may be one of several emotional links creating a bond
between all of the essays (and essayists) in these four volumes. The
theory occurs in the midst of a discussion of Luther's "passivity," which

Erikson emphasizes is not mere indifference but the activation of perceptions and their emotional counterparts that existed before Luther's—and other children's—development of will and willfulness. Thus, it is the "passivity" of active reception, the kind of reception that occurs when readers allow a biblical text to "speak" to them. Erikson asks:

> Is it coincidence that Luther, now that he was explicitly teaching passivity, should come to the conclusion that a lecturer should feed his audience as a mother suckles her child? Intrinsic to the kind of passivity we speak of is not only the memory of having been given, but also the identification with the maternal giver: "the glory of a good thing is that it flows out to others." *I think that in the Bible Luther at last found a mother whom he could acknowledge: he could attribute to the Bible a generosity to which he could open himself, and which he could pass on to others, at last a mother's son.* (1958, 208, my emphasis)

Noting that Luther spoke of being reborn "out of the matrix of the scriptures," Erikson adds, "matrix is as close as such a man's man will come to saying 'mater'" (208).

As we have seen, for editors Ellens and Rollins, the psychological process to which the psychological-critical approach attends occurs in the biblical authors and their communities, in the texts they have produced, in the readers and interpreters of these texts and in their communities, and in the individual, communal, and cultural effects of these interpretations. This psychological process *is* the very matrix of the Scriptures. Thus, the essays included in these four volumes attest to the generosity of the Bible, to the fact that it is, indeed, the "good book" (although by no means perfect book) that richly rewards those who come to examine it, assess it, and take its measure. Undoubtedly, its greatest rewards are reserved for those who are unabashedly— perhaps hopelessly—in love with it. In the course of reading these essays, the reader will find, however, that examination, assessment, and love—all three together—are integral to the psychological process to which the Bible itself gives testimony.

Decades from now, our successors will surely wonder how such a monumental undertaking as these four volumes on psychology and the Bible could ever have come about. This undertaking is a reflection of the organizational and administrative acumen that the two editors have also displayed in their work on behalf of the Psychology and Biblical Studies program unit of the Society of Biblical Literature. It is also a tribute to the respect in which they are held by their colleagues. But these four volumes also testify to the editors' exquisite sense of timing. As Jesus' own illustration of the children in the marketplace attests (Matt. 11:16–17), one can pipe a tune, but if no one is either willing or able to dance, nothing much happens. According to my count, aside from the editors themselves, thirty-two responded to their invitation to write essays, and some more than once. Had Abraham done even half as well, the city of Sodom would have been spared. Ellens and Rollins clearly discerned that there are scholars out there who, if asked, are not only willing but able to set aside their inhibitions and fear of self-embarrassment and to venture out on the dance floor, secure in the knowledge that there is safety in numbers. May this monumental undertaking inspire others to make a similar venture.

References

Bakan, D. (1966). *The Duality of Human Existence: An Essay on Psychology and Religion.* Chicago: Rand McNally.

Bakan, D. (1968). *Disease, Pain, and Sacrifice: Toward a Psychology of Suffering.* Chicago: University of Chicago Press.

Ellens, J. H. (1997a). Psychology and the Bible: The Interface of Corollary Disciplines. *Pastoral Psychology, 45,* 159–162.

Ellens, J. H. (1997b). The Bible and Psychology: An Interdisciplinary Pilgrimage. *Pastoral Psychology, 45,* 193–209.

Ellens, J. H., ed. (2004). *The Destructive Power of Religion: Violence in Judaism, Christianity, and Islam* (4 vols.). Westport: Praeger Publishers.

Erikson, E. H. (1958). *Young Man Luther: A Study in Psychoanalysis and History.* New York: Norton.

Erikson, E. H. (1974). *Dimensions of a New Identity.* New York: Norton.

Rollins, W. G. (1996). *Rationale and Agenda for a Psychological-Critical Approach to the Bible and Its Interpretation, Biblical and Humane,* D. Barr, L. B. Elder, & E. S. Malbon, eds. Atlanta: Scholars Press, 153–172.

Rollins, W. G. (1999). *Soul and Psyche: The Bible in Psychological Perspective.* Minneapolis: Fortress.

Series Foreword

J. Harold Ellens, PhD

The interface between psychology, religion, and spirituality has been of great interest to scholars for a century. In the last three decades a broad popular appetite has developed for books that make practical sense out of the sophisticated research on these three subjects. Freud expressed an essentially deconstructive perspective on this matter and indicated that he saw the relationship between human psychology and religion to be a destructive interaction. Jung, on the other hand, was quite sure that these three aspects of the human spirit—psychology, religion, and spirituality—were constructively and inextricably linked. Anton Boisen and Seward Hiltner derived much insight from both Freud and Jung, as well as from Adler and Reik, while pressing the matter forward with gratifying skill and illumination. Boisen and Hiltner fashioned a framework within which the quest for a sound and sensible definition of the interface between psychology, religion, and spirituality might best be described or expressed (Aden & Ellens, 1990). We are in their debt.

This set of general interest books, so wisely urged by Greenwood Press, and particularly by its editor Debbie Carvalko, defines the terms and explores the interface of psychology, religion, and spirituality at the operational level of daily human experience. Each volume in the set identifies, analyzes, describes, and evaluates the full range of issues, of both popular and professional interest, that deal with the psychological factors at play in the way religion takes shape and is expressed, in the way spirituality functions within human persons and shapes both religious formation and expression, and in the ways that spirituality is shaped and expressed by religion. The primary interest is psychological. In terms of the rubrics of the discipline and the science of psychology, this set of superb volumes investigates the operational dynamics of religion and spirituality.

The verbs *shape* and *express* in the previous paragraph refer to the forces that prompt and form religion in persons and communities, as well as to the manifestations of religious behavior in personal forms of spirituality, in acts of spiritually motivated care for society, and in ritual behaviors such as liturgies of worship. In these various aspects of human function, the psychological drivers are identified, isolated, and described in terms of the way they unconsciously and consciously operate in religion and spirituality.

The books in this set are written for the general reader, the local library, and the undergraduate university student. They are also of significant interest to the informed professional, particularly in corollary fields. The volumes in this set have great value for clinical settings and treatment models as well.

This series editor has spent an entire professional lifetime focused specifically on research into the interface of psychology, religion, and spirituality. These matters are of the highest urgency in human affairs today, when religious motivation seems to be playing an increasing role, constructively and destructively, in the arena of social ethics, national politics, and world affairs. It is imperative that we find out immediately what the psychopathological factors are that shape a religion that can launch deadly assaults on the World Trade Center in New York and murder 3,500 people, or a religion that motivates suicide bombers to kill themselves and murder dozens of their neighbors weekly, or a religion that prompts such unjust national policies as preemptive defense—all of which are wreaking havoc on the social fabric, the democratic processes, the domestic tranquility, the economic stability and productivity, and the legitimate right to freedom from fear in every nation in the world today.

Of course not all of the influences of religion now or throughout history have been negative. Indeed, most of the impact of the great religions upon human life and culture has been profoundly redemptive and generative of great good. It is just as urgent, therefore, that we discover and understand better what the psychological forces are that empower people of faith and genuine spirituality to give themselves to all the creative and constructive enterprises that, throughout the centuries, have made of human life the humane, ordered, prosperous, and aesthetic experience it can be at its best. Surely the forces for good in both psychology and spirituality far exceed the powers and proclivities toward the evil that we see so prominently in our world today.

This set of Greenwood Press volumes is dedicated to the greater understanding of psychology, religion, and spirituality, and thus to the profound understanding and empowerment of those psycho-spiritual drivers that can help us transcend the malignancy of our pilgrimage and enormously enhance the humaneness and majesty of the human spirit, indeed, the potential for magnificence in human life.

Reference

Aden, L., & Ellens, J. H. (1990). *Turning Points in Pastoral Care: The Legacy of Anton Boisen and Seward Hiltner*. Grand Rapids: Baker.

CHAPTER 1

INTRODUCTION

J. Harold Ellens and Wayne G. Rollins

"There was a great teacher, and gathered around him was a small group of faithful followers. They listened to his message and were transformed by it. But the message alienated the power structure of his time, which finally put him to death but did not succeed in eradicating his message, which is stronger now than ever." That description would apply equally to Jesus and Socrates. But nobody's ever built a cathedral in honor of Socrates.

—J. Pelikan (1985, 17)

Christ would never have made the impression he did on his followers if he had not expressed something that was alive and at work in their unconscious. Christianity itself would never have spread through the pagan world with such astonishing rapidity had its ideas not found an analogous psychic readiness to receive them.

—C. G. Jung (1953–1978, 11:713)

A riddle lies at both ends of the spectrum between the historical figure of Jesus of Nazareth and the imperial figure of the Christ as *pantokrator*, creator of all things. The former is now enshrined in a panoply of recent scholarly books. The latter may be found readily, resplendent in gold leaf in the rotunda of a Byzantine church. The riddle at the more recent end is how the "divine man" emerged from the historical man. The riddle at the far end is how the historical man gave birth to the manifold glories of the "divine man." Both riddles are profoundly psychological. They are rooted in a process of great interest to those of us in psychology and biblical studies, namely, the psychic process by which a Galilean teacher, or as John Meier describes him, a "marginal Jew," is spoken of as the Word, the Truth, the Light, Son of God, Saviour, the Anointed One (*Christos*); all within a century of his birth. How did he so quickly come to be identified as the embodiment of the ultimate purpose that informs all creation?

Such a development illustrates a habit of the psyche evident in all religious traditions, namely the irrepressible urge and need to capture in archetypal imagery the immense meaning that a figure like the Jesus of history has catalyzed in the human mind, imagination, and will. Jesus quickly became much more than he ever was, which is the legitimate psychological function of any tradition that finds a treasure and wants to refract its worth in images that pass it on, images that express the world of discourse and experience of the tradents. It is widely assumed by biblical scholars that one of the reasons Jesus never wrote anything down, nor asked to have anything written down, is that he was suspicious of the inflated projections made on the written word (John 5:39). A second factor is that he trusted the power of the human soul and the human imagination to take the ball, run with it, and do interesting new things. The Gospel of John reports of Jesus telling his disciples that they would do "greater works" than those he had done (John 14:12). His parables, his style of teaching, and his invitations to run-of-the-mill entrepreneurial fishermen all point to Jesus' trust in the lively processes at work in the human soul. As William Sloane Coffin remarked, "It is a mistake to look to the Bible to close a discussion; the Bible seeks to open one" (Coffin, 1999, 49). In similar fashion, Jesus' business was never to provide final answers to questions nor shut down debate, but to get the juices running along with the moral and spiritual imagination in the hearer, each in his or her own voice and personal way. The result in Christendom is described by Yale historical theologian Jaroslav Pelikan in *Jesus through the Centuries: His Place in the History of Culture*. This book takes us through the past twenty centuries, listing the dozens of images that seemed appropriate to the art and imagination of one generation after another, for capturing what the man from Galilee had catalyzed in their visions from "rabbi" to King of Kings; from "cosmic Christ" to the universal man; from Prince of Peace to the liberator; and from the "mirror of the eternal" to the teacher of common sense (Pelikan, 1985). However, it is at the distant end of the Christ–Jesus continuum that the story of this volume begins. Its authors want to get back to the primordial event. We want to smell the turf and unveil some of the psychodynamics in the life of the Galilean, vis-à-vis John the Baptist, Peter, the disciples, the structures of power, women, tax men, religious authority, marginalized humans, even Mary Magdalene. We want to observe the ways he related to issues of sexuality, religion, the wilderness experience, and his own fatherlessness. We want to move away from the mythic, archetypal, symbolic, celebrative super-structure of Nicene Christianity. We want to set in stark relief the ordinary moment in time, like all other ordinary moments, in their diurnal simplicity; even homeliness, in which a person like Jesus appears and lets something loose with an archetypal power that is too subtle to identify but too powerful to ignore. We want to look at that moment through the lens of psychology, with "psychological realism" as Hal Childs, a clinical psychologist and biblical scholar, calls it, delineating the outlines of the man in history, always wondering what it was in this original event, this real human being, that smacked of the holy and inspired those around him to holiness. These psychological questions about the psychodynamics at work in every human situation, including the past, are part of the set of tools the historian must use when trying to comprehend the realities in any human setting.

The present volume, fourth in this set on *Psychology and the Bible: A New Way to Read the Scriptures*, focuses on a psychological approach to the Gospel accounts of the life of Jesus of Nazareth. It opens with a review of the "Jesus Quest" as a major wing of New Testament research, followed by an introduction to "psychobiography," its importance and its necessity within the repertory of historical critical research. Two classic psychobiographies by Donald Capps and John Miller are presented, followed by overviews of three other "portraits," unveiled through the psychological lenses of Albert Schweitzer, Jay Haley, and Erik Erikson. It adds to this picture Andries van Aarde's reflections on Jesus as "fatherless child" and Walter Wink's archetypal focus on "the original impulse of Jesus." The volume concludes with imaginative essays by Hal Childs and Paul Anderson, who reflect on the role of the primordial figure of Jesus in the meaning he catalyzed in generations of "readers," in a kind of hermeneutical circle from Christ to Jesus, to today's reader, and back again, in a never ending process of the evolution of consciousness about that distant figure and ourselves. Nine scholars have joined us to develop this volume, all sharing the common desire to bring into focus the meaning and message of the Bible through the lens of psychology. To introduce these authors and their ideas, we offer the following brief overviews of their chapters.

Donald Capps wrote the Foreword for all four volumes in this set. Capps expresses in detail his developing interest in reading the Bible through the lens of psychology, and the great knowledge he received from Wayne Rollins's (1999) book, *Soul and Psyche: The Bible in Psychological Perspective*, Erikson's (1958) *Young Man Luther: A Study in Psychoanalysis and History*, Ellens's (1982) *God's Grace and Human Health*, and other related works.

Following this Introduction, J. H. Ellens discusses the complexities of scholarly research into the story of Jesus as a person who actually lived in history about two thousand years ago, and Jesus as a literary character who walks the pages of four Gospel narratives in the New Testament. He critiques the quest for the historical Jesus and raises two interesting and crucial questions. The first question is about whether it is possible for us to work our way back through history and see clearly, from the perspective of our own time and cultural conditioning, the person who lived in the first century C.E. Ellens refers to the definitive work of Hal Childs regarding the psychological and cultural limitations every human has to deal with in trying to understand any person or moment in history. As Childs indicates in Chapter 12 of this volume, we can never reconstruct the exact situation of a past moment, and we must always view it through the eyes of our own experience. Hence, the past person or event we think we see is only ever the one we imagine, on the basis of the limited historical data available to us. Ellens argues that we can, nonetheless, heuristically construct a model of Jesus that can be more or less accurate and trustworthy, depending on how well we qualify our sources. In the end, however, Ellens contends that the second question may be more important: What kind of character must Jesus have been to legitimately carry the freight of the stories told about him? That question drives us to the literary character of Jesus as he moves through the narrative of the Gospels, and forces us to ask what gives that narrative its constructive power and irrepressible persistence. Such a search of the literary data implies a certain conclusion about what sort of character the historical Jesus must have been to generate the Jesus story, just as it took shape in the four Gospels.

It is appropriate that such an inquiry should be followed by J. H. Charlesworth's chapter, teasing out the great variety of trajectories, methods, and models of the man from Nazareth, who was proclaimed to be the Christ of God. Charlesworth describes the rise of the First Quest for the Historical Jesus centering in the work of Albert Schweitzer, its development into the New Quest for the Historical

Jesus initiated by the work of James Robinson and Charlesworth's own early research, and its continuation in what has become the Third Quest for the Historical Jesus in which Charlesworth's recent work stands out. The great strength of Chapter 3 is that it offers us a comprehensive and articulate historical-critical overview of the long history of modern Jesus research from the mid-nineteenth century to this present moment. Moreover, Charlesworth did Jesus scholarship the great favor of developing an apologia for psychobiography as an essential component in historical-biblical criticism.

The next two chapters discuss psychological biographies of Jesus. Donald Capps claims that Jesus' illegitimacy resulted in his growing up in an alienating and shaming environment in which he suffered from having no real father until he finally found that need fulfilled, spiritually, in his perceived relationship with God. His life and ministry unfolded in terms of his seeking certification and vindication vis-à-vis the authority figures in his world, who were the identified sources of his shame in that they prevented him by Jewish law from having a legitimate place in society. Jesus identified his quest for justice and vindication with the cause and kingdom of God, asserting a preferential option for the underprivileged and socially wounded. This need to certify himself and the cause of God, his father, over the religious authorities led Jesus to the symbolic attack on the establishment through his violence in the temple. This led directly to his crucifixion, but represented once and for all a triumph over his shame by asserting the victory of God and his identification with God as his faithful son.

John Miller contests Capps's claim that Jesus was a fatherless child shaped by shame and disenfranchisement. He suggests, rather, that Joseph adopted Jesus as his son and that because of the excellence of this father-son relationship, Jesus identified readily with God as his father. The crucial dynamics of his development, therefore, were related primarily to his pressing the claims of God's kingdom on earth, the causes of justice, mercy, and righteousness. Miller claims that we need not speculate about Jesus' nature since we know he was shaped in word and action by a deep experience of compassion, which arose from his own experience of God as a compassionate father.

Chapters 6 through 8 by Donald Capps provide a psychological critique of the picture, or model, of who Jesus was as set forth by Albert Schweitzer, Jay Haley, and Erik Erikson, respectively. Schweitzer chastised the psychiatrists of his day for devaluing the historical Jesus without taking seriously the real data available about him, and doing so merely on the grounds that any transcendental considerations were, perforce, ridiculous. Schweitzer insisted that we must at least come to terms with the actual information we have and find out how to put the most positive and honest construction upon it.

The psychiatrists were persuaded that Jesus was delusional. Schweitzer emphasized that it was common in Jesus' day to find one's identity by "ideas of reference" in which one interjected qualities and characteristics of persons one idealized. Capps argues that Jesus developed his identity as a fictive personality, imagining an image and model of himself which then became progressively his own ego structure. This emphasizes the positive aspects of developing an idealized self, which is quite different from delusional ideation. Jay Haley contended that Jesus was a skilled power tactician capable of extraordinary persuasion, management, and manipulation. Haley claims that Jesus miscalculated in confronting the religious authorities, manifesting self-defeating impulsivity. Capps picks up this theme in terms of Jesus' skill at displacing his absent human father with the present divine father. However, Capps believes Jesus did not miscalculate in his confrontation with the authorities, but instead he took over the power process of their mutual conflict by the kind of surrender which shames and impugns the integrity of those who seem the victors.

Capps has a high appreciation for the work of Erik Erikson, particularly his book entitled *Young Man Luther*. Erikson wrote definitively on Jesus' self-concept as the Son of man. Both Haley and Erikson emphasized the family systems dynamics in Jesus' life, a perspective congenial with Capps's own primary perspective on Jesus. Erikson held that Jesus' notions about the kingdom of God were simply the transformation of his childhood model of family and religious ideology. Capps extends this idea by suggesting that Jesus himself replaces the human mother as the object of trust and the model of security, thus becoming a numinous presence to his familiar circle of his disciples and to the psychosocially and spiritually disenfranchised in his society. This landed him in the historic role of the prophet who speaks for God and runs the risks, in his case fatal, of being a challenge to the traditional modes of his world and a source of unacceptable turbulence to the establishment. This got him killed and gave Christianity its raison d'etre.

Walter Wink follows Capps's tour de force with an incisive chapter titled "The Original Impulse of Jesus." He claims that something essential has gone wrong in Christian history, resulting in the church departing radically from Jesus' mission. Wink argues that Jesus' business in the world was proclamation of a divine kingdom that was to put a definitive end to all forms of domination and oppression, from subtle slighting of others in institutionalized ways to abuse and enslavement or economic repression of the disadvantaged. Wink is sure that our standard ways of reading the Bible, doing theology, and understanding human personality obstruct freedom and enhance repression. He declares that far more important than discovering the Jesus of history is discerning the original impulse Jesus let loose in history, with the intention of sowing such a culture of freedom as to turn all natural human psychosocial inclinations toward power structures upside down.

Andries van Aarde returns us to the theme of Jesus as the fatherless child and interprets Jesus' life and work in terms of the psychological models of social identity formation, status envy, and other aspects of individual and communal psychohistory. He suggests that if we wish to understand the real Jesus, we cannot recover the figure of the first century because the historical resources are not adequate. However, he suggests that by using the Ideal Type model we can raise the questions regarding what Jesus was most likely like, given what the narratives say about him and what he is reported to have said and done. For example, he trusted God as his father, destroyed conventional patriarchal values, cared for the fatherless and widows, and generally evidenced the characteristics which would be natural to a man who had been an unempowered fatherless child. This tells us much about him which the narratives about him do not specifically detail but which can be read from the psychology of an ideal type.

Van Aarde continues by suggesting that we can critique the narratives about Jesus to smoke out indications of inflation and idealization of the story about him, things which are obviously gratuitous and unnecessary to the narrative. From these considerations and sociological models of envy and social identity we can critique the Gospels to discern how the models fit Jesus as the literary character he appears to be in the story. Applying cross-cultural criteria to this assessment, we can finally ask, "What model explains the story and its character most adequately?" Thus we can come to a refined sense of who it is with whom we have to deal in this mysterious and inescapable character, Jesus of Nazareth.

In Chapter 11, Paul Anderson introduces us to the contribution cognitive and developmental psychology can make to the solution of a long-standing riddle in the Gospel of John. His essay, "A Way Forward in the Scientific Investigation of Gospel Traditions," is developed in four parts, two of which are written by colleagues J. Harold Ellens and James Fowler. The riddle is the apparent theological contradiction in John between a high Christology and a low one, between Jesus as subordinate to the Father and Jesus on equal footing with the Father, and between a realized and a futuristic understanding of the "last things" (eschatology), along with puzzling discontinuities in the text. This theme of "contradiction" or "paradox" inspired the title of Anderson's magnum opus *The Christology of the Fourth Gospel: Its Unity and Disunity in the Light of John 6* (1996). The paradox has led to two explanations. One that was popular for decades (Rudolf Bultmann) held that John's Gospel is a pastiche of Gospel pieces from different times in early Christian history, pasted together haphazardly and representing disparate points of view. The new theory, proposed by Anderson, with the help of James Fowler's theories of "stages of faith" and James Loder's crisis-transformational model, is that the paradoxical perspectives held in tension in John's Gospel are due to cognitive changes and crises within the Gospel author and/or his community for which he was writing.

In the introductory section of the essay, Anderson makes a case for getting beyond traditional historical critical method in order to ask new kinds of questions of the text. Anderson argues that "good history" must also be the history of cognitive development, using the best available cognitive theory. In the second section of the chapter, J. Harold Ellens offers an engaging sketch of Anderson, his book, and his inclusion of cognitive-critical analysis in the mix of literary, historical, and theological exegetical tools. In the third section, Anderson returns with a "field report" on forty-three critical reviews of his books, with special attention to the pros and cons in response to his focus on cognitive-critical tools in Gospel research, and his scholarly approach may be key.

The fourth section provides a vigorous conclusion with a cameo appearance from James Fowler presenting a firsthand account of his theory of the stages of faith: "synthetic-conventional faith," "individuative-reflective faith," and "conjunctive faith," marking the latter as the most mature in its ability to integrate opposites, contradictions, paradoxes and ambiguities, and as the key to understanding the riddle of John's paradoxical Christology. Hal Childs appropriately follows, in Chapter 12, with his tightly argued claim that all our historical quests for Jesus can produce only myths shaped by our own assumptions, belief systems, cultural metaphors, and psychological archetypes.

However, myths are crucially important, according to Childs. They are the informed confessional statements we make about those things that constitute the underpinnings and superstructures of our personal and communal worldviews. Therefore, we ought not to shrink back from our quest for understanding by means of myth-making, but we should announce our personal and communal-cultural assumptions at the outset and, in the end, acknowledge the psychosocial limitations inherent in all our models and mythic confessions or claims.

So we must settle with the fact that we will have many stories and perspectives regarding the Jesus whom we seek, all apprehended in wonder and marvel as they fashion new myths of meaning in us at each new stage of our reflection upon them. We need to accept the psychological evidences of our own internal responses to this quest, individually and communally, and acknowledge the new hermeneutical key which these experiences afford us, freeing us to live fully, in the context of the always mysterious Jesus narrative, as creators of our own sense of him and of our own unfolding selves.

Paul Anderson's *Jesus and Transformation* follows nicely on Childs's hard-hitting assessment of historiography, arguing persuasively that, despite the variety of models of Jesus and his ministry floated by modern scholarship, the claim of the Gospels is quite clear that the impact Jesus had upon his society centered in his skill at inducing growth-producing dissonance. Anderson outlines a number of forces Jesus set into play in this regard. His trajectory of thought moves us to the point of understanding the transformative dynamism Jesus turned loose in the culture of his time. He concludes with a constructive appreciation of the continually astonishing psycho-spiritual necessity to understand Jesus' surprising role in history, and to take its claims and consequences seriously. Finally, the power of the verbal and acoustic imagery of the Bible is the subject of Schuyler Brown's work titled "The Bible and the Alchemy of Language in Psychological Perspective." Analytical psychologists, litterateurs, and liturgical specialists have long instructed us in the capacity of religious symbolism to enchant, stir the imagination, and awaken awareness in a way that appeals to regions of the mind inaccessible to argument.

Freud and Jung confirmed that religious symbols, not to mention everyday language, are the bearers not only of simple and univocal meanings, but also of a complex of meanings drawn from the psychic and linguistic context of speaker and audience, of writer and reader. A special point Brown brings to the table, often ignored in our logocentric worldview, is that "the emotional impact of biblical language has to do not only with visual imagery but also with acoustic images." Jung's work on word association and Freud's on "suggestion" reinforce Brown's point, noting that acoustic associations (for example, "violet" and "violate") often enter the picture as much as denotative meanings, as a client goes about interpreting what has been seen or heard. It is safe to say that the broad success of the Book of Common Prayer and the public reading of the King James Bible in Western tradition can also be attributed to the psycho-acoustic power of the word to "catch the ear" and move the mind, the imagination, the conscience, and the will. The mantric tradition in Far Eastern spirituality reinforces the point. In our own culture, one that has largely been impervious to the enjoinder to "let him who has ears, hear," Brown's study awakens us to a new/old dimension of our experience with the virtuosity of the alchemy of language.

Conclusion

In this volume, eleven scholars offer a variety of perspectives on the way in which the lens of the psychological sciences can be focused in numerous new ways upon ancient Hebrew and Christian scripture text. This volume focuses on the story and person of Jesus. It is a devoted and serious endeavor to read the Bible more clearly, faithfully, and understandably. The long human quest is an irrepressible lust for meaning and truth, which means our mutual hunger is for greater light and more satisfying insight. We have turned the psychological lens toward the biblical text so as to channel good light, new vision, and amplified illumination to it. We both hope and expect that this endeavor will produce a more heavenly and user-friendly sense of the clarity and value of our daily earthly pilgrimage, a more profound reckoning with the role of Jesus of Nazareth in that historic pilgrimage, and a more honest vision of "our common human terror and our common hope" (Mertz, 1966, 367).

References

Anderson, Paul. (1996). *The Christology of the Fourth Gospel: Its Unity and Disunity in the Light of John 6*. Tübingen: Mohr.

Coffin, W. S. (1999). *The Heart Is a Little to the Left*. Hanover: University Press of New England.

Ellens, J. H. (1982). *God's Grace and Human Health*. Nashville: Abingdon.

Erickson, E. (1958). *Young Man Luther: A Study in Psychoanalysis and History.*
   New York: Norton.
Jung, C. G. (1953–1978). *The Collected Works of C. G. Jung,* R. F. C. Hull, trans.
   Princeton: Princeton University Press.
Mertz, B. (1966). *Red Land, Black Land.* New York: Dell.
Pelikan, J. (1985). *Jesus through the Centuries: His Place in the History of Culture.*
   New Haven: Yale University Press.
Rollins, W. (1999). *Soul and Psyche: The Bible in Psychological Perspective.* Min-
   neapolis: Fortress.

CHAPTER 2

FROM CHRIST TO JESUS: THE JESUS QUEST

J. Harold Ellens

Introduction

Early in the development of the various original Christianities, it seems to have become clear to most faith communities that this new religion's salvific strength lies in the intuitive psycho-spiritual insights of its confessional myths rather than any corpus of historical data about its founder or origins. By the fourth century and the rise of the ecumenical councils which defined the orthodox creeds, the Imperial Church, under the influence of Alexandrian Christianity particularly, decided that the redemptive task of the church was to formulate, as its foundational structure, a mythic confessional theology rather than a historical narrative. This theological foundation was crafted on the model of Plato's rational idealism, a wholly speculative model of reality, which was reified as ontology by both Plato in his philosophical model and by the church in its philosophico-theological formulations. Thus was created, as the substructure of the Christian movement, a speculative, confessional, mythic system, reified as objective mundane and transcendental reality. It was this move—rather typical, and even predictable, given the Platonic philosophical envelope in which the first centuries B.C.E. and C.E. unfolded in the ancient world—that ultimately led the church to conceive of everything from Plato to Augustine as divinely inspired and authoritative. This mythic corpus was treated in turn throughout the ancient and medieval periods whenever the issues of Christianity's historical and historiographical qualities arose, as if the myth were also historically warrantable; historiography being the discussion of the method of writing history, while the historical is the content of the narrative that reports the past.

Exposition

This early reification of the mythic confession of the church as ontology forced the emphasis of the church's praxis not only toward speculative theology but even more radically toward liturgy. Perhaps in an earlier and more primitive form, liturgy was also the spawning ground for the mythic confession. The aesthetics and poetry of liturgy could speak for the heart and inspire redemptive intuition and faith that no amount of history, on its own, had the energy to do. Moreover, the mythic worldview, translated into the aesthetic drama of liturgy, offered the tools of metaphor and symbol into which could be poured the entire range of human anguish, imagination, longing, expectation, hope, trust, and faith. So Christianity flourished redemptively, affording the consolations that empowered and sustained people and communities through the direst of abject suffering and loss in the tragic adventure of human existence, without needing to challenge the historicity of its myth, and while emphasizing the quality of its poetic or metaphoric liturgies.

The Protestant Reformers proposed to tame the mythic and speculative Christian tradition by grounding it in a history-based theological corpus. They undertook to discover or create a new historiographical method which would offer a way to read the Bible that distilled from it the historical base for Christianity. Hence one of the battle cries of the Reformation: *Sola Scriptura*. It is this historical and historiographical endeavor that produced the historical-critical and literary-critical methods of the eighteenth, nineteenth, and twentieth centuries, and which is the ground and assumption of the work of the Jesus Seminar and the Quests for the Historical Jesus. This should not surprise us, for it was this same genius of the Protestant Reformation which contended that the material world was tractable and gave rise to objective scientific research, the enlightenment, and the scientific, industrial, and technological revolutions.

As historical and historiographical endeavors, the Jesus Seminar and the Quests for the Historical Jesus are worthy undertakings and will undoubtedly continue to produce useful data. However, as efforts to ground the Christian faith or movement in history, they are doomed to failure precisely because there is not adequate historical data in the biblical or historical sources. The best such endeavors can do is to demythologize various aspects of the tradition by means of that analysis of the sources which can discredit some details of the mythic reports in scripture or the creeds. This reality must be faced honestly as a deconstructionist, not constructionist, enterprise. For example, on the basis of literary and historical analysis of the Gospels, it would be possible to demonstrate that the early church could tell the whole story of Jesus three generations after his death, without a virgin birth narrative or stories of resurrection appearances. That is how it appears in Mark's Gospel, apparently the earliest. However, four generations after Jesus' death, when Matthew and Luke were written, it was no longer possible to tell the whole story without a virgin birth and resurrection narratives. One must raise the question, therefore, as to whether the virgin birth and resurrection narratives are historical reports (not a very likely possibility) or evidence of the expanding myth-development process of the worshipping community's consciousness and its panoply of salvific metaphors (a likely possibility).

Of course, John's Gospel, written another generation or so later, has no virgin birth either, for the obvious reason that it has glorified Jesus into a pre-existent and transcendental divine being in exactly the same way that Rabbinic Judaism glorified the Torah. In any case, we can deconstruct certain aspects of the confessional faith tradition of the historic church community and institution via literary and historical-critical methods, thus distilling from it some clarity about what is or might be historic, and what might not be or is certainly not. It is questionable, of course, what good this does and whether this enhances or detracts from the capacity of the mythic tradition with its dynamic liturgies, metaphors, and symbols to afford humans an adequate range of sustaining and redemptive stimuli for processing human anguish, imagination, longing, expectation, hope, trust, and faith. Can you bury your child and recover any kind of life with the Gospel of the Jesus Seminar, however admirable the work of that group of devoted scholars? Can you face your own mortality accompanied by any of the numerous Jesuses of the Quests? Obviously Nietzsche's panoply of questions is the right one here. Is the courage to be, in the end, the capacity to stand on the brink of the abyss of nothingness and hear without flinching the announcement that God is dead? Moreover, it is interesting that there is so great a variety of Jesuses produced by the quests for the historical Jesus. These are contrived by scholars who generally agree on the historical-critical, literary-critical, and form-critical strategies for the historiographical methods that should be employed in this work. One does not need to analyze these scholarly products very deeply before it becomes clear that the Jesus-image which is produced by each one is not a product of a pristine historiography, but is rather a product of the mythic assumptions at the root of each worldview that shaped the scholar who produced any given image of Jesus—that is, the mythic faith assumptions with which each scholar began the scholarly endeavor. Such a scholarly process is legitimate, of course, as long as the scholar announces up front his or her faith assumptions, predispositions, and presuppositions on the matter.

It is not surprising, therefore, that Hal Childs, in his recent book, *The Myth of the Historical Jesus and the Evolution of Consciousness* (2000), should chasten the scholars who attempt to find the historical Jesus by claiming that, at best, they can only find the Jesus of myth or their own psychological projections. Childs's book is a remarkable piece of brilliant, courageous, innovative, and challenging scholarship. He has created a psychoanalytic model based largely on Jung as the platform from which to launch a broadside critique of all historical research, particularly that which quests for the historical Jesus, and most particularly that of John Dominic Crossan, a noted and prolific Jesus scholar. Childs identifies the problems of historical research as inadequately distinguishing, first of all, between three terms: historic, historical, and historiographical. He insists, probably correctly, that the first term refers to the actual event or person of history—a thing that can never be recovered or reconstructed in our modern research enterprise. The second term is a name for the mythic narrative we create when we attempt to report some kind of account of an event or person of history, an account always fraught with and shaped by our own personal, communal and cultural presuppositions, predispositions, and projections. Historiography is a term that refers to the process of composing the historical mythology, which we generally refer to as a history of something in the past. Second, Childs contends that the other problem of historical research is the fact that we can never escape the myths and myth-making nature inherent in all our perception processes, and thus an inevitable part of our construction of any description of events or persons of the past.

Childs aggressively analyzes the enterprise of Historical Jesus research and points out in a thoroughly analytic manner how impossible it is for any modern day scholar to penetrate his or her own personal paradigm and the cultural paradigm of our collective unconscious to get at the real Jesus of history. Indeed, he makes a convincing case that this problem has plagued scholarship regarding Jesus from the beginning and throughout the last two thousand years. Even the Gospel writers, who wrote their accounts between two and five generations after Jesus had departed the scene of history, were in no better place to access the real Jesus than are we. Even they were already separated from the original historic events by both a mindset and set of master stories that had grown up around the memory of Jesus in their faith community. The narratives had formed, meeting deep inner psycho-spiritual needs within individual believers and within the communal unconscious that inevitably functioned as the screen through which the narrative had to be seen.

I am certain that Childs's emphasis is necessary and appropriate. I am less certain that its application is quite as radical and unrelenting as Childs claims. One week after the attack on the World Trade Center, my brother Gordon was referred by his dentist to an oral surgeon who prescribed an antibiotic for an infected tooth. One week later, he was dead from that antibiotic. On the day before we terminated his life-support, the family was gathered around his bed. At 3 p.m. that afternoon my brother-in-law, Orville, got up from the family circle to do an errand for a friend. At 6 p.m., he was brought back into the same ICU on a stretcher, having fallen from a roof. For all practical purposes he was already dead, though life-support technology preserved his organs for harvesting the next day. The next morning we terminated both within twenty minutes of each other. That is not my imagination or projection, nor a mythic product of Jungian unconscious. They are dead. We buried them. There are gravestones, death certificates, multiple attestations which all say the same thing. The historical fact is also historic truth, clear and uncomplicated, though desperately horrific. Empirical data, documentation, testimony, heuristic evidence, phenomenological evidence. By Childs's own definitions, historic fact, not mythic truth.

However, I think Childs would agree that such certainty is possible when the event is one of personal experience, and not so distant as to have acquired mythic interpretation. Moreover, only the fact that they are dead and buried is historic truth. If you asked each witness what it means, or feels like, or how it should be interpreted, the function of the personal and collective unconscious in myth-making—in interpreting the event and desperately trying to give it meaning—would be very much at play already, in approximately the way Jung suggested. Childs might go further to say that it is a quite different matter if the past event is reported to us by other witnesses, empirical, heuristic, or phenomenological. Perhaps there is something to that. However, it seems to me that a historical report is not just the projection of personal and collective or universal unconscious. It is also the report of a combination of various forms of data, which stand in various degrees of independence of one another, at various levels of empirical objectivity and thus present themselves with various qualities of reliability. When John Dominic Crossan reports his methodological approach to Historical Jesus research, then proceeds to examine the data for reliability, he is not claiming that he is establishing a picture of ultimate objective reality. As I understand it, he is claiming that, given the documents, the variety and quality of witnesses, the empirical, heuristic, and phenomenological evidences, and the degree to which these all comport in support of a specific picture of Jesus, said picture gives us an experience of the real historic Jesus that is worth the trouble. Moreover, Crossan's employment of a method or system for qualifying the witnesses and evidence gives warrant to his endeavor, even if it does not certify that in the end we have a photographic portrait of Jesus of Nazareth, a Galilean Jew of the first century of our Common Era.

To put it more analytically and perhaps more succinctly, not everything about Crossan's picture of Jesus is the projection of his personal or our collective unconscious, standing as we do in the twenty-first century, laden with the traditional ways of thinking about Jesus. Part of Crossan's picture is shaped by the data of early documents, archaeological witnesses, comparative analysis of all these data, literary and historical critique of the whole, and a scientific distillation from the evidence of a basis for according more warrant to some aspects of the story and less to others. That is to say, the historian's task is to generate that "evidence," weigh its relative dependability or reliability, and so determine the quality of the evidence. Crossan does not claim to speak for God, revealing some kind of ultimate truth, but rather to quest on our behalf for some proximate approach to the best quality of truth about Jesus of Nazareth of which humans are capable with the methods of properly disciplined historiography.

One cannot help but profoundly appreciate and greatly esteem Childs's tour de force in rigorous scholarship, but the construction of his thesis, method, and analytic conclusions are as subject to distortion by his own assumptions, projections, predispositions, and presuppositions as he claims the methods and products of the historians to be. Childs would likely agree with that statement, and declare that he acknowledged his assumptions and biases up front and so has established both the method and right to launch his critique. In that he would be correct. So has Crossan, I think—and for the same reasons—a legitimate prerogative to pursue his historian's task and project.

Childs seems to have allowed the psychologist to swallow up the historian. That would be no more legitimate than for the historian to eat the psychologist. Psychologizing is as readily mistaken in its models as historiography can be. As a psychologist and a biblical scholar myself, I am well aware of the fact that psychologizing everything does not give us a basis for dogmatic statements about anything. For example, there is no empirical, heuristic, or phenomenological evidence that Jung's notion of the collective unconscious, or any kind of universal phenomenon like it, actually exists. It functions merely as a theoretical hypothesis that may or may not work to give us useful insights about what we see or experience. We have taken the concept and reified it. It may well be the case that everything we have tried to understand better by the use of that Jungian hypothesis may be much more accurately interpreted by quite a different hypothesis that no one has as yet devised. Nonetheless, Childs has reified the Jungian notion, almost to the point of giving it a kind of ontic quality and function—certainly a normative one. He sets it as the formulating principle of all epistemology, and therefore creates what he seems to consider a standard and paradigmatic definer of the imperatives and deficiencies of the historians and the historical research methods. In any case, Childs's work gives us a new dimension of insight regarding the interface of the mutually illumining disciplines of psychology and biblical studies. For this, I congratulate and thank him.

Note

An earlier form of this chapter appeared under the same title in *Pastoral Psychology*, *51*(6), 435–440, and is published here with permission.

References

Childs, H. (2000). *The Myth of the Historical Jesus and the Evolution of Consciousness*. Dissertation Series, Atlanta: SBL.

Crossan, J. D. (1991). *The Historical Jesus: The Life of a Mediterranean Jewish Peasant*. San Francisco: HarperSanFrancisco.

Crossan, J. D. (1994). *The Essential Jesus: Original Sayings and Earliest Images*. San Francisco: HarperSanFrancisco.

Crossan, J. D. (1994). *Jesus: A Revolutionary Biography*. San Francisco: HarperSanFrancisco.

CHAPTER 3

Psychobiography: A New and Challenging Methodology in Jesus Research

James H. Charlesworth

We do not yet grasp what historical forces brought forth and determined early Christianity. But beside and within this external history there is an inner history.... Anyone who thinks that this religion can be illumined historically and factually without psychological reflection is just as much in error as one who pretends that everything about this religion can be said in this fashion.

—G. Theissen (1987)

Introduction

As I assess the present state of Jesus Research, identified by some as the Third Quest of the Historical Jesus, I am surprised to encounter a new method. It is the appearance of psychobiography.[1] The title of this chapter contains two technical terms that should be defined at the outset: Jesus Research and psychobiography.

Jesus Research, which appeared around 1980, asks historical questions about the powerful Jew named Jesus that is portrayed in the Gospels.[2] While the First Quest and the Second Quest were motivated and shaped by theological agendas and needs, Jesus Research is not (or should not be) tied to theological claims or concerns, nor is it primarily interested in a portrayal of Jesus that would be attractive to Christians. More is explained about Jesus Research later in the chapter, when I review the study of the historical Jesus over the past three centuries.

Numerous terms of scholarly jargon are employed throughout the chaper. In order to avoid confusion, it is helpful to give three more definitions: (1) the *Jesus of History* denotes the Jew, the actual and real man of history, who lived in Palestine in the first century C.E.; (2) the *Historical Jesus* signifies the Jesus who is a construct of scholarly research; and (3) the *Christ of Faith* is the person Jesus Christ who is confronted in preaching and known to the believing Christian.

Psychobiography is a new and seldom defined methodology for studying a person. It is a subdivision of psychohistory (the application of psychological methodologies to reconstructions of historical persons or groups) which asks questions, using psychological insights and methodologies, to obtain something like a biography. I define this method as the study of persons in the attempt to obtain a story or biography of them. To employ psychobiography in our effort to understand and describe Jesus, we must do so by looking at all data generated by the enlightening advances made since Albert Schweitzer offered his devastating critique of nineteenth-century psychiatrists in *The Psychiatric Study of Jesus* in 1913 (Schweitzer, 1948).

Exposition

Having defined the two major terms in the title of this chapter, we may now explore what a psychobiographical study of Jesus of Nazareth is, and how it differs from the earlier attempts to psychoanalyze Jesus. Often, the old psychological approach to Jesus was uninformed of the proper means of interpreting the New Testament and was agnostic or influenced by atheism. The new method, psychobiography, attempts to be informed of "Gospel Criticism" and is often theistic, even sensitively alive, to the claims of traditional Christendom. I am convinced that a psychobiographical approach to Jesus is warranted because other methods have given us such a variety of portraits of Jesus of Nazareth, and because virtually every attempt at describing the historical Jesus is shaped implicitly by psychological factors or assumptions, often unperceived or hidden. Miller and Capps, as we shall see, use psychobiography to explain some apparent anomalies in what can be known about the Historical Jesus. Now we must remember that "the Historical Jesus," as indicated above, is a construct offered by critical scholars and is distinct from the real Jesus who lived and taught before 30 C.E., that is, the Jesus of History.

My interpretation of psychobiography reflects the perspective of a New Testament scholar who has been devoted to the study of pre-

135–136 C.E. Jewish phenomena. Perhaps another definition would also be helpful. W. M. Runyan of the University of California in Berkeley offers a refined definition of psychobiography that improves upon the attempts made by Anderson, Friedlander, Glad, and Tucker to define this method. In his *Life Histories and Psychobiography*, Runyan offers the following definition:

> In light of these considerations [a critique of the definitions offered by others], psychobiography may be defined as the explicit use of systematic or formal psychology in biography. Three aspects of this definition should be noted. First, the field is defined by the use of psychology, which may or may not be psychoanalytic. Second, the use must be explicit or visible, in order to distinguish psychobiography from all those biographies which make implicit use of commonsense psychology. Third, the definition refers not to the application of personality theory but to the use of psychology, which is intended to include within psychobiography those works drawing upon the full range of resources from the field of psychology, including psychological concepts, data, and methods, as well as theory, from developmental, social and personality psychology. (Runyan, 1984, 202)[3]

Before we can explore new aspects of Jesus Research, we need to review the study of the historical Jesus from circa 1835 to the present. The limitations of this essay demand brevity, but perhaps such focus will help serve one of the reasons for this essay: to encourage others to become involved in the study of the historical Jesus and to approach this area of scholarship from various scientific and theological perspectives.

Almost a century ago, Albert Schweitzer once referred to the "chaos of modern lives of Jesus." He was referring to the books on Jesus that appeared after his magnum opus on the historical Jesus. Schweitzer was not a prophet; he was merely prescient. As one sees the veritable flood of books on Jesus, one may be forgiven for thinking that the field is in more chaos today than when Schweitzer wrote. Some specialists in the New Testament think the study of the historical Jesus is a dead end. Others parade their ignorance by assuming that in the second century C.E., Papias, whose work is most unfortunately lost, and Irenaeus, who was a defender of the faith, accurately reported that at least two Gospels were composed by eyewitnesses of Jesus.[4] Jesus Research is neither as impoverished as the first group of scholars concluded nor as richly documented as the latter group imagines. In the field of Jesus Research, as well as in archaeology, we confront the minimalists and the maximalists. Most experts shun either alternative as unbalanced and unperceptive of the sources and proper methodology used in Jesus Research.

In this short review essay I shall attempt to point out how and why both minimalists and maximalists have followed the blind and fallen into a pit (cf. Matt. 15:14). I also wish to point out that behind the apparent chaos is an unparalleled consensus on methodology, and on some major aspects of Jesus' life and thoughts. The differences between a book by a scholar and one by a non-scholar are the amount of attention given to methodological issues and the degree to which a scientific, unbiased method is followed in asking historical, literary, and theological questions. All scholars who focus their research on the historical Jesus acknowledge that the historical-critical method needs to be employed. Too few scholars recognize and attempt to supplement their Jesus Research by including insights obtained from sociology, anthropology, archaeology, rhetoric, and, perhaps, psychobiography.

The field of Jesus Research is vast. No one has read all the publications. In fact, it may be impossible now even to claim to have read all the important publications, as they are so numerous, scattered in so many different fields, and written in over 20 languages. Fortunately, we have a useful bibliographical guide to most publications up until 1996: C. A. Evans's *Life of Jesus Research* (1996).

My inaugural at Princeton Theological Seminary in 1984 focused on Jesus Research. I stressed that from 30 C.E., the date of the crucifixion, to 1835, the date of the first critical life of Jesus (D. F. Strauss's *Das Leben Jesu* [1835]), the approach to Jesus was devotional.[5] That is to say, Christians, who were the only ones attracted to Jesus, had approached Jesus by worshiping him as the Christ, the Son of God. In the early centuries, scholars claimed, and thence it was presupposed, that eyewitnesses composed the Gospels: Matthew and John were apostles, Mark was the assistant of Peter, and Luke was the companion of Paul.

The period of excitement with the historical search for Jesus extends from 1835 until 1906. Strauss initially, and others intermittently, dreamed of giving persons in the pew a reliable biography of the one they followed. Many, including Strauss, were finally led to question whether an informed and enlightened person could still remain a Christian according to triumphalist orthodoxy.

Some scholars claimed that Mark was the most reliable biographer of Jesus; others defended John. Many arguments published by scholars looked erudite but were hardly scholarly, self-critical, or focused on an objective assessment of Second Temple Judaism and Jesus' place within it. Some New Testament experts even claimed that Judas was the Beloved Disciple of the Gospel of John. The distinguished Frenchman Ernst Renan opined that Jesus' painful last moments in Gethsemane may have been due to his regret over the women he should have loved in Galilee. Famous church historian Adolph Harnack claimed that Jesus taught the fatherhood of God, the brotherhood of humankind, and the ethic of love. Readers of Renan and Harnack—and they were widely read and highly influential—were not hearing the voice of the Galilean Rabbi; they were in touch with French romanticism and German idealism. The attentive reader pondered why Jesus was so misunderstood by his followers, and why the Prince of Peace could have been crucified. This period (1835–1906) is called "the Old Quest for the Historical Jesus."

In the first edition of his study on the historical Jesus in 1906, Albert Schweitzer showed that all who had written during the nineteenth century were simply offering a view of Jesus that they could appreciate, understand, and admire. Schweitzer's monumental work, *The Quest of the Historical Jesus* (1910), is not only a classic, it is perhaps the most influential study of Jesus ever published. Today, almost a hundred years later, virtually every scholar who has been working independently has come to agree with Schweitzer that Jesus was deeply influenced by Jewish Apocalypticism.[6]

George Tyrrell, an Irish modernist and Roman Catholic, insightfully emphasized a statement that is too often associated with Schweitzer. In Tyrrell's review of Harnack's *What Is Christianity*, he stated that those who had written a putative historical work on Jesus had merely peered down the well of history and seen the reflection of their own face (Tyrrell, 1909/1963, 49).[7]

Thus, immediately after World War I the historical search for Jesus died in many seminaries and universities, especially in the influential and leading German institutions. Formative judges like Bultmann, Barth, and Tillich announced not only that the historical Jesus was merely a scholarly creation, but also that reliable knowledge about the Jesus of history was also irrelevant for Christian faith.[8] A slogan seemed to be heard: all Christians need to know is that they are saved by "faith alone." This cliché misrepresents the complex theologies of Luther and Paul,[9] and opens up a mandate to forgo the arduous task of historical research. Sadly, these perspectives, now clearly disproved by biblical scholars and theologians, can be heard as ghostly echoes in lectures and sermons. An important new methodology for studying the New Testament is Rhetorical Criticism, but it can become a way of avoiding the claims of the kerygma, the proclamation that Jesus is the Christ, the Son of God, and looking not at history but at the Jesus in the story.

From 1919 (the date of Barth's commentary on Romans) and the 1920s (the beginnings of Bultmann's school) until 1953, the theology of Karl Barth and Rudolf Bultmann flourished, but they and their followers tended to denigrate historicism. Although many New Testament scholars, especially the Frenchman Pierre Benoit and the Norwegian Nils A. Dahl, stressed the importance of historical research on Jesus before 1950, it is widely recognized that Ernst Käsemann opened up "the New Quest for the Historical Jesus" in 1953. He did so boldly – before his teacher Bultmann and at a celebratory gathering of his students. Käsemann showed that there is far more history in the New Testament than Bultmann had allowed. Käsemann argued that Christian theology was grounded not in ideas or existentialism. He was able to convince many New Testament experts that Christianity was founded on real history, and that there was some continuity between Jesus' own words and the words of the Palestinian Jesus Movement (my term).

The New Quest for the Historical Jesus did not engage most theologians, and slowly sank from view. Why was the New Quest ineffective? Obviously, the failure of this approach was due to advocates' preoccupation with theological interests, which continued to be marred by a misperception of the importance of history that was typical of existentialism. Lack of dedication to sociology, anthropology, and archaeology, and too much interest in Christology, marred a putative search for an understanding of the pre-30 C.E. historical Jew called Jesus of Nazareth. Retrospectively, it is obvious that the methods used by the new "questers" were not in line with strict scientific historiography.

Around 1980, something new appeared in scholarship.[10] I have called it "Jesus Research." Regardless of their own theology or beliefs, many scholars around the world, including Jews who do not perceive Jesus polemically, find it interesting and important to ask historical questions about pre-70 C.E. Palestinian Jews, including Jesus of Nazareth. Those who examine the pre-70 C.E. pavements and streets, found unexpectedly in Jerusalem, raise questions of what kind of people walked them about two thousand years ago. The discovery of first-century stone houses in Capernaum and palatial abodes in Jerusalem's Upper City stimulates reflections about life in them before 70 C.E. The recognition of Mikvaot (Jewish ritual baths for spiritual purification) in Jerusalem and elsewhere raises reflections on Jewish religious life before 70 C.E. The recovering of stone vessels for the Jewish rites of purification caused a new reading of John 2, and of the Jesus who was reputedly present at a wedding in Cana.

Jewish and Christian historians independently, and in many places—especially Germany, the United States, and Israel—pondered about what can be known concerning the founder of the Qumran Community, the anonymous Righteous Teacher; about Hillel, the Pharisee just before Jesus who held theological ideas similar to those attributed to Jesus; about Gamaliel, reputedly the teacher of Paul; and Johanan ben Zakkai, the one who chaired the first rabbinic academy at Jamnia. The modern experts asked similar questions about Jesus of Nazareth.

How was the new approach distinct from the previous ones that had dominated the field? The answer is clear. In contrast to the Old Quest and the New Quest, Jesus Research was not tied to a theologically motivated "search" for Jesus. Jesus Research was often stimulated by studies of the Dead Sea Scrolls, early Rabbinics, Josephus, and other early Jewish writings, particularly the Old Testament Apocrypha and Pseudepigrapha. This study was not a "search"; it was a result of "research"—that is, archaeology, anthropology, and sociology became important in the study of the historical Jesus.

Sometime in the late 1980s, Jesus Research was infiltrated—some might say contaminated—by authors, some of whom are scholars who basically took up the Old Quest, seeking to find a Jesus whom they could follow or worship. The most attractive of these books may be Marcus Borg's *Jesus: A New Vision* (1987). It is understandable why some scholars call the new period of the study of the historical Jesus the "Third Quest," or "Third Search."

To what extent is a distinction between the study of Jesus before and after 1980 misleading? The year 1980, in contrast to 1970, does not mark a cataclysmic event in history. Distinguished scholars such as Guignebert, Goguel, Loisy, Strauss, and Bauer would reject the claim that their studies were motivated by theological agendas. It is not fair to brand Bultmann as one whose Christological concerns and existential theology simply dictated his historical research. It is surely debatable to what degree Marcus Borg and John Dominic Crossan, and others such as Luke Johnson, are true historians whose work on the historical Jesus is not in any way shaped by Christological perspectives.

What I wish to stress is that more concern for "disinterested" research in Jesus is more apparent today than it was before approximately 1980. By disinterested, I mean a study of Jesus that is objective and inductive. Questions are asked without any presupposition regarding possible answers. Honest questions are asked, and sometimes Christian scholars are not pleased with some historical answers. Certainly, scholars working in Jesus Research are capable of solid historical research; at the top of the list I would place E. P. Sanders, Richard Horsley, James Dunn, John Meier, Gerd Theissen, Petr Porkorný, and Craig Evans. Moreover, the publications by Jews are now essential reading; two important Jews who have worked significantly and fruitfully in this area of scholarship are Geza Vermes of Oxford and David Flusser of Jerusalem.

Some illustrations are necessary to clarify that the paradigm shift is real and not merely apparent, and that the new wave of research is different, not only because of more primary data like the Dead Sea Scrolls and other archaeological discoveries that antedate 70 C.E., but in both content and methodology. Originally, Flusser could end his study of the historical Jesus with Jesus' death. Now his book requires an epilogue in which he suggests how the ideas of the historical Jesus evolved into the faith of the early Christians (Flusser & Notley, 1998). Formerly, Father Marie-Joseph Lagrange, founder of the École Biblique et Archéologique Française in Jerusalem, had to keep one eye looking for possible Vatican censorship. Now Roman Catholic scholars are free to explore historical issues. Ray Brown and John Meier can query the historicity of the Virgin Birth (and yet confess it liturgically), and in the École Biblique J. Murphy-O'Connor is free to publish a life of Paul that is in no way designed to please the Papacy.

There are, of course, vast substantive differences within contemporary Jesus study, as compared with that of a quarter century ago. At the outset, one can try to divide scholars into those who, like E. P. Sanders, want history and not confessionalism, and those who, like Borg, mix history and Christology. But finally all such neat categories such as liberal versus conservative distort rather than re-present. Books in the field of Jesus Research, like those by Flusser, Charlesworth, Meier, Horsley,[11] and Sanders, appear alongside other publications on Jesus that resist categorization, such as those by Witherington, Crossan, Wright, and Fredriksen.

A century ago, Albert Schweitzer summarized the study of the historical Jesus during the nineteenth century in one volume. The review of the study of the historical Jesus during the twentieth century is a monumental task. Three experts now seek to assess what has transpired. Walter P. Weaver, Pendergrass Professor of New Testament, Emeritus, at Florida Southern College, completed the first book in

1999. It is entitled *The Historical Jesus in the Twentieth Century.* Weaver reviews the study of the historical Jesus from 1900 to 1950. Carsten Claussen, a New Testament scholar in Strasbourg, will cover the period from 1951 to 1980, and Charlesworth will assess the period from 1981 to 2000. It is clear that there is so much development in the study of the historical Jesus from 1900 to 2000 that it takes three scholars and multiple volumes to adequately access the scholarly publications devoted to Jesus during the twentieth century.[12]

What Can Be Known about Jesus' Actions?

A remarkable consensus has appeared among many leading scholars regarding Jesus' actions. Here are some Jesus traditions that seem to be, if not virtually *bruta facta*, at least highly probable conclusions:

- Jesus grew up in Nazareth.
- He was baptized by John the Baptizer.
- He was obsessed with doing God's will.
- He was "intoxicated" with God and identified himself as a prophet.[13]
- He chose twelve men to be his disciples.
- He was very close with Mary Magdalene.
- He performed healing miracles.
- He taught in synagogues (at the beginning only, perhaps), small dwellings, and on the fringes of villages (not cities).
- In shocking contrast to many Pharisees and the Essenes, he associated with the physically imperfect (deaf and lame) and those deemed socially unacceptable (whores and thieves).
- He went to Jerusalem to celebrate Passover and worship within the Temple cult.
- He frequented the Temple, worshiped there, and taught in the porticoes.
- When he was in Jerusalem, he attacked some corruptions in the Temple cult.
- His meals were often religious events, and his last meal with his disciples was at Passover time in Jerusalem.
- He seems to have been denied by Peter.
- He was forcefully taken by some men, including Jews related to the cult.
- He was crucified by Roman soldiers outside the western walls of Jerusalem.[14]
- He died on Friday afternoon before the beginning of the Sabbath.

After thirty years of lecturing on Jesus and The Twelve, and pointing out that Peter is always first and Judas last, I strove to convince
my students that Jesus' followers created the concept of The Twelve.
Since it is undeniable that Judas is in the list and is often referred to as
one of The Twelve, I now conclude that Jesus chose twelve. I am
pleased to observe that Sanders and Meier—leading experts in Jesus
Research—independently came to the same conclusion. That means
that Jesus certainly had some political agenda. In *Who Was Jesus?*
Hendrikus Boers points to the evidence that Jesus' followers "were
armed in Gethsemane," and thus it is "difficult to deny that he himself
may have been involved in armed resistance against Rome" (Boers,
1989).

Did Jesus have a political agenda? I find it absurd that leading scholars stress, on different occasions, two mutually exclusive ideas. On
some occasions, I hear them claim that Jesus was in no way interested
in, or linked to, political causes. On other occasions, I hear them argue
that politics and religion in first-century Judaism cannot be distinguished or separated.[15] Fortunately, this absurd inconsistency has
been exposed and rejected by two major publications: one is Borg's
Conflict, Holiness, and Politics in the Teachings of Jesus (1984); the other
is a collection edited by E. Bammel and C. F. D. Moule entitled
Jesus and the Politics of His Day (1984). Thus, it is clear to me that
Jesus may not have been interested in political issues, but his message
had deep political ramifications.

Moreover, if he chose twelve men, maybe he did have politics in
mind—that is, twelve is a political number that brings to recollection
the twelve tribes of Israel. This number, made even more popular by
the composition of *The Testaments of the Twelve Patriarchs* (an apocalyptic book from ancient Judaism) is attributed to one of the twelve
sons of Jacob. Jacob's name in the biblical story, of course, was
changed to Israel. In ascertaining Jesus' relation to politics, one cannot forget two facts: first, James and John (the sons of Zebedee) ask
Jesus for the thrones on his left and right; second, Jesus was crucified
as a political criminal.

Debates certainly continue regarding other actions attributed to
Jesus. Some revered experts conclude or are associated with the perception that Jesus was a marginal Jew, or that he was a Mediterranean
peasant. I cannot agree that Jesus was either a marginal Jew[16] or a
peasant.[17] Jesus was devoutly Jewish and affirmed the centrality of the
Temple. Furthermore, he was far too sophisticated, learned, and
involved with urban life to be a peasant. These conclusions sometimes

appear without the seasoning of scholarly dialogue and nuanced sophistication.

Central to the previous reflections are methodological searches to authenticate Jesus' activities. Fortunately, Bruce Chilton and Craig A. Evans have edited a book that will be essential in any future search for Jesus' actions. In *Authenticating the Activities of Jesus* (1999b), nineteen established New Testament experts share their own methods and conclusions. The purpose of the collection is "to clarify what procedures should be undertaken to distinguish tradition and meaning that stem from Jesus from those which stem from later tradents and evangelists" (Preface). One third of the book addresses Methods and Assumptions, and two-thirds focus on Authenticating the Activities of Jesus.

Seventeen essays appear in the Chilton-Evans volume; eleven are new and six have been revised. J. D. G. Dunn and most scholars who contributed to the volume and its companions are convinced that the goal of Jesus Research, or the Third Quest, will most likely succeed, if it has not already done so. M. Hengel and C. A. Evans present papers to show that Jesus did have a messianic mission. Personally, I am convinced that while Jesus never declared himself to be the Messiah (the Christ), he may have had a messianic self-understanding.[18]

W. Klassen brilliantly raises again a perplexing question: "What did Judas betray?" He disagrees with Marcus Borg, Ruth Tucker, John Dominic Crossan, and others regarding this issue. Klassen rightly points out that the New Testament verb used to describe Judas' act is *paradidomi*, which means "to hand over," or "transmit"—it does not mean "betray." The Greek word for betray is *prodidomi*, a verb that does not appear in the New Testament. An obviously incorrect reading in Mark 14:10 can be found only in Codex Bezae, an important, but divergent manuscript of the Gospels. Thus, Klassen is convinced that "Judas acted in obedience to Christ's will and that in his act of handing over could have been obedient to God's will" (Chilton & Evans, 1999a, 386).

Klassen is correct to point out that Judas is a much more positive character than Christian traditions allow. Judas was certainly one of the Twelve, and he may have been the treasurer of Jesus' group (John 12:6; 13:29). The tendencies of the later strata of the Gospels do certainly increase the vilification of Judas. Narrative exegesis and the rhetorical thrust of the Gospels clarify that Judas left Jesus' group, joined his enemies, and initiated a process that eventually led to Jesus' crucifixion. We have no way of knowing Judas' motives, or Jesus' final evaluation of him.[19] Was Judas a betrayer? If so, what did he betray?

He could not have betrayed Jesus' identity. He was too well known. He could not have betrayed a secret spot where Jesus prayed. Jesus went out of Jerusalem to pray; it was his customary place to pray and the place was a public olive grove.

It is important, of course, to seek to know what can be reliably ascertained about the reasons for Jesus' horrible death in 30 C.E.[20] Jesus ascends to Jerusalem from Galilee in order to celebrate Passover. Pontius Pilate brings thousands of his soldiers from Caesarea Maritima to the Holy City for crowd control during the celebration. Pilgrims flood in from everywhere, especially Parthia in the East and Rome in the West, to celebrate. The city becomes electric with messianic and eschatological fever as the Jews begin to celebrate—actually relive—how God acted on their behalf and saved them from the Pharaohs, bringing them out of Egypt "with his strong hand and his outstretched arm." In his well-written *Jesus: A Revolutionary Biography*, Crossan captures the social setting.

> Caiaphas and Pilate would no doubt have agreed before such a festival that fast and immediate action was to be taken against any disturbance, and that some examples by crucifixion might be especially useful at the start. (Crossan, 1995a)

For Caiaphas and Pilate, who must preserve order amid potential crises, and most likely against the wishes of most in the Sanhedrin, Jesus was deemed to be dangerous because of his ability to arouse unruly crowds (the most unstable of social institutions), and was quickly taken from the public arena and placed in prison. Is it conceivable that some Jewish leaders who wanted him imprisoned hoped to protect Jesus from danger? Did a good intention turn out wrong? What is the relation between the two crowds during Jesus' last week: the crowd who hailed his entry into Jerusalem, and the crowd who shouted for his crucifixion?

What Can Be Known about Jesus' Teaching?

R. Bultmann and those in the Bultmann School, which fundamentally controlled the agenda of New Testament scholarship from the 1940s to the 1970s, tended to de-emphasize the importance of what can be known about the historical Jesus. Bultmann wrote the following:

> I do indeed think we can now know almost nothing concerning the life and personality of Jesus (daß wir vom Leben und von der Persönlichkeit Jesu so gut wie nichts mehr wissen können), since the early Christian sources show no interest in either, are moreover fragmentary and often

legendary; and other sources about Jesus do not exist. (Bultmann, 1934, 1958)[21]

This dictum is often alluded to, but is seldom quoted accurately. In some ways, it does not represent other statements by Bultmann. For us now, let it suffice to point out that Bultmann's claim was highly influential throughout the world, especially after World War II, and is still considered axiomatic today by some New Testament experts.

Why is it important to mention Bultmann's conclusion now? His claim is a benchmark against which to judge the "new" in psychobiography, which takes a paradigmatically different interpretation of our sources.

Christians take the life of Jesus seriously, concluding that faith in him is faith in a particular human person who did something particularly important for those who believe in him. Thus, it is imperative to know something about Jesus the man, what he did, why the crowds slowly left him, and why he died on a cross near the western wall of Jerusalem. While Bultmann eschewed any study of Jesus' actions, and while Sanders brought the actions of Jesus back into focus,[22] it is those who are using psychobiography who have helped us comprehend or speculate why Jesus acted the way he is reputed to have acted. Near the end of this chapter, we shall access this new dimension of Jesus Research. Suffice it here to report that psychobiography includes Jesus' actions, brings them back into focus, and in doing so is certainly not motivated by Christian Dogmatics.

Now it is fundamentally important to point out that, while Jesus' actions are important and must be included in any critical evaluation or summary of his life, it is equally central—and perhaps more important for many scholars, as Bultmann claimed—to examine what can be known regarding the teaching of Jesus. Psychobiographers urge us to ask, "What can be comprehended about the mind of Jesus?"

A major turning point in the study of Jesus by a Jew is seen in the brilliant and challenging trilogy written by Vermes: *Jesus the Jew* (1973), *Jesus and the World of Judaism* (1983), and *The Religion of Jesus the Jew* (1993).

A turning point in this aspect of Jesus Research is unknown to most psychobiographers. The shift was made by a pioneer in Jesus Research, the late David Flusser. He was an incredibly erudite and creative professor at the Hebrew University in Jerusalem. In my celebration of his work, long before he died, I reported that in Jerusalem, Flusser was hailed in many quarters as both a somewhat crazy showman and yet an incomparable genius. He is the only scholar with whom I have discussed the text of the New Testament who habitually knew the

major variants in the Gospels—and not just from the *apparatus criticus,*
but from reading the manuscripts.

In the major revision of his book *Jesus* (Flusser & Notley, 1998),
Flusser focused on Jesus' concept of love. This is quite remarkable in
view of the fact that at the beginning of the twentieth century, Jewish
scholars cast aspersions on Jesus as a foolish teacher because he told
his followers to love those who could kill them. For example, in 1910,
C. G. Montefiore, who had been president of the Liberal Jewish Synagogue and who had a deep respect for Jesus, treating him fairly,
claimed that to love our enemies "cannot be done" (1910, 57–58).[23] He
opined that it was foolish to teach disciples an ethical norm that is neither attractive nor possible.

In contrast to earlier Jewish authors who rejected Jesus because of
his apparently absurd command to love our enemies (Matt. 5:44),
Flusser crafted a sensitive and scholarly book that is one of the best
discussions of Jesus' understanding of love ever written. Flusser saw
a markedly "new sensitivity" among Jews who were Jesus' contemporaries. Like them, Jesus knew that love must include all and be like
God's mercy (Luke 6:36, Matt. 5:4).

From years of discussing Jesus with Flusser, I perceived Jesus'
teachings more clearly. Jesus taught that love that is defined by
boundaries may only be a self-serving affection. As we mature and
reflect on our own lives, we may discern that we cannot know who
may be our friends or our enemies, and that such a bifurcation of
humanity distorts reality. Moreover, if we do not strive to love our
enemies, how are we to live in a world without enemies? Hence, rather
than an insane teaching, the injunction to love our enemies is the
proper perspective from which to envision a New World Order. Such
a love is aligned with Jesus' injunction to turn the other cheek; thus,
Jesus is a great thinker who was consistent. If love is not costly, then
how can it be love that is genuinely empowered by God's love?

Jesus' influence on the brilliant and highly trained Jews who followed him was precisely on this point: the concept of love. Paul constantly emphasized the importance of faith, but when he compared
faith, hope, and love, he stressed that the greatest of these is love (1
Cor. 13). The author of the Fourth Gospel stressed the importance of
the verb "to believe." He also felt the power of Jesus' concept of love.
This author claimed that Jesus taught a new commandment. Jesus'
followers are commanded to love one another as he had loved them
(John 13:34–35; 15:12, 17).

It is obvious that Jesus stands out in the history of Jewish thought.

His major ethical teaching was to love others, even enemies. While the liberal lives of Jesus that appeared in the late nineteenth century over-emphasized this aspect of Jesus' life and teaching (especially Harnack), and missed the apocalyptic dimension of his teaching, it is clear that Jesus placed more emphasis on love than did other Jews, including those who are behind the high ethical teachings in *The Sayings of the Fathers (Pirke Abot)*. What is most remarkable to me is that Jesus presented his teachings within such a tortured social context: Jews suffered from occupation of Palestine by Roman militant forces and from oppression by scribes and priests who controlled the citadel of learning and tradition centralized in Jerusalem.

Flusser's influence continues: one of his students has written a perceptive assessment of Jesus' parables. Brad Young's *The Parables: Jewish Tradition and Christian Interpretation* (1998) focuses on the attempt to understand Jesus in light of what can be known of Jesus' own time. Young rightly points out that Christian interpretations, even by the early Greek scholars, often missed Jesus' message because they removed him from his Jewish environment. There should be no doubt that the parables originate with Jesus, though edited by the evangelists. Many scholars, including C. W. Hedrick (1994), rightly see Jesus' own personal creativity in these parables.

What is Jesus' fundamental message or teaching? Most scholars concur that Jesus' central message is the dawning of God's Rule, the establishment of the Kingdom of God on earth in practical and operational ways. Matthew's Gospel refers to this goal as the coming of "the Kingdom of Heaven." Thus, among the most certain aspects of Jesus' teachings are the following:

- Jesus' fundamental proclamation was the dawning of God's Rule. He inherited much reflection about God as "King" and God's Kingship from early Jewish thought.
- Like some of the early Rabbis, his custom was to speak pictorially, using parables.
- He knew some Greek (if he spoke to Pilate), and Hebrew (he read scripture in the synagogue), but his usual language for teaching was Aramaic.
- He seems to have taught his disciples a special way to pray [the Lord's Prayer], and it is conceivable he may have learned this from John the Baptizer, as Luke 11:1 may indicate, and perhaps indirectly from the Qumran Community.
- In line with ideas implicit within the teaching of other early Jews, Jesus taught his followers that they should love their enemies.

- He often argued with the Pharisees because his theology was close to theirs.
- Jesus' teachings are often similar to those of Hillel, a Pharisee who died before Jesus' ministry; but Jesus' mind, unlike Hillel's, was impregnated with apocalyptic and eschatological concepts and perceptions.
- He was influenced by some Essene thoughts, as reflected in the Dead Sea Scrolls, especially CD (particularly the Qumran fragments), but would have been highly critical of the Qumran hatred of others, their predestinarian beliefs, and their exclusivism.[24]
- He apparently perceived his mission, and that of his followers, to be focused on Israel alone ("go nowhere among the Gentiles" in Matt. 10:5).
- He argued against the Jerusalem-based elevated concept of purity, and most likely attacked the money changers in the Temple because of their pollution of the "Father's House."

Of course, every aspect of this list—and also of the previous one—can be, and has been, debated.[25] What I present is only a consensus I observe among experts who have been independently involved in Jesus Research in Israel, Germany, France, Canada, Australia, the United States, and elsewhere within established institutions of higher learning.

The list contains one item that is now hotly debated. Some scholars, such as Borg, are convinced that Jesus' message was not eschatological. I am personally convinced, and most experts in Jesus Research would concur, that Jesus' teaching was eschatological and apocalyptic. This issue is unfortunately no longer a major consensus among authors, but it is clearly a consensus among scholars who have studied Early Judaism and the earliest stratum of Jesus traditions. W. Klassen is certainly correct to stress that members of the Jesus Seminar try "to free" Jesus from "the shackles of Jewish apocalypticism" so that they may "tailor Jesus to their own likes" and so "find him more palatable" (Klassen, 1999).

To deny a Jesus with eschatological teachings (because it brings into focus a Jesus that is unattractive to us moderns) violates the point made by Schweitzer: scholars must be wary of concluding about Jesus what they had hoped to conclude. The wish must not be allowed to become the parent of the thought. If an apocalyptic Jesus is offensive, is that conclusion any more offensive than a Palestinian Jew who refuses to include Gentiles in his mission? Surely, one of the attractions of a psychobiographical approach to Jesus is that it allows our insights to lead us to surprising answers, free of controls that undermine any honest intellectual questioning.

To me, an apocalyptic and eschatological Jesus is demanded by a disinterested examination of the Jesus traditions in the New Testament and an exploration of his place within pre-70 C.E. Palestinian Judaism. Such a perspective is attractive and not embarrassing; it allows us to see Jesus as a Jew who had a magnificent vision. Jesus was concerned as much about the present as the future, and as much about the future as the present. Some engaged in the study of Jesus have failed to study the Jewish apocalypses. The authors of these works often stress that apocalypticism is directed more to the present than the future. For example, Enoch sees what is about to happen, learns wisdom, and shares these insights with those who are suffering on earth (1 Enoch 91–107). These reflections reveal some of the chaos now marring the study (or search) of the historical Jesus. The massive disagreements in published books lead us to ponder how one can access Jesus' message.

A particular point that has bothered scholars lies in the question, "Did Jesus invite sinners and not urge them to repent?" This is a major claim by E. P. Sanders, with whom I share much. Yet I must confess that I agree here with N. T. Wright and that I disagree with Sanders. I am persuaded that Jesus called sinners to repent (cf. John 7:53-8:11). This claim or declaration in the Fourth Gospel has as strong a case for representing Jesus as any other section of the New Testament, even though it is not original to the Gospel of John.

What Can We Really Say about the Man from Nazareth?

Is my list of what can be known about Jesus' teaching idiosyncratic or representative of the field? Other, often strikingly similar lists are provided by Wright and Sanders. I agree with C. A. Evans, in adding to the list "that Jesus was viewed by the public as a prophet, that the Romans crucified him as 'King of the Jews,' and that following Easter, his followers regarded him as Israel's Messiah." Thus, the pendulum has swung from the declarative, "We cannot know anything about Jesus," to the interrogative, "How much can we reliably know about the historical Jesus?" Perhaps the central issue once again concerns methodology. How do we know we are hearing Jesus' own voice and not merely distorted echoes passed on by those who never knew him?

A search for such answers is aided by Bruce Chilton and Craig A. Evans's edited work entitled *Authenticating the Words of Jesus* (1999a).

Again, the purpose is to seek behind the edited versions of the Evangelists' four Gospels some reliable traditions that derive ultimately from Jesus himself. The book includes seventeen essays, almost all of which are by leading experts who write in English. Essays on methodology are presented by C. A. Evans, B. D. Chilton, B. J. Malina, and T. Holmén.[26] The chapter by Malina is particularly superb. Two of the essays discuss the Lord's Prayer.

Only one essay is devoted to "the Son of Man"; it is by Chilton, who makes some important contributions. Chilton, however, fails to realize that today most experts on the Pseudepigrapha conclude that the author of 1 Enoch 37–71 tends to identify the Messiah with the Son of Man, and that this tradition antedates Jesus' own authentic words. If this document, the so-called "Parables of Enoch," is prior to or contemporaneous with Jesus, then "Christian" theology is much closer to some forms of Judaism than we might expect, and we may have an invaluable source for grasping Jesus' self-understanding.

Bultmann began his *Theology of the New Testament* (1951, 1955) with a conclusion: "*The message of Jesus* is a presupposition for the theology of the New Testament rather than part of that theology itself."[27] I find it practically impossible to comprehend why Bultmann made such a claim, having written a book on Jesus which focused on his teachings, and it would have been helpful to have him explain what the relation is between this claim, which begins his first paragraph in his two-volume work on New Testament theology, and the final sentence of the same paragraph that appears to be a non sequitur: "Jesus' message cannot be omitted from the delineation of New Testament theology." To make sense of Bultmann's first paragraph and its place within his complex system of thought, I must take his first sentence to be misleading and a way to shock his readers into reading the rest of his work attentively.

While Bultmann concluded that Jesus is the presupposition of New Testament Theology, I have learned that early Jewish thought is the presupposition of Jesus' message. That is, what Bultmann and especially the Bultmannians attributed to the creativity of "the early Church," I have found to be an aspect of the creativity of early Jewish theology in Palestine before 70 C.E. I believe that this is especially true of the brilliant perceptions and *termini technici* found in the Pseudepigrapha and the Dead Sea Scrolls. Moreover, Jesus' self-understanding was shaped by his knowledge of early Jewish speculations that are focused on the Son of Man, the Messiah, and the Righteous One. Finally, Jesus' teachings are the beginnings of New Testament Theology, as Jeremias (especially Goppelt) and others have shown.[28]

Having made these claims, I prescind briefly to consider a creative suggestion by J. C. O'Neill in *Who Did Jesus Think He Was?* (1995, 164–187). O'Neill is convinced that Jesus' claims in the Gospel of John do not derive from Jesus, but from Jewish documents that antedate Jesus.[29] While much in the Gospel of John derives from earlier sources and is grounded in history, the echoes of Jesus in this Gospel are almost always the sound of the Evangelist's own voice.

Only one essay in *Authenticating the Words of Jesus* is directly on the Parables. In one of the best essays in these two volumes on authenticity, W. Klassen demonstrates how the command to love our enemies is both authentic to Jesus and also rooted in the Greek theater, as well as in the new morality appearing in early Jewish theology around the time of Jesus, as Flusser's book also demonstrates.[30]

Both of the volumes by Chilton and Evans appear in a series inaugurated and still edited by Bruce M. Metzger: *New Testament Tools and Studies*. Each is obviously intended as a reference work for scholars. The essays are mostly in English, but one is in German. The discussions unfortunately often demand knowledge of Hebrew and Greek philology. It is a pity that all who have contributed to these volumes seem to be from the Christian community. This ignores the superb work on Jesus that is being published by Jews and by others who defy the traditional Christian labels.

These two major flagships in publishing on Jesus, in central focus just now, unfortunately follow the old traditional approaches to Jesus. More research should have been grounded on sociology and archaeology—a dimension of Jesus Research that will be corrected by the proceedings of the millennium celebration in Jerusalem.[31]

What are the tendencies of the essays presented in these two volumes? There is a move to distance research from the popular, and often journalistic, publications of the Jesus seminar which, inter alia, has sought objective proofs and announces, with distorted methodology, that Jesus must be divorced from Jewish apocalypticism. Many readers will agree with N. T. Wright that the Jesus Seminar employs a misleading methodology, and has five gospels but "no Gospel." Yet there is also some good that comes out of the Jesus Seminar, and R. W. Funk's initiative and desire to take the historical Jesus seriously is commendable.[32]

The essays show a willingness to consider Jesus' messianic self-understanding. There is an awareness that Jesus was thoroughly Jewish, and that the New Testament Gospels incorrectly tend to shift the blame for his death to "the Jews." There is also a tendency to avoid positivism—claims to something like objective unedited data regarding Jesus—while also endeavoring to keep clear of the distorting claim that all conclusions are merely tenuous speculations by scholars.

We are now in a new day in the study of the historical Jesus. The world of the twenty-first century is different from the world of the twentieth century. One difference is placarded by some words written by H. Gunkel, the great German biblical scholar in the first half of the twentieth century. It is riveting to read Gunkel's words: "To us, for whom war has become the solution for the problems of today, this book (the Old Testament) can become a source of strength. Our people also will remain invincible if we know both: the heroism of the sword and the heroism of faith."[33] I am convinced that the world leaders today—especially after the invasion of Iraq (no matter how apparently necessary)—have learned that war is not "the solution for the problems of today." Even so, no one would be so foolish as to suggest that peace will soon appear in the Middle East or elsewhere on our fragile globe, as every place is now threatened by terrorism.

Scholars should be thankful to Chilton and Evans for the two books highlighted in this review essay, namely *Authenticating the Activities of Jesus* and *Authenticating the Words of Jesus*. This adds to the attractiveness of their other works, especially their earlier edited collection of essays: *Studying the Historical Jesus: Evaluations of the State of Current Research* (1994), and *Jesus in Context: Temple, Purity, and Restoration* (1997). Reading the contributors to these books leaves one with an impression that there is much creative diversity among the world specialists devoted to Jesus Research.

Jesus Research and the Appearance of Psychobiography

Chilton and Evans's two volumes, *Authenticating the Activities of Jesus* and *Authenticating the Words of Jesus*, provide a benchmark for evaluating where scholars are at present regarding the study of the historical Jesus. While many of the contributions are solid and informative, the volumes could have been much better. It is neither wise nor easy to separate the story of Jesus into his deeds and his words. Sometimes Jesus' message is more articulate in his actions than in his verbal expressions. This point is made especially strongly when one looks at the books that study Jesus from the sociological and psychological point of view—perspectives noticeably absent in the two volumes by Evans and Chilton.

Before World War II, Shirley Jackson Case introduced the sociological approach to Jesus.[34] Case died in 1947, before he could complete his

second book on Jesus. In 1978, Gerd Theissen, in a brilliant monograph entitled *Sociology of Early Palestinian Christianity*,[35] initiated the
new wave of studying Jesus in light of sociology.[36] In 1989, Richard A.
Horsley added a major contribution to this field with his book *Sociology and the Jesus Movement*. In 1999, another major study of Jesus,
which included sociology, was published. It is by E. W. Stegemann
and W. Stegemann. They investigate the social world of Jesus. Their
work is entitled *The Jesus Movement: A Social History of Its First Century*.

These three books were not written by sociologists, but rather by
New Testament experts informed by sociological analysis. No book
has been dedicated to a sociological biography of Jesus, and I am not
familiar with a word such as "sociobiography."

Therefore, major monographs on sociology and Jesus are still waiting to be written. After teaching courses on the sociology of the Palestinian Jesus Movement before 70 C.E., I have observed the need for
four major studies. First, we need an examination of Jesus and the
crowds. This study would bring to bear the insights of G. Le Bon and
other sociologists on the sociology of the "crowd." That would help
clarify Jesus' popularity in Galilee, his entry into Jerusalem, and the
mob's shouting that led to his crucifixion. Second, we need an in-depth
study of the sociology of pilgrimage and how such insights help us
comprehend Jesus' last trip to Jerusalem. Third, we need to revisit
Weber's insights that Jesus was a charismatic. This pioneering work
can be enriched fruitfully in the light of the apocalyptic erudition
found in the Enoch Groups and the Qumran Community, as well as in
the fanatical groups such as the Zealots (see the works by Hengel and
Rhoads). Fourth, Mary Douglas's contributions on the relation between
purity and danger are seminal for Jesus Research. Her sociological
insights help us better comprehend the growing evidence of the
Jewish rites for purification in Palestine (stone vessels and mikvaot)
and the fear of becoming impure (*Temple Scroll*, col. 50) among Jews
before 70 C.E. Such a background, I am convinced, helps us perceive
the reason for Jesus' strong resistance to such an elevation of what it
means to be holy and pure. This resistance is surely one of the reasons
why he was imprisoned at Passover, and perhaps why he was eventually crucified.

While a careful sociological study of Jesus is lacking among the
hundreds of books on Jesus that have appeared over the past twenty
years, a psychological assessment of Jesus has recently assumed some
prominence. After being dormant for over fifty years, the psychological way of studying Jesus has taken on new methodologies that tran-

scend the programs of both Freud and Jung. It is certainly clear that no one should attempt to psychoanalyze Jesus. It is simply impossible to place him on a couch and cross-examine him. Yet it is essential to complete a study of Jesus by adding what one trained in psychology may see or query.[37] Jesus Research (or the Third Quest) has been converging with psychobiography and psychohistory. Two superb attempts at a psychobiography of Jesus have appeared, which deserve highlighting, if only briefly.

John W. Miller's *Jesus at Thirty: A Psychological and Historical Portrait* (1997), is one such attempt. Miller, who was formerly director of Psychiatric Rehabilitation Services at a hospital and taught religion at the college level, is convinced that the proper method to use in writing a psychological biography of Jesus is a refined method adapted from Freud, Fromm, Erikson, and Levinson.

Especially important for Miller is Freud's insight into the oedipal complex. Miller attempts to demonstrate that Jesus was estranged from his family, lost his father at an early age, and became surrogate father and husband. Later, Jesus had a powerful pneumatic experience during his baptism by John the Baptizer. He eventually broke with his mother at about thirty years of age. Jesus, however, resisted the temptation to be the Messiah, did not marry because his father was not available to perform the normal Jewish familial search for a spouse, and he achieved peace and wholeness in recognizing that he had found a heavenly Father.

New Testament critics will point out that Miller places too much historical validity on Luke's portrayal of Jesus. The Third Evangelist alone reports that Jesus began his ministry at age thirty, which Miller admits may have been between twenty-eight and thirty-three (Miller, 1997, 80). This Evangelist is committed to clarifying the order of Jesus' life; but there is no evidence that he had sources superior to those used by Mark and John.

Experts in the Judaism of Jesus' day will also need more discussion on the report that Jesus' public ministry began when he was thirty. According to the *Cairo Damascus Document*, the priest who is to preside over The Many is to be between thirty and sixty years old (CD 14.6-7). According to the *Temple Scroll*, the age of maturity is twenty, not thirty. Note this representative passage:

> From twent[y] years and upwards they shall observe it (17.8)
> on the day on which they make h[im] king of the sons of Israel,
> (those who are) between thirty and sixty years of age. (58.2-3)[38]

Most likely, the quotation specifies those who are to be included in a census; hence, a male is counted only when he reaches twenty years of age.

It is evident that this tradition, because it is found in the Temple Scroll, represented more than Qumran sectarian beliefs, since this scroll is not like the Rule of the Community or the Hodayot, which represent quintessential Qumran theology. Moreover, one should observe that the Temple Scroll, in the passage just cited, is most likely exegetically dependent on, yet creatively divergent from, Leviticus 27:3, which specifies the obligations of males, qualifying that they must be between twenty and sixty (cf. also Baba Bathra 121b).

New Testament scholars will find Miller's analysis unconvincing, because he misses the "Tendencies of the Evangelists" [*Redaktionsgeschichte*]. It is certain that each of the four canonical evangelists not only received traditions, some of which may be reliable historically, but that they also shaped and edited what Jesus did and said. No one can simply read the Gospels as if they are objective biographies. The Jesus traditions were too challenging, defining, and convincing for the Evangelists not to mix interpretation with tradition. That is to our advantage, since we have first-century accounts of Jesus that are somewhat coherent, and most importantly, meaningfully interpreted. To try to dissect the Jesus of History out of the Christ of Faith not only misunderstands the creative dimension of all our sources, but misses the point that Jesus was important because of what he claimed and what was claimed about him. Bultmann's adage that in the post-Easter community the Proclaimer became the proclaimed is right on target in one sense, but in another sense is misleading. *Jesus was the Proclaimer who proclaimed.*

Miller focuses on an aspect of Jesus' teachings, the fatherhood of God, which was a feature of the psychological study of Jesus during the Old Quest of the Historical Jesus that ended in 1906 with Schweitzer's book, *The Quest of the Historical Jesus.* Miller, however, misses the advancements made since Jeremias' research on "Abba,"[39] and incorrectly claims that only women were with Jesus at the cross (John 19:26f.; p. 72).

There is much that scholars may learn from Miller's book. He does show that one can obtain some insight into Jesus' early years by looking at what is reported about him after he joined John the Baptizer. Miller brings into shocking focus the apparently reliable evidence that Jesus was estranged from his mother and siblings, but not from his father.

In *Fatherless in Galilee* (2001). A. van Aarde is influenced by Miller but "profoundly uneasy" with his methods and conclusions. Van Aarde is critical of Miller because he does not know how to study the New Testament and makes assumptions that would be demolished by cultural historians of pre-70 C.E. Palestine and New Testament exegetes. He highlights four major problems with Miller's work (Miller, 1997):

1. Miller uncritically accepts the historicity of the patristic claim that Joseph died when Jesus was young;

2. Miller uncritically assumes that Jesus must be the firstborn;

3. Miller assumes that Jesus became a "surrogate father";

4. Miller postulates that Jesus enjoyed an "emotionally secure childhood."

In each of these claims, van Aarde is basically correct. He proves that psychobiographers must learn how to study the New Testament and perceive how it took shape, from Aramaic oral traditions to the Greek text. The Evangelists were not eyewitnesses (Luke 1:1-4), and they edited what they received, including re-writing what Jesus had said, as can be seen, for example, from how differently Matthew and Luke edit Mark 9:1.

Van Aarde suggests that we might start with the birth narratives in Matthew and Luke because questions about Jesus' identity first appear in these stories. He is convinced that Jesus appears in the Gospels as "a fatherless figure." He asks us to ponder one focused question: "What would it be like for someone in first-century Herodian Palestine to bear the stigma of being fatherless, but who trusted God as Father?" Van Aarde (2001) is convinced that "Jesus filled the emptiness caused by his fatherlessness with his trust in God as father." With such claims, many bridges connect the works of Miller and van Aarde.

I too wonder why Jesus chose almost always to call God "Father," and not Yahweh, Lord, or Elohim. Why and how did Jesus' failures to prove his parentage to those who claimed he was a *mamzer* (not a bastard, but one who could not prove convincingly to authorities who his parents were) affect his psychological personality?[40] If Jesus was judged by the scribes and priests to be a *mamzer*, then he was lost in the interstices of Jewish society, which would adversely affect his psychological development.

Even more challenging is Donald Capps's *Jesus: A Psychological Biography* (2000). Capps, a professor at Princeton Theological Seminary and a leading specialist on the psychology of religion, carefully assesses what advances have been achieved by those dedicated to Jesus Research. He chooses to focus on Jesus' role as healer. Capps certainly demonstrates that Jesus scholars have inadvertently been drawing conclusions about Jesus that impinge on the field of psychology. He shows also that psychological theories are not only legitimate but essential in the historical re-assessment of the man known as Jesus of Nazareth.

More sensitive to the way the Evangelists' communities and the Evangelists themselves shaped and edited the Jesus traditions than Miller, Capps rightly claims that Jesus, as most scholars contend, performed healing miracles. Capps explores Jesus' role as exorcist-healer and makes some fascinating suggestions.[41] His discoveries are often fresh and a stimulus to more explorations.

Capps's book is controversial and certainly is not controlled by Christian orthodoxy or tradition. For example, Capps is convinced that Jesus' birth was illegitimate,[42] that Joseph failed to adopt him, and that "Jesus was a melancholic male who turned to an alternative religious formulation, based on belief in Abba [God as Father] to address and overcome his melancholia" (Capps, 2000, 260).

What is most impressive about the studies by Miller and Capps? Perhaps the fact that they are not mere reports on personality pathologies, or what Schweitzer and the psychiatrists he critiqued called "pathographies." Such reports would merely be studies of historical figures that focused on their pathogenic personalities to the exclusion of virtually all that might be said about their important or notable qualities that made them worthy of study in the first place. Miller, in fact, views Jesus as a healthy male. Capps suggests that Jesus "treated" his own "melancholia" in a truly restorative and therapeutic course of action, through his cathartic explosive anger in the Temple. That event, of course, almost certainly set in motion the sequence of actions that led directly to his death. Miller and Capps, therefore, present a portrait of Jesus as one who overcame major psychological problems and emerged as a relatively healthy male.

Conclusion

Luke Timothy Johnson, in his book *The Real Jesus* (1996), appropriately stresses the fundamental truth of the story in the Gospels. Story is essential not only for the individuals we meet in Scripture,[43] but also for all humans.[44] As I review human history from caveman to modern man, I am persuaded that story rates very high among the needs of humans. Everywhere, and in every vehicle for expression—etchings on cliffs and cave walls, hieroglyphics, and the world of sophisticated symbols—humans need story. This is evident from the so-called ballads that give us Homer's masterpieces to the daily news we receive in story form. Humans need sustenance above all, but the need to tell a story counts next, probably before shelter, safety, sex, and clothing. The study of the Gospels is a study of Jesus' story as remembered by those who were challenged and excited by him. Rhetorical analysis of the Gospels, now in its heyday, focuses on the power of the rhetorical presence of the man from Nazareth who proceeded from Galilee to Judaea.

As we study the Jesus traditions, nothing could be clearer than the perception that we are able to obtain meaning only when we put data into a meaningful framework or story. Johnson wisely points out that "the most critical thing about a person is precisely what most eludes the methods of critical historiography, namely, the *meaning* of a character" (1996, 133). Indeed, I agree with Johnson that our "problem is not the lack of data, but the inaccessibility of meaning" in the vast primary data of the Jesus story. "Meaning derives from the interpretation of the facts rather than the facts themselves. And such interpretation depends on story." Have not the psychologists of religion helped us see that psychobiography is important in comprehending any biography, especially the story of Jesus? Have they not challenged those who are disappointed in the old and trite to explore creatively the psychic power of the man and message?

We need to comprehend that history is accessible only through tradition, and comprehensible only through interpretation.[45] Tradition and its interpretation are conveyed and rediscovered only in and through story. Thus, we need to ask, is the New Testament witness so powerful to so many because the story is not only historic, but also historical and real? Is not the story of Jesus fundamentally founded on some real, un-interpreted events in history?[46] I am persuaded that the answer is yes.

Thus, despite the great value of his work, I must disagree with Johnson on a key issue. He is too focused on exposing the problems with the Jesus Seminar when he advises that "Christian faith, then and now, [in New Testament times and the modern age] is based on religious claims concerning the present power of Jesus." That statement can be used out of the context in which Johnson has carefully crafted it; if so, it can lead to Docetism (a non-historical mysticism) and idealism, which leads to the notion that Jesus was a divine or heavenly figure whose humanness was merely apparent and not real. I am convinced we should add to Johnson's assessment that these "religious claims" must be grounded not only in what is putatively the "real Jesus," but also in the history of Roman Imperialism and ancient Judaism. We professors, especially those who teach in seminaries, must not teach something that would make our students sound foolish in the halls of the Hebrew University in Jerusalem.

Why is Jesus Research necessary? Jesus Research should begin with purely historical and scientific methods and honest questions. It must be "disinterested" in the sense that one should not lead the evidence to obtain a pre-set, desired conclusion. When scientific research is completed, if only temporarily, there is more to do, at least for Jews and Christians; and what is left is the need for a personal assessment of what answers have really been discovered. We need to be alert, and to explore how sacred traditions and faith are informed by the ramifications of the scientific study of antiquity, especially the life and teachings of Jesus in the first half of the first century C.E. In the process, all methodologies that inform us of who we have been and who we are as humans must be employed, from sociology to psychobiography, and from archaeology to theology.

Christians need to avoid the perennial pitfalls. On one hand, we must not err by seeking to ground Christian faith on some mirage of objective scientific knowledge. To remove from Christian faith the scandalous and gnawing uncertainty of a personal and total commitment drains faith from authentic spirituality. On the other hand, authentic Christian faith is more than a Kierkegaardian leap of faith. If one is to follow Jesus, then some reliable knowledge about how he lived and what he thought is imperative. Some existentialists might have thought Christians would be content to know only one unassailable fact about the historical Jesus: the pure givenness of Jesus' crucifixion. This fact leaves us with only a corpse, and fails to account for the rest of the Jesus story.

If Christianity is to survive or blossom in our increasingly secular world, it must be more aware of its origins in first-century Jewish culture. It must also be grounded and enriched by absorbing the truths authentically embodied in Jesus' life and message.[47] After living in Jerusalem intermittently since 1968, I have learned to avoid the fallacy of thinking that the main vehicle for understanding Jesus is his words. We should also comprehend that his meaning comes to life when we experience and imagine his environment and circumstance. While the Dead Sea Scrolls, for example, never mention Jesus or any of his followers, they nevertheless provide us with the intellectual and psychic environment of Jesus' time. Moreover, the spirituality of the

Qumran Community, and of Jesus' world in general, is preserved for us on leather scrolls once held by Jews who were contemporaneous with Jesus.

Belief in Jesus Christ is rooted in faith in a Jew named Jesus. The belief is dedicated to a faithful, honest, and, above all, scientific and disinterested inquiry into the *What* (*Was*) and the *How* (*Wie*) that gives meaning to the starkness of a public crucifixion. That secular event is only part of the *That* (*Das*) which provides for both the story of Jesus and the "good news" (Gospel) about him. Schweitzer, who perceived Jesus to be incomparably great, saw problems with the historical Jesus for the person of faith who intends to be faithful to our traditions and sources. Unable to solve those problems, he withdrew from Europe into a world of mysticism and wonderful service to Africans.[48]

Did Schweitzer accurately see the chaos in the lives of Jesus that postdated his own magnum opus? On the one hand, Schweitzer and his generation were correct to point out that we cannot ultimately define Jesus or exhaustively understand him by mere psychiatric methods.[49] On the other hand, it is also unwise to follow Bultmann and his school in refusing to consider Jesus' own self-consciousness, on the grounds that his earliest followers and the earliest sources are claimed by Bultmann to have had no objective interest in Jesus' personality or personal development.

As I pointed out in *Jesus within Judaism* (1988), every person has some self-understanding; hence, the historian and not only the theologian is entitled to ask about Jesus' self-understanding. Now, with the new methods developed by psychologists of religion, we can explore the psychobiographical possibilities as we imagine Jesus, the man, in his earthly context.

Perhaps the following are only minor questions: What were Jesus' relationships with his father, Joseph, and his mother, Mary? What were his relations with John the Baptist and Mary Magdalene? Did he have an elevated ego, and did he claim that he was the Son of Man or the designated Messiah? Surely historical research leads us to ask questions that have been charted by the psychologists of religion.

At the beginning of the twenty-first century, we may, at first glance, see an even greater chaos among Jesus scholars than Schweitzer envisioned. With patience and more pellucid perception, we may comprehend a challenging consensus that helps us see through the mists of history more clearly. Certainly there is at least a consensus regarding the big questions: Who was Jesus? Who did he think he was? What was his purpose? How did he think he was related to God? Why did he act and speak the way he does in our Gospels?

Can any of these questions be adequately assessed without any concern for psychobiography? Is it not certain that those who work on a Jesus psychobiography must be thoroughly trained in the archaeology and history of first-century Palestinian culture? I am convinced that most experts on the historical Jesus would today answer "yes" to both questions. It is becoming apparent that as New Testament exegetes need philology and archaeology, those devoted to Jesus Research need not only sociology—a given for decades—but also psychobiography.

Notes

1. I wish to dedicate this chapter to my longtime friend and colleague, Dr. Donald Capps, the William Harte Felmeth Professor of Pastoral Psychology at Princeton Theological Seminary. He knows far more about psychobiography than I do; I am grateful to him for helping me improve my presentation.

2. A. van Aarde, who apparently does not know my published research, rightly though inadvertently cites me when he reports that some scholars, correctly in his judgment, have announced a paradigm shift in the study of Jesus in 1980. See A. van Aarde (2001).

3. I am indebted to Professor Donald Capps for bringing Runyan's work to my attention.

4. This perspective appears in the uninformed, uncritical, and journalistic book by L. Strobel, *The Case for Christ: A Journalist's Personal Investigation of the Evidence for Jesus* (1998). Strobel moved from atheism or skepticism to Christianity by his own search for Jesus, but his search is far from objective and critical, despite the promises of the attractive anecdote that begins the book.

5. Of course, Schweitzer was correct to point out that Reimarus was the inaugurator of the Old Quest.

6. One needs to be careful not to confuse the German second edition with the English second edition, which was based on the German first edition.

7. G. Tyrrell had focused his thoughts on the Liberal Protestant, Harnack: "The Christ that Harnack sees, looking back through nineteen centuries of Catholic darkness, is only the reflection of a liberal Protestant face, seen at the bottom of a deep well" (1909/1963). Of course, Tyrrell's own fiery spirit and some tension between Catholics and Protestants are not well hidden in this outburst. See Tyrrell (1909/1963, 49). I am grateful to W. P. Weaver for discussions on Tyrrell's pellucid insight.

8. See H. Anderson (1967) for one of the best examinations of the denigration of historicism by Barth and Bultmann.

9. For recent discussion that attempts to show that Paul possibly knew about Jesus' life and teachings, and not only about his passion and resurrection, see D. Wenham (1994).

10. B. Tatum rightly sees the shift from a theologically loaded "Quest" toward a new approach to the historical Jesus. He calls it "post-quest" and places the date at 1985 because of two dates: the appearance of Sanders' *Jesus and Judaism* (1985), and the first session of the Jesus Seminar. While they did not initiate the new movement, both were part of it. See Tatum (1982, 1999). Tatum's statement could not have been in his first edition, and his own book, in its first edition, signifies that something new in the study of the historical Jesus has begun.

11. See especially R. A. Horsley (1987).

12. For those who cannot spend months working through the erudite and exhaustive volumes on Jesus by John Meier (1991–2003), a little book by Charlesworth and Weaver (2000) may be attractive. This book, entitled *Jesus Two Thousand Years Later*, contains essays that are written for the general public. Five well-known scholars present their ideas in the newest volume in the Faith and Scholarship Colloquies that are held each year at Florida Southern College: Walter P. Weaver, John Dominic Crossan, E. P. Sanders, Amy-Jill Levine, and James H. Charlesworth.

13. I am convinced that Jesus identified himself with the Old Testament prophets.

14. It is certain that Romans are responsible for Jesus' crucifixion. See J. D. Crossan (1995b).

15. See the important insights found in D. Mendels's *The Rise and Fall of Nationalism* (1992).

16. The title of J. Meier's book, *The Marginal Jew*, is not representative of Meier's erudite insights. When Meier uses "marginal," he means that Jesus' life would not have been featured on CNN and that he was not a typical Jew.

17. J. D. Crossan argues that Jesus was a peasant. See especially Crossan (1991).

18. I wish to add agreement with P. Stuhlmacher when he points out that any attempt to build bridges of understanding between Christians and Jews must be honest. For example, we dare not claim as Christians that Jesus must not be allowed to make messianic claims. See Stuhlmacher (1993).

19. J. Spong is convinced that Judas was a name (and story) invented by Christians. See Spong (1996).

20. In addition to the other works already cited, see Brown (1993) and Rivkin (1997).

21. For the German original, see Bultmann (1926, 1929).

22. Bultmann wrote that his study of Jesus would not show any interest in Jesus' life or personality, but only (nur) in his teaching and preaching. See Bultmann (1926, 1929, 15), in the German edition.

23. See also Anderson (1967).

24. See the contributions in Charlesworth (1992, 1995).

25. For a list of presuppositions of the Third Quest regarding the character of sources of the study of Jesus that represents the Jesus Seminar, see Funk and Smith (1991).

26. Those interested in methods for ascertaining authentic Jesus tradition should also consult Evans (1995, 1–49).

27. The German of the first sentence is as follows: "Die Verkündigung Jesu gehört zu den Voraussetzungen der Theologie des NT und ist nicht ein Teil dieser selbst."

28. L. Goppelt rejected Bultmann's starting point with these words: "If we desire to represent New Testament theology in keeping with its intrinsic structure, then we must begin with the question of the earthly Jesus (nach dem irdischen Jesus zu fragen)" (Goppelt, 1981, 1982). Hence, volume 1 of Goppelt's *Theology of the New Testament* is subtitled *The Ministry of Jesus in Its Theological Significance.*

29. I do not agree that the Gospel of John was put together by "only collectors and dramatists" (185). For the German version, see Goppelt (1985, 33–35). This German edition has a new opening section containing insightful comments on Bultmann.

30. For a discussion of Jesus' morality, see Harvey (1990).

31. It is focused on Jesus and Archaeology, and most of the leading archaeological experts participated. The proceedings will be published by Eerdmans. A very helpful but dated guide to Jesus and archaeology is Rousseau and Arav (1995). Also see Charlesworth (1988). For more recent treatments of Jesus and archaeology, see especially Reed (2000) and Charlesworth (2003).

32. It is interesting to observe that the two volumes by Funk and the Jesus Seminar and the two volumes edited by Chilton and Evans are divided into Jesus' acts and Jesus' words. I am dubious that a comparison of the four books would be fruitful: they are not responding to each other, and too many other important related works would be ignored.

33. A translation by W. Klassen of this work appears in *New Testament Tools and Studies 28*(1), 392.

34. Early portions of it are at Florida Southern College. I am grateful to W. P. Weaver for the opportunity to study these pages.

35. Also, for superb reading to obtain a feeling of life in ancient Palestine during the time of Jesus, see Theissen (1987).

36. As J. D. G. Dunn correctly reports, "To Gerd Theissen must go the credit for making the first effective attempt to study NT texts from a sociological perspective" (Dunn, 2003, 54). Also, see Dunn's discussions of Barth and Bultmann in light of the study of the historical Jesus; consult the index.

37. Contemporary visions of Mary are well known, but visions of Christ are habitually kept secret and unexamined. For a recent attempt to take these "Christic visions" seriously and study them in light of earlier books by Spar-

row and Huyssens, as well as in light of P. Feyerabend's work in the philosophy of science, see Wiebe (1997).

38. My translation; for the Hebrew (and another translation), see Yadin (1983).

39. See the contributions in Charlesworth (1994).

40. This question is central to me now, since I have just finished editing *Some Works of the Torah* (MMT) for publication, and in it there are challenging rules for the *mamzer*, including his exclusion from the Temple.

41. There is no doubt that Jesus did perform amazing healings; his opponents admitted that when they said he was able to perform such healings because he was possessed. For a recent study of Jesus' healings, see Davies (1995). Also, see Theissen (1983).

42. This position was developed by Schaberg (1990).

43. J. Licht's examination of the craft of the biblical storyteller is full of deep insight. See Licht (1978, 1986).

44. Profound insight into the foundations of language, especially when words are "resurrected" with new meaning in a story, is found in Aichele (1985).

45. I am here indebted to conversations with Ernst Käsemann (personal communication).

46. See my further reflections in Charlesworth (2000).

47. I have tried to avoid referring to non-English publications, but one work is extremely important to note. Criteria for authenticating Jesus' traditions behind the Jesus traditions are assessed in Theissen and Winter (1997). Also see Theissen and Merz (1998).

48. Especially see Schweitzer (1964).

49. In 1913, Schweitzer rejected the methods and conclusions of four psychopathologists who supposed Jesus had a mental disorder. According to their claims, he suffered from hallucinations and some paranoia. They failed to perceive Jesus within his time, which was a time of excessive messianic claims (often by bandits), apocalyptic hopes, and social and military oppressions. See Schweitzer (1948). Schweitzer was critical of these psychopathologists not because of psychology, but because of their misperceptions of the history of the gospel tradition and how to comprehend biblical studies. See Capps (Chap. 6, this vol.). Capps demonstrates that Schweitzer did not judge Jesus to be delusional. Certainly, Capps is correct, since for Jesus to claim that "something greater than Solomon is here," a saying that clearly goes back to Jesus because it is not created by the kerygma, and to ask, "who do you say that I am," indicates that Jesus' perception of himself and his questions to his disciples about who they thought he was are not that of a paranormal or delusional character, especially one in Palestine before 30 C.E. Schweitzer and Bultmann were deeply influenced by M. Kähler, who concluded that one should distinguish between the Christ of faith and the Jesus

of history, that only the proclaimed Christ should matter to Christians, and that a biography of Jesus is impossible since we have no sources that help us speculate on Jesus' psychological makeup. See Kähler (1964). The distinction between "Christ" and "Jesus" may be found in Strauss's critique of Schleiermacher's *Jesus*. See Strauss (1977).

References

Aichele, G., Jr. (1985). *The Limits of Story*, SBL Semeia Studies. Chico: Scholars Press.

Anderson, H. (1964). *Jesus and Christian Origins*. Oxford: Oxford University Press.

Anderson, H., ed. (1967). *Jesus*. Englewood Cliffs: Prentice Hall.

Bammel, E., & Moule, C. F. D. (1984). *Jesus and the Politics of His Day*. Cambridge and New York: Cambridge University Press.

Black, M., & VanderKam, J. (1992). *The Messiah*, J. H. Charlesworth, ed. Minneapolis: Fortress.

Boers, H. (1989). *Who Was Jesus?* San Francisco: Harper & Row.

Borg, M. (1984). *Conflict, Holiness, and Politics in the Teachings of Jesus*. Studies in the Bible and Early Christianity, vol. 5. New York and Toronto: Mellen.

Borg, M. (1987). *Jesus: A New Vision*. San Francisco: Harper & Row.

Borg, M. (1994). *Jesus in Contemporary Scholarship*. Valley Forge: Trinity Press International.

Borg, M., ed. (1997). *Jesus at 2000*. Boulder: Westview Press.

Borg, M., & Wright, N. T. (1999). *The Meaning of Jesus: Two Visions*. San Francisco: HarperSanFrancisco.

Brown, R. E. (1993). *The Birth of the Messiah: A Contemporary on the Infancy Narratives in the Gospels of Matthew and Luke*. Anchor Bible Reference Library. Philadelphia: American Interfaith Institute.

Brown, R. E. (1994, 1998). *The Death of the Messiah: From Gethsemane to the Grave*, 2 vols. Anchor Bible Reference Library. Philadelphia: American Interfaith Institute.

Bultmann, R. (1926, 1929). *Jesus*. Berlin: Deutsche Bibliothek.

Bultmann, R. (1934, 1958). *Jesus and the Word*, L. P. Smith & E. H. Lantero, trans. London: Scribner's Sons.

Bultmann, R. (1951, 1955). *Theology of the New Testament*, K. Grobel, trans., 2 vols. New York: Scribner's Sons.

Canetti, E. (1978). *Crowds and Power*, C. Stewart, trans. New York: Seabury.

Capps, D. (2000). *Jesus: A Psychological Biography*. St. Louis: Chalice Press.

Charlesworth, J. H. (1988). *Jesus within Judaism: New Light from Exciting Archaeological Discoveries*. Anchor Bible Reference Library. New York: Doubleday.

Charlesworth, J. H. (1990). David Flusser's Vision. *Explorations*, 4 (1). Philadelphia: American Interfaith Institute.

Charlesworth, J. H. (1994). A Caveat on Textual Transmission and the Meaning of Abba: A Study of the Lord's Prayer, *The Lord's Prayer and Other Prayer Texts from the Greco-Roman Era*. Valley Forge: Trinity Press International, 1–14.

Charlesworth, J. H. (2000). The Historical Jesus: Sources and a Sketch, *Jesus Two Thousand Years Later*, J. H. Charlesworth and W. P. Weaver, eds. Harrisburg: Trinity Press International.

Charlesworth, J. H. (2003). Jesus Research and Near Eastern Archaeology: Reflections on Recent Developments, *Neotestamentica et Philonica: Studies in Honor of Peder Borgen*, D. E. Aune, ed. Leiden: Brill, 37–70.

Charlesworth, J. H., ed. (1992, 1995). *Jesus and the Dead Sea Scrolls*. New York: Doubleday.

Chilton, B., & Evans, C. A., eds. (1994). *Studying the Historical Jesus: Evaluations of the State of Current Research*. New Testament Tools and Studies 19. Leiden: Brill.

Chilton, B., & Evans, C. A., eds. (1997). *Jesus in Context: Temple, Purity, and Restoration*. AGJU 39. Leiden: Brill.

Chilton, B., & Evans, C. A., eds. (1999a). *Authenticating the Words of Jesus*. New Testament Tools and Studies 28.1. Leiden: Brill.

Chilton, B., & Evans, C. A., eds. (1999b). *Authenticating the Activities of Jesus*. New Testament Tools and Studies 28.2. Leiden: Brill.

Crossan, J. D. (1991). *The Historical Jesus: The Life of a Mediterranean Jewish Peasant*. San Francisco: HarperSanFrancisco.

Crossan, J. D. (1995a). *Jesus: A Revolutionary Biography*. San Francisco: HarperSanFrancisco.

Crossan, J. D. (1995b). *Who Killed Jesus?* San Francisco: HarperSanFrancisco.

Dahl, N. (1991). *Jesus the Christ: The Historical Origins of Christological Doctrine*, D. H. Juel, ed. Minneapolis: Fortress.

Davies, S. L. (1995). *Jesus the Healer: Possession, Trance, and the Origins of Christianity*. New York: Continuum.

Dunn, J. D. G. (2003). *Jesus Remembered, Christianity in the Making*, vol. 1. Grand Rapids: Eerdmans.

Evans, C. A. (1995). *Jesus and His Contemporaries*. AGJU 25. Leiden: Brill, 1–49.

Evans, C. A. (1996). *Life of Jesus Research: An Annotated Bibliography*. New Testament Tools and Studies 24. Leiden: Brill.

Fenn, R. (1993). Crowds, Time, and the Essence of Society, *Secularization, Rationalism, and Sectarianism: Essays in Honour of Bryan R. Wilson*, E. Barker, J. A. Beckford, & K. Dobbelaere, eds. Oxford: Clarendon; New York: Oxford University Press.

Flusser, D., & Notley, R. S. (1998). *Jesus*. Jerusalem: Magnes.

Fredriksen, P. (1988). *From Jesus to Christ*. New Haven and London: Yale University Press.

Fredricksen, P. (1999). *Jesus of Nazareth, King of the Jews.* New York: Alfred A. Knopf.

Funk, R. W. (1996). *Honest to Jesus: Jesus for a New Millennium.* San Francisco: HarperSanFrancisco.

Funk, R. W. (1998). *The Acts of Jesus.* San Francisco: HarperSanFrancisco.

Funk, R. W., & Hoover, R. W. (1993). *The Five Gospels: The Search for the Authentic Words of Jesus.* New York: Macmillan.

Funk, R. W., & Smith, M. H. (1991). *Gospel of Mark: Red Letter Edition.* Sonoma: Polebridge Press.

Goppelt, L. (1981, 1982). *Theology of the New Testament,* J. Alsup, trans., 2 vols. Grand Rapids: Eerdmans.

Goppelt, L. (1985). *Theologie des Neuen Testaments* (3rd ed.). Göttingen: Vandenhoeck & Ruprecht.

Gunkel, H. (1916). *Israelitische Heldentum und Kriegsfrömmigkeit im alten Testament.* Göttingen: Vandenhoeck & Ruprecht.

Harvey, A. E. (1990). *Strenuous Commands: The Ethic of Jesus.* Philadelphia: Trinity Press International.

Hedrick, C. W. (1994). *Parables as Poetic Fictions: The Creative Voice of Jesus.* Peabody: Hendrickson.

Horsley, R. A. (1987). *Jesus and the Spiral of Violence.* San Francisco: Harper and Row.

Horsley, R. A. (1989). *Sociology and the Jesus Movement.* New York: Crossroad.

Johnson, L. T. (1996). *The Real Jesus.* San Francisco: HarperSanFrancisco.

Kähler, M. (1964). *The So-Called Historical Jesus and the Historic Biblical Christ,* C. E. Braaten, ed., trans. Philadelphia: Fortress. (Original work published 1896)

Käsemann, E. (1964). The Problem of the Historical Jesus, *Essays on New Testament Themes: Studies in Biblical Theology,* W. J. Montague, trans. London: SCM.

Le Bon, G. (1960). *The Crowd: A Study of the Popular Mind.* New York: Viking.

Licht, J. (1978, 1986). *Storytelling in the Bible.* Jerusalem: Magnes.

Meier, J. P. (1997). The Circle of the Twelve: Did It Exist during Jesus' Public Ministry? *Journal of Biblical Literature, 116*(4), 635–672.

Mendels, D. (1992). *The Rise and Fall of Nationalism.* New York: Doubleday.

Miller, J. W. (1997). *Jesus at Thirty: A Psychological and Historical Portrait.* Minneapolis: Fortress.

Montefiore, C. G. (1910). *Some Elements of the Religious Teaching of Jesus According to the Synoptic Gospels.* London: Macmillan.

Nickelsberg, G. W. E. (2000). *Encyclopedia of the Dead Sea Scrolls,* vol. 1. London: Oxford.

O'Neill, J. C. (1995). *Who Did Jesus Think He Was?* vol. 6. Leiden: Brill.

Reed, J. L. (2000). *Archaeology and the Galilean Jesus.* Harrisburg: Trinity Press International.

Rivkin, E. (1997). *What Crucified Jesus?* New York: UAHC Press.

Rousseau, J. J., & Arav, R. (1995). *Jesus and His World: An Archaeological and Cultural Dictionary.* Minneapolis: Fortress.

Runyan, W. M. (1984). *Life Histories and Psychobiography: Explorations in Theory and Method.* New York and Oxford: Oxford University Press.

Sacchi, P. (1990). *L'Apocalittica Giudaica e la sua storia.* Brescia: Paideia.

Sanders, E. P. (1985). *Jesus and Judaism.* London: SCM; Philadelphia: Fortress.

Sanders, E. P. (1993). *The Historical Figure of Jesus.* London and New York: Penguin Press.

Schaberg, J. (1990). *The Illegitimacy of Jesus: A Feminist Theological Interpretation of the Infancy Narratives.* New York: Crossroad.

Schweitzer, A. (1910, 1911). *The Quest of the Historical Jesus: A Critical Study of Its Progress from Reimarus to Wrede* (2nd ed.), W. Montgomery, trans. London: Black.

Schweitzer, A. (1948). *The Psychiatric Study of Jesus,* C. R. Joy, trans. Boston: Beacon.

Schweitzer, A. (1964). *The Mystery of the Kingdom of God,* W. Lowrie, trans. New York: Schocken. (Original work published 1914)

Spong, J. (1996). *Liberating the Gospels.* San Francisco: HarperSanFrancisco.

Stegemann, E. W., & Stegemann, W. (1999). *The Jesus Movement: A Social History of Its First Century.* Minneapolis: Fortress.

Strauss, D. F. (1835). *Das Leben Jesu.* Tübingen: Osiander.

Strauss, D. F. (1977). *The Christ of Faith and the Jesus of History,* L. E. Keck, ed., trans. Philadelphia: Fortress. (Original work published 1865)

Strobel, L. (1998). *The Case for Christ: A Journalist's Personal Investigation of the Evidence for Jesus.* Grand Rapids: Zondervan.

Stuhlmacher, P. (1993). *Jesus of Nazareth—Christ of Faith,* S. S. Schatzmann, trans. Peabody: Hendrickson.

Tatum, B. (1982, 1999). *In Quest of Jesus* (rev. ed.). Nashville: Abingdon.

Theissen, G. (1978). *Sociology of Early Palestinian Christianity,* J. Bowden, trans. Philadelphia: Fortress.

Theissen, G. (1983). *Miracle Stories of the Early Christian Tradition,* F. McDonagh, trans. Edinburgh: T. & T. Clark.

Theissen, G. (1987). *The Shadow of the Galilean: The Quest of the Historical Jesus in Narrative Form.* Philadelphia: Fortress.

Theissen, G., & Merz, A. (1998). *The Historical Jesus: A Comprehensive Guide,* J. Bowden, trans. Minneapolis: Fortress.

Theissen, G., & Winter, T. (1997). *Die Kriterienfrage in der Jesusforschung.* NTOA 34. Freiburg: Universitatsverlag Freiburg.

Tyrrell, G. (1909/1963). *Christianity at the Crossroads.* London: Longmans Green.

Uhlig, S. (1984). *Das Äthiopische Henochbuch.* JSHRZ 5.6. Gütersloh: Gütersloher Verlagshaus Gerd Mohn.

van Aarde, A. (2001). *Fatherless in Galilee: Jesus as Child of God.* Harrisburg: Trinity Press International.

Vermes, G. (1973). *Jesus the Jew.* London: Collins; Philadelphia: Fortress.

Vermes, G. (1983). *Jesus and the World of Judaism.* London: SCM Press; Philadelphia: Fortress.

Vermes, G. (1993). *The Religion of Jesus the Jew.* London: SCM Press; Minneapolis: Fortress.

Weaver, W. P. (1999). *The Historical Jesus in the Twentieth Century, 1900–1950.* Harrisburg: Trinity Press International.

Wenham, D. (1994). The Story of Jesus Known to Paul, *Jesus of Nazareth: Lord and Christ–Essays on the Historical Jesus and New Testament Christology,* J. B. Green & M. Turner, eds. Grand Rapids: Eerdmans, 297–311.

Wiebe, P. W. (1997). *Visions of Jesus: Direct Encounters from the New Testament to Today.* New York and Oxford: Oxford University Press.

Witherington III, B. (1995). *The Jesus Quest: The Third Search for the Jew of Nazareth.* Downers Grove: InterVarsity Press.

Wright, N. T. (1992, 1996). *Jesus and the Victory of God.* London: SPCK; Minneapolis: Fortress.

Wright, N. T. (1996). *Who Was Jesus?* Grand Rapids: Eerdmans.

Yadin, Y., ed. (1983). *The Temple Scroll,* vol. 2. Jerusalem: Israel Exploration Society.

Young, B. H. (1998). *The Parables: Jewish Tradition and Christian Interpretation.* Peabody: Hendrickson.

CHAPTER 4

A PSYCHOBIOGRAPHY OF JESUS

Donald Capps

I should like in this chapter to summarize the main arguments of my book, *Jesus: A Psychological Biography* (2000), centering especially on the portrait of Jesus presented in the third section. The book itself belongs in the genre of *psychobiography*, referred to by Charlesworth in the previous chapter, and which is one of the two main branches of psychohistory (Capps, 2000).

Psychobiography deals with the study of individuals, while group psychohistory deals with the psychological characteristics or formative experiences of groups. Psychobiography, according to William McKinley Runyan, "is the explicit use of formal or systematic psychology in biography" (1984, 201). The predominant psychological framework in psychobiography has been that of psychoanalysis, which is the framework I employed in my book on Jesus. The working title of the book was *Young Man Jesus*, an allusion to Erik H. Erikson's classic psychobiographical study of another religious man, *Young Man Luther: A Study in Psychoanalysis and History* (1958).

Exposition

Jesus: A Psychological Biography (2000) is based on the claim that more explicit use of psychological concepts in historical Jesus studies is helpful precisely at those points where scholars find themselves at an impasse. When historical Jesus studies turned to the social sciences, they embarked on a journey that leads to psychology; for the questions now being posed, especially concerning the identity of Jesus, cannot be adequately answered in terms of sociological theories alone.

The book first summarizes the "portraits" of Jesus formulated by four major contemporary scholars: Sanders, Meier, Crossan, and Borg, taken as representative of the field. It then makes a case for the legitimacy of psychobiography and the psychohistory of groups, illustrating the central methodological issues involved with studies of family and village life in early American Puritan communities. A chapter on the social world of Jesus' day provides the larger sociocultural context for the psychological portrait of Jesus, which centers on the hidden years of his childhood and youth, his role as exorcist-healer, and his utopian-melancholic personality.

Conclusions drawn include the following:

- Joseph was not Jesus' natural father and did not adopt him, thus consigning him to a marginal role in the family and community;
- his baptism was both a purification of his socially ascribed sinfulness owing to his illegitimacy and a symbolic adoption by the Father (Abba);
- anxiety played a central role in the etiology of the diseases and illnesses he treated and these anxieties were attributable to familial, interfamilial (or village), and class conflicts;
- he was neither an apocalypticist nor a social reformer, but a peasant-style utopian without a social agenda; and
- the temple disturbance that issued in his execution was both a symbolic destruction of the Temple motivated by his (and other men's) exclusion from the temple religion and a symbolic cleansing of his mother's body; thus a reparative act on Mary's behalf, whose conception of Jesus ostracized her as well. The temple disturbance was therefore both the culmination of his work as exorcist-healer as empowered by Abba and a symbolic subversion of the effects of his illegitimate birth.

A Psychological Portrait of Jesus

Now I would like to elaborate a bit on these conclusions. In effect, I will comment on only the third section of the book, entitled "A Psychological Portrait of Jesus."

The Fatherhood Question

The first chapter in the third section is titled "The Hidden Years: The Fatherhood Question." Here I take issue with John P. Meier's suggestion that the reason we do not know much about Jesus' childhood and youth is that it was unsufferably normal. On the contrary, I argue that Jane Schaberg, and more recently Gerd Lüdemann are correct in their view that Jesus was illegitimate (Schaberg, 1987; Lüdemann, 1998). Where I take a step beyond Schaberg, however, is in my proposal that Joseph, who proceeded with his marriage to Mary, did not adopt Jesus as his own. Andries van Aarde provides support for this conclusion in an article published in Ellens's *Pastoral Psychology* on Jesus as belonging to a category of fatherless sons (1997). Van Aarde has a recently published book on this topic entitled *Fatherless in Galilee: Jesus as Child of God* (2001). I also suggest that illegitimacy was an increasingly serious social problem in first century Palestine, here drawing on social historian Edward Shorter's study of illegitimacy rates among peasant classes in modern Europe (1971). Shorter shows that illegitimacy rates dramatically increased in countries with a high concentration of land ownership in the hands of a few, and he focuses especially on master-servant exploitation versus peasant bundling or premarital intercourse between engaged couples. I posit that Mary worked in the fields, and like peasant women working the fields in modern Europe, she was vulnerable to master-servant exploitation. Shorter suggests that seducers were unlikely to include landowners themselves, but rather foremen, who could force compliance by threatening women with negative work reports or other sanctions. I also argue that Galilean laws regarding sexual relations between engaged couples, being less stringent than comparable laws in Judaea, left Galilean men like Joseph with limited legal recourse. For Joseph to prove that he was *not* the father—namely, that this was not a case of peasant bundling—was very difficult. So he proceeded with the marriage.

In my view, however, Joseph did not adopt Jesus because he was under no legal obligation to do so and would have had a personal aversion to it as well. Since writing the book, I came across a book by Martin Daly and Margo Wilson citing evidence from various species of mammals and birds that stepparents have no biological propensity to love or care for stepchildren, as this care, among other things, typically comes at the cost of their own offspring. They note that the risk of child abuse by stepparents is highest for infants. This observation challenges the common assumption that conflicts between stepparents and stepchildren are "primarily created by obstreperous adolescents" (1998, 30). In my book, I argue that Matthew's Joseph is Matthew's own ideal, and may bear little if any resemblance to the real historical Joseph.

The following is a brief summary of the conclusions I draw from this view of the fatherhood question:

1. Jesus was chronologically the *firstborn*, but his half-brother, James, was accorded that status. Birthorder theory supports this claim, as Jesus did not behave like a firstborn. James does behave like a firstborn, as Crossan points out (1994, 23–24). In certain respects, Jesus was more like a middle-born, whom Monica McGoldrick describes as competitive, having no special or ascribed family status, and vulnerable to maladjustment if he or she cannot find a place to stand; resourceful and independent, but also craving attention—sometimes leading to behavior the family rules do not allow. He or she may therefore become the "identified patient" or "symptom bearer" of the family (1995, 221–224).

2. As a dispossessed son, Jesus became a carpenter. I argue that we should not assume this was Joseph's trade. As Crossan notes in *The Historical Jesus*, carpentry was a trade open to the dispossessed (1991). Jesus fits this category.

3. Joseph did not carry out the traditional duties of a father; most notably, he failed to arrange Jesus' marriage. That Jesus was illegitimate is a more plausible explanation for his presumed unmarried state than that Joseph had died before he had opportunity to arrange a marriage, as argued by Miller in *Jesus at Thirty: A Psychological and Historical Portrait* (1997). Nor did Joseph teach Jesus a trade. Mark 6:3 has the citizens of his own village referring to him as "the carpenter, the son of Mary," which is doubly derogatory. If he were known in the community as the son of Joseph, Joseph's death or physical absence from the scene would not alter how he was identified on this occasion. But Matthew, working from Mark's text, has them say, "the carpenter's son" (Matt. 13:55) and Luke, also working from Mark, has them refer to him as "Joseph's son" (Luke 4:22). Together, Matthew and Luke have deftly normalized Jesus' status within his family of origin. When all three texts are harmonized, a picture forms of the boy Jesus working with hammer and chisel alongside his kindly father Joseph. Fortunately, comparison of the three texts also enables us to reconstruct the making of a myth.

4. Jesus was a perfect candidate for John's radical movement in the desert, one where young men formed an alternative religion to that of

the official temple religion, from which Jesus, owing to his illegitimacy and non-adoption, would be excluded. Its central ritual was, of course, baptism in the River Jordan.

5. Jesus found the solution to his fatherlessness in Abba, and John's baptism ritually purified him of the original sin of his illegitimate conception. Abba is the true adoptive father, as Paul also later emphasized.

Jesus as Exorcist-Healer

The second chapter in the third section focuses on Jesus' role as exorcist-healer. It is titled "Disabling Anxiety: Jesus as Village Healer." Disabling has a double meaning: Anxiety disables, and Jesus disabled *it*. I initiate this discussion by examining the distinction between disease and illness derived from medical anthropology and employed by biblical scholars to explore healing practices in the New Testament Era (Pilch, 2000), including the healings that Jesus performed (Crossan, 1994, 84; Crossan and Watts, 1996, 69–80). I critique Crossan's view that Jesus did not heal diseases (for example, organic dysfunctions), but *did* heal illnesses—that is, the social devaluation to which a diseased person is subject. I argue that what is missing from this distinction is a psychological dimension, and suggest that if we view disease as psychobiological and illness as psychosocial, we may assert that Jesus did heal diseases, as they were *psycho*biological in origin, due to the somatizing of anxiety. Also, Jesus' method of healing required an awareness of the diseased individual as not only a social being, but also, and more fundamentally, a *psycho*social being; one whose illness is rooted in psychological processes, especially involving intergenerational and intra-village conflicts. Thus, the healing of illness was a psychosocial process. I argue that the primary cause of the illnesses Jesus healed was fear that manifested itself in *anxiety*. Following Freud, I suggest that these anxieties were aggression, sexually-based, or both. To make this case, I focus on the symptomatology of the illnesses Jesus encountered. Centering on the healings that John P. Meier identifies as authentic in his extensive discussion of the healings (1994), I draw the following conclusions:

1. The symptomatology of demon possession suggests repressed rage in the case of the teenage son in Mark 9:14–29 against his father. The son wants to kick and hit his father and hurl invectives at him, but he does not. Hence, physical writhing and foaming at the mouth.

2. The symptomatology of paralysis suggests both forms of anxiety—that is to say, a passive-aggressive refusal to work for someone

one despises but also a reaction-formation against illicit sexual acting-out, thus, a mechanism of self-control. If you are paralyzed, you cannot go to work and you cannot indulge in illicit sexual behavior. I also note the effect of Jewish flatfootedness on the propensity toward paralysis of the legs, especially.

3. Blindness is a defensive reaction to the aggressive impulses in the use of the evil eye. If one is blind, one is invulnerable to the curse of the evil eye and to charges that one is cursing others. Crossan suggests that belief in the evil eye was widespread throughout Mediterranean countries. Blindness may also have a sexual basis as an extreme form of gaze aversion. It addresses the problem of lustful eyes, especially with regard to the incestual implications of some forms of gazing. It was imperative that a family be able to certify at the time of betrothal that a sister/daughter had not been sexually violated by a brother or father. Also, since a mother might be only twelve years or so older than her eldest son, sons' sexual attraction to their mother was certainly not out of the question.

4. The raising of Jairus's daughter, age twelve, is also an instance of hysteria or conversion disorder, a diagnosis available to Jesus' own contemporaries. She is an interesting counterpart to Mary, considered by most scholars to have been about twelve years old when she married Joseph. Hysteria was believed to be caused by a wandering uterus which a fetus would keep in its place. Marriage was thus designed to forestall hysteria in young pubescent girls.

5. I also discuss the high incidence of hypochondria among Jews. Contemporary hypochondria studies indicate that Jews, followed by Italians, have the highest incidence of hypochondria. I note the relation of hypochondria to skin lesions, suggesting that it has bearing on the problem of leprosy. In a recent review of the literature on hypochondria in *Somatization and Hypochondriasis* (1986), Robert Kellner describes the skin lesions produced by hypochondriacal patients in their attempts to remove dreaded parasites with pins, tweezers, scissors, and scalpels. "Leprosy," however, could also have applied to venereal diseases caused by sexual promiscuity. As John J. Pilch notes in his discussion of "biblical leprosy," "in Leviticus, three topics relate to bodily openings or orifices: clean and unclean foods (mouth); childbirth/menstruation (female genitals); bodily discharges (male and female genitals)" (2000, 50). He further notes that in stories of Jesus healing lepers, "the concern is not contagion but pollution"—a distinction that is particularly relevant to venereal diseases (51).

Since writing the book, I came across Mary Kilbourne Matossian's

Poisons of the Past (1989). Matossian argues that food poisoning due to contaminated grains explains why one village could experience an epidemic and another village in the same general vicinity would not, thus virtually ruling out a virally transmitted disease. She also notes that among the more serious symptoms would be skin eruptions, bleeding from body orifices, and central nervous system disorders, including delirium, stupor, convulsions, depression, and disorientation. Her argument has relevance to first-century Palestine, and thus to Jesus' role as exorcist-healer, in that food poisoning causes physical symptoms found in "biblical leprosy" and mental aberrations found in demon possession. The fact that it strikes one community but not another supports belief in localized demonic agencies.

6. Key to Jesus' healings was the name of Abba, a magical name due to its reversibility, its preoedipal associations, and its alphabetical priority to Belelzebul, the name by which the chief of demons was known; Satan was a more universalized appellation. I invoke Freud's observation that the talking cure works because words retain their original magical qualities. Children believe, for example, that saying "I wish you were dead" could cause another to die. Conversely, a single word or phrase such as, "Yes, I will marry you," is a blessing beyond words. Unlike healers who used complex verbal incantations, Jesus healed in the name of Abba, whom I associate with Freud's "father of personal prehistory," the father of whose presence we were aware before we were able to make out the contours and characteristics of our human father (Freud, 1962, 21). In effect, Jesus countered anxiety through the invocation of the protective name, Abba. We need not be anxious, for Abba has placed his protective circle around us. He protects against both external threats and illicit internal desires.

Jesus as a Melancholic-Utopian Personality

The third chapter in the third section is titled "Utopian-Melancholic Personality: The Temple Disturbance." It focuses on Jesus as a melancholic-utopian, and on the relevance of this personality structure to the temple disturbance that almost certainly cost him his life.

Briefly, I attribute male melancholia to a boy's loss of his emotional attachment to his mother, exacerbated by the fact that, as Freud says in his essay on mourning and melancholia, she is still in the neighborhood—that is, not physically dead (1962). (Since this emotional separation occurs early in life and is experienced by most if not all boys, melancholia is ontological and therefore different from clinical depression, which is a mood disorder.) Thus, more than girls do, boys feel abandoned by their mothers, and Jesus, the homeless man, was such a melancholic. The woman's counterpart would be agoraphobia, or confinement to the home. I look briefly at the table and meal, explaining their erotic implications, especially for men, for whom food is associated with their first sexual experience of mother. I also consider the missing mother theme in the parable of the prodigal son and the Kingdom of God idea to support my view that Jesus was a melancholic, as were, I assume, his male cohorts. I cannot go into these discussions in any detail here, but they are designed to make the point that melancholia needs to be understood on three levels: psychophysiological, psychosocial, and sociopolitical.

I also note the longstanding historical association of melancholia and utopian desires, and argue that Jesus as a melancholic was a utopian not in sociological or communitarian terms, but in psychological terms. Utopia, meaning "no place," is most fundamentally a state of mind, which for Jesus is a state of living beyond anxiety. The idea that it is located in some future time, thus having primarily eschatological meanings, is a very late development in the evolution of the concept. Thus, I do not rule out that Jesus may have thought in catalysmic terms, as this would be entirely consistent with the utopianism of the poor, which involves "endless meditation, even obsessional thinking about another world" (Cioran, 1987, 82). But I primarily emphasize that a peasant, the class to which Jesus belonged, must resort to a psychological utopia and not concern himself with social reform, which has more proximate as well as long-term goals. Social utopians assume that social change and reform are possible, and may even believe that they are inevitable. Peasants have no such expectations. They look for "utopia" in day-to-day relief from hunger, pain, disease, depression, boredom, and petty conflicts. Much discussion of Jesus as a social reformer reflects, in my view, a middle-class mindset that was foreign to that of Jesus and the persons and groups with whom he associated.

I use Freud's discussion of mania as a response to melancholia, and employ recent studies of impulsivity to set the stage for my consideration of the *temple disturbance*, a symbolic act with two levels: one clearly conscious, the other perhaps less so. First, in the name of Abba, Jesus claimed the temple for all those dispossessed sons and daughters of Abraham who had been excluded from temple religion and all that it represented. This is the *father–son dynamic*. Here I follow essentially the views of Crossan as presented in his *Jesus: A Revolutionary Biography* (1994). Second, the temple symbolizes the mother's body. Thus,

Jesus inaugurated a ritual cleansing or purification of Mary, his mother. This was a *reparative act* on behalf of her and all mothers who have been similarly ostracized. Melanie Klein's discussion (Klein, 1986) of reparation informs this argument, as does David J. Halperin's *Seeking Ezekiel: Text and Psychology* (1993).

I suggest that the words, "It is finished," attributed to Jesus on the cross, are words that should have been placed on his lips as he awaited his arrest. *This* was the culmination of his life's work. Whereas the crucifixion was *done* to him, the temple disturbance was *his* last act. Perhaps he anticipated that his action would arouse his heavenly Father's rage as well, thus initiating a divine purificatory act of immense proportions and consequences. But, in any case, his own action was *symbolic*, and as such, it made "Utopia" real, if only briefly, in the here and now. Through this act, he affirmed that one can indeed change one's fate, as if to say, "I'm occupying a space which they said I could never occupy." Moreover, if the temple disturbance claimed the temple for his father Abba and was also a reparative action in his mother's behalf, it was the symbolic solution to his own illegitimacy and the culminating act of his role as exorcist-healer. Thus, there is a deep continuity between his own personal tragedy, his public role, and the symbolic action that led to his death. Through this action, he completed his life's work and realized his utopian dreams.

It is understandable that Christianity has found its symbolic center in the cross of Christ, and I do not wish to minimize the horror of his death, as this was the price he paid for his moment of utopian bliss. But Christianity's preoccupation with the cross has obscured the power of the temple disturbance, the scene of realized utopia. Moreover, the fact that it was a personal triumph for Jesus has itself been obscured by apocalyptic theorists, who believe his view that the Kingdom of God was imminent was mistaken, and by social reform theorists, who cannot avoid the conclusion that Jesus' vision of a just society has yet to be realized some 2,000 years later, despite the fact that the religion bearing his name has been the official religion of the West throughout that era. As Christianity cannot blame other religions for this outcome, it has "scapegoated" secularism instead. In my view, Jesus' symbolic action that day was complete unto itself, and therefore a crowning success. He made utopia happen. Any lesser Jesus—a Jesus who miscalculated his heavenly Father's plans, or a Jesus who started something that has taken us nowhere—is, in my view, hardly worth believing in.

The Resurrection Appearances

A brief discussion of dreams as the most likely source of resurrection stories follows. I cite Bert O. States's view in *Seeing in the Dark* that dreams, like daily life, may be viewed as a continual tension or reciprocity between *motive* and *contingency* (1997). A motive would be: "Today, I must go to the hardware store." A *contingency* would be: "On my way to the hardware store, who suddenly walks up to me but my friend John." I suggest that Jesus "appeared" to his friends and family members in dreams. Because these appearances were experienced as contingent, they were felt to be under his, not their, volition. I also point out that dreams are the "no-place" where utopias occur. As Erik H. Erikson has suggested, while dreams are the locus of nightmares, they are also reparative. Where else but here does a loved one return to assure us that he is in good hands and that we need not be anxious for him?

Incidentally, I do not rule out visual and auditory hallucinations as another likely basis for accounts of Jesus' appearances. However, the fact that any one of his followers could experience his appearance in a dream, together with the fact that all would have been traumatized by his death, thus increasing the likelihood of dreaming about him, led me to emphasize dreams as the most likely source of the appearance reports. Of course, I recognize that Gospel stories of his appearances may resemble hallucinatory experiences more than they do dreams, but these stories are the work of skillful writers. My concern was to account for the widespread oral tradition of appearances that preceded the written tradition, and dreams are simply more common and universally attested to than hallucinations.

Conclusion

As for the question of Jesus' identity with which I launched my study, I hazarded my own answer in the epilogue. I took the liberty of doing so because Jesus himself seems to have been acutely aware (painfully so) of what modern authors on identity have noted, that "if identity is something that is assigned by persons to other persons, the initial question to which we call 'identity' an answer, namely 'Who am I?', acquires a strong connotation of 'Who am I in the eyes of others?'" (de Levita, 1965, 7). Because his ascribed identity was that of an illegitimate man, I suggested that he was a man in search of an identity by which he could be legitimated in his own eyes. Thus, I draw on Jay Martin's work on the "fictive personality," a term he developed in working with patients who had "made up" an identity for themselves as a means and source of personal inspiration and empowerment (1988).

Erik Erikson asked a patient who created a fictitious Scottish identity for herself why she did this. She replied in a thick brogue, "Bless you, sir, I needed a past" (Erikson, 1980, 141). I suggest that Jesus discovered and adopted the identity of "Son of Abba" because he needed a *future*. Little could he have known how long that future would extend, or how many persons would experience him as the means by which they too would be afforded a livable present and a viable future. Following my suggestion that perhaps the most stunning of Jesus' "fatherlike performances" (a term borrowed from van Aarde, 1997, 460) was his declaration that all children are "the sons and daughters of the heavenly Father" (Matt. 18:10), I concluded, "His refusal to see himself as unique in this regard may be the very nucleus of his identity" (Capps, 2000, 271).

References

Capps, D. (2000). *Jesus: A Psychological Biography*. St. Louis: Chalice.

Childs, H. (2000). *The Myth of the Historical Jesus and the Evolution of Consciousness.* Atlanta: Society of Biblical Literature.

Cioran, E. M. (1987). *History and Utopia*, R. Howard, trans. Chicago: University of Chicago Press.

Crossan, J. D. (1991). *The Historical Jesus: The Life of a Mediterranean Jewish Peasant.* San Francisco: HarperSanFrancisco.

Crossan, J. D. (1994). *Jesus: A Revolutionary Biography*. San Francisco: HarperSanFrancisco.

Crossan, J. D., & Watts, R. G. (1996). *Who Is Jesus?* Louisville: Westminster/John Knox Press.

Daly, M., & Wilson, M. (1998). *The Truth about Cinderella: A Darwinian View of Parental Love.* New Haven: Yale University Press.

de Levita, D. J. (1965). *The Concept of Identity*. New York: Basic.

Erikson, E. H. (1958). *Young Man Luther: A Study in Psychoanalysis and History.* New York: Norton.

Erikson, E. H. (1980). *Identity and the Life Cycle.* New York: Norton.

Freud, S. (1962). *The Ego and the Id*, J. Riviere, trans. New York: Norton.

Halperin, D. J. (1993). *Seeking Ezekiel: Text and Psychology.* University Park: Pennsylvania State University Press.

Kellner, R. (1986). *Somatization and Hypochrondriasis.* New York: Praeger.

Klein, M. (1986). A Study of Envy and Gratitude, *The Selected Melanie Klein*, J. Mitchell, ed. London: Penguin Books, 211–229.

Lüdemann, G. (1998). *Virgin Birth? The Real Story of Mary and Her Son Jesus.* Harrisburg: Trinity Press International.

Martin, Jay. (1988). *Who Am I This Time? Uncovering the Fictive Personality.* New York: Norton.

Matossian, M. K. (1989). *Poisons of the Past: Molds, Epidemics and History.* New Haven: Yale University Press.

McGoldrick, M. (1995). *You Can Go Home Again: Reconnecting with Your Family.* New York: Norton.

Meier, J. P. (1994). *A Marginal Jew: Rethinking the Historical Jesus,* vol. 2. New York: Doubleday.

Miller, J. W. (1997). *Jesus at Thirty: A Psychological and Historical Portrait.* Minneapolis: Fortress.

Pilch, J. J. (2000). *Healing in the New Testament: Insights from Medical and Mediterranean Anthropology.* Minneapolis: Fortress.

Runyan, W. M. (1984). *Life Histories and Psychobiography: Explorations in Theory and Method.* New York: Oxford University Press.

Schaberg, J. (1987). *The Illegitimacy of Jesus: A Feminist Theological Interpretation of the Infancy Narratives.* San Francisco: Harper & Row.

Shorter, E. (1971). Illegitimacy, Sexual Revolution, and Social Change in Modern Europe, *The Family in History: Interdisciplinary Essays,* T. K. Rabb & R. I. Rotberg, eds. New York: Harper & Row, 48–84.

States, B. O. (1997). *Seeing in the Dark: Reflections on Dreams and Dreaming.* New Haven: Yale University Press.

van Aarde, A. (1997). Social Identity, Status Envy and Jesus' Abba, *Pastoral Psychology,* vol. 45, J. Harold Ellens, ed. New York: Human Science Press, 451–472.

van Aarde, A. (2001). *Fatherless in Galilee: Jesus as Child of God.* Harrisburg: Trinity Press International.

CHAPTER 5

JESUS: A PSYCHOLOGICAL AND HISTORICAL PORTRAIT

John W. Miller

To achieve a deepened understanding of Jesus' mission, recent studies have emphasized the importance of a correct interpretation of certain prior transitional events that occurred soon after he left his parental home: his baptism, temptations, and temporary association with, above all, John the Baptist (Jeremias, 1971; Meyer, 1979; Hollenbach, 1982). However, in the investigations to date, not much attention has been paid to Luke's suggestion that he might have been "about thirty years old" at the time (Luke 3:23),[1] even though we now realize, thanks to developmental psychology, that abrupt changes of this kind frequently occur in men's lives right at this point for reasons that are inherent to the process of becoming a mature adult (Erikson, 1963; Levinson, 1978b; Greenspan & Pollock, 1980). Might then an inquiry into this facet of Jesus' life, in this light, sharpen our perceptions of what he was contending with at this time, and thereby enrich our picture of him at maturity?[2]

An answer, I suggest, will depend on our response to three additional questions: (1) What is now known about the developmental issues facing men generally at this stage of their lives? (2) Is what is generally known, based as it is on studies of men in modern societies, at all relevant to an understanding of someone living as long ago in another culture as did Jesus? and (3) What can be said about the Jesus of history that might be at all germane to such an inquiry?

I will try to address each of these questions in the paragraphs that follow, and conclude with a few comments regarding the contemporary relevance of such a psycho-historical probe.

The Age Thirty Transition

What in general is known about the transitions men often experience at this time of their lives? It was Daniel Levinson's careful study of a cross-section of forty American men that first alerted us to the unique importance of "about thirty" as a specific life stage (Levinson, 1978b, 71–135). Building on the life stage research of Sigmund Freud, Carl G. Jung, and especially Erik Erikson, Levinson sought, through in-depth "biographical interviews," to gain a fuller picture of what these men had experienced during their adult years from seventeen to forty-five. Since he began his study predisposed to the traditional notion that a crucial transition in adult life occurs around forty, the discovery that earlier and equally significant transitions often take place was somewhat surprising. More specifically, he observed that during their twenties and early thirties, these men already typically approached adulthood in two clearly distinguishable phases: an initial casual, exploratory mode during their early and middle twenties, when a first provisional life structure was fashioned; and then a more serious, urgent mode during their later twenties and early thirties, followed by making stronger commitments and forming deeper roots and a new life structure (Levinson, 1978b, 84). Between the structures of the first provisional phase and those of the "settling down" period in the early thirties, Levinson noted an often turbulent "age thirty transition." What seemed, at least in part, to bring it about was a dawning sense of mortality, the now persistent awareness that life is short, and that a start will have to be made soon if what one hopes to accomplish in life is going to get done before it is too late. As a consequence, the life stage structures and achievement of the initial phase were tested and often found to be wanting and in need of radical change (85).

In his discussion of the tasks or objectives that typically engaged these men during this time of their lives, Levinson observed, as had Erikson, the central importance of establishing a truly meaningful vocational identity as well as "forming love relationships, marriage and family" (Levinson, 1978b, 101–110). The wider significance of the latter had been especially stressed by Erikson, for it was through this process, he had written, that "generativity" emerges—that quality of "caring for," or "taking care of" (that which has been generated), which is so essential to the life and well-being of the succeeding generation (Erikson, 1963, 266–268).

But two additional issues of equal importance surfaced in Levinson's research. He noted that, in one way or another, all of the men he had interviewed were preoccupied during their age thirty transitions with what he termed "forming a Dream and giving it a place in the life structure," as well as with "forming mentor relationships" that would assist them in this task. This Dream, Levinson wrote, had "the quality of a vision, an imagined possibility that generates excitement and vitality" (1978b, 91). At the beginning of the age thirty transition, it was often still poorly articulated or encased in grandiose aspirations only tenuously connected to reality, as in the myth of the hero. But whatever the form, he observed that the age thirty transition was experienced as a time when it was urgent to define the Dream and live it out quite concretely. Therefore, the extent to which the initial life structure was "consonant with and infused by the Dream, or opposed to it" was a matter of great consequence. For if the Dream had remained unconnected to their lives, Levinson wrote, it might simply die, and with it their sense of "aliveness and purpose" (92).

While mentoring relationships have long been recognized as important to emotional development earlier in life—during adolescence, for example—Levinson's research indicated they were crucial during this age thirty transition as well. Ideally the mentor at this stage in life is neither parent nor crypto-parent, he noted, but a slightly older peer who fosters the younger adult's development "by believing in him, sharing the youthful Dream and giving it his blessing, helping to define the newly emerging self in its newly discovered world, and creating a space in which the young man can work on a reasonably satisfactory life structure that contains the Dream" (1978b, 99).

For a few men, the age thirty transition went smoothly, according to Levinson, although all of the men he interviewed experienced significant changes. For the great majority, this period was extremely stressful; the interviewees felt like men alone in the water between two islands, unable to move one way or the other, and on the verge of drowning (1978b, 86). A man's difficulties may be accentuated "by specific aspects of his situation—economic recession, discrimination, the rivalries of a highly competitive world—and by his own emotional problems of committing himself to an occupation, relating to women and separating from parents" (82).

Relevance

To what extent are these observations, based as they are on the study of men in twentieth-century North America, valid for a deepened understanding of a historic figure like Jesus, living as he did in first-century Palestine? As noted, a heightened sense of mortality and urgency to do something authentic while there is still time appears to be a critical factor in the changes that occur in this period. This could be related to the fact that bodily maturation, along with reproductive capacities, reach their peak in humans in their mid-twenties, after which a slow physical decline sets in. If so, this in itself would suggest that a species-wide genetic clock, and not culture alone, may be a triggering factor in the age thirty transition (Levinson, 1978b, 326–330). Levinson admits, however, that whether men in all cultures do in fact experience this time of their lives in analogous ways is as yet hard to verify. Still, he points out, there are a number of texts from a variety of cultures that seem to at least allude to this age-specific transition. In the Talmudic "Sayings of the Fathers," for example, the stages of life from 5 to 100 are carefully outlined, and thirty is mentioned as the time in life when "full strength" is attained (*Avot* 5.24). In a Confucian text, Confucius himself traces the stages of his life from fifteen to seventy, and says that it was in his thirtieth year that he had planted his feet "firm upon the ground" (Analects, book 2). Thirty is also mentioned by Solon of Greece in a similar sketch of the life cycle as "the season for courting and begetting sons who will preserve and continue his line" (Levinson, 1978b, 324–326). In Israel, thirty was specified as the lower limit for the census of those fit to bear arms who were liable for service in the temple (Num. 4). Among the Jewish sectarians at Qumran, a man was eligible for communal office at twenty-five, but it was not until thirty that he was deemed ready to render judgments or function as a tribal commissioner (Manual of Discipline for the Future Congregation of Israel). A scattering of anecdotal data adds color to these transcultural hints. Gautama Buddha experienced his famous life-changing encounter with suffering and death at twenty-nine. To this example may be added, from biblical tradition alone (apart from Jesus), the allusions to similar age-thirty type transitions in the lives of Joseph (Gen. 41:46), David (2 Sam. 5:4), Ezekiel (1:1), and possibly Moses, Hosea, and Isaiah, all of whom were married and having their first children at the time they were called to be prophets.

This does not mean, obviously, that there are no differences at all in the process of becoming an adult in modern America and the small first-century Galilean village where Jesus grew up. Life, we imagine, was much simpler then than today, and the social structures shaping adult transitions were firmer and more stable. Were we to imagine, however, that our world and his were too different in this respect, a single story, Jesus' parable of the prodigal son (Luke 15:11–32), should remind us that then, too, becoming an adult was not easy. In any case, neither the rebellious prodigal of this story who left home, nor his obedient brother who stayed behind, reached adulthood, it seems, in a single bound. The prodigal had first to experiment with being an adult in the wider world before returning to his father's farm, ostensibly to settle down there; his elder brother, while remaining home, was also obviously not altogether content with his initial choice, as his bitter complaint to his father at the time of his younger brother's return reveals. The relevance of contemporary life-stage research to the experience of a first-century Palestinian Jew is hardly thereby proven. It does suggest, however, that its heuristic value ought not to be summarily dismissed.

Jesus' Age Thirty Transition

Granted the possible relevance of this data, how much do our sources for the life of Jesus actually tell us that might be germane to this theme? Factual information regarding Jesus' life during his childhood, adolescence, and young adulthood is, of course, notoriously scarce. Indeed, even the few accounts we do have of his birth and adolescence are regarded suspiciously by most historians. However, there is no reason to doubt Luke's reference to his role as his parents' firstborn (Luke 2:7), nor that his family eventually included four younger brothers and several sisters (Mark 3:31–35; 6:3; Wilson, 1984, 72; Brown et al., 1978, 65–72). Nor need we question that his father was a carpenter (Matt. 13:55), or that Jesus worked at that trade as well (Mark 6:3). This does not necessarily mean, however, that he was a simple village carpenter, or poor, as often imagined. Buchanan has sought to demonstrate that "carpenter" might also mean "contractor," and that Paul's allusion to his having once been rich (2 Cor. 8:9) could be historical (Buchanan, 1984; 1985). If so, this would be congruent with the preponderance of middle-class figures who people his parables: owners of vineyards with managerial worries (Matt. 20:1–16); fathers with wealth to be distributed (Luke 15:11–32); traveling merchants (Luke 10:29–37; Matt. 12:45–46); farmers with servants (Matt. 13:24–30; 24:45–51); and rich entrepreneurs (Matt. 25:14–30).

But why then by thirty had Jesus not married and founded a family? Some have argued that he had, on the basis that it is inconceivable in an age where marriage by twenty was virtually mandatory that he would not have (Phipps, 1970; 1973). Yet the silence of our sources regarding a wife and children is deafening, and can hardly be construed otherwise than that there were none. The possible reasons for this ought, however, to be analyzed more carefully than they generally are. Virtually all discussions of this topic focus on the motives Jesus might have had at thirty for remaining single (Sloyan, 1983, 129–132; Wilson, 1984, 96–97; Buchanan, 1984, 184–190). But the Talmud states that it was the father's responsibility to see that his son got married, and to do so while the son was young and amenable to the father's advice.[3] Were traditions of this kind at all in vogue among the Jews of Jesus' day—and there is no reason to think otherwise—the question would then be not so much why Jesus at thirty had not yet married, but why his father, much earlier, had failed to make arrangements to this end.

A likely answer is that Joseph had died before it would have been appropriate to do so. That he died prior to Jesus' mission at thirty is almost certain, for he is missing from all the accounts of this period, even those where members of Jesus' family are explicitly identified (Mark 3:312–35; 6:1–6). David Flusser comments that it is his impression that this death took place quite early in Jesus' life, when he was still "quite a child" (Flusser, 1969, 17). But that would not have been possible were it true that there were six younger siblings, as Mark 6:3 implies. That Jesus was still unmarried at thirty suggests that his father's death occurred during his early teens, before the time had arrived when a marriage would have certainly been arranged for him, were his father still alive.

According to the traditions of his times, Jesus would have then become, as eldest son, the head of his deceased father's family (Connick, 1974, 131; Wilson, 1984, 71). With this possibility we arrive at what might well have been the most important factor of all in Jesus' personal development during his growing-up years. The loss of a father by anyone at any time in life is a difficult experience. In a relatively large first-century Jewish family, the loss of a father by an eldest son during his early teens must have been traumatic. Can we imagine what some of the more obvious consequences of such a death might have been for such a son under such circumstances? Although it is admittedly conjectural, the attempt to do so may shed light on several otherwise puzzling features of the life of the "about-thirty"-year-old Jesus.

To begin with, if it is true that prior to his father's death Jesus was indeed working with him in carpentry or contracting, as the Gospels intimate, it would now fall to Jesus to shoulder this trade by himself, for he would have become his family's chief means of support. Not just financially, but in other ways, too, the leadership once vested in his father would now gravitate toward him. This could be a stimulus to the development of latent talents. He would have to learn quickly how to care for and manage the family and the business in an efficient, competent manner.[4]

On the other hand, such a demanding role may pose certain risks, or "temptations," as well. To suddenly become "father" in a world in which it would still be normal to be "son" sets the stage for a reawakening of oedipal ambivalence. A son might respond with a sense of over-responsibility or grandiosity. In any case, an inner debate is sure to rage over which is to have priority, and for how long: remaining as head of his father's family or founding one of his own, concern for his father's wife or finding a wife of his own, and caring for his father's children or having children of his own? As a result, personal plans for marriage are almost sure to be postponed beyond the time ordinarily set for them, as I have personally observed in the case of several Middle Eastern and North American men in similar circumstances.[5] As time goes on, such a son's relation to his mother may prove to be especially problematical, as she, on her part, tries to cope with her own needs and frustrations by leaning more and more on this highly resourceful firstborn. This will not only intensify his ambivalence, but also exacerbate sibling rivalries. A welter of other emotions may accompany these developments: anger at the premature loss of his father, guilt at taking his place, fear of going too far or not far enough in this complex new role, idealization of the lost father, and anxiety over unknown catastrophes yet to come (Lammers 1977, 75–76).

To summarize, the available evidence, while meager, strongly suggests that during his adolescence, Jesus, as eldest son, became the head of his father's family. An especially significant consequence of this would be that, while vocationally successful, he would not be free at the appointed time to marry and found a family of his own. As can be readily gathered from the fact that at "about thirty" he left his parental family, quite abruptly it seems, to join the masses who were going to the Jordan to be baptized, he would have been, during these years, increasingly uneasy and dissatisfied with the course his life was taking. Clearly, he would not yet have fulfilled *his* dream.

Jesus at Thirty

A hypothesis is only as good as its power to illumine perplexing data. Does the developmental scenario just outlined do this? I will try to indicate a few of the ways I think it does, and add several comments regarding how looking at Jesus in this light may serve to highlight certain otherwise neglected features of his life and mission.

An especially puzzling aspect of the Gospel portraits of Jesus at thirty are references to tensions that seem to have existed at this stage of his life between himself and his mother, brothers, and sisters. His brothers did not believe in him, the fourth Gospel reports (John 7:5), and Mark 3:19–21 states that at one point during the height of his public mission, his family thought him "beside himself" and were determined to seize him and bring him back home.[6] We are then also told, as a sequel, that on their visit to his headquarters at Capernaum, ostensibly to carry out their plan, Jesus would not even see them, but sharply distanced himself from them when he said: "Who are my mother and my brothers? . . . Here are my mother and my brothers! (Mark 3:33–35).[7] Additional hints of this estrangement may be found in the report of his abortive visit to Nazareth (Mark 6:1–6), as well as those sayings that stress the absolute priority of doing God's will over family ties (Matt. 10:35; Luke 9:60/Matt. 8:22; Luke 11:28; 12:51–52; 14:26; 18:29–30). The pathos of this unexpected development is summed up in John's Gospel: "He came to his own home, and his own people received him not" (John 1:11).

All this is consistent, I suggest, with the developmental scenario just outlined. Few situations in life are as demanding and emotionally complex as that of a son caught up in the necessity of assuming his father's role with his mother and her family. If his mother, brothers, and sisters were mystified at this time by his radical shift in loyalty from their family to God's family and thought him "beside himself," then this only means that they, and the mother especially, like others in their predicament, perhaps were more attuned to their own needs and necessities than to his.

John the Baptist's role in Jesus' life may also come into sharper focus in this light. Of no one else, it would appear, did Jesus speak so exuberantly. John is a prophet, Jesus is quoted as saying, yes, more than a prophet, indeed, the greatest man who ever lived (Matt. 11:9, 11/ Luke 7:26, 28). Yet after working briefly with John in Judea, even perhaps baptizing as John did (John 3:22), he returned to Galilee (John 4:3) and there continued his mission in a manner increasingly unique to himself. While traditionally regarded as Jesus' forerunner, John's part in Jesus' age thirty transition also corresponds precisely to that of the mentor who helps awaken and realize the still latent Dream.[8] John's person and preaching were, our sources suggest, the catalyst Jesus needed to break free of an increasingly sterile role in his deceased father's family so that he could at last fulfill his own unique destiny and mission.

What Jesus is said to have experienced as a consequence of his association with John, his baptism and temptations especially, may also take on added meaning when looked at more closely in the context of the age thirty transition. Immediately following Jesus' baptism, we are told, God became experientially real to him as gracious father through divine words of acceptance and approval that broke into his consciousness while he prayed (Luke 3:21–22).[9] During the temptations that followed, he wrestled with Satan over whether to turn stones into bread, throw himself from the pinnacle of the temple, or rule the world (Matt. 4:1–11/Luke 4:1–13).[10] These were, we may conjecture, thaumaturgical fantasies of a type widely current in his time, for to produce mighty signs and rule the world were the then prevailing expectations of what the Messiah would do when he appeared.[11]

Grandiose thoughts such as these on the part of Jesus would accord with the fantasies of greatness, which, as we have seen, are endemic to the struggle for self-definition of the age-thirty male. In Jesus' case, these might have been exacerbated by his assumption of his father's role at the time of his death.[12] Nor is it to be doubted that with the help of his baptism and the disclosure experience he had at that time ("Thou art my beloved son"), he was finally able to fight free of these fantasies, reconnect with the "Father," and experience what it meant to be a trusting "son" once again. Viewed in this way, something like the battle with Satan described here would help explain Jesus' unprecedented certainty during the time of his mission that Satan was retreating and God's fatherly care was being revealed to the world through him.[13]

Regarding the mission itself, what Erikson has written of Gandhi's achievement at a similar stage in his life may apply to Jesus as well. "The true saints," he writes in his book about Gandhi, "are those who transfer the state of householdership to the house of God, becoming father and mother, brother and sister, son and daughter, to all creation, rather than of their own issue" (Erikson, 1969, 399). Erikson was referring to the way Gandhi extended his emerging sense of generative care from his wife and children to the needs of India during a time of crisis. If our conjecture is correct, Jesus too had been a "householder" of sorts; not in a family of his own, but in his deceased father's family. As a result, both ripe experience and a pent-up generativity were still waiting to be released. John was the catalyst; his years as head of his deceased father's family were the apprenticeship, his baptism and temptations were the turning point. Through finally taking matters into his own hands, going out to John and thereby being set free of his past, he was poised and ready now to create a family of his own; one born, however, not of flesh, nor of blood, nor of the will of man, but of God (John 1:12–13).

The focus of his mission, initially at least, was "the lost sheep of the house of Israel" (Matt. 10:6); the sick and the sinners, or the poor, as he preferred to call them.[14] Their numbers were large, for times were tumultuous. Gentiles occupied the Israelite homeland, and to many, God seemed distant. Only a dedicated few could live up to the high standards of God's Torah and find meaning—the rest lived in a religious twilight zone. The result was that they frequently suffered from guilt, sickness, confusion, or worse (Borg, 1984, 51–72). Obviously Jesus' own life experience had prepared him to understand their condition well. All that we know about him during this phase of his life testifies to his swift, uncanny insight into the inner world of these disaffiliated ones. Often, it appeared, only a word was needed for amazing things to happen (Mark 2:5–12). In fact, his charismatic effectiveness with this sector of the population quickly thrust him into the center of the Jewish struggle for self-definition, where his subjective inward approach to Torah soon rendered him suspect among the Jewish elite.[15] When this happened, he did not retreat, but defended his approach with irenic skill (Farmer, 1982, 32–48). There are hints that satanic delusions of grandeur continued to haunt him, but he would not succumb (Mark 8:33).[16] He disliked honorific titles (Matt. 23:6–12),[17] rebuked those who called him "good" (Mark 10:18), and warned against emulating "great men" who lord it over others (Mark 10:42–45). His exuberant thanksgiving at one point in his mission for the way God's fatherly love was being revealed to the world through him (Matt. 11:25–27/Luke 10:21–22) would suggest that he was, in that moment at least, a man at last at peace with himself and his God, doing now what he knew he did best, God's gracious will for his life (Matt. 6:33; Luke 12:31).[18]

Concluding Comments

Already the author of Hebrews saw nobility in Jesus being tempted as we are (Heb. 4:15) and maturing through the things he suffered (Heb. 5:8), but prior to the advent of developmental psychology, our knowledge of *how* we are tested, and tempted and grow through various life stages from early childhood onward, was limited. As a result, biographies tended to be long at the end in their accounts of the culminating achievements of a man's life, but short at the beginning on analysis of the events leading up to those accomplishments.

This is certainly true of the Gospels. They too focus almost exclusively on Jesus' final public mission and the events leading up to his death. And yet even they insist that there were developments leading up to these climactic events without which they cannot properly be understood or appreciated. Although Jesus had lived the greater part of his life in Nazareth, they inform us, his mission did not begin there. Prior to his mission at thirty, he had left Nazareth and gone out to the Jordan where he was baptized, tempted, and associated for a time with one of the great men of his world. And it was then, the Gospels intimate, that something happened without which there might possibly have been no mission. Jesus had to face and surmount certain inner problems: fantasies of power and miracle-working greatness above all. Only after that, and the arrest of his mentor, John the Baptist, did he return to Galilee "in the power of the Spirit" and begin that mission for which he became famous (Luke 4:14–15/Mark 1:14/Matt. 4:12).

A sharper focus on Jesus' age-thirty transition could have contemporary relevance, for problems of this nature—pseudoattachments, misshapen identities, and fantasies of power in men of this age group—remain with us as one of our intransigent problems. A recent psychobiography informs us that the world-famous martyr-theologian Dietrich Bonhoeffer was also conflicted in this way at this time of his life (Green, 1977, 169). Theology itself was initially embraced by him, we are told, partly as a tactic for surpassing his prestigious father and brothers. In a memoir written when he was twenty-six, he refers to the "contemptible vanity" that had plagued him in doing so. "How often," he lamented, "he had sought to master it [this vanity]. But it always crept back again and . . . forced an entry into the house of his soul and made him afraid" (Green, 1977, 169). Only through a deep-seated conversion to the God of the Bible and to Jesus was he released from this agonizing state of mind and set free at last to pursue his life's work.

Pope John XXIII also tells, in his posthumously published *Journal of a Soul*, of the "fantastic dreams" of "positions and honors" that assailed him all his life (Pope John XXIII, 1965, 187). His "enemy within," he called them. "In the end," he says, "I was able to get the better of it. But I was mortified to feel it constantly returning" (xvii). Hitler may be cited as an example of someone who, beset by similar problems and grandiose dreams, not only yielded, but in yielding brought the world with him to the brink of destruction. It would appear that the great men who fail in this crucial encounter with hubris, especially at this time of their lives, may descend to the depths and become the tragic antichrists of history, while those who instead come "to their senses" (Luke 15:127 NIV) are the pillars upon whom whatever sanity the world has is continually being built and rebuilt.

Through the centuries, the portraits of Jesus have varied from age to age and place to place: "good shepherd" during the early church persecutions; "cosmic ruler" during the triumph of Christianity in the Roman Empire; "the crucified" in the late Middle Ages (Bainton & Devasahayam, 1974). A psychohistorical probe of the kind undertaken here may help us appropriate still another dimension of Jesus' achievement; one of special importance, perhaps, in an age grasping for ways to check the indulgent and sometimes dangerous ambitions of too many of its age-thirty-and-over males. Jesus, "the tempted one," who at the right time finds a wise mentor, humbles himself in baptism, says no to grandiosity, and with God's help goes on to become what he was meant to be: the prototypical, caring, "generative man."[19]

Notes

This chapter was previously published as "Jesus and the Age Thirty Transition" in the *Journal of Psychology and Christianity*, J. H. Ellens, ed., vol. 6, no. 1, 1987, 40ff; as well as in *Christian Perspectives on Human Development*, L. Aden, D. G. Benner, and J. H. Ellens, eds., (1992), Grand Rapids: Baker, 237–250. It is republished here by permission of the former publishers and the author.

1. On the basis of papyri evidence, where ages are often given in multiples of five, J. Cadbury (1963, 275–276) suggests that Luke's "about thirty" was meant to convey that Jesus was between twenty-five and thirty-five at the time.

2. The importance of utilizing psychological insights in historical Jesus research is astutely analyzed and defended by J. McIntyre (1966, 114–143). For a review of psychohistorical research generally, see Gilmore (1984); Rollins (1999); Capps (2000); Childs (2000); and *Pastoral Psychology*, J. H. Ellens, ed., vol. 50, no. 6 (2002), 51, no. 2 (2002), and 51, no. 6 (2003). The

three numbers of *Pastoral Psychology* each address at length in a number of articles an evaluation of the work of D. Capps, W. G. Rollins, and H. Childs, respectively. All are related to seeing Jesus and Sacred Scripture through the lens of psychology. Among the sporadic attempts at understanding Jesus in this light, the following should be mentioned: Berguer (1923); Boisen (1936); Erikson (1981); and Vitz and Gartner (1984). To this end, no one to date, so far as I know, has made use of Levinson's research.

3. In *Kiddushin* it is stated, "the father is bound in respect of his son, to circumcise, redeem, teach him Torah, take a wife for him, and teach him a craft. Some say, to teach him to swim too" (Epstein, 1961, 291). It is also reported in *Kiddushin* that "Raba said to R. Nathan b. Ammi: Whilst your hand is yet upon your son's neck, [marry him], viz., between sixteen and twenty-two. Others state, between eighteen and twenty-four" (30a).

4. Parental loss as a factor in high achievement has been carefully researched by Eisenstadt (1978). In a study of 573 "eminent individuals," he discovered that parental loss among this group was at a significantly earlier age than among the general population. Surprisingly, the statistics for this group were similar to the age of parental loss among psychotic, severely depressed, or suicidal patients. The reason, he concluded, is that a child faced by the loss of one or both parents is suddenly compelled to master a new environment. For some, this challenge may prove to be overwhelming, leading to mental and emotional breakdown. But others are able to respond by going through what Eisenstadt calls a process of "creative mourning" and "overcompensation." The potential genius, he writes, translates this struggle for mastery, following the death of a parent, into a personal development that leads to a high degree of competency in an occupational field.

5. In one instance, a son whose father was killed in a farming accident when he was an adolescent told me that the dilemma he felt over how long to remain at home was resolved only when his mother remarried. He was twenty-five at the time, but "it was as though a burden had been lifted from my shoulders," he said, and it was this that gave him the emotional freedom soon thereafter to marry and establish a home of his own.

6. For a review of the problems involved in translating Mark 3:19b–21, see Brown et al. (1978, 51–58). Geza Vermes (1973) comments that "the scandalous incongruity of this statement is the best guarantee of its historicity" (33). For a further understanding of the historical Jesus, see Hengel (1981, 64).

7. According to J. Klausner and H. Danby (1925), "respect for his mother, a prominent trait among the Jews, ranked in the Ten Commandments on the same level as respect for the father, required that he should go to her at once" instead of responding in this manner (280).

8. The mentor at thirty is invariably "a transitional figure," writes Levinson (1978b, 99), due to the innate drive of the age thirty male to find himself and realize his destiny. This would suggest that there was no one

"root cause" of Jesus' eventual independence and differentiation from John, such as the "disconfirmation" of John's eschatological expectations (Riches, 1980, 165, 180), or his exorcisms (Hollenbach, 1982, 209–216), or the audition and vision at the time of his baptism (Jeremias, 1971, 55). These may well have been factors, but at thirty the mentoring relationship is almost always very temporary.

9. The way Matthew's Gospel has changed what was undoubtedly a private audition ("*Thou* art my beloved Son" Mark 1:11/Luke 3:22, italics added) into a public event ("*This* is my beloved Son" Matt. 3:17, italics added) has often been observed. For a defense of the historicity and life-changing importance of this experience, see especially Jeremias (1971, 51–56); Dunn (1975, 62–65); and Wilson (1984, 87).

10. While it is difficult to imagine who in the early church might have invented stories of Jesus being tempted by Satan in this manner, an analysis of Jesus' mission points to a victorious battle over "Satan" as one of its presuppositions (see note 14). For further arguments for historicity, see Manson (1953, 55); McCasland (1964, 31); and Marshall (1978).

11. Josephus writes in *The Jewish Wars* (1987, 6:312) that the chief inducement for the Jewish rebellion against Rome in the years prior to the fall of Jerusalem in A.D. 70 was an "oracle also found in their sacred scriptures, announcing that at that time a man from their country would become ruler of the world." While Josephus is vague regarding the relevance of this oracle for the various prophetic-messianic type revolutionaries he describes elsewhere as active during the fourth and fifth decades of this first century (see 2.118, 258–265), it is apparent that there must have been some connection. In 2.259, for example, these latter are described as "deceivers and imposters, claiming divine inspiration" and as men who "fostered revolutionary changes by inciting the mob to frenzied enthusiasm and by leading them into the wilderness under the belief that God would show them omens of freedom there." This is as plausible a background for understanding Jesus' wilderness temptations as could be hoped for. Seen in this light, Jesus' temptations would appear to be not "temptations of the Messiah," as traditionally thought, but "temptations to messianism." In other words, a spiritual ordeal is alluded to in which Jesus, after his encounter with God as gracious Father at his baptism, came to recognize messianic delusions of grandeur as satanic and thrust them from him.

12. It is worth noting that Satan, in these narratives, represents patricidal ambition. He tempts Jesus to usurp the role of his true Father (God) and rule the world in his stead. This is precisely the dilemma a son would face in taking charge of a deceased father's family, as we conjecture Jesus did. Suddenly powerful in a realm where only a short time before he had been a subordinate, his identity as "son" will inevitably be threatened by the heady "impossible possibility" of "ruling" in his father's place. Understandably, a son in such circumstances will find himself contending with fantasies of greatness, which he knows in his more sober moments to be illusory. If he should happen to live

in a time when hopes for the coming of a miracle-working Messiah are high, these may well determine the more precise form such fantasies might take.

13. That a satanic figure was extremely real to the historical Jesus, and had in fact, in his view, already in some sense been defeated, is evident from the following passages: Mark 3:27/Luke 11:21; Luke 10:18; Mark 8:33; Luke 22:31–31. Regarding God's fatherly power, see Matt. 6:10/Luke 11:2 ("Father . . . thy kingdom come!"); Matt. 12:28/Luke 11:20; Luke 17:20–21. For a penetrating discussion of Jesus' "Abba-experience" as "source and secret of his being, message, and manner of life," see Schillenbeeckx (1979, 256–271).

14. Regarding this alienated sector and the reasons for its alienation, see Jeremias (1971, 108–113); Oppenheimer (1977); and Sanders (1985, 186–211), who call attention to the failure of earlier discussions of this topic to differentiate between "sinners" and "common people" ('am ha-aretz).

15. Again, M. J. Borg's judgment is similar (1984). Whereas, he writes, the other renewal movements of the time "intensified the Torah in the direction of holiness, emphasizing various forms of separation: from society as a whole, from the Gentiles, from impurity within society; Jesus intensified the Torah primarily by applying it to internal dimensions of the human psyche: to dispositions, emotions, thoughts and desires" (238). For a comparable analysis, see Vermes (1984, 47).

16. The emotional dimension of Jesus' reaction to Peter's insistence on projecting a messianic identity upon him are too seldom noted. It can be argued, I suggest, that Jesus not only did not think of himself as Messiah (Vermes, 1973, 149), but that he was inwardly tormented over this issue and feared succumbing to such an identity. It was, so to speak, the dark side of his inner world, one which he thrust from him on this occasion (Mark 8:33) with an outburst of emotion that apparently startled his disciples ("Get behind me, Satan! For you are not on the side of God, but of men").

17. According to Jeremias (1971, 258), "the only title used by Jesus of himself whose authenticity is to be taken seriously" is "Son of Man," but Vermes (1973, 160–191; 1984, 89–99), has shown that even this (Aramaic: bar enash) was not a title in a world of Jesus, but an idiom meaning "man," "someone," or used occasionally as a self-effacing circumlocution for "I."

18. Jeremias (1978, 45) documents the "turning of the tide" in favor of the historicity of these important texts. See also Jeremias (1971, 57–59); Dunn (1975, 27–34); and Meyer (1979, 152).

19. For an incisive discussion of this prototype and its contemporary relevance, see Browning (1973).

References

Aden, L., Benner, D. G., & Ellens, J. H. (1992). *Christian Perspectives on Human Development*. Grand Rapids: Baker.

Bainton, R. H., & Devasahayam, S. (1974). *Behold the Christ: A Portrayal in Words and Pictures.* New York: Harper & Row.

Berguer, G. (1923). *Some Aspects of the Life of Jesus From the Psychological and Psychoanalytic Point of View.* New York: Harcourt, Brace.

Boisen, A. (1936). *The Exploration of the Inner World: A Study of Mental Disorder and Religious Experience.* New York: Harper.

Borg, M. J. (1984). *Conflict, Holiness and Politics in the Teaching of Jesus.* New York: Edwin Mellen.

Brown, R. E., Donfried, K. P., Reumann, J., & Fitzmyer, J. A., eds. (1978). *Mary in the New Testament: A Collaborative Assessment by Protestant and Roman Catholic Scholars.* Philadelphia: Fortress.

Browning, D. S. (1973). *Generative Man: Psychoanalytic Perspectives.* Philadelphia: Westminster.

Buchanan, G. W. (1984). *Jesus, the King and His Kingdom.* Macon: Mercer University Press.

Buchanan, G. W. (1985). Jesus and the Upper Classes. *Novum Testamentum,* 7, 195–209.

Cadbury, H. J. (1963). Some Lukan Expressions of Time: Lexical Notes on Luke-Acts 7. *JBL 82,* 272–278.

Capps, D. (2000). *Jesus, A Psychological Biography.* St. Louis: Chalice.

Childs, H. (2000). *The Myth of the Historical Jesus and the Evolution of Consciousness.* SBL Dissertation Series 179, Atlanta: SBL.

Connick, C.M. (1974). *Jesus, the Man, the Mission, and the Message* (2nd ed.). Englewood Cliffs: Prentice Hall.

Dunn, J. D. G. (1975). *Jesus and the Spirit: A Study of the Religious and Charismatic Experience of Jesus and the First Christians as Reflected in the New Testament.* London: SCM.

Eisenstadt, J. M. (1978). Parental Loss and Genius. *American Psychologist,* 33(3), 211–213.

Ellens, J. H., ed. (1987). *Journal of Psychology and Christianity* 6(1).

Ellens, J. H., ed. (2002, 2003). *Pastoral Psychology,* vols. 50(6), 51(2), 51(6). New York: Human Sciences Press.

Epstein, I., ed. (1961). *The Babylonian Talmud.* London: Soncino Press. (English translation of the Kiddushin)

Erikson, E. H. (1963). *Childhood and Society* (2nd ed.). New York: Norton.

Erikson, E. H. (1969). *Gandhi's Truth: On the Origins of Militant Nonviolence.* New York: Norton.

Erikson, E. H. (1981). The Galilean Sayings and the Sense of "I." *Yale Review,* 70, 321–362.

Farmer, William R. (1982). *Jesus and the Gospel: Tradition, Scripture, and Canon.* Philadelphia: Fortress.

Flusser, D. (1969). *Jesus.* New York: Herder and Herder.

Gilmore, W. J. (1984). *Psychohistorical Inquiry: A Comprehensive Research Bibliography.* New York and London: Garland.

Green, C. (1977). Bonhoeffer in the Context of Erikson's Luther Study, *Psychohistory and Religion: The Case of the Young Man Luther*, R. H. Bainton, ed. Philadelphia: Fortress.

Greenspan, S. I., & Pollock, G. H., eds. (1980). *The Course of Life: Psychoanalytic Contributions towards Understanding Personality Development*, vol. 3: *Adulthood and the Aging Process*. Adelphi: NIMH.

Hengel, M. (1981). *The Charismatic Leader and His Followers*. New York: Crossroads.

Hollenbach, P. (1982). The Conversion of Jesus: From Jesus the Baptizer to Jesus the Healer. *Aufstieg und Niedergang der Romischen Welt*, 2(55), 196–219.

Jeremias, J. (1971). *New Testament Theology, Part One: The Proclamation of Jesus*. London: SCM.

Jeremias, J. (1978). *The Prayers of Jesus*. Philadelphia: Fortress.

Josephus, F. (1987). *The Works of Josephus, Complete and Unabridged*, W. Whiston, trans. Peabody: Hendrickson.

Klausner, J., & Danby, H. (1925). *Jesus of Nazareth: His Life, Times, and Teaching*. London: Allen and Unwin.

Lammers, W., Jr. (1977). The Absent Father, *Fathering, Fact or Fable?* E. V. Stein, ed. Nashville: Abingdon.

Levinson, D. J. (1978a). Eras: The Anatomy of the Life Cycle. *Psychiatric Opinion*, 15, 39–48.

Levinson, D. J. (1978b). *The Seasons of a Man's Life*. New York: Knopf.

Manson, T. W. (1953). *The Servant-Messiah: A Study of the Public Ministry of Jesus*. Cambridge: Cambridge University Press.

Marshall, I. H. (1978). *The Gospel of Luke: A Commentary on the Greek Text*. Grand Rapids: Eerdmans; Exeter: Paternoster.

McCasland, V. (1964). *The Pioneer of Our Faith: A New Life of Jesus*. New York: McGraw Hill.

McIntyre, J. (1966). *The Shape of Christology*. London: SCM.

Meyer, B. F. (1979). *The Aims of Jesus*. London: SCM.

Oppenheimer, A. (1977). *The 'Am Ha-aretz: A Study in the Social History of the Jewish People in the Hellenistic Roman Period*. Leiden: Brill.

Phipps, W. E. (1970). *Was Jesus Married? The Distortion of Sexuality in the Christian Tradition*. New York: Harper.

Phipps, W. E. (1973). *The Sexuality of Jesus: Theological and Literary Perspectives*. New York: Harper.

Pope John XXIII. (1965). *Journal of a Soul*. Montreal: Palm Publishers.

Riches, J. (1980). *Jesus and the Transformation of Judaism*. London: Darton, Longman, & Todd.

Rollins, W. G. (1999). *Soul and Psyche, The Bible in Psychological Perspective*. Minneapolis: Augsburg Fortress.

Sanders, E. P. (1985). *Jesus and Judaism*. Philadelphia: Fortress.

Schillenbeeckx, E. (1979). *Jesus: An Experiment in Christology*. New York: Seabury.

Sloyan, G. S. (1983). *Jesus in Focus: A Life in Its Setting*. Mystic: Twenty-Third Publications.

Vermes, G. (1973). *Jesus the Jew: A Historian's Reading of the Gospels*. New York: MacMillan.

Vermes, G. (1984). *Jesus and the World of Judaism*. Philadelphia: Fortress.

Vitz, P. C., & Gartner, J. (1984). Jesus as the Anti-oedipus. *Journal of Psychology and Theology, 12*, 4–14.

Wilson, I. (1984). *Jesus: The Evidence*. London: Weidenfeld and Nicolson.

CHAPTER 6

BEYOND SCHWEITZER AND THE PSYCHIATRISTS: JESUS AS FICTIVE PERSONALITY

Donald Capps

This is the first of three chapters on views of Jesus presented by twentieth century psychologists. The trilogy lifts up three central themes: pathology, power and presence. This chapter addresses the pathology issue by focusing on Albert Schweitzer's influential text, *The Psychiatric Study of Jesus* (1948). Schweitzer and the psychiatrists whom he severely critiqued shared the belief that Jesus identified himself as the coming Messiah. Unlike the psychiatrists, however, Schweitzer did not therefore judge Jesus to have been delusional. I agree with Schweitzer on the grounds that "ideas of reference" were a common feature of the religious milieu in which Jesus lived. I then introduce the psychoanalytic concept of the "fictive personality" as relevant to Jesus' identification of himself as the coming Messiah. In contrast to delusional theories, this concept emphasizes the positive uses of such identifications, especially as means of self-empowerment.

In *Jesus: A Psychological Biography* (Capps, 2000), I lamented the fact that the use of psychology in current research on the historical Jesus lags far behind the use of disciplines like sociology and anthropology. This neglect of psychology as a whole is unfortunate, because many of the key questions now being raised about Jesus' identity cannot be answered in sociological and anthropological terms alone, as they are fundamentally psychological. While the question of Jesus' understanding of his own identity requires consideration of the types of religious authority available to him—such as prophet, teacher, healer, and messiah—there is also a psychological element involved in his self-identification with one or more of these types.

In this chapter, I will discuss Albert Schweitzer's *The Psychiatric Study of Jesus* (Schweitzer, 1948), because his critique in this text of psychiatric studies of Jesus originally published in the first decade of the twentieth century discouraged others from making similar attempts. Over the decades that have followed, this critique has continued to cast a long shadow over the use of psychological theories and concepts in historical Jesus research. In my discussion, I will show that the fundamental disagreement between Schweitzer and the psychiatrists centered on the question of whether or not Jesus was delusional. I will argue that the answer to this question hinges on whether "ideas of reference" can be held to be delusional when they are an integral feature of the religious culture in which Jesus lived. I contend that twentieth and twenty-first century psychiatrists cannot answer this question in the affirmative, but that Jesus' own contemporaries could do so on the basis of their own criteria. These criteria, however, would not be expected to be applied with scientific neutrality, but would instead reflect the sociopolitical biases of those who applied them. I suggest in conclusion that another psychological construct—the fictive personality—*is* applicable to Jesus, and because it does not involve the claim that Jesus was delusional, is a construct that we may apply to him despite the fact that we are not his contemporaries. In fact, it may be argued that the "fictive personality" concept articulates his own self-understanding as well as the understanding of him held by his disciples and supporters. Schweitzer's *The Quest of the Historical Jesus: A Critical Study of Its Progress from Reimarus to Wrede* (1968), was followed seven years later by *The Psychiatric Study of Jesus*. In the seven-year interval between the publication of these two books, Schweitzer had been studying medicine so that he would be trained for medical work in Africa. *The Psychiatric Study of Jesus* was his thesis for the degree of Doctor of Medicine at the University of Strassburg.

Exposition

As Wayne G. Rollins points out (1999), Schweitzer had criticized studies of Jesus that employed modern psychological theories in his earlier 1901 book, *A Sketch of the Life of Jesus*, noting that such efforts are a "patchwork of opinions" produced by "mediocre minds" who "with much else that is modern" have "transferred to [Jesus] our modern psychology, without always recognizing clearly that it is not applicable to him and necessarily belittles him" (62). He "reinforced his attack" in 1913 with the publication of *The Psychiatric Study of Jesus*. According to Rollins, Schweitzer "did not intend to condemn psychology as a whole, only 'faulty' and 'amateurish' instances of it." But the effect of his critique on biblical scholars "was a virtual ban on things psychological . . . for the better part of the century" (63). Rollins cites evidence of an "attitudinal change" beginning in the late 1960s toward the psychological interpretation of the Bible (65–87). But most of it applies to Paul, not to Jesus (127–130).

If Schweitzer's book on the psychiatric study of Jesus had the effect of "a virtual ban on things psychological among professional biblical scholars for the better part of the century," it makes sense that we return to this book to find out why it had this effect, whether intentional or not, and try to determine whether this effect was justified.

As we enter into our discussion of Schweitzer's text, we should keep in mind that this critique of the psychiatric studies was mounted by a scholar who had embraced historical-critical methods. But Schweitzer was highly critical of David E. Strauss, the scholar who is typically viewed as the inspiration behind the first sustained scholarly quest for the historical Jesus. When Strauss's *The Life of Jesus Critically Examined* (1972) appeared in 1835, it was met with a storm of protest, resulting in his dismissal from his professorship in New Testament at the University of Zurich. Schweitzer was born in 1875, forty years after Strauss' work was published. By this time, the historical-critical method had gained a solid foothold in German theological faculties, and Schweitzer was introduced to this method during his theological studies in the early 1890s at the University of Strassburg in Alsace, which was then under German rule. Heinrich Julius Holtzmann was lecturing there on the Synoptic Gospels. He was a proponent of the theory that Mark, not Matthew, is the earliest Gospel, a theory that continued to be contested throughout the nineteenth century, but is now almost universally accepted by biblical scholars.

Schweitzer did not dismiss the historical-critical method, but his independence of mind led him to question some of its fundamental conclusions about Jesus. In 1894, when he was serving his compulsory year of military service in the German army, he worked in preparation for an examination in the Synoptic Gospels at the beginning of Winter Term. One day, while reading Matthew 10–11, he began to question Professor Holtzmann's view that this material was not historical but derived from the early church. Schweitzer concluded that this discourse in which Jesus sends his disciples out, telling them that they would be persecuted and that they "will not have gone through all the towns of Israel, before the Son of man comes" (Matt. 10:23) was authentic. He based this judgment on the fact that the Messianic Kingdom did not appear before the end of their journey, and the disciples were not persecuted. As the translator of *The Psychiatric Study of Jesus*, Charles R. Joy points out, "Schweitzer was sure that no later generation would ever have attributed to Jesus statements proved false by events" (Schweitzer, 1948, 20).

Schweitzer also concluded on the basis of Jesus' reply to John the Baptist's query, "Are you the one to come or should we look for another?" that Jesus was thinking of two different worlds—"the natural world in which they all lived, where John was the greatest of all, and the Messianic Kingdom that was to come soon, where the least of the supernatural beings who should people that world would be greater than John" (1948, 21). When he reached home after military maneuvers, Schweitzer felt that "new horizons" had been opened up to him. He was certain "that Jesus had announced no kingdom that was to be founded and realized in the natural work by himself and the believers, but one that was to be expected as coming with the almost immediate dawn of a supernatural age" (21).

Schweitzer concluded that the disciples' return without having suffered any persecution caused Jesus to rethink his position, and that he came to believe that he himself must suffer death before the appearance of the kingdom, thereby atoning for the sins of the elect and saving them from the days of tribulation. The new conviction that he was to suffer death and then become the Messiah when God's kingdom is ushered in was disclosed to the disciples at Caesarea Philippi, and when he left his retirement to join the band of pilgrims from Galilee en route to Jerusalem, only the disciples knew what he believed himself to be (Schweitzer, 1948, 22). Schweitzer's subsequent reflections elaborated on his belief that Jesus was profoundly eschatological and that his eschatological understanding was deeply apocalyptic, anticipating the end of the world as we know it and the beginning of the reign of God.

Schweitzer knew that this conception of Jesus would be unpopular with his professors and the church leaders of his day, as they promoted a view of Jesus as envisioning a Kingdom of Heaven that was to be achieved gradually here on earth. But according to Joy, he was unprepared for the "superficial thinkers wearing the garb of psychology and psychiatry" who "would find in his eschatological picture of Jesus support and comfort for their contention that we have to do in this man of Narzareth [*sic*] with mental derangement, with hysteria perhaps, with paranoia certainly. This new school of psychopathology found here a man who suffered from hallucinations, from ideas of reference [i.e., claiming to be a person that he is not], from delusions of grandeur" (Schweitzer, 1948, 24). In the first decade of the twentieth century, "books appeared that disturbed Schweitzer profoundly. They asked if Jesus was an ecstatic, they frankly pronounced him to be an insane man, they analyzed the Gospels for evidence of psychopathic symptoms" (Schweitzer, 24). But "they were little qualified for their task. They had no critical understanding of the sources. They based their findings on historically discredited material. *Yet Schweitzer's friends pointed out to him that his own studies were in part responsible for them*" (25, my emphasis).

Joy suggests, therefore, that for Schweitzer the writing of this book was "an inescapable duty. He himself was sure that Jesus was completely sane. That Jesus shared the Messianic ideas of late Judaism, that he who was really a descendent of David had come to believe that in the world to come he was destined to be the Messiah, are in no rational sense evidences of mental disease." Thus, *The Psychiatric Study of Jesus* "came out of a deep inner compulsion. It had to be written" (Schweitzer, 1948, 25).

In the preface to the 1913 edition of *The Psychiatric Study of Jesus*, however, Schweitzer pointed out that his primary target was not the more recent psychiatric studies of Jesus. Rather, it was David F. Strauss' conjecture in *The Life of Jesus Critically Examined* that "the Jesus who lived in the world of ideas contained in the Book of Daniel and in the late Jewish apocalyptic literature and who considered himself the 'Son of Man' and the 'Messiah' soon to appear in supernatural glory is to be adjudged in some fashion as psychopathic" (Schweitzer, 1948, 27). Yet in the text itself, Schweitzer indicates that Strauss actually tempered his position in his second *Life of Jesus* in 1864. In the first life of Jesus, published in 1835, Strauss had declared that Jesus "lived with the quixotic idea that he was destined to appear in the near future in a blaze of supernatural glory, surrounded by angels, on the clouds of heaven, to judge the world as the expected Messiah and to establish the kingdom which was to follow" (Schweitzer, 34). Therefore, Jesus was "a fanatic." Strauss, however, tried "to explain that the Nazarene, even though the fanatical idea had gripped him, can be considered, nonetheless, as one in full possession of all his facilities, partly because of the fact that his expectation has its roots in the general conceptions of late Judaism" (35).

But when he wrote his second *Life of Jesus* in 1864, Strauss was "so vividly conscious of the fanatical in the thought of the second coming that . . . he was inclined to consider the idea as very close to madness, and accordingly doubted whether the sayings that refer to this really originated with Jesus" (Schweitzer, 1948, 35). Thus, by doubting that these sayings were authentic, he was able to preserve his conviction that Jesus was "in full possession of all his faculties." However, his decision to let these sayings about the second coming "fall completely into the background in his portrayal of Jesus" was "reproached by various critics for apostasy from the better judgment he showed in 1835" (Schweitzer, 35). In effect, the price Strauss paid for his preservation of his conviction that Jesus was mentally sane was the loss of Jesus' own anticipation of his second coming and his self-identification as the expected Messiah.

Schweitzer joins in this reproach, for "historical research has more and more clearly perceived that the expectation of the second coming of the Messiah is at the center of Jesus' thought, and that it dominates his feeling, his will and his action far more rigorously than we had previously supposed" (1948, 35). Schweitzer does not make specific reference here to his own contribution to this perception, but he notes in the preface that in his *The Quest of the Historical Jesus*, he "had brought out the apocalyptic and what in modern concepts is considered the visionary in the Nazarene's thought world more vividly than any of the investigators who formerly worked in this field" (27). In the text itself, he acknowledges that these new developments have been reproached for having resurrected the earlier views of Strauss. By placing in the foreground what Strauss calls "the quixotic and the fanatical in the world of Jesus' ideas," the new perception of Jesus "pictures a personality with clearly revealed morbid traits" (35).

Schweitzer cites as authors of such reproaches his own professor, Heinrich J. Holtzmann, Adolf Jülicher, and others who have "constantly reminded" him that "I have portrayed a Jesus whose object world looked like a structure of fantasies." Moreover, they have made "warning allusions" on occasion "to the medical books which believed that the 'paranoia' of the Jewish Messiah had been proved" (Schweitzer, 1948, 27). In effect, Schweitzer was being accused of abetting those who consider Jesus to have been insane.

For Schweitzer, the discussion turns almost entirely on the degree to which such ideas attributed to Jesus may be considered authentic: "Indeed, a series of attempts have been made which essentially represent the Messianic claims of Jesus and the expectation of his second coming as unhistoric. According to this hypothesis, the Nazarene was a simple Jewish teacher, whose followers after his death elevated him to the rank of Messiah and then proceeded to place in his mouth allusions and expressions relating to it" (1948, 36). He cites William Wrede's *The Messianic Secret in the Gospels* as "the most ingenious attempt of this sort." Ingenious as these efforts may be, "this kind of distinction between authentic and unauthentic words in the sources cannot be maintained. It must, therefore, be admitted that Jesus considered himself to be the Messiah and expected his majestic return on the clouds of heaven" (36).

While Schweitzer clearly felt that this issue was hardly debatable, it has proven to be one of the most challenging and vexing issues in subsequent Jesus research. Almost a century later, it remains both controversial and divisive. My immediate concern is that his view that Jesus *did* see himself as the coming Messiah left him open to the charge that he was providing support, however unintentionally, for the psychiatrists' view of Jesus as insane. Thus, he had a great deal at stake in mounting his critique against the authors of the psychiatric studies of Jesus.

Schweitzer's *The Psychiatric Study of Jesus*

In the following discussion of Schweitzer's *The Psychiatric Study of Jesus*, I will focus mainly on the issue of Jesus' understanding of himself as the coming Messiah, on how this understanding contributed to the psychiatrists' view of him as delusional, and on Schweitzer's view that Jesus could understand himself as the coming Messiah and yet be perfectly sane (or non-delusional).

Schweitzer begins with some general comments about the application of the psychopathological method to historical figures. This method, which involves the investigation of the mental aberrations of significant personalities in relation to their works, has "recently fallen into disrepute" (1948, 33). This is not the fault of the method itself, which "with proper limitations and in the hands of professional investigators can produce and has produced valuable results," but is because "it has been faultily pursued by amateurs. The prerequisites which are essential for successful work in this field—exact source knowledge, adequate medical, and particularly psychiatric experience, both under the discipline of critical talents—are very seldom found together." Because most practitioners of this methodology lack one or another of these prerequisites and sometimes lack all of them, one often encounters in this field of study "misconceptions of the grossest kind" (33).

For example, forming a judgment about a person on the sole basis of his acts is contrary to all psychiatric practice and "has always something suspicious about it." If this is true for the present age, "how much more restraint must be exercised when we are dealing with people from a very distant epoch and with imperfect and uncertain traditions!" (Schweitzer, 1948, 33). Most psychiatrists today are disinclined to use the method, partly because "they do not consider psychiatry so perfected and stabilized that they can find a useful criterion in it for all the acts of mankind," and partly because "they know that every vital human activity must be understood within the conditions of its own age" (Schweitzer, 34).

In Schweitzer's view, these caveats have even greater applicability to Jesus. As he intends to show, there are "special reasons" for not engaging in a psychopathological study of Jesus, and these "take on extraordinary emotional value when it is a question of dealing psychopathologically with the life of Jesus" (1948, 34). This is all the more reason for assuring ourselves that the practitioner has the prerequisites enumerated above. The objective of his book, therefore, is to examine the opinions advanced by the medical writers who have dealt with Jesus, and to do so from both the psychiatric and historical-critical point of view.

He discusses three texts: A German text by George de Loosten, *Jesus Christ from the Standpoint of the Psychiatrist*, published in 1905; an English text by William Hirsch, *Conclusions of a Psychiatrist*, published in 1912 and translated into German under the title *Religion and Civilization from the Standpoint of the Psychiatrist*; and a French text by Charles Binet-Sanglé, *The Dementia of Jesus*, published in four volumes in 1910–1915. He also cites Emil Rasmussen's *Jesus: A Comparative Study in Psychopathology*, a Danish text published in German translation in 1905. Because Rasmussen was not a psychiatrist but a student of religion, Schweitzer does not discuss this work in detail. He did, however, append a footnote on Rasmussen's views when the thesis was published, noting the difficulty of discussing Rasmussen's views in detail because of "the chaotic condition of the concept of psychiatry in his own mind" (1948, 74). As Rasmussen's views add little to those of the three psychiatrists, I will not discuss Schweitzer's critique of his views in this article.

De Loosten: Jesus as Psychic Degenerate

Schweitzer begins with de Loosten's view that Jesus was "evidently a hybrid, stained from birth by heredity, who even in his early youth as a born degenerate attracted attention by an extremely exaggerated self-consciousness combined with high intelligence and a very slightly developed sense of family. . . . His self-consciousness slowly unfolded until it rose to a fixed delusional system" (1948, 37). Its peculiarities "were determined by the intensive religious tendencies of the time and by his one-sided preoccupation with the writings of the Old Testament" (37). For de Loosten, Jesus' psychopathology became full-blown when he came into contact with John the Baptist. Either directly encouraged by John or by the relationship he offered, Jesus "was moved to express his ideas" and "proceeding step by step" he finally arrived "at the point of relating to himself all the scriptural promises, which had become vital again through national misfortune, and on whose ultimate glorious fulfillment all hearts hoped" (37).

De Loosten concluded that "Jesus regarded himself as a completely supernatural being," for only in this way can we understand his behavior when he arrogated to himself divine rights like the forgiveness of sins. As for indications in the Gospels (Matt. 9:2; Mark 2: 5–12; Luke 5:20, 7:48) that Jesus "kept the Messianic dignity which he claimed as much as possible to himself," he explains this reticence psychologically on the grounds that "Jesus did not believe he had a large enough following at the time to enable him to realize his claims" (Schweitzer, 1948, 37).

From Jesus' response to the young man who wanted to attend to the burial of his father, "Follow me and let the dead bury the dead" (Matt. 8:22) and comparable sayings, de Loosten infers "that Jesus takes it for granted that the beginning of his divine Utopia was immediately imminent" and "that he was no longer conscious of his human nature" (Schweitzer, 1948, 38). Both are reflected in his journey to Jerusalem, which was prompted by the "foolhardy idea of achieving by a certain stroke of violence his long cherished, and a thousand times expressed, claims" (Schweitzer, 38). Driving the money changers out of the temple was "a shocking act of violence," which led to his arrest. Before his arrest, Jesus was in "a highly nervous, excitable state. He knew what a risky game he played and suffered greatly under the weight of fears and ominous misgivings" (38). The completely senseless cursing of the fig tree was reflective of this mood. Taking out "his ill-humor on a defenseless tree" can only be explained "as the boiling over of severe spiritual excitement" (38–39). Also, feelings of persecution, apparently irrational, are evident in his accusation that the crowd around him was looking for an opportunity to kill him, to which they respond, astonished, "You have a demon! Who is trying to kill you?" (John 7:19–20).

In Gethsemane, he experienced a moment of depression, and then his "psychosis" erupted in all its old strength when the police came to arrest him. His "mental disorder" was revealed during the examination before the high council when he suggested to the high priest that his judges will see him sitting at the right hand of God as the Son of Man and coming on the clouds of heaven (Schweitzer, 1948, 38).

Thus, Jesus' temperament was extremely variable, and he was prone "to strange and apparently groundless moods of depression." John 12:27 ("Now, my soul is troubled . . .") supports this claim. He also suffered from hallucinations, such as the occurrences at his baptism, "a vision which obviously exercised a decisive influence upon Jesus' later decisions." In this particular case, the hallucination was both visual and auditory and therefore reveals "a greatly excited mind" (Schweitzer, 1948, 39). While acknowledging that we do not know how frequently Jesus had these hallucinations, de Loosten "considers it probable that Jesus depends upon them for his decisions and that similar visions like those at the baptism occurred later" (Schweitzer, 39). It is also highly probable that Jesus suffered from voices which seemed to him to come out of his own body, as though he had a spirit residing inside of him that determined what he should and should not do, and which he obeyed. Also, on the basis of Mark's account (5: 25–34) of Jesus' perception that power had gone out of him and into the woman who suffered from a hemorrhage, he conjectures that Jesus "had felt some kind of abnormal peripheral sensation, perhaps of the skin, and that he was trying to find an explanation for it." Schweitzer specifically disputes this conjecture, noting that Jesus merely asserts that someone had touched his clothes, adding that it was "a naive conjecture of the Evangelist that he said this because of a feeling that power had gone out of him" (39).

Finally, de Loosten believes that Jesus' own "lack of sex-consciousness" is proven by his reference to persons who are eunuchs by choice for the sake of the kingdom of heaven (Matt. 19:12). Tying this lack of sex-consciousness together with his lack of family loyalty, he considers this a sure sign of "psychic degeneration *par excellence*" (Schweitzer, 1948, 40).

Unlike today's readers, Schweitzer's original readers would have known what de Loosten meant by "psychic degeneration." The degeneration theory was formulated in the 1850s by the French psychiatrist Benedict Morel, who used it to explain all forms of chronic mental illness. He believed that mental deterioration was inherited, and that the characteristics of the degenerate were passed from one generation to the next in a progressive diminution of the family lineage until it became extinct. Physicians should therefore inquire into the pathological heredity of the parents rather than search for organic causes of mental illness. Because it provided an all-inclusive explanation for every mental disorder, Morel's idea took hold and dominated French psychiatry in the 1880s, then came into vogue throughout Europe, in England, and to a lesser extent in America.

De Loosten attributed Jesus' alleged degeneracy to his "hybrid" heredity. In his discussion of the psychiatrists' use of spurious sources, Schweitzer notes de Loosten's view that Jesus' father was a Roman soldier. De Loosten's picture of Jesus' lack of sexual consciousness, of family loyalty, and his erratic behavior and emotional volatility is also consistent with the degeneracy theory, which held that degenerates are likely to become subject to "impulses and obsessive ideas" and experience "anxiety and dread if the idea is not obeyed," for otherwise "harm will follow" (Taylor, 1984, 133–139). Thus, degeneracy was presumed to have a special relationship to paranoia.

Hirsch: Jesus as Paranoid Psychotic

According to Schweitzer, William Hirsch makes a flat-out diagnosis of paranoia. In his view, Jesus' delusional system can be traced to his boyhood. Jesus was "a boy with unusual mental talents" who was "predisposed to psychic disturbances," leading to the gradual formation of delusions. He spent "his whole leisure in the study of the Holy Scriptures, the reading of which certainly contributed to his mental illness. When at the age of thirty he first made a public appearance, his paranoia was completely established" (1948, 40). His paranoia was apparently one of those cases where sudden and formless psychotic ideas are present, but where some external shock and strong emotion are needed for a systematic structure of paranoia to form. This shock was provided by another paranoid, John the Baptist, whom Jesus went out to join when he heard of this "forerunner of the Messiah."

When he was baptized by John, "the aberration which had so long filled the mind of Jesus, that he was the Son of God and that God had ordained him to be the Savior of mankind, was from now on converted into visual and auditory hallucinations." Besides his hallucinations at his baptism, he "must have been in a state of continual hallucination" during the following forty days in the wilderness. All of his utterances claiming direct inspiration from God were "spoken with reference to preceding auditory hallucinations" (Schweitzer, 1948, 42). The transfiguration story (Mark 9:2–8) was also a hallucinatory experience, for when others heard thunder, he heard a voice from heaven proclaiming his coming glorification (John 12:28–30).

Jesus' forty-day sojourn in the wilderness solidified his paranoia. Up to that time, his delusions were isolated and unrelated to one another. From that time forward, they "merged into a great systemic structure of delusions; doubtless Jesus had at that time repeated conversations with God the Father who had commissioned him and whose doctrine he preached. Such a development of his illness, a transition from the latent to the active stage of paranoia, is quite characteristic of this psychosis" (Schweitzer, 1948, 40–41). In the three years following his wilderness experience, a ceaseless megalomania "formed the center around which everything else turned," and "no textbook on mental disease could provide a more typical description of a gradually but ceaselessly mounting megalomania than that afforded by the life of Jesus" (Schweitzer, 41).

Hirsch supports his diagnosis of megalomania by means of an exposition of several "I" statements in the Gospel of John, and by various "ideas of reference," or instances where Jesus ascribes to himself the predictions of prophets, especially regarding the king who should rule over the world. Hence, he "manifests one of the actual peculiarities of paranoids, who apply to themselves everything possible that they see or read." His claim to be of the family of David is typical of youthful paranoids who "substitute for their real descent a highly colored fanciful one" (Schweitzer, 1948, 41). His cursing of the fig tree is also typical of a paranoid.

Binet-Sanglé: Jesus as Religious Paranoid

While Hirsch viewed Jesus as a typical paranoid, Binet-Sanglé advanced the diagnosis of "*religious* paranoia," distinguishing three stages in its formation: the period of conception and of systematization; the hallucinatory period; and the period of personality change. To the extent possible, he treats the delusions and hallucinations separately. In his view, "the primary delusion (the primordial fixed idea) appears *ex abrupto*, without previous reflection. The further development of the delusion is apparently coherent, and though proceeding from a false hypothesis is thoroughly logical in its consequences. It develops by the progressive extension of the primary idea but without undergoing any transformation and without losing its original stamp" (Schweitzer, 1948, 42–43). How did it happen?

Various incidents and factors brought it about, including John the Baptist, his own miraculous cures, the amazement of those who were healed of their diseases, and the enthusiasm of the disciples. By these means, Jesus was brought "to the point of believing himself to be the Messiah, the king of the Jews, the Son of God, God's interpreter, God's witness, and finally of identifying himself with God" (Schweitzer, 1948, 43). The threats of the fanatical Pharisees and Scribes "also awakened in him the notion that he was the sacrificial lamb which by its death was to take away the sins of Israel" and the idea "that after his resurrection he would ascend into the heavens, there to be revealed in his complete glory" (Schweitzer, 43).

Like de Loosten and Hirsch, Binet-Sanglé emphasized Jesus' hallucinations, beginning with his baptism. This particular hallucination demonstrates a typical characteristic of religious paranoia, namely that "the object of the visual hallucination almost always appears to have a certain exalted character" (Schweitzer, 1948, 43). In Jesus' case, the hallucination comes from above and is of an encouraging nature: "You are my Son, the Beloved; with you I am well pleased" (Mark 1:11). Also, Jesus' flight into the wilderness after his baptism was a period in which he experienced a series of hallucinations: "Here, under the influence of protracted abstinence and loneliness, of the quiet and monotony of the wilderness which placed him at the mercy of all his obsessions, perhaps also under the added influence of weariness and heat, multifarious mental disturbances took form" (Schweitzer, 1948, 43). Binet-Sanglé identifies seven hallucinations in the account— two purely visual, and five that are described as both visual and auditory-verbal. None were wholly verbal, which is consistent with religious forms of paranoia, where "it is very rare for verbal hallucinations to appear alone without the conjunction of visual hallucinations" (Schweitzer, 43–44). Also, their content always refers to religious objects, especially the devil. They may be separated into the fearsome and the comforting, with the comforting ones being visual. At the baptism a dove appears, in the wilderness the angel of God appears, and in Gethsemane he is strengthened by an angel (Luke 22:43).

Binet-Sanglé doubts that the recorded hallucinations were the only ones Jesus experienced, for "insane mystics almost always suffer from hallucinations of muscle-sense" (Schweitzer, 1948, 44). Thus, in later periods, secondary psychomotor symptoms develop, "constituting a kind of theomanic possession." As examples, he cites "sensory hallucinations," in which Jesus says the Father speaks through him.

Like de Loosten, Binet-Sanglé focuses on Jesus' desire to keep his Messianic claims secret, viewing this as typical of the secretiveness of the paranoid. Thus, he was "brought to admit his system of delusions only under the stress of emotion, as, for example, in the proceedings at the trial" (Schweitzer, 1948, 44).

Schweitzer's Rejoinder

In his rejoinder to the psychiatrists' profiles of Jesus, Schweitzer makes two strategic moves. The first is to show how their lack of knowledge about the methods and findings of historical-critical research on the Gospels led them to make assertions and develop interpretations that are simply untenable. The second is to meet them on their own ground and contend that they misuse psychiatric diagnoses, especially relating to paranoia, in their applications to Jesus. The first move plays a much more prominent role in his rejoinder, as it is designed to demonstrate that no one should make assertions about Jesus, especially concerning his emotional stability and soundness of mind, if they have not taken the trouble to familiarize themselves with the work of scholars in historical Jesus research. The second move, however, is also important, as it issues a very strong warning to psychiatrists that they risk dishonoring themselves and their profession when they apply their diagnostic categories to historical figures. This second prong of his attack has the effect, whether intentional or not, of marginalizing the psychiatric study of historical figures in the field of psychiatry itself, because the available evidence will never be sufficient to enable one to achieve the same level of confidence in the accuracy of one's diagnosis expected in clinical work with living patients.

In the opening sentence of his rejoinder, Schweitzer indicates that his fundamental problem with the psychiatric portraits of Jesus is that none of the three authors is familiar with what has been going on in historical Jesus studies for several decades: "De Loosten, Hirsch, and Binet-Sanglé busy themselves with the psychopathology of Jesus without being familiar with the study of the historical Jesus. They are completely uncritical not only in the choice but also in the use of sources" (1948, 45). Thus, "before we can enter into a psychiatrical discussion of their studies, we must recall what they neglected." Schweitzer devotes the next eight pages of his forty-page text to a summation of "the results achieved by the criticism of sources and by the scientific study of the life of Jesus" (45).

Beginning with the issue of sources, he notes that the Talmud and the noncanonical Gospels should not be considered at all; and yet de Loosten is indebted to the statements handed down in Talmudic and pagan tradition through Celsus in the second century for the belief

that Jesus was the natural son of Mary and the Roman legionary Pan-
thera. This was the basis for his conclusion that Jesus was a "hybrid"
and "born degenerate." Schweitzer notes that Binet-Sanglé is even
more uncritical than de Loosten in his choice of sources, using documents such as the so-called "Judgment of Pilate" that were long ago
proved spurious (Schweitzer, 1948, 45).

Schweitzer also notes their uncritical use of the canonical sources.
For example, the Gospel of John must be omitted if one's purpose is to
reconstruct the life of the historical Jesus. This is because "the Jesus
painted there, as critical investigation since Strauss has more and
more recognized, is in the main a freely imagined personality who is
designed to improve and supplement the Jesus appearing in the first
three Gospels" (1948, 45). This "imagined personality" of Jesus is
inherently enigmatic, and therefore there is much in this image that is
"peculiar, unnatural, and studied." Thus, the psychiatrists were taken
in by this inherently enigmatic portrait, as their ascriptions of mental
illness to Jesus are largely based on citations from John: "Three-quar-
ters of the matter studied by de Loosten, Binet-Sanglé and Hirsch
come from the Fourth Gospel" (46).

The Gospel of Luke is also essentially expendable, as it "agrees in
the main with the Gospels of Mark and Matthew" and "whenever it
goes beyond them it makes a doubtful contribution, which moreover
is without any great significance for the criticism of Jesus and so can
be left out of consideration" (Schweitzer, 1948, 46). For example, the
story of the twelve-year-old Jesus in the temple (Luke 2:41–52) "cannot be considered historical for a variety of reasons." As the "stories of
the birth and childhood in Matthew (Matt. 1, 2) also belong to legend,
not to history" (Schweitzer, 1948, 46), a similar caveat applies to the
infancy narrative in Luke 1–2.

What remain useful sources are the Gospels of Mark and of Matthew (with the clear exception of Chapters 1–2). These two Gospels
"agree with one another in their construction," though Matthew goes
beyond Mark in a series of valuable discourses, which he alone has
handed down to posterity. In addition, both Gospels date from
between 70 and 90 C.E. While both go back to still older sources, their
reports are in general trustworthy, and "even though here and there
later misunderstandings and cloudy traditions are to be observed, the
exact similarity of certain details is startling" (Schweitzer, 1948, 46).

This is not the place to comment on Schweitzer's own assumptions
about the canonical Gospels, especially the Synoptics. But it is worth
noting that he places Matthew on at least a par with Mark, thus

departing from his professor H. J. Holtzmann's view that Jesus' life and teaching could best be understood from the Gospel of Mark, since Mark was the oldest of the Gospels and was the foundation on which Matthew and Luke had built (Schweitzer, 1948, 20). In contrast, Schweitzer refers to Matthew and Mark as "the two oldest Gospels" (Schweitzer, 48), implying that they were contemporaneous documents, and makes no reference to Matthew's dependence on Mark. An obvious reason for making Matthew contemporaneous with, and seemingly independent of, Mark is that it was his reading of Matthew 10–11 while on military maneuvers that led to his "discovery" that Jesus understood himself to be the coming Messiah.

Schweitzer next moves to what can be said about Jesus on the basis of "the scientific study of the life of Jesus." Of Jesus' early life, little is known: "He came from a carpenter's family in Nazareth and himself plied that trade" (1948, 46). He appears not to have engaged in studies leading to his role as a teacher, for when he returned to his hometown in the role of a prophet, the townspeople wondered at the wisdom displayed by a man they knew only as a carpenter (Mark 6:1–5). His knowledge of the Scriptures, however, could have been acquired from listening to the Sabbath readings as he was growing up. Also, prior to this public appearance he had possibly spent a longer period of time elsewhere, where he presumably gained the knowledge he presented on this occasion.

Four brothers and several sisters are mentioned (Mark 6:3, 3:31), but there is no mention as to where his age placed him among the children. That he was descended on his father's side from David "may be considered assured." But there is nothing especially extraordinary about this descent, as various prophetic texts indicate that members of the royal family were well-represented among the returnees from the Babylonian captivity under Cyrus. His descent from David is attested in Mark 10:47–48 and Matthew 21:9 and accords with the witness of Paul in Romans 1:3. We know nothing about his physical appearance or the state of his health.

The fact that neither Matthew nor Mark mention other journeys to the Passover Feast in Jerusalem during the course of his public ministry (besides the one that led to his death) supports the assumption that his ministry lasted a year or less. How long he spent among the followers of John is not known, but when John was taken prisoner, Jesus returned to Galilee and preached the same message that John had proclaimed by the Jordan River: "The Kingdom of God is at hand." This proclamation remained the centerpiece of his message from the beginning to the end of his ministry, and the phrase "the Kingdom of God" is synonymous with the "Messianic Kingdom." The proclamation of its nearness signified that the end of the world was near (Schweitzer, 1948, 48).

Schweitzer provides a brief description of the concept and image of "Kingdom of God," emphasizing that a supernatural period of time is expected to occur after the natural order has ended. But he notes that Jesus would not have needed to describe this future in any detail, and that his hearers would have known what it was all about as soon as the statement "The Kingdom of God is at hand" was spoken, its details having been well established from the books of the prophets and the apocalypses. He specifically cites the book of Enoch, which dates from the beginning of the last century B.C.E.; and the book of Daniel, 165 B.C.E., as influences upon "the idea world in which Jesus lived" (1948, 49). His listeners would have understood that the last days in the course of the natural world would be filled with terrible wars and unprecedented miseries. Thus, the content of the Gospel he preached was the nearness of the Kingdom, the judgment that would come in its wake, and the fact that he himself must endure great disgrace and persecution. He implores his followers not to be led astray at that time, but to remain loyal to him (Mark 8:34, 9:1).

In effect, Jesus reconciled two traditions—the older prophetic way of looking at things and the newer apocalyptic way. The older view asserted that the Messiah would come from the royal family of David. The newer view, as presented in Daniel and Enoch, recognized that without a reigning family, no ruler could be raised up to the position of Messiah; therefore, God would confer this status in the coming world to an angelic being who has human form and looks like "the Son of Man" (Dan. 7:13–14). What Jesus did was to claim that, while he as a normal man is not in his lifetime the Messiah, he was ordained to this dignity and would be revealed as the Messiah at the end of the world and the beginning of the Kingdom of God. Thus, Jesus endorsed both the older view that the Messiah would be a descendent of David; and the newer view that "the Son of Man," an angelic being having human form, would be the highest power in the kingdom which is to come. Jesus did not think of himself as Messiah or "Son of Man" in his natural lifetime, as he was "a normal man." But he believed that he was destined to be the coming Messiah when the kingdom of God itself became a reality. "In the natural era of the world the Messiah can be no more present than the Kingdom of God itself" (Schweitzer, 1948, 51).

For Schweitzer, "one of the most certain results of modern critical research" is that Jesus did not permit the conviction that he was destined to be the Messiah to play a part in his message. He avoided any such pronouncement or self-display by referring to the "Son of Man" in the third person. Since he was not yet this "Son of Man," this was literally accurate. So to the general public he was "the prophet of Nazareth," and nothing more. Even those who opposed him had no suspicion of his claims. If he had made such claims public, the High Priest should have been able to summon a witness at his trial to testify to this effect, but he failed to do so.

Yet even his disciples knew of it only a few weeks before his death, when he set about going to Jerusalem (Mark 8:27–30). Judas betrayed this confidence to the High Council, and Jesus was arrested on the basis of this disclosure. According to Jewish law, the High Priest required two witnesses for the accusation, and had only Judas. Therefore, everything depended on whether Jesus admitted his guilt. While he could have saved himself by saying nothing, he had come to Jerusalem with the settled purpose of dying. His death was to be an atonement, exempting humankind from the general misery which is to precede the Messianic Kingdom. Then, either at the moment of his death or three days later, he would enter into the supernatural life, achieve the Messianic honor, and usher in the end of the world (Schweitzer, 1948, 52).

At this point, Schweitzer advances his theory that Jesus changed his views as a consequence of his disciples' return from their successful journey to the districts of Israel, preaching that the kingdom was at hand. As they were not persecuted, and the great distress that was to occur before the Kingdom became a reality did not happen, Jesus reconsidered his position and came to the view that he, as the coming Messiah, was called upon to suffer and die for others, "thus accounting for the nonarrival of the period of trouble and of the Kingdom of God" (Schweitzer, 1948, 53). Schweitzer believes that the two most decisive influences in his formulation of this thought were the death of John the Baptist "which occurred after the sending out of the disciples" and Chapter 53 of the book of Isaiah, "which speaks of the servant of God who suffers for the guilt of the people" (53). Between his disciples' return and his departure for Jerusalem—that is, during the autumn and winter seasons—Jesus remained secluded in "heathen territory, in the neighborhood of Tyre and Sidon and Caesara Philippi, without preaching and intent only on remaining unknown" (53). Schweitzer's position in *The Psychiatric Study of Jesus* is therefore identical to the view he formulated when on military maneuvers nearly two decades earlier.

Critique of the Three Psychiatrists

Schweitzer asks: Is it possible from the foregoing sketch of the life and self-understanding of Jesus, as well as many details that he could not take into consideration, to draw the sorts of conclusions that the three psychiatrists had reached? His answer, of course, is no. His introductory critique of the psychopathological method as applied to significant historical figures and his comments on the psychiatrists' naïveté regarding sources have already given reasons why we should be highly skeptical of these studies. But he proposes to go into the substance of these writings "in order to form a clear opinion" (1948, 53).

He begins this critique by noting that the psychiatrists' deductions from Jesus' childhood and youth concerning his predispositions and development have no validity whatsoever. Luke's story (2:41–51) of the behavior of the twelve-year-old Jesus in the temple is a case in point. All three psychiatrists focused on this incident, and Binet-Sanglé was inclined to find in it "the account of a hebephrenic crisis" (Schweitzer, 1948, 53).[1] Also, the Gospel of John must be completely discarded; yet it has allowed the psychiatrists to assume that we can follow Jesus' mental development through the course of three years, when, in fact, his public appearance was somewhat less than a year. With this three-year time span, they could "draw a personality continually occupied with his ego, placing it in the foreground of his discourses, asserting his divine origins, and demanding of his hearers a corresponding faith" (Schweitzer, 54). By amalgamating the portrait of Jesus in John with those of the older Gospels in which Jesus does not speak of himself or of his dignity, the psychiatrists came to the conclusion that Jesus sometimes proclaimed himself the Messiah, and sometimes refrained from doing so, interpreting this conduct in terms analogous to those which are appropriately applied to paranoids. Also, whatever claims de Loosten and Binet-Sanglé make concerning Jesus' ideas of persecution and inexplicable depressed moods, these claims are derived exclusively from the Gospel of John. So is Hirsch's example of auditory hallucination (John 12:28–30) when Jesus hears a voice from heaven. The affected and unnatural manner of speaking to which Binet-Sanglé alludes, and which is frequently found in paranoid schizophrenia, is also peculiar to the Gospel of John (Schweitzer, 1948, 54).

In regard to the psychiatrists' claims based on reliable texts—

Matthew and Mark—both de Loosten and Binet-Sanglé emphasize
the statements of Jesus' own contemporaries: that he was out of his
mind, citing the effort of family members to restrain him because the
people were saying that "he has gone out of his mind" (Mark 3:21), and
the statement by the scribes from Jerusalem who claimed that he was
demon possessed (Mark 3:22). The only inference we may draw from
these verses is that the scribes wanted to discredit Jesus with the people, and that family members "perceive a change in him and are not
able to explain to their satisfaction how it comes about that he sets
himself up as a teacher and a prophet" (Schweitzer, 1948, 54–55). In
addition, no one declares that Jesus is beside himself because he
considers himself to be the Messiah. After all, they know nothing
whatsoever about this claim which he has kept to himself and only
revealed to his disciples when he announced his intention to go down
to Jerusalem.

All three psychiatrists emphasize Jesus' forty days in the wilderness, to which Mark 1:12–13 briefly alludes, but Matthew 4:1–11 and
Luke 4:1–13 greatly elaborate upon. Yet "even if we assume the historicity of the sojourn in the wilderness," the claim that Jesus experienced "numerous hallucinations" is "a wholly vague hypothesis" that
"allows them to affirm a hallucinatory phase in the development of his
psychosis" (Schweitzer, 1948, 55). Furthermore, to call these historical utterances of Jesus "hallucinations" is arbitrary, and the psychological explanation that Binet-Sanglé advances to explain the origin of
these alleged hallucinations is wholly artificial. Schweitzer has reference here to Binet-Sanglé's view that the hallucinations were caused
by Jesus' excitability, which was exacerbated by the night, his solitude, and his abstinence from food and drink (44). "To offer with
assurance such a mechanical explanation of the appearance of hallucinations even in a living patient with mental disease, a many-sided and
comprehensive analysis of the individual would be necessary" (56).
This is hardly possible on the basis of the wilderness account in
Matthew. Since Schweitzer doubts the very historicity of the
sojourn in the wilderness accounts, his critique of Binet-Sanglé's
interpretation of the wilderness story is meant for readers who
believe it occurred.

Schweitzer next takes up all three psychiatrists' contentions,
strongest in Hirsch and Binet-Sanglé, that Jesus suffered from paranoia. He notes that the question of paranoia is one of the most difficult
problems in modern psychiatry and is still very far from solution.
Controversies over the nature of paranoia are "in no small degree also

a controversy over words." On the other hand, "a considerable number of the kinds of paranoia are sufficiently well known in the way they progress to permit a profitable discussion of differential diagnosis among those who are concerned not with the words but with the facts" (1948, 56).

In addressing the application of paranoia to Jesus, Schweitzer makes a disclaimer. The purpose of his study is not "to express an opinion for or against the existence of any particular form of mental disease in Jesus, or to discuss a clinical diagnosis." Rather, its purpose is "merely to test the elementary symptoms which the three authors have used to support their diagnosis for their historic authenticity, and in case this is established, for their clinical value" (Schweitzer, 1948, 56). The alleged symptoms are (1) delusions; (2) hallucinations; (3) emotional attitude; and (4) other characteristics. Each, he says, will be treated separately.

Before proceeding, however, he addresses the psychiatrists' claims concerning the origins of Jesus' paranoia. De Loosten's view that Jesus' paranoia has a hereditary basis has "very little probability," as his source for his claim that Jesus was a "hybrid" (Jewish mother, Roman father) is a second-century document of dubious value. Hirsch's view that it may be traced to Jesus' boyhood—suggesting that his unusual mental talents caused him to spend his leisure in the study of the Holy Scriptures, which contributed to his mental illness—has no reliable textual support either. It is unlikely that Jesus read the Torah as a boy, though he probably listened to it being read on Sabbath day. Binet-Sanglé's citation of a large number of clinical observations of sick people who have suffered from religious paranoia is equally irrelevant. Such cases tend to be "hospitalized soon after the onset of the illness," and "these forms of mental disease are exactly the type which do not win supporters and disciples and found sects" (Schweitzer, 1948, 57). Their numerous hallucinations, catatonic symptoms, and the effects of dissociation also make them incapable of consecutive activity.

Conversely, persons who suffer from delusions of persecution, as Jesus is alleged to have suffered, tend not to become dysfunctional and they very seldom draw the practical conclusion from their hallucinations and delusions of persecution that they should defend themselves, either legally or illegally, from their persecutors. If, in some fleeting moment, they do defend themselves, it happens because of some state of excitement and not from conscious or logical inferences from the delusions themselves. Schweitzer wants his reader to keep these well-

supported clinical facts in mind as he considers the first, and most serious, contention of the psychiatrists: that Jesus suffered from delusions.

The Question of Delusions

Schweitzer begins this discussion of Jesus' alleged delusions by taking up the psychiatrists' views on how his paranoia developed once it
was formed. While de Loosten speaks of a continually mounting progression of the illness, Binet-Sanglé and Hirsch regard the forty days
in the wilderness as a dormant period and propose a later development
to which it was connected. No one speaks of a period filled with ideas
of injury and persecution. This is very striking, for clinical experience
with paranoid patients indicates that these are characteristics of the
first phase of this psychosis. What the psychiatrists present instead is
a paranoia comprised largely of megalomania, centered around Jesus'
view of himself as the Messiah. But such a one-sided form of paranoia
is very infrequent, as delusions of grandeur are characteristically
accompanied by corresponding feelings of persecution. Furthermore,
the psychiatrists' view of either a mounting progression (de Loosten)
or of successive stages (Hirsch, Binet-Sanglé) of the illness is not supported by the clinical evidence. While delusions of grandeur may per-
sist for long periods of time, there is no progression as such. Thus,
Binet-Sanglé's view that Jesus' delusions of grandeur progressed from
belief that he was the Messiah-king, to the Son of God, to the Agent
of God, and then to God Himself lacks clinical support (Schweitzer,
1948, 59).

If we set aside the progression claim, are there grounds for saying
that his words and actions, those authenticated by historical criticism,
indicate a "pathological distortion of the content of consciousness?"
(Schweitzer, 1948, 60). Schweitzer says no, for "the ideas of religion
which Jesus shares with his contemporaries and which he has accepted
from tradition may not be considered as diseased, even when they
appear to our modern view entirely strange and incomprehensible. De
Loosten, Hirsch, and Binet-Sanglé repeatedly transgress this fundamental rule" (Schweitzer, 60). Because they consider Jesus' understanding of himself as the future Messiah to be central to his delusional system, Schweitzer focuses on this aspect of Jewish religion,
noting that "the Messianic expectations belong to the stock of late
Jewish dogmas" (Schweitzer, 1948, 61). Not all Jews believed that
these events were imminent, but this conviction was widespread
within the specifically Jewish movement that originated with John the
Baptist. In Jesus' time, there were various views concerning the

details of Messianic ideas. For example, it was not clearly attested in the apocalyptic and rabbinical sources that the Messiah must suffer. But this idea becomes more plausible when, as some believed, the Messiah would experience an anonymous life on earth before his period in glory. In that case, he would have to suffer with the chosen the misery that preceded the Messiah.

Also, the oldest Messianic tradition held that the Messiah was to be a member of the royal family of David. As the "oldest traditions" affirm that Jesus was a descendent of David, it is perfectly understandable that he might come to believe that he was destined to become the future Messiah, especially if he belonged to the community that believed the Messianic Kingdom was imminent. Furthermore, when the Messiah is called the Son of God, this has nothing to do with descent from God in any metaphysical sense, as occurs in subsequent Christian theology: "The Son of God is only a title that indicates that his place of honor originates in God. In this sense the Jewish kings were already the Sons of God" (Schweitzer, 1948, 62).

Thus, when Jesus' view of himself as the coming Messiah is seen in context, the claim that it was delusional has no basis. His so-called "delusions of grandeur" and "paranoid ideas of persecution" are perfectly understandable within the context of ideas to which he, as a member of John the Baptist's community, would have subscribed. Of course, his view that, of all living descendants of David, he was the coming Messiah was certainly "a striking thing." But what makes it striking is not that a carpenter's son would believe that he is the future Messiah, for the apocalyptic view explicitly required that the future Messiah would be a nonentity in this life: "He who was to occupy the highest place in the future world should here in the natural course of the world belong to the despised and common people. Therefore, only a descendant of David living in lowly poverty could be considered as the possible future Messiah." Moreover, "If the end of the world were thought of as being very near, then it must be that this man had already been born and had to be sought within the generation which was to experience the end of the era" (Schweitzer, 1948, 63). An already born lowly carpenter who was a descendent of David fit the Messianic portrait. How many others met all three criteria is impossible to determine, but they were a finite number. So, it was not unreasonable for Jesus to become persuaded that he was, in fact, the coming Messiah.

Still, it *is* remarkable that he applied the messianic prophecies to himself. Why he did so is largely inaccessible to us from the available sources. Schweitzer chooses not to speculate on this. But what the sources *do* tell us is that paranoid ideas of injury and persecution never arose, for the conviction that he was to suffer derived from his belief that the coming Messiah must suffer along with the chosen when the apocalyptic era began. The change in his views in this regard was "conditioned by outward circumstances"—his disciples' return, the death of John the Baptist—and represents "completely logical consequences in harmony with the total picture" (Schweitzer, 1948, 64). The change is one in "the notion of suffering." Jesus no longer assumes that he is to suffer the "woes of the Messiah" together with the chosen ones (his supernatural character already evident). Instead, he believes that "by virtue of his suffering, the others will be spared the suffering they were to have gone through." There is nothing inherently paranoid in either view. Moreover, the change in his views from believing that all the chosen will suffer, including himself, to the view that through his suffering others would be spared, is no indication of a "progression" in his alleged paranoia. In fact, this "modification of his views presupposes a susceptibility to influence which does not accord with the forms of paranoia which develop in accordance with a firmly established type" (Schweitzer, 64). That is, it is typical of paranoia that external circumstances have no appreciable effect on the delusional system.

Moreover, there is no overt antagonism toward others, which is a common feature of paranoia. Of course, Jesus had enemies and opponents because he spoke out against the narrow-minded and external piety of the Pharisees. But in relation to these opponents, who are real and not imaginary, he conducts himself in a fashion diametrically opposite to the conduct of a sick man with a persecutory trend. Unlike sick persons who believe themselves to be persecuted, he does not remain inactive and limit himself to a defensive attitude. Instead, he seeks by actions which have a provocative character, such as driving the lenders and money changers from the forecourt of the temple and the discourses against the Pharisees, to bring on a conflict with the authorities, thus forcing them to take steps against him, until "in the end he brings the high council to the decision to get rid of him even before the festival." Schweitzer rejects the view that this effort to achieve his own death is a "morbid self-sacrifice" reflecting a diseased mind, for "this sacrificial death represents a necessary constituent part in the Messianic thought and action of Jesus" (1948, 65).

The Question of Hallucinations

Schweitzer next takes up the question of hallucinations. Once again, he focuses on the source issue, noting the degree to which the psychiatrists depend on the Gospel of John, "doing great violence [even] to this material" (1948, 65). He also challenges Binet-Sanglé's detailed discussion of the auditory hallucination in Gethsemane, contending that "we are dealing here with a legendary elaboration of the scene which precedes the arrest." Of greater importance to the hallucinatory theory, however, is the forty-day sojourn in the wilderness. But this too must be set aside, as these accounts are also unhistorical, belonging "to the prehistoric legend," as Strauss "has already rightly remarked" (66).

What about the accounts of Jesus' baptism? These are also of doubtful historical validity. Jesus emerged into the light of history for the first time on the day that he appeared as a preacher in Galilee, and "everything that comes before that belongs to dark and uncertain tradition" (Schweitzer, 1948, 67). The voice from heaven sounds remarkably like Psalm 2:7—"You are my son; today I have begotten you"—which is usually interpreted in a Messianic sense. Yet when he discloses his messiahship to his disciples (Mark 8:27–30), Jesus makes no mention of his baptism. Also, the story of the transfiguration (Mark 9:2–8) does not point to a hallucination by Jesus. Instead, the earliest tradition of the scene points to Peter, who also "has the first vision of Jesus after his death" (Schweitzer, 1948, 67). Of course, by thus shifting the focus from Jesus to Peter, Schweitzer implies that Jesus associated with men who had hallucinatory experiences.

If we were to assume that the baptism hallucination is authentic—Schweitzer thinks it cannot be categorically ruled out—even Binet-Sanglé recognizes that emotionally colored hallucinations "are not to be found only in the mentally diseased." They also occur "in individuals who are very excitable emotionally, but who nevertheless can still be considered as fitting entirely within the category of healthy people" (1948, 67). We should also keep in mind "the great excitement which rose with the expectation of the immediate coming of the end of the world" and its role in facilitating "the rise of hallucinations in individuals predisposed to them" (68).

Emotional Instability and Other Symptoms

Schweitzer next takes up the view of both de Loosten and Binet-Sanglé that Jesus' alleged emotional instability was "of a morbid kind." The first question is whether emotional instability can be substantiated at all. Admittedly, as presented in the Gospels of Matthew and Mark, there appears to be "no consistent ordered activity" in Jesus' public ministry. It seems to dissolve "into a rather disordered running to and fro, in which he now appears on the east bank and now returns to the west bank, until in the end he takes himself off to the solitude of the north" (1948, 68). This disorderly itinerary and alternation between public activity and quest for solitude is sufficiently puzzling that one might be tempted to confuse it with emotional instability. But the explanation is quite simple. For reasons that are still in part perceptible on the basis of surviving sources, Jesus sought to avoid gatherings of people. One of the principle reasons for this "is that he wished to shun the people because they brought the possessed and the sick from all sides in order that he might heal them. The encounter with the former especially was extremely distasteful to him as appears from significant details in Mark's account" (Mark 1:34, 3:12). Schweitzer does not speculate as to why this would be, but he would obviously reject the idea that the "possessed" were distasteful to Jesus because they reminded him of his own mental disease.

The only other "evidence" of morbid emotional symptoms that Binet-Sanglé and de Loosten put forward center on Jesus' attitude toward his family and his seeming lack of sexual consciousness. As for absence of family loyalty, this can be explained by the fact that they want to take him home and obstruct his public ministry (Mark 3:21). Moreover, when he declares that the bonds knit between those who share a common faith in the imminence of the Kingdom of God are holier than blood ties, this is not accounted for psychopathologically. Instead, it is a "special point of view to be explained by perceptions contemporarily conditioned," relating to the belief that in the Kingdom, the usual claims of privilege based on blood lines will not be honored. As for the striking statements he made regarding eunuchs, this has nothing whatever to do with "morbid sexual feeling," for prior to making these statements about eunuchs (Matt. 19:3–9), he had "spoken about marriage in a very natural and affirmative way" (Schweitzer, 1948, 69). Moreover, the key to this "much discussed and much misunderstood saying" is provided by passages in the Old Testament and later Jewish writings. If Deuteronomy 23:1 rules that eunuchs are excluded from the religious community, the later, post-exilic prophetic writings (Isa. 56:3–5; Wisd. Sol. 3:14) take a more accepting attitude toward eunuchs, promising them that "in compensation for their lack of posterity [they] will not only be made equal to the others in the expected future but will even be set above them" (Schweitzer, 1948, 70).

Jesus' own opinions move in the same direction. He sees in the eunuchs "the despised ones who, like the children, are destined to honor in the Kingdom of God because formerly they had been among the rejected ones," and makes the rather "mysterious surmise that men have placed themselves in the class of these despised ones in order to participate in that special future honor." But this has nothing whatever to do with Jesus himself, as he expects a high position in the Kingdom of God through his descent from David. He does not personally identify with voluntary or involuntary eunuchs, and his words about them "have nothing to do with sex feeling, but are to be explained by the ideas found to be present in late Judaism" (Schweitzer, 1948, 70).

Finally, Schweitzer addresses the apparently senseless act of cursing the fig tree. This is a reflection of late Jewish apocalyptic expectations that even the natural world would participate in the transformation and become capable of a wonderful fertility. Thus, the Apocalypse of Baruch tries to imagine the future yield of a single grapevine. Schweitzer believes that the historical kernel of this story is a judgment against a tree that, by means of its rich foliage, deceived the future Messiah in his hunger. His judgment against it is therefore an anticipation of his future power over the natural order, similar to his decision in advance to appoint the twelve disciples who will have jurisdiction over the twelve tribes of Israel (Matt. 19:28): "In these and similar words we have to do with promises and judgments which he thinks to carry out as soon as he is established in his Messianic power." The cursing of the fig tree is merely one of a whole series of such utterances, and the "more they strike us as remarkable, the more understandable they are from the point of view of Jesus' late Jewish ideas" (Schweitzer, 1948, 71).

Schweitzer concludes his study with a very brief itemization of the results of his critique of the psychiatric studies of Jesus. It consists of four basic conclusions:

1. The material (in the Gospels), which is in agreement with these books, is for the most part unhistorical.

2. From material that is certainly historical, a number of Jesus' acts and utterances impress the authors as pathological because they are too little acquainted with the contemporary thought of the time to be able to do justice to it. A series of wrong deductions also springs from the fact that they lack any understanding of the peculiar problems inherent in the course of his public ministry.

3. From these false preconceptions and with the help of entirely hypothetical symptoms, they construct pictures of sickness that are themselves artifacts which, moreover, do not conform exactly with the clinical forms of sickness diagnosed by the authors.

4. The only symptoms that may be accepted as historical, and thus possibly can be discussed from the psychiatric point of view—the high estimate that Jesus has of himself, and perhaps also the baptism hallucination—fall short of proving the existence of mental illness.

These conclusions indicate Schweitzer's confidence that he has effectively distanced his own picture of Jesus, as that Jesus sees himself as the coming Messiah, from the psychopathological pictures formulated by the three psychiatrists. The first two conclusions focus on their lack of knowledge about historical matters, especially relating to sources and the late Jewish context within which Jesus' own views were formed. The third relates to the psychiatrists' own field, particularly their application of their own diagnostic categories in imprecise and invalid ways. But the fourth conclusion leaves the door open, if ever so slightly, for future psychiatric approaches to Jesus. It notes that Jesus' high estimate of himself and possibly the baptismal hallucinatory experience are discussable from the psychiatric point of view, though not as evidence of mental illness.

A Religion of Referential Ideas

Of the two small openings that Schweitzer specifically mentions, I believe that Jesus' "high estimate of himself" is the most promising, as it has direct bearing on the question of whether he was delusional (i.e., reflecting an alternation of megalomanic and paranoidal ideation). The best way to approach this subject, however, is to focus on what psychiatrists then and now have called "ideas of reference" or "referential ideas." As noted earlier, Hirsch cited instances in the Gospel of John where Jesus is said to have ascribed to himself the predictions of prophets. In so doing, he "manifests one of the central peculiarities of paranoids, who apply to themselves everything possible that they see or read" (Schweitzer, 1948, 41).

Contemporary psychiatric diagnostic protocols for paranoid type of schizophrenia and for delusional disorder include ideas of reference or "referential delusions." As *The Diagnostic and Statistical Manual of Mental Disorders* published by the American Psychiatric Association notes, such ideas of reference may involve the belief that certain gestures, passages from books, newspapers, song lyrics, or other environmental cues, are specifically directed at oneself, or that random events are of special significance, and the interpretation of these events is usually consistent with the individual's delusional beliefs (1994, 275).

What makes Jesus' case different from contemporary diagnoses of paranoid schizophrenia and delusional disorder, however, is that ideas of reference were prevalent in Jesus' sociocultural milieu. If the socio-cultural milieu itself promoted ideas of reference, what effect does this have on the psychiatrists' claim that Jesus was delusional because he believed that he was the coming Messiah referred to by the prophets? In effect, this is the nub of Schweitzer's argument that the psychia-trists "are too little acquainted with the contemporary thought of the time to be able to do justice to it" (Schweitzer, 1948, 72). Significantly, *The Diagnostic and Statistical Manual of Mental Disorders* agrees. As its description of paranoidal schizophrenia notes, "Ideas that may appear to be delusional in one culture (for example, sorcery and witchcraft) may be commonly held in another. In some cultures, visual or auditory hallucinations with a religious content may be a normal part of reli-gious experience (for example, seeing the Virgin Mary or hearing God's voice)" (1994, 281).

This suggests that the psychiatrists' claim that Jesus was delusional because he held ideas of reference about himself would need to be set aside on the grounds that only Jesus' own contemporaries would be in a position to judge whether or not such ideas are delusional. In fact, if we assume that there was general agreement among those who cared about this matter in his own day that the Messiah had not already come, then there is nothing in principle to preclude someone then liv-ing from believing that he was the Messiah. It would be an entirely different matter if Jesus had claimed to be the Roman Emperor. On the other hand, given the great importance the society ascribed to this belief in the coming Messiah, it would be perfectly understandable if the question of whether Jesus is delusional would become a matter of controversy among his own contemporaries. The controversy would not be whether "ideas of reference" are inherently delusional, but whether Jesus is self-deluded when he ascribes the Messianic prophe-cies to himself.

Significantly, Schweitzer believes that suspicions that Jesus may have been mentally ill had nothing to do with "ideas of reference." Rather, his family's suspicions concerned their perception of a change in him that they could not explain, and the scribes' allegations were politically motivated. While the issue of who he believed himself to be came up at the trial, the allegation that he claimed to be the coming Messiah did not result in the official judgment that he was mentally insane (i.e., self-deluded).

In *The Historical Figure of Jesus*, E. P. Sanders cites an episode which occurred about thirty years after Jesus was executed in which another Jesus, the son of Ananias, went to the temple during the Feast of

Booths (Tabernacles) and proclaimed the destruction of Jerusalem and the sanctuary. This action led to his being interrogated and flogged, first by the Jewish authorities, then by the Romans. He answered questions by reiterating his dirge over the city, and was finally released as a maniac (1993, 267). The grounds for his release indicate that Jesus' own contemporaries had their own methods and criteria for judging a person sane or insane, and the very fact that Jesus was executed suggests that he, unlike Jesus, the son of Ananias, was considered sane—that is, not suffering from delusions. Instead, the authorities evidently believed that he was exploiting the tradition of referential ideas for his own political self-aggrandizement.

In a sociocultural milieu in which ideas of reference were not considered inherently delusional, their use would need to be judged on a case-by-case basis, and it is very unlikely that there could be any consensus as to the validity of an individual's expression of them (for example, attribution of prophetic writings to himself). Those who believed Jesus was not the coming Messiah might say that he was deluded because there were things that were true about him that disqualified him from possible consideration as the coming Messiah. Others, however, might contend that he was not deluded because the belief that someone else was the coming Messiah was itself an error, or that the evidence presented to disqualify Jesus was itself erroneous, or even lent support to the claim that he was the coming Messiah. The very fact that the issue could be debated, however, indicates that ideas of reference were not held to be inherently delusional, as would be the case if one of our contemporaries were to assert that he is Napoleon.

To someone who did not believe in the Messiah idea, such debates would seem rather pointless. But for someone who took the idea with great seriousness, such debates were hardly nonsensical or inconsequential. The Gospels manifest this very sociocultural context. When Jesus is reported to have asked his disciples who the people claim the Son of Man—evidently a reference to himself—to be, they answer, "Some say John the Baptist, others say Elijah, and others Jeremiah or one of the prophets" (Matt. 16–14). No one says, "He is the carpenter from Nazareth." Instead, the question is with which of these predecessors is Jesus to be identified, and are any of these attributions valid or true?

In short, if Schweitzer emphasized that Jesus' views were based on "the contemporary thought of the time," ideas of reference were an integral part of Jesus' own worldview and figured prominently in his own self-understanding (1948, 72). Such ideas of reference were implicated, for example, in Schweitzer's contention that Jesus viewed the death of John the Baptist as signaling the imminence of the Kingdom of God, for in John "Jesus had recognized the Elijah who had been promised for the last days" (53). As Malachi 4:5 puts it, "Lo, I will send you the prophet Elijah before the great and terrible day of the Lord comes." Another belief was that an ordinary person might be a supernatural being incognito. This is suggested in Schweitzer's view that Jesus "regarded himself as the man who would enter upon the supernatural inheritance of the family of David" (Schweitzer, 1948, 63).

Schweitzer claims that a "psychological analysis of this attitude" on Jesus' part "is not possible for reasons already discussed," namely, that Jesus based this view of himself on the apocalyptic view of late Judaism. The most that can be said is that "the exaggeration of an idea does not in itself justify our considering it the manifestation of a psychosis" (1948, 63–64). If by "psychological" Schweitzer means viewing this attitude of Jesus' as a sign of mental illness, I would certainly agree. This does not, however, rule out "psychological analysis" altogether. If it did, one need only claim that an idea or habit of thought is already present in the culture and thereby checkmate any effort to gain a psychological understanding of this idea, or of the person who holds it. Gaining such understanding might begin with an imaginative projection of ourselves into Jesus' own religio-cultural milieu. If we ourselves lived in a social context in which there was widespread belief that someone known to us might be the reincarnation of a historical personage or a supernatural being incognito, this would create the very ambiguity and intrigue that the Gospels manifest. This intrigue is due largely to the fact that nothing is quite as it seems. John the Baptist *might* simply be a prophet in his own right. On the other hand, he *might* be Elijah, and if so, the prophecy of Malachi 4:5 applies directly and immediately to him. Similarly, Jesus *could* simply be another prophet in his own right. Then again, he *could* be the coming Messiah.

In other words, an individual may be the person he is known to be— the carpenter from Nazareth—and nothing more; or he might be this person and someone else as well. He might wonder if he actually is this other "person," and ask for evidence from God one way or the other. Or others might say that he is this other "person," and ask him for confirmation of their belief. If he says that he believes he is this other "person," he is likely to be challenged to prove it or be accused of being an imposter, guilty of false self-representation. In either case, it is not the fact that he is "the carpenter from Nazareth" that is being challenged (as may happen, for example, when someone falsely claims that he has had medical training and performs surgeries on the basis of this false claim), but the fact that he is this "mysterious other."

I doubt that we can fully appreciate the full psychological impact of the fact that "ideas of reference" were integral to the religious culture in which Jesus lived. In our culture, we assume that someone who believes that he is someone else is mentally ill. We have difficulty imagining a criminal trial in which a person is asked if he believes he is someone else. Should this occur, we would assume that its purpose is to establish that this person is mentally incompetent to stand trial. Yet this is precisely what the Gospel writers claim happened to Jesus before he was taken out to be executed.

Conceivably everyone knew that, when they entertained ideas of reference, they were not speaking literally but metaphorically; that John the Baptist is not literally Elijah come back from the dead, but that John is reminiscent of Elijah or that Elijah's spirit lives in John. It appears, however, that the line between metaphor and identity is a fuzzy one in this religious context, and there is little difference between Jesus asking the disciples to "compare me to someone and tell me whom I am like" (Thomas 13) and the query at Caesarea Philippi, "Who do people say that the Son of Man is?" and "But who do you say that I am?" (Matt. 16:13–17).

Then there is the added element of secrecy. Whether this element goes back to Jesus himself or originated with the Gospel writers, the idea that an ordinary man is a supernatural being incognito is itself a remarkable notion. But the idea that he was aware of having this other "identity" while keeping it to himself adds another level of ambiguity and intrigue. The Gospels create a picture in which there is not only praise for those who are able to "see" what others cannot see, but also suspicion, distrust, errors in discernment, and even disillusionment. Individuals were continually in danger of being perceived as imposters, false claimants, opportunists, and dupes.

What does all this mean for a psychological perspective on Jesus himself? As Schweitzer convincingly argued, the view that Jesus was delusional fails to take the sociocultural context into consideration. Nonetheless, there is something quite odd, at least from our own vantage point, about a religious environment in which "ideas of reference" play such a prominent role. It is quite appropriate to ask what it may have been like to live in a religious culture in which "ideas of reference" were encouraged, and even rewarded. How does it affect the individual who believes that he has an identity other than his socially ascribed identity? And if it is not a delusion, what would we call the psychological process involved? A useful key to answering these questions is precisely the ambiguity noted above between a *metaphorical* self-reference and one that claims an *identity* that is not one's socially ascribed identity. It is the "fuzzy line" between these two that the concept of "the fictive personality" takes into account and the "delusional" concept does not.

The Fictive Personality; Or, on Not Being Who They Say You Are

If the assumption that Jesus' self-identification with the coming Messiah is ipso facto evidence of "mental illness needs to be set aside," is there another psychological concept or theory that is applicable to this self-identification? Schweitzer's view that Jesus had a "high estimate of himself" is suggestive in this regard, especially if it is linked to his observation that the Gospel of John paints a portrait of Jesus that is "in the main *a freely imagined personality* who is designed to improve and supplement the Jesus appearing in the first three Gospels" (Schweitzer, 1948, 45, my emphasis). If we shift the focus from the author of John's Gospel to Jesus himself, might we not say that Jesus himself may have been the author of "a freely imagined personality," one that accorded with his "high estimate of himself"? If so, the psychoanalytic concept of the "fictive personality" then becomes relevant to the historical Jesus and, specifically, to the role that referential ideas played in his own self-understanding.

Jay Martin (1988) explores this phenomenon of the fictive personality in the writings of psychoanalytic thinkers from Alfred Adler to Heinz Kohut, and cites the cases of several of his patients who lived fictive lives. One patient operated on the theory "that the world had three shapes, corresponding to her three favorite books—*Little Women, Gone With the Wind,* and *The Wizard of Oz.* One had only to select the appropriate book and passage to interpret whatever aspect of the world a problem brought to hand, and the way of dealing with it would become evident." The difficulty with her theory was that her way of dealing with the problem often did not work, yet she insisted that "the 'key' remained right, though the world might be wrong" (Martin, 1988, 74). The situation began to change, however, as she continued in psychoanalysis. Formerly, she "had treated the world *as if* it were real; now, in psychoanalysis, she began to come from behind the veil and live in the world's reality." A complaint she often voiced was that psychoanalysis "had robbed her of the ability to live her other fantasy lives." Yet interestingly enough, she did not entirely abandon fictions but instead began to use them differently. She learned to make a "crucial distinction between fantasies that supplant reality and fantasies of power that helpfully release anxiety" (Martin, 1988, 76). This is also the crucial distinction between a delusional person— one whose delusion supplants reality—and one who has formed a "fictive personality"; one that is inherently empowering in one's dealings with the world.

In *Jesus: A Psychological Biography*, I argued that Jesus' healing ministry was based on the "disabling" of the anxiety that disabled the person who was diseased or incapacitated (Capps, 2000, 165–217). In a similar way, Martin suggests that these "fantasies of power . . . helpfully release anxiety" (Martin, 1988, 76). When one adopts a delusional system, there is no such "release of anxiety." In fact, the delusional system *increases* one's sense of anxiety. In psychiatric terms, one becomes paranoidal. This is not what appears to have happened in Jesus' case. Whether the "coming Messiah," for which Schweitzer contends, or the "Son of Abba," for which I contend in *Jesus: A Psychological Biography*, his "fictional personality" enabled him to live "beyond anxiety" (Erikson, 1950, 403–424). Thus, his "fictive personality" was of a piece with his healing ministry.

In addition to the release of anxiety, however, a "fictive personality" may also empower one to challenge the ability of one's socially ascribed identity to determine one's fate in life (van Aarde, 1997; 2001, 119–127). In *Jesus: A Psychological Biography*, I cited Erik H. Erikson's case in *Identity and the Life Cycle* (1959) of a young woman of middle European descent who assumed a fictive Scottish identity. When Erikson asked her how she managed to marshal all the details of her early "life" in Scotland, she replied, "Bless you, sir, I needed a past" (Erikson, 1959, 41). In affording her a past different from the one she had actually lived, her 'fictive' identity gave her the necessary leverage she required to change her fate (Erikson, 1964, 183). Thus, it promised a different future as well.

Delusional systems tend to paralyze or render impotent those who have them. Persons are under their delusions' control. In contrast, a fictive personality may take the form of a fantasy of power that makes a real difference in how this person engages the world's reality. Schweitzer's view of Jesus as active and exercising control over events is relevant in this regard: "In relation to these opponents, not imaginary but genuine, Jesus conducts himself in a fashion diametrically opposite to the conduct of a sick man with a persecutory trend. He does not remain inactive and does not limit himself to a defensive attitude like so many of the sick who believe themselves possessed, but rather seeks by actions which have a provocative character . . . to bring on a conflict with the authorities and to force them to take steps against him, until in the end he brings the high council to the decision to get rid of him before the festival" (1948, 65).

Jesus' own contemporaries could still, if they chose, decide that he was delusional. In the terms of their cultural worldview, he might be viewed in that case as demon possessed (a religious assessment) or as a false claimant (a political assessment). The psychoanalyst may, however, view his self-proclaimed identity as the coming Messiah or as the Son of Abba as a fictive personality, one based not on fantasies that supplant reality, but on fantasies of power that helpfully release anxiety and alter one's fate. Such fantasies of power, especially if used to empower others, may be dangerous, even as a delusional person with a "persecutory trend" may be dangerous to others. But Jesus' response to John the Baptist's emissaries who had relayed his question whether he was the one to come or should he wait for another—"Go and tell John what you hear and see: the blind receive their sight, the lame walk, the lepers are cleansed, the deaf hear, the dead are raised, and the poor have good news brought to them"—indicates that his fictive personality mainly posed dangers for the powers that be.

Note

1. Hebephrenia is a form of schizophrenia characterized by childish or silly behavior, disorganized thinking, delusions, and hallucinations, usually beginning in adolescence.

References

American Psychiatric Association. (1994). *Diagnostic and Statistical Manual of Mental Disorders* (4th ed.). Washington, DC: American Psychiatric Association.

Binet-Sangle, C. (1910-1915). *La folie de Jesus*, 4 vols. Paris.

Capps, D. (2000). *Jesus: A Psychological Biography*. St. Louis: Chalice.

de Loosten, G. (1905). *Jesus Christus vom Standpunkte des Psychiaters*. Bamburg.

Erikson, E. H. (1950). *Childhood and Society*. New York: Norton.

Erikson, E. H. (1959). *Identity and the Life Cycle*. New York: Norton.

Erikson, E. H. (1964). *Insight and Responsibility*. New York: Norton.

Hirsch, W. (1912). *Conclusions of a Psychiatrist*. New York.

Martin, J. (1988). *Who Am I This Time? Uncovering the Fictive Personality*. New York: Norton.

Rasmussen, E. (1905). *Jesus, Eine vergleichende psychopathologische Studie*, A. Rothenburg, trans. Leipzig.

Rollins, W. G. (1999). *Soul and Psyche: The Bible in Psychological Perspective.* Minneapolis: Fortress.

Sanders, E. P. (1993). *The Historical Figure of Jesus.* London: Penguin.

Schweitzer, A. (1948). *The Psychiatric Study of Jesus: Exposition and Critique,* C. R. Joy, trans. Boston: Beacon. (Original work published 1913)

Schweitzer, A. (1968). *The Quest of the Historical Jesus: A Critical Study of Its Progress from Reimarus to Wrede,* W. Montgomery, trans. New York: Macmillan. (Original work published 1906)

Strauss, D. (1972). *The Life of Jesus Critically Examined,* P. Hodgson, ed., G. Eliot, trans. Minneapolis: Augsburg Fortress. (Original work published 1835)

Taylor, E. (1984). *William James on Exceptional Mental States.* Amherst: University of Massachusetts Press.

van Aarde, A. (1997). Social Identity, Status Envy and Jesus' *Abba,* J. H. Ellens, ed., *Pastoral Psychology,* 45, 451–472.

van Aarde, A. (2001). *Fatherless in Galilee: Jesus as Child of God.* Harrisburg: Trinity Press International.

CHAPTER 7

JAY HALEY'S PSYCHOLOGICAL
PORTRAIT OF JESUS:
A POWER TACTICIAN

Donald Capps

This chapter focuses on family therapist Jay Haley's contention that Jesus was a skilled "power tactician" who demonstrated this skill in his ability to build an organization, gather a following, and critique the religious authorities of his day in a manner that left him invulnerable to their reprisals and enabled him to gain support among a tradition-oriented public.[1] Haley also argues, however, that Jesus made a fatal miscalculation when he confronted the religious authorities in Jerusalem, a miscalculation that he attributes to Jesus' somewhat impatient or impulsive personality. I expand on Haley's view of Jesus as a skilled tactical leader by noting that a key to Jesus' ability to build an organization was his tactical displacement of the human father. I argue, however, that Haley's view that Jesus miscalculated the outcome of events in Jerusalem is incorrect, and that a feature of Haley's own theory of power dynamics supports this conclusion.

Exposition

In the previous chapter, I suggested that Albert Schweitzer's stinging critique of psychiatric studies of Jesus published in the first decade of the twentieth century (Schweitzer, 1948) has cast a very long shadow, as it has discouraged the use of psychological theories and methods in historical Jesus studies. When such studies *have* appeared, they have received little attention, and their status in historical Jesus

studies has been extremely marginal. In this chapter, I will discuss Jay
Haley's essay "The Power Tactics of Jesus Christ" (Haley, 1986),
originally published in 1969, thus coinciding with a renewed interest
among biblical scholars in the study of the historical Jesus. In my
view, this essay by a leading authority in strategic family therapy
offers an insightful psychological portrait of Jesus, as it focuses on
Jesus as a man who was skilled in the use of power. After presenting
Haley's portrait of Jesus, I will discuss an important implication of his
view that all organizations are hierarchical, namely that Jesus was
uncompromising in his opposition to all human *paternal* authority. I
will also address his contention that Jesus miscalculated the outcome
of the temple disturbance.

Haley's Portrait of Jesus

Haley is known in family therapy circles for his emphasis on the
problem of how to change the locus of power in a family. If such a
change is to be realized, the therapist must use "power tactics" to
counter the "power tactics" of the family. These tactics, however, need
to be subtle and often indirect, as the overt use or exhibition of power
is likely to be counterproductive. An example of the therapist's use of
power is defining the problem to which the therapy will be directed in
such a way that it not only expresses what the family or the individual
client wants changed, but is also "put in a form that makes it solvable"
(Haley, 1989, 38). Another is establishing himself as the gatekeeper of
information: "In actuality or illusion, he should be defined as the one
who allows or permits information to pass. Therefore, his power is
enhanced if he is provided with secrets to be protected. The more an
individual or group gives a therapist information it wishes concealed,
the more power and status the therapist is given" (Haley, 1989, 240).

Haley also discusses the relationship between power and organization, noting that "if there is one generalization that applies to humans
and other animals, it is that all creatures capable of learning are compelled to organize. To be organized means to follow patterned, redun-
dant ways of behaving, and to exist in a hierarchy. Creatures that
organize together form a status or power ladder in which each creature has a place in the hierarchy, with those above and those below"
(Haley, 1986, 107–108). While groups will have more than one hierarchy because of different functions, "the existence of hierarchy is
inevitable because it is in the nature of organization that it be hierarchal. We may dream of a society in which all creatures are equal, but

on this earth there are status and precedence and inequality among all creatures" (Haley, 108).

As hierarchy is unavoidable, all groups "must deal with the issue of organizing in a hierarchy, and rules must be worked out about who is primary in status and power and who is secondary" (Haley, 1986, 110). When "the status positions in a hierarchy are confused, or unclear, there will be a struggle that an observer would characterize as a power struggle" (Haley, 110). An observer "who has a theory of innate aggression or of a need for power may say that the participants are satisfying an inner drive by struggling for power." But a more useful theory is that this struggle is "an effort to clarify, or work out, the positions in the hierarchy of an organization" (110).

How Jesus Acquired Power

Haley's title, "The Power Tactics of Jesus Christ," makes clear that he intends to understand Jesus' public career from the same perspective that informs his therapeutic work with families, focusing on power and power relationships. He defines power in this way: "A person has achieved 'power' when he has established himself as the one who is to determine what is going to happen" (Haley, 1986, 37). Power tactics are "those maneuvers a person uses to give himself influence and control over his social world and so make the world more predictable" (Haley, 37). Thus, "a man has power if he can order someone to behave in a certain way, but he also has power if he can provoke someone to behave in that way. One man may order others to lift and carry him, while another might achieve the same end by collapsing. Both men are determining what is to happen in their social environment by the use of a power tactic" (37–38).

Gaining power appears to be more important to some individuals than any subjective distress they might experience. For example, "The alcoholic who says to the bartender, 'If you want me out of here, throw me out,' may suffer pain and indignity, but *he* determines the outcome of the interchange" (Haley, 1986, 38). It is even possible to determine what is going to happen from beyond the grave, "as victims of wills and those whose intimates have committed suicide will testify" (Haley, 38). Haley concludes: "When we examine the tactics of Jesus, it is useful to consider power tactics defined this broadly" (38).

Besides the Synoptic Gospels, Haley's primary sources for his analysis of Jesus' power tactics are Schweitzer's *The Psychiatric Study of Jesus* (1948) and *The Quest of the Historical Jesus* (1961), and Josephus' *The War of the Jews, or the History of the Destruction of Jerusalem* (1987).

He also has footnote references to Eric Hoffer's *The True Believer*, which focuses on leaders of mass movements and their followers. Haley recognizes that what we know of Jesus is based on the writings of members of his organization, so questions about Jesus' own contribution to organizational strategy can always be raised due to doubts about the objectivity and authenticity of these writings. Still, one can discern the basic pattern of Jesus' organizational strategy. Basically, what Jesus was able to do, where others had failed, was to organize the poor and powerless into a force capable of a sustained threat to the establishment rather than the occasional sporadic riot. How did he do this? It involved several stages.

Stage 1: Becoming Known

The problem that any aspiring leader who was not born into a royal or priestly family faces is that of becoming known. Jesus had several factors going for him in this regard. One was the discontent of the populace, which was directed to a large degree against "a priestly hierarchy made up of families which were exploitative and were maintained in power by the occupying Roman colonists" (Haley, 1986, 23). Another was that the power structure was divided. The geographical division after the death of Herod had left conflict and resentment. The "wealthy class and the priests had their differences, the priestly hierarchy was in internal conflict, and the Romans were sufficiently hated to cause a cleavage between the governor and the populace. The establishment could not offer a united front against a bid for power" (Haley, 23).

A third was the mythology of the time—that is, the "persistent myth among the populace that all difficulties could be magically alleviated by the Lord or a Messiah who would relieve all misery, strike down all enemies, and place the tribes of Israel in power. . . . At the time Jesus stepped into the public road, there seems to have been an accepted general belief that a single man could arrive and put everything right" (Haley, 1986, 23). In thus emphasizing Messianic expectations, Haley seems to be drawing very explicitly on Schweitzer's portrayal of Jesus.

A fourth was that in Judaism a man could rise from low to high estate by following a religious life. This is the path chosen by Jesus, who was outside the pale of organized power, but appeared in public as a religious prophet, using the popular tradition of itinerancy which stood against and contrasted with the settled and entrenched establishment with its power base in the cities. This tradition was also helpful if one wished to gain a reputation before too much opposition was aroused: "The state and the priestly hierarchy were accustomed to criticism within the prophetic framework so that by custom a man could be heard without being immediately extinguished" (Haley, 1986, 24).

In order to attract and keep an audience, an itinerant prophet would need to speak in a certain way. If he said only what was orthodox, no one would listen because they could hear the same or similar ideas from the established religious leaders; to say the unorthodox, however, risked losing an audience by antagonizing a people devoted to an established religion that was built into their lives and very being. Jesus handled this dilemma with unusual adroitness by managing "to call attention to himself as an authority who was presenting new ideas" while "defining what he said as proper orthodoxy" (Haley, 1986, 24). He achieved this feat in two ways. He insisted that he was not advocating a change and then he called for change, and he claimed that the ideas he was presenting were not deviations from the established religion but a truer expression of the ideas of that religion.

His skill in calling simultaneously for conformity and change is best expressed in his discussion of the law and its demands (Matt. 5:17–22). On one hand, he claimed that he was not advocating the destruction of the law, but its fulfillment. Thus, whoever breaks even the least of the commandments and teaches others to do so will be called "the least in the kingdom of heaven," but whoever teaches and does them "shall be called great in the kingdom of heaven" (Matt. 5:17–19).[1] On the other hand, if Jesus had only "conformed to this teaching, no one could have had the slightest objection to what he might have said. He would have been collecting followers for the establishment rather than himself" (Haley, 1986, 25). So he proceeded to offer himself as the authority by providing major revisions of the law. He said, "You have heard that it was said to those of ancient times, 'You shall not murder'; and 'Whoever murders shall be liable to judgment.' But I say to you that if you are angry with a brother or sister, you will be liable to judgment; and if you insult a brother or sister, you will be liable to the council; and if you say, 'you fool,' you will be liable to the hell of fire" (Matt. 5:21–22). One could hardly consider this anything but a basic revision of the law, for he is saying that persons should be punished for their thoughts as well as their deeds. He also advocates revisions in the laws of adultery, divorce, revenge, the procedure for taking oaths, for giving charity, the method of prayer, and the way to fast. In fact, "little is left of the established law when he has redesigned it—after stating that he has not come to change a letter of the Law" (Haley, 1986, 26). Thus, "by calling for conformity to the law, Jesus disarms opposition. By then redesigning the law, he sets himself up as an equal in power and authority to the entire religious establishment of the state" (Haley, 27). Not surprisingly, Matthew claims that his listeners were "astonished at his doctrine. For he taught them as one having authority, and not as the scribes" (Matt. 5:28–29).

The culture that Jesus inherited provided him a special opportunity to be an authority, as it was assumed in Israel that the laws to be followed had been established in the beginning and one could only discover and interpret them. In other cultures, similar laws may be viewed as the product of consensus; the citizenry makes its own laws, and agree more or less to abide by them. But when "it is assumed that laws exist independent of man and one can only discover what they are, a single individual can speak with as much authority as an establishment because he can claim to have discerned the true law" (Haley, 1986, 27). He can therefore request or even demand a change by claiming that his opponents have deviated from the law. Throughout his career, then, "Jesus attacked the leaders of the establishment consistently and cleverly, but he based his attack within their religious framework. He said they deviated from the true religion, setting himself up as the authority on what the true religion should be" (Haley, 27). Nowhere in the Gospels does Jesus compliment any established religious leader, except those long deceased: "The nearest to a compliment he pays [to a contemporary] is to his fellow and competing prophet, John" (27). Yet, even here, while asserting that John is the greatest among those born of women, he adds that in the kingdom of heaven the one who is least of all is greater than John (Matt. 11:11).

Jesus brought himself to the attention of the populace by making use of the popular tradition of the itinerant prophet. But this would not account for the fact that he appears to have become much better known than other itinerant Galilean prophets. Saying things that people haven't heard openly voiced before may arouse an audience, but an insurgent religious leader also needs to offer something tangible and concrete. What Jesus had was an ability to cure people of their physical and mental distress. Thus, "the reputation of Jesus as a healer gave him his greatest notoriety. It is the nature of the healing trade to strike a deep chord of wishful thinking in people. Legends build quickly and success in healing breeds belief in success and therefore more success. Certainly once a man had a reputation as a healer, a touch of his robes could produce cures (which was why a guard was maintained to keep the masses of diseased people from touching the robes of the Roman emperor)" (Haley, 1986, 28). Whether Jesus had more than usual skill is impossible to determine, "but the fact that he chose to be a healer demonstrates his ability to select a way to become immediately famous. Perhaps no other device would have spread his name so quickly, particularly in an age when medicine was inadequate against disease and people were emotionally wrought up over the possession of devils" (Haley, 28). Moreover, "Since illness knows no class, this reputation also gave him access to the rich and he was begged for his assistance by the leader of a synagogue" and others (28).

The fact that Jesus downplayed his cures was also evidence of his strategic ability. In refusing to boast about his cures and so arouse investigations and resistance, he advised his patients to keep their cure a secret. Since no one who has been cured of a lifelong distress is likely or able to conceal the cure, the result was that cures were broadcast by others. As a result, only the statements of others could be refuted. It was only when messengers sent by John to ask if he was "the one who was to come" that Jesus referred to his healings as evidence, and even then he makes no claims relating to himself. He merely states: "The blind receive their sight, and the lame walk, the lepers are cleansed, and the deaf hear" (Matt. 11:4–5).

There is another power tactic that an unknown can use if he wishes to become known quickly, but it has certain risks: "If a man wishes to be thought of as an equal, or a superior, to a powerful opponent, he can make audacious personal attacks upon him. The more audacious the attack, the more prominent does the attacker become if it is widely known" (Haley, 1986, 29). Such attacks may place the leader of a small mass movement on the same plane as the powerful opponent. Jesus used this tactic when he called the established religious leaders serpents, a generation of vipers who will not escape the damnation of hell (Matt. 23:33); and when he made a physical assault on the religious hierarchy by attacking the money changers in the temple. Haley believes, however, that this attack was a tactical miscalculation that cost Jesus his life. Thus, an audacious attack on a powerful opponent may pay great dividends, but it can also backfire.

Stage 2: Building an Organization

Haley next takes up the fact that Jesus built an organization. He contrasts Jesus with prophets like John the Baptist, a solitary man who lived outside of society, who are dependent on transient followers who "might be attracted to them out of curiosity or because they sought a touch of divinity" (Haley, 1986, 29). As a member of John's group, Jesus may have perceived that it was too loosely organized and did not require long-term loyalty and commitment. In any event, he began his own public career by choosing men to join him in his movement. According to Matthew (Matt. 4:18–19), one of his first acts was to recruit a cadre who would recruit others. He had at least twelve in his organization, and if Luke is to be believed (10:1–17), he had an additional seventy, "which is an organization of some size" (Haley, 1986, 30).

In his selection of this elite, he did not recruit among the members of the establishment but from the lower strata of the population, from which he was also gathering his public following. "When he recruited his men, he asked of them what is now typically asked of any small revolutionary cadre. They had to give up everything related to ambition in the society as it was and abandon all other commitments to others, including family ties, when they joined him" (Haley, 1986, 30). Thus, he declared that anyone who loved father, mother, son, or daughter more than they loved him was not worthy of him (Matt. 10:37), and he said to the young man who wanted to do his filial duty to his father before joining his movement, "Let the dead bury the dead" (Luke 9:60). In making this demand, however, he did not ask more of the others than he asked of himself. When informed that his mother and brothers were outside and wished to speak with him, he said, "Who is my mother? And who are my brothers? Again he stretched forth his hand toward his disciples, and said, 'Behold my mother and my brethren'" (Matt. 12:48–49).

In return for their absolute commitment, Jesus gave his men elite status. They had authority to heal the sick, cleanse lepers, cast out demons, and raise the dead, all the activities from which he had achieved personal fame. He also melded them together with promises. When Peter is said to have asked what they would gain by following him, he promised them that they would sit on thrones of their own, as judges over the twelve tribes of Israel (Matt. 19:28). Thus, his promise to his men included what they would achieve once he came into power, and not merely what they might gain from listening to him, as they might to a teacher. He also effectively threatened them, saying, "But whoever denies me before others, I also will deny before my Father in heaven" (Matt. 10:33). As the story of Peter's denials suggests (Matt. 26:69–75), this was a threat that would come back to haunt the men following his untimely death.

He also kept his men unsure as to their personal future in the kingdom. By raising doubts about whether they would be finally acceptable to him, he insured that they would remain actively dedicated in following him. As Matt. 7:22–23 puts it: "On that day many will say to me, 'Lord, Lord, did we not prophesy in your name, and do many deeds of power in your name?' Then I will declare to them, 'I never knew you; go away from me, you evildoers'." He also used the persecutory actions of others as a tactic for securing group unity, declaring that he sent them out as sheep in the midst of wolves, and enjoining them therefore to be as wise as serpents, but as harmless as doves (Matt. 10:16). This dual approach to their adversaries was itself the device of a shrewd tactical leader.

Another indication of his careful attention to tactics was in instructing his men to go out as poor men without money or extra clothes (Matt. 10:9–10). The point was not that they were to present themselves as ascetics akin to John the Baptist, but that they were to present themselves as being just as poor as the people among whom they were seeking to win a following: "One can take a second coat and still cure, but one cannot win followers among the poor with money or a second coat or even shoes" (Haley, 1986, 33).

If he taught his cadre his own methods and encouraged them to use them, how did he insure that no member of his group tried to usurp his position? If there were power struggles in the group, why were they not directed against him? Haley thinks that Jesus forestalled any challenge to his leadership position by putting his men in their places by criticizing their obtuseness in not understanding his teachings, their inability to heal people properly, and their jealousy over who was closest to him now and who would hold the highest rank next to him when success came. Even as Jesus paid no member of the religious establishment a compliment, he paid no special compliment to any member of his cadre. The nearest thing to such a compliment is his response to Peter's suggestion that Jesus was "the Christ, the Son of the Living God," declaring that Peter is surely blessed, as this insight was revealed to him by Jesus' Father in heaven (Matt. 16:17). Yet when Peter protested Jesus' subsequent declaration that he must go to Jerusalem and be put to death, he charged that Peter was now speaking with the voice of Satan and was therefore "an offense" to him (Matt. 1:6:23).

Whether Jesus was justified in criticizing his men in this way is "open to interpretation," but, in any case, the Gospels indicate that he did not succeed in training them to be as skillful as he was at handling the criticism of others: "Whenever Jesus was attacked or questioned, he responded with attack or question, always putting his critics in their places and never using defensive behavior" (Haley, 1986, 34). Yet, after his death, when his men were amazing a crowd by speaking in various tongues, a critic said, contemptuously, "These men are full of new wine." Peter responded to this attack for the whole group, noting that they could not be drunk because it was only the third hour of the day (Acts 2:13–15). Haley dryly observes: "That was hardly a reply worthy of the master" (Haley, 1986, 34).

Stage 3: Collecting a Following

Haley next takes up Jesus' method of collecting a following. Ordinarily, if a man seeks power in a society he must work his way up within the existing established political structure. Some might argue that Jesus did not seek political power because he made no attempt to secure a position within the established religious hierarchy, just as he emphasized the more supernatural "Son of Man" rather than the more political "Son of David." But this is to overlook the new strategy that he employed, one that bypassed the current political establishment and appealed for support among the dispossessed of society: "His basic tactic was to define the poor as more deserving of power than anyone else and so curry their favor. With the first statements of his public life he pointed out that the poor were blessed" (Haley, 1986, 34), that they were "the salt of the earth, the light of the world," and that they, the weak, "would inherit the earth." By the same token, he consistently "attacked the rich, saying that they would have difficulty entering his kingdom, and speaking to audiences of the last he emphasized that the last would be first. Not only did he send his elite out as poor men, but he himself gained a reputation for wining and dining with the outcasts of respectable society. Nowhere does he criticize the poor, but only the rich, the learned, and the priestly establishment" (Haley, 35).

He offered those who agreed with him "the opportunity to suffer for a good cause" by pointing out to them that their reward would be great in the kingdom if they are reviled, persecuted and falsely accused for his sake (Matt. 5:11–12). In return, he "offered to take all problems upon himself" (Haley, 1986, 35), encouraging his hearers who labor and are heavy laden to come to him and he would give them rest (Matt. 11:28–30). He also assured them that if they heard his words and acted on them, they would be like the man who built his house on a rock; but if they didn't, he warned that they would be like the man who built his house on sand so that it comes crashing down in the turbulent times to come (Matt. 7:24–27).

Jesus' manner of collecting a following indicates that he was establishing long-range plans for his organization. This is evident from the fact that he pinned his hopes on "separating the young from ties to their parents and the current establishment" (Haley, 1986, 36). Leaders of mass movements have typically emphasized reaching the young people and have used the young against dissidents among their own followers. Jesus "called for the breaking of family ties and the pitting of the young against their elders. The conservative force of the family is an impediment to any mass movement, and only after becoming the establishment does a revolutionary group call for family solidarity" (Haley, 36). Also, revolutionary leaders generally say that they are not to be followed for their own person but for what their person represents. Thus, as individuals, they do not take full credit or blame for what they say, "because they are only spokesmen for a greater force" (37). Jesus "insisted that he did not speak for himself but only expressed the will of his heavenly Father" (37). But this meant that he defined opposition to himself as opposition to his Father, and he inhibited resistance to himself and accusations of self-aggrandizement by consistently pointing out that he was a mere instrument. He also defined himself as the *only* instrument able to interpret the heavenly Father correctly, because he was on intimate terms with the Father.

Finally, an important tactic Jesus used in collecting a following was to point to the inevitability of his coming to power. This way, the irresistible was on his side. This is a tactic other revolutionary leaders have subsequently employed: "By arguing that they are only shortening the time of arrival, or clarifying the progress of an inevitable event, such leaders encourage recruits to accept an established fact and inhibit opponents who might fear going against the course of history" (Haley, 1986, 37). Because Jesus endorsed the same tradition to which the religious establishment and the overwhelming majority of the people subscribed, he could count on the reluctance of the religious establishment to challenge him, not only because they feared his power among the people, but also because they feared that he might be right, both in his interpretations of this tradition and in what these interpretations predicted regarding the coming of the Kingdom of God. After all, they shared his view that earthly powers and principalities would one day be supplanted by the reign of God. Evidence of their reluctance to silence him altogether is the fact that, while they disputed things he said, he was allowed to teach in the synagogues.

The Major Tactical Contribution of Jesus

Haley believes Jesus' major tactical contribution, used by all revolutionary leaders subsequently, was to mobilize the poor against the establishment. While revolutionary leaders have condemned Jesus for the tactics he introduced, these objections "are not based on a study of the tactics as Jesus used them, but on the way established powers learned to use them later" (Haley, 1986, 38). Established powers, often using Christian rhetoric, have been able to remain in power by persuading the oppressed to look to a future life for their reward. In contrast, while Jesus "promised a paradise in some ill-defined future" for those who followed him, he "implied that the day was in the not too distant future" (Haley, 35). If he was pinning his hopes on the younger generation, he nonetheless declared that some persons standing in his midst would not taste death until the Kingdom of God comes into power (Mark 10:1). Thus, unlike later Christian established powers who promised a reward in heaven, Jesus envisioned a new world order with the arrival of the Kingdom of God on earth. Therefore, when he promised a reward, he did not use this as a way of persuading the poor to accept their misery, but to enlist them in accelerating the coming of the Kingdom. He also presented them with a choice having real consequences. He promised that if they followed him and resisted the establishment, they would be amply rewarded, but that if they followed the establishment, they would suffer dire consequences. As Matthew 13:41–43 puts it: "The Son of Man will send his angels, and they will collect out of his kingdom all causes of sin and all evildoers, and they will throw them into the furnace of fire, where there will be weeping and gnashing of teeth. Then the righteous will shine like the sun in the kingdom of their father. Let anyone with ears listen!"

Revolutionary leaders who have condemned Christians for using tactics of weakness also misunderstand Jesus' own strategic position: "While Bolsheviks might argue that force must be met by force, and when Hitler said that terror must be met with equal terror, they were adapting to a quite different situation" (Haley, 1986, 39). There was no way that Jesus could marshal force against the force of Rome or terror equal to the actions of the establishment: "A leader at that time might achieve sporadic riots, but organized attack against the occupying Roman force was futile, as Roman executions regularly demonstrated" (Haley, 39). Insofar as the Romans were supporting the religious establishment and permitting it authority over the people, those who opposed the religious establishment risked being exterminated: "In this situation Jesus developed the surrender tactic, a procedure which has been used by the powerless in the face of the invincible to this day" (39).

The Surrender Tactic

Haley gives considerable attention to the specific tactic of surrender, as he believes it played a significant role in Jesus' personal confrontation with the establishment and was a major factor in his execution. What is the surrender tactic? Noting that Jesus advises his listeners to consider the beasts of the field and the birds of the air and to emulate them, Haley suggests comparing this particular tactic to those employed by animals. Citing the observations of the ethnologist Konrad Lorenz, he notes that when two wolves are in a fight and one is about to be killed, the defeated wolf will suddenly lift his head and bare his throat to his opponent: "The opponent becomes incapacitated and he cannot kill him as long as he is faced with this tactic. Although he is the victor, the vanquished is controlling his behavior merely by standing still and offering his vulnerable jugular vein" (Haley, 1986, 40). The turkey does the very same thing.

In his study of Gandhi's tactics of nonviolence, Erik H. Erikson also invokes Lorenz's studies, citing not only the example of wolves, but also the antler tournament of the Damstags. This is a contest that ends when the loser "concedes the tournament by a ritualized disengagement which normally stops the attack of the victor" (Erikson, 1969, 426). Yet Erikson cites Lorenz's observation that the ritual may fail and end in "violence to the death. Skeletons of stags whose antlers are entwined in death have been found; but they are victims of an instinctive ritual that failed" (1969, 426).

Haley cites Lorenz's own connection between Jesus and animal behavior. Commenting on the lessons to be learned from the behavior of wolves, Lorenz wrote, "I at least have extracted from it a new and deeper understanding of a wonderful and often misunderstood saying from the Gospel, which hitherto had only awakened in me the feelings of strong opposition. 'And unto him that smiteth thee on the one cheek offer also the other' (Luke 6:29). A wolf has enlightened me: not so that your enemy may strike you again do you turn the other cheek toward him, but to make him unable to do it" (Haley, 1986, 40).

Haley points out that Jesus did not originate the surrender tactic. In his *Antiquities* (Book 18, Chapter 3), Josephus reports that Pilate's troops surrounded a mob of protesters and told them that they would be killed if they did not disperse. Instead of dispersing, the unarmed protesters "flung themselves in a body on the ground, extended their necks, and exclaimed that they were ready to die rather than to transgress the [ancient Jewish] Law" (Haley, 1986, 42). By extending their necks, they were acting precisely as the wolf did in Lorenz's example. The banners of Caesar, which Pilate had erected in Jerusalem, the provocation for this protest, were taken down.

The "surrender tactic" is not merely a device by animals and humans to suffer defeat without being extinguished, for "it is also possible to see the procedure as a way of determining what is to happen. You cannot defeat a helpless opponent; if you strike him and your blows are unreturned, you can only suffer feelings of guilt and exasperation as well as doubt about who is the victor" (Haley, 1986, 40). This tactic has proven itself effective by anxious parents who find that helplessness will enforce their directives more tyrannically than giving orders. And of course, "the extreme tactic of threat of suicide falls in a similar category" (Haley, 40).

It is not, however, without its risks. It seems to be a tactic that either wins, or provokes murderous extermination. The fact that Jesus, Gandhi, and Martin Luther King died violent deaths just as surely as if they had lived by the sword does not seem coincidental. Why, then, does it work in some situations and not in others? Haley believes that "the use of weakness to determine what is to happen in a power struggle works most effectively if there is a threat of violence in the background to support the meek tactic" (Haley, 1986, 41). If the opponent believes that he will not be able to control the violent actions that may follow from the murderous extermination of the one who surrenders, or will suffer an unacceptable number of casualties in achieving this control, he is more likely to allow the user of the surrender tactic to win and may explain his seemingly weak behavior as an act of mercy. Thus, the opponent needs to believe that his extermination of the one who bares his neck, so to speak, carries unacceptable risks. But if he believes that he will be able to control any residual consequences of the extermination without unacceptable risks to himself, he may take advantage of the opportunity that has been handed him, virtually on a silver platter, and exterminate his tormentor.

There is also the risk that even if the one to whom one surrenders capitulates, he may not be in a position to insure that others will do likewise. An individual or group who is enraged by the fact that the surrender succeeded may decide to do what the original adversary would not do. Thus the surrender tactic is risky, because one cannot control every aspect of the process that it sets in motion. A case in point is Josephus' account of what happened after the protesters achieved their goal of forcing Pilate to remove the banners of Caesar. Pilate sought to bring "a current of water" to Jerusalem, paying for the project with sacred money. Tens of thousands of Jews, displeased by this action, "made a clamor" against Pilate, and also publicly "reproached" and "abused" him. So he organized his soldiers to surround them, and when the crowd refused to disperse but instead hurled more reproaches upon him, Pilate gave the soldiers a prearranged signal to move against the crowd. But the soldiers "laid upon them much greater blows than Pilate had commanded them," and they indiscriminately attacked those who were "tumultuous, and those that were not." They "did not spare them in the least; and since the people were unarmed, and were caught by men prepared for what they were about [i.e., carried concealed daggers], there were a great number of them slain by this means, and others of them ran away wounded; and thus an end was put to this sedition" (Josephus, 1987, 480). Thus, Pilate lost control over his own soldiers, and *this* confrontation, unlike the previous confrontation, ended in bloodshed. In the very next paragraph, Josephus mentions that Jesus appeared at "about this time," and at "the suggestion of the principal men" around him, Pilate condemned him to the cross.

The Climax of the Struggle for Power

Following his discussion of Jesus' surrender tactic, Haley focuses on the outcome of Jesus' struggle for power against the establishment. In his view, the preceding examination of Jesus as a tactician not only increases our understanding of the nature of the power struggle in which he was engaged, but also suggests "a possible resolution" of some of the contradictions in the Gospels relating to the final days of his life: "In their determination to prove him innocent [the Gospels] neglect to state what charges were made against him, and their attempts to fit his actions into complicated prophecies about the Messiah compound the confusion" (Haley, 1986, 43). But what is clear is that when Jesus went into "the final struggle he arranged a situation where there was no hope of compromise. He condemned the clergy, he condemned the temple, and finally he made a physical assault on the temple" (Haley, 43). While he "took care" not to call for open rebellion against the priestly hierarchy, he "thoroughly discredited them" (43). As Matthew 23:4 indicates, he made this accusation against them: "They tie up heavy burdens, hard to bear, and lay them on the shoulders of others; but they are unwilling to lift a finger to move them." A series of "woe to you" condemnations follow, in which he declares that they are "blind guides" and "hypocrites."

Such verbal attacks would have rung hollow if he did not also take action with his "audacious assault on the temple." In attacking the commercial aspect of the temple and not violating the altar or intruding on the Holy of Holies, he chose his opponents' "most vulnerable area for his attack," thus again demonstrating "his skill as a tactician." Accusing them of "turning a house of prayer into a robber's cave," he "could win immediate fame throughout the city while not giving his opposition an advantage. It was awkward for the priesthood to retaliate against him for his violent ways because he was quoting their own scripture to them, attacking a point difficult to defend" (Haley, 1986, 44). In addition, he offered himself as an alternative to the establishment, pointing out that he could tear the temple down and rebuild it in three days, thus ushering in a new order to replace the old, corrupt order presided over by the priests who had forfeited their claim to legitimacy. The message was clear: He and his men would replace the old establishment with a new rule whose legitimation derived from the heavenly Father, not from Rome.

The position he had taken was too extreme for the establishment not to take action of some kind. Apparently, they sought to lay their hands on him but "feared the multitude" who had come for the Passover (Matt. 21:46). There was an attempt to stone him, but he escaped. The only remaining alternative was to arrest him. His successful escape from stoning but surrender to arrest indicates that he sought the publicity of arrest and trial. Despite the confusion in the Gospels about the events that followed his "audacious assault" on the temple, these points are reasonably clear (Haley, 1986, 44–45):

1. Over his followers' objections, Jesus insisted on going to Jerusalem to be arrested. When he arrived, he behaved in such an extreme manner that he forced his arrest. He either arranged that the arresting officers would find him, or waited patiently for them to come to him. He may even have planned Judas's betrayal by, in effect, designating him as the betrayer (i.e., the one who was to lead the authorities to where he was staying) during the final week with his disciples. After all, he announced the fact that there was a betrayer in their midst, yet apparently did nothing to stop him. This is not to say that he manipulated Judas into revealing his whereabouts to the authorities, but he did take advantage of Judas's weakness.

2. He was tried and condemned to death by the Sanhedrin and was passed to the Roman government for execution.

3. Pilate declined to execute him since he found no evidence that he had broken Roman law.

4. Pilate turned to the populace for a decision and the crowd called for Jesus' death (44–45).

Up until the time of his trial, Jesus' behavior could have been interpreted several ways, all consistent with his aggressive behavior and willingness to be arrested: (1) He was actually the coming Messiah, and this meant he must therefore go through the prophetic pattern of being handed over to his enemies and executed; (2) he was sacrificing himself for the sins of the world as part of the messianic pattern, and this was his individual choice; (3) he went mad and decided that he was the Messiah and must die so that the Kingdom of Heaven would immediately arrive; or (4) he did not intend to die, but wanted to be arrested because he was pitting himself and the strength of his organization in a final power struggle with the establishment (Haley, 45).

In Haley's view, Jesus' behavior *after* his arrest indicates that only the fourth interpretation fits the facts: "After permitting, or arranging, his arrest, he made it almost impossible for the establishment to condemn him and execute him" (Haley, 1986, 46). If he merely wished to be executed as part of the Messianic prophecy or to sacrifice himself for the sins of the world, he could have announced that he was the Messiah, opposed Roman rule, and his execution would have been routine. Or, if he had gone mad and sought to sacrifice himself in a suicidal manner, he would have behaved in a provocative way and made the execution simple. But according to the Gospel accounts, Jesus neither announced that he was the Messiah, nor acted in a manner that would force the authorities to kill him. Rather, he refused to say that he was the coming Messiah and to speak in opposition to Rome: "In fact he behaved in such a way that execution appeared impossible—after amicably surrendering himself into the hands of the establishment" (Haley, 46). He did not curse or revile the religious and political establishments, or individual members of them, and did not even defend himself or assert his own authority. He said nothing through many hours of interrogation and the futile calling of witnesses. His response to direct questioning about whether he claimed to be the Messiah was noncommittal. His response, "You have said so," is taken as affirmative by the high priest and as a denial by Pilate. Since only one of the four Gospels have him making this claim (Mark 14:62), while all agree that he maintained a remarkable silence throughout the proceedings, Haley concludes that he made no such admission, and that this would be consistent with indications that he had never announced that he was the Messiah in his whole career.

Therefore, Jesus was counting on the strict application of rules of evidence to gain his acquittal, and thus to prove that the religious authorities were powerless to control him: "By remaining silent and providing only a final and ambiguous answer, Jesus made it legally impossible for them to condemn him to death" (Haley, 1986, 47). Thus, in handing him over to Pilate for execution, they broke their own rules, acting "in a fit of pique, on impulse" (Haley, 48).

A remarkably similar situation occurred when he was brought before the Roman governor: "Although the establishment was given surprising autonomy for a subjected colonial people, they could not execute a man except with permission of Pilate. Once again, if Jesus was determined to be executed, he would have to persuade Pilate to give the order. Instead, he made it extremely difficult, if not impossible, for Pilate to order his execution" (Haley, 1986, 48). Throughout his public career, Jesus had been extremely circumspect in his behavior with the Romans. Nowhere in the Gospels is there a statement by him that could be considered an attack on Rome. He did not stir up the populace against Rome, or oppose Roman taxation, though he did object to the temple tax (Matt. 17:26). At most, he included the Romans among all Gentiles and placed them outside the pale, instructing his disciples to deal only with Jews, saying, "I was sent only to the lost sheep of the house of Israel" (Matt. 15:24). Attempts to provoke him into expressing anti-Roman sentiments are cleverly countered (Matt. 22:19–21).

While Haley considers the possibility that the Gospel writers did not want to antagonize Rome and therefore suppressed Jesus' anti-Roman sentiments, he believes, instead, that Jesus made no statements against Rome, and did so for tactical reasons. "Roman power must have appeared clearly invincible and a power strategist does not directly attack invincible power, he seeks other means of undermining it" (Haley, 1986, 49). Attacking the more vulnerable religious establishment that worked closely with the Roman governor was a much better strategy.

Without evidence that Jesus had even spoken against the Roman government, much less advocated action against it, Pilate had no legal grounds for executing him. But this placed him in a political quandary, one that Jesus may well have intended to provoke, as it pitted Pilate and the priestly hierarchy against each other. (In family systems' terms, Jesus used the method of triangulation.) Placing the decision in the hands of the crowd that had gathered for the public trial was a counter move by Pilate designed to extricate himself from the dilemma into which Jesus' behavior had placed him.

Haley acknowledges that the crowd's decision to call for Jesus' death is a puzzling one, especially if he was so popular that he had to be arrested secretly. He cites Schweitzer's explanation in *The Quest of the Historical Jesus* that the crowd was informed that Jesus had claimed at the private trial before the Sanhedrin that he was the Messiah, and on the basis of this misinformation they called for his death on the grounds of blasphemy, the very basis on which the high priest judged him guilty (Matt. 26:65–66). While more or less persuaded by Schweitzer's explanation, Haley remains sufficiently puzzled by the crowd's action to wonder if the episode is authentic, especially since there is no known tradition of a release of a prisoner at Passover. But in the end he concludes that "the Gospel version would seem as adequate as any other," basing this conclusion on the assumption that Jesus' actions would "have forced the priestly hierarchy to deal with him, and the Romans must have had a problem legally executing him when he had broken no Roman law" (Haley, 1986, 49).

Instead of offering his own solution to the puzzle, Haley turns the issue around and suggests that, precisely because this outcome was puzzling, Jesus may not have considered it in his strategic planning, or if he did so, would not have thought it very likely. He proposes that we place ourselves in Jesus' position prior to his arrest and strategically examine "what we would gain and what we would lose by arranging to be arrested," with our gains and losses estimated "in terms of the probabilities in a situation where the outcome was uncertain" (1986, 49). The most probable outcomes, in the order in which they were most likely to happen, are these:

1. Faced with no adequate witnesses and a silent victim, the Sanhedrin would be forced to release Jesus for lack of evidence. He would prove the impotence of the religious establishment in the face of his movement and of his aggressive statements and his physical assault on the temple.

2. The Sanhedrin might, in exasperation, break their own laws and condemn him even without evidence. They would take him to the Roman governor for execution. Since he had been careful to break no Roman law, the governor would order him released and at most scourge him. He would have discredited the temple hierarchy and proven its impotence, and he would be released as a leader who could openly oppose the temple and be tolerated by Rome.

3. By chance, and therefore it could not be predicted, the unexpected might happen and Pilate would put the decision up to the crowd. With the following Jesus had built, he would be freed by the

populace and triumphantly lead a popular movement which could not be defeated by the temple hierarchy.

4. The Sanhedrin might convict him illegally, Pilate might turn to the crowd, and the crowd might call for his death. This seems the least likely possibility. Yet if the Gospel accounts are to be believed, this is what actually happened (Haley, 1986, 50).

This being the case, Haley concludes: "It would seem possible to interpret the execution of Jesus as the result of a miscalculation on his part. Who could have guessed the Sanhedrin would condemn him without evidence, that Pilate would happen to ask the crowd for a decision, and that the crowd [Jesus] had never wronged would ask for his death? Even a master tactician cannot take into account all the possibilities, including chance occurrences" (50). Thus, the very fact that the crowd's demand for Jesus' death is so puzzling is grounds for believing that Jesus did not consider this outcome in his strategic planning, or if he considered it, did not think it very likely.

If Jesus made a fateful miscalculation, Haley suggests that the reason for this miscalculation may be discovered by examining his life more carefully. When we do so, we recognize that "it would fit his character to move prematurely to gain the whole world. All the evidence indicates that Jesus was a man with a passion to determine what was to happen in his environment" (Haley, 1986, 50). The ultimate resistance to him resided in Jerusalem, the seat of religious and political power, and he chose that place for what was to be his final struggle for power. His arrest occurred at a place and time of his own choosing. It was provoked by his actions, and therefore determined by them. After his arrest, he behaved in such a way that his opponents were incapacitated and forced to respond to his terms. What else could they do but release him, allowing him to walk out a free man, exonerated of all charges against him, and proclaiming victory before the massive crowd that was gathered in Jerusalem for the Passover celebration?

His basic miscalculation was his failure to factor into his strategic planning "the desperation of his opposition" when he forced them into a corner. They could not legally condemn him, *but neither could they release him* without seriously damaging their power and control. By leaving them no graceful way out, he created a situation where what happened was beyond his control. Invoking his cry from the cross, "My God, my God, why have you forsaken me?" (Matt. 27:46), Haley also implies that a related factor in Jesus' miscalculation was that he believed his heavenly Father would surely not allow the situation to get out of control. Moreover, even those who argue that he deliberately sought his execution, a view that Haley discounts, "support the argument that Jesus was determined to control whatever happened to him" (Haley, 1986, 51). Until this final and fateful miscalculation, he had succeeded brilliantly in this regard.

Haley concludes his analysis of Jesus' power tactics, however, by noting that even though it appears that his plans failed on those last days, there was still the fact that he had built an organization, and in this he did not fail. In fact, the very act of being executed extended his control from beyond the grave. Haley does not consider whether such extension of his control may have played a part in Jesus' calculation, but he does suggest that this extension of his control from beyond the grave "fits the character of a man who would finally say, 'All power is given unto me in heaven and on earth' (Matt. 28:18)" (1986, 51).

The Tactical Displacement of the Father

I will now take up two issues in Haley's portrait of Jesus as power tactician. The first concerns an implication of his view that all organizations are hierarchical: if Jesus created an organization that placed the heavenly Father at the top of the hierarchy, the primary target of this organization is the human father, the person who held the top position in the human family.

For Haley, a key element in Jesus' recruitment of the men who would form the core of his movement was that he "asked of them what is now typically asked of any small revolutionary cadre. They had to give up everything related to ambition in the society as it was and abandon all other commitments to others, including family ties, when they joined him" (1986, 30). He adds, "Once they have done this, it is difficult for them to defect and abandon the movement; they have sacrificed too much and have no place to go" (52).

If we were in Jesus' position, and wanted to have clear evidence that a young man has in fact "given up all ambitions in the society as it is" and "abandoned all other commitments to others," where would we look for it? Quite simply, in the young man's severance of his ties with his father. Why is the tie to the father so important? Because a young man's father would hold the key to his ambitions in the existing society. A Jewish father had five principal responsibilities toward his son: to circumcise him, redeem him, teach him Torah, teach him a trade, and find him a wife. By pledging himself to Jesus and his movement, a young man renounced or set aside these paternal blessings. In addition, a son's social position was determined by his father's position and the promise and bestowal of a portion of his property. In return, the son would be expected to fulfill certain obligations to his father, such as working for him, marrying the daughter of a man of use to his father's own ambitions, and so forth.

If we were in Jesus' place, we would want concrete, indisputable evidence that a recruit had broken his emotional and legal ties to his father. He would be expected to make a clear, irrevocable choice: either his human father and all that this represents, or the heavenly Father and all that this implies. "No one can serve two masters. Either he hates the one and loves the other, or he is loyal to the one and despises the other" (Matt. 6:24; Luke 16:13). The importance of breaking both legal and emotional ties to one's father is expressed in the most stark and uncompromising terms in Jesus' response to the son who agreed to follow him but proposed to attend to his father's burial first: "Let the dead bury their own dead; but as for you, go and proclaim the Kingdom of God" (Luke 9:59–60; also Matt. 8:21–22). The implication is not merely that others can see to the care of the dead, but that if *he* cannot treat as "dead" his claims on his father and obligations to him, he is not yet ready to join Jesus' organization. Haley's view that power and control can be exercised from beyond the grave is especially relevant here.

An illustration of sons who *were* ready to sacrifice the claims and obligations of the father–son relationship is the story in Mark 1:19–20 where Jesus sees "James, son of Zebedee and his brother John, who were in their boat mending the nets." When he called them, "they left their father, Zebedee, in the boat with the hired men and followed him." Whether authentic or not, this story indicates that it was the father–son relationship that Jesus required his men to sacrifice. In leaving their father, they abandoned their claims to property—symbolized by the boat—that would be theirs on their father's death. The hired men, who received wages rather than a paternal legacy, remained with Zebedee.

Later, the brothers demonstrate that they have in fact transferred their ambitions and commitments associated with their father Zebedee's world to the world in which the heavenly Father is the highest authority. This is indicated in the story of their request to be placed immediately to Jesus' right and left in the kingdom of the Father (Mark 10:35). Matthew's account of the same episode (Matt. 20:20–28) adds a wrinkle to the story that, even if more imaginative than factual, underscores the point that it was the severing of the son's relationship to his father that proved he was ready to join Jesus' organization. This is

Matthew's suggestion that it was "the mother of the sons of Zebedee" who "came to him with her sons, and kneeling before him, she asked a favor of him" (v. 20). That it was their mother, not their father, who asked this favor indicates that breaking the tie to the father was the essential thing. Jesus tolerated, possibly even welcomed, the son's continuing tie to his mother, as she may well have encouraged her son to join the organization, thus subverting the father's authority over his son. Thus, Jesus—the skillful tactician—may have used the mother–son relationship to his advantage.

John Dominic Crossan's discussion in *The Historical Jesus* under the heading "Against the Patriarchal Family" is relevant in this regard (1991, 299–300). While he wants to argue that Jesus' pronouncements on family issues reflect his "social egalitarianism," in which women are fully included, his citation of the various relevant texts makes clear that the central feature of these pronouncements was the breaking of the filial tie between son and father. For example, Crossan cites the Gospel of Thomas versions of two narratives that also appear in Luke 14:25–26 and Mark 3:31–35, respectively. The first reads: "A woman from the crowd said to him, 'Blessed are the womb which bore you and the breasts which suckled you.' He said to [her], 'Blessed are those who have heard the word of the father and have truly kept it" (Thomas 79:1–2). The second reads: "The disciples said to him, 'Your brothers and your mother are standing outside.' He said to them, 'Those here who do the will of my father are my brothers and my mother. It is they who will enter the kingdom of my father'" (Thomas 99). In the first case, Luke has "the word of God" rather than "the word of the father," and in the second case, Mark has "the kingdom of God" instead of "the kingdom of my father." Thus, the Gospel of Thomas makes explicit what the other Gospels obscure; that in these narratives where family relations are paramount, Jesus emphasizes the word and kingdom of the heavenly Father.

Crossan notes that what the text in Mark and parallel text in Thomas both agree upon is "excluding the father." But then he adds, "This exclusion might be interpreted in many ways: Joseph was busy that day, was already dead, or was omitted to protect either the virgin birth or God as Jesus' true father." Therefore, Crossan wants to emphasize "less the father's exclusion than the mother's inclusion" (1991, 299). Even so, he goes on to say that "however we explain the literal absence of Jesus' father, his new metaphorical family lacks one as well" (1991, 299). Thus, even though his point is that women were to be *included* in the kingdom, these texts actually emphasize the *exclusion* of the human father and the central prominence of the heavenly Father. Gospel of Thomas 16, a variant form of Matthew 10:34–36, makes this unmistakably clear. "Jesus said, 'Men think, perhaps, that it is peace which I have come to cast upon the world. They do not know that it is dissension which I have come to cast upon the earth: fire, sword, and war. For there will be five in a house: three will be against two, and two against three, *the father against the son, and the son against the father*. And they will stand solitary" (my emphasis). Crossan claims that this single example—"the dominant male one"—obscures the saying's point; that is, that the split is not only *between* the generations but also across *genders*. But the fact that the "dominant male" division *is* the single example cited must certainly reflect the fact that this is the one with which Jesus and his closest cohorts were most concerned. Either a man serves his human father or his heavenly Father. No man can serve two masters.

The variant form of this statement in Matthew makes the same point: "Do not think that I have come to bring peace to the earth; I have not come to bring peace, but a sword. *For I have come to set a man against his father*, and a daughter against her mother, and a daughter-in-law against her mother-in-law; and one's foes will be members of one's own household" (my emphasis). Crossan cites Bruce Malina's astute observation that there is no mention of the son-in-law, since it was the new wife who moved into her husband's house, not the husband who moved into the wife's house (1991, 300). But again, this obscures the basic point that the central division will be between son and father, and that other divisions will follow. It may also be noted that an even more conspicuously absent relationship here than of the son-in-law is that between a man and his *mother*. This makes the division between the son and his *father* all the more striking.

Crossan concludes that it is "the normalcy of familial hierarchy that is under attack," and that Jesus threatens to "tear the hierarchal or patriarchal family in two along the axis of domination and subordination" (1991, 300). But following Haley's argument that all organizations are necessarily hierarchical, Jesus' attack on the hierarchical family does not mean that he replaces this hierarchy with an "egalitarian" form of organization. Rather, what the kingdom is fundamentally about is the displacement of the father—paternal authority and power—by establishing the heavenly Father at the top of the hierarchy. If Jesus does not emphasize that he has also come to set a man against his mother, this is less because he is interested in the inclusion of women in his organization than because he recognizes that the son–

mother alliance is one means by which the power of the father has traditionally been effectively undermined.

In fact, Crossan provides evidence that supports this very point. In
his chapter on "Bandit and Messiah," he cites Josephus' account of "a
somewhat paradigmatic encounter in Galilee between Herod the not
yet Great and the bandit chief Ezekias" shortly after Herod was
appointed ruler of Galilee in 48 B.C.E. by his father Antipater, prime
minister under Hyrcanus II. Herod caught Ezekias and put him and
many of his brigands to death. When he was accused by "a number of
malicious persons at court" for having killed people without trial "in
violation of Jewish law," Hyrcanus acquitted him on orders from the
Syrian legate, for the brigands were ravaging the district on the Syrian frontier. But the episode angered Hyracanus because it underscored his political weakness, and his "anger was further kindled by
the mothers of the men who had been murdered by Herod, for every
day in the temple they kept begging the people to have Herod brought
to judgment in the Synhedrion for what he had done" (Crossan, 1991,
175). Crossan views this appeal by the mothers as evidence that
Ezekias had great popular support. It also suggests that this support
was especially strong among the murdered men's mothers. We might
ask: Where were the fathers of the murdered men? Why did they not
come forward?

A parable often used to make the case that for Jesus the human
father is a figure for the heavenly Father is that of the two sons (Luke
18:1–18). In *Jesus at Thirty: A Psychological and Historical Portrait*
(1997), John W. Miller claims that "a strong, fatherly-type man is a
recurrent figure in the forty or so stories" that Jesus told, and cites in
this regard "that unforgettably gracious father in the story of the
prodigal son and his upright elder brother" (39). While noting that
several of the men who play the leading role in these parables "are not
of especially good character," nonetheless, "the dominant figures in
the great majority of Jesus' stories are fatherly types in positions of
responsibility who are shown executing these responsibilities in force-
ful, competent, but often surprisingly gracious ways" (39). Miller
believes that Jesus could not "have spoken of fathers and the father-
child relationship so often and in such utterly realistic yet positive
terms, had he not had a deeply meaningful experience somewhere
along the way with his own personal father" (40–41).

Miller also points to several individual sayings, besides the stories,
where "fathers are explicitly referred to and instruction given regarding them" (1997, 40). One is Jesus' citation of the command to honor

father and mother in his reply to a young man who asked him what he should do to inherit eternal life (Mark 10:19; parallels in Matt. 19:19 and Luke 18:20). Another is his critique of the practice among the rabbinic elite whereby a son could avoid financial obligations to his father or mother by dedicating the support he owed them to the temple instead (Mark 7:9–13). He acknowledges Jesus' saying in Luke 14:26 (also Matt. 10:37) that one's father, all other relations, and even life itself, must be "hated," but suggests that Jesus enjoins such hate *if this would prevent someone from becoming his disciple.* He cites the "most sharply formulated saying of this type," Jesus' "leave the dead to bury the dead," but claims that, "at issue, perhaps, was [Jesus'] treasured new-found experience of God as gracious father, devotion to whose will (as this was unfolding through his mission) takes priority over everything else" (Miller, 1997, 40). He adds, "A moving testimony to the depth of his faith in this regard is his beautifully off-hand statement about the greater goodness of God as father compared to the flawed goodness of human fathers" (Miller, 40). Miller makes reference here to Matthew 7:9–11 (with a parallel in Luke 11:11–13): "Is there anyone among you who, if your child asks for bread, will give a stone? Or if the child asks for a fish, will give a snake? If you then, who are evil, know how to give good gifts to your children, how much more will your Father in heaven give good things to those who ask him!"

In my view, Miller's effort to portray Jesus as a religious leader who held human fathers in high esteem is fundamentally misguided. The first two sayings that he adduces in support of his view that Jesus' attitude toward human fathers was "unusually positive" may be accounted for by Haley's point that Jesus insisted that the ideas he was presenting were not deviations from the established religion but a truer expression of them. Thus, to the young man's question about what he needed to do to inherit eternal life, Jesus cited, among others, the commandment to honor his father and mother (Exod. 20:12; Deut. 5:16). In the discussion of the son's financial obligations to his father and mother, he opposed the diverting of these monies to the temple instead. Both responses reflect Haley's point that revolutionary leaders need to "define what they do as orthodox while making the changes necessary to establish a power position" (Haley, 1986, 24). Moreover, since Jesus positioned himself against the temple establishment, he invoked the tradition against its recent innovations.

Miller's interpretation of the "hatred" saying introduces the very sort of qualifications Jesus would have considered evidence that the speaker was not yet ready to join his movement. His suggestion that

Jesus is merely saying one must "hate" a family member if, otherwise, he would be unable to commit himself to Jesus' movement, is in fact directly countered by the "let the dead bury the dead" saying, which makes very clear that one cannot have it both ways: either your loyalty is to your father, or to the heavenly Father. There is no middle ground. In contrast, Miller introduces another qualification: that of priorities. Whereas Jesus is demanding an absolute commitment—one where there is no turning back, for the recruit has burned his bridges behind him—Miller suggests that Jesus made this harsh sounding comment because of his own experience of God as a gracious father, "devotion to whose will . . . *takes priority over everything else*" (1997, 40, my emphasis). A leader cannot depend on a member of his organization who merely promises that devotion to the head of the organization—in this case, the heavenly Father—will "take priority" over all other persons to whom he is also devoted. Such an arrangement is simply unacceptable. Had the son in this story agreed to Jesus' terms and *not* gone off to bury his father, he would then have met the critical test for membership in Jesus' organization.

As for Miller's interpretation of the saying (supported by previous examples) about fathers who give good gifts to their children, Jesus *does* make a comparison between the heavenly Father and earthly fathers. But this is not a comparison between the "flawed goodness" of the one and the "greater goodness" of the other, but between "evil" fathers and the "good" heavenly Father. As Haley indicates, the leader of a revolutionary movement must promise rewards in return for the sacrifices he requires, and the rewards must be of such magnitude that the things that have been sacrificed pale in comparison. There is an implied disparagement, if not ridicule, in Jesus' examples of the father who gives bread and fish, not stone and serpent, in response to his son's entreaties. Since giving a stone or serpent would be downright perverse, the father's gift of bread and fish is better than the hypothetical alternatives. But giving his son exactly what the son requests can hardly be compared with the manner in which the heavenly Father gives gifts, or with the magnificence of the gifts themselves. Jesus promised his men that they would one day be rulers with him in the kingdom of the Father. For this, they were willing to sacrifice whatever "gifts" they might receive from their earthly fathers—gifts that, in any case, have strings attached.

In short, Jesus' tactical displacement of the human father both supports and gives concreteness to Haley's point that, in joining Jesus' organization, a young man would be giving up "everything related to ambition in the society as it was and abandon all other commitments to others" (1986, 30). The requisite evidence that such a sacrifice had been made is that a man had severed emotional and legal ties to his father. In stark contrast to their father, Zebedee, who fishes for fish, James and John will "fish for people" (Mark 1:16). As Haley puts it, in exchange for this sacrifice, the leader "gives them a sense of mission and purpose in life" (52). In turn, he places "his hopes in the young who do not yet have an investment in the establishment, and he deliberately incites the young against their elders, to break the family ties that solidify the strength of the establishment" (52). What is perhaps most remarkable about Jesus in this regard is his candor: "Do not think that I have come to bring peace to the earth; I have not come to bring peace, but a sword. *I have come to set a man against his father*" (Matt. 10:34, my emphasis). A leader could not be any more explicit than this.

Did Jesus Miscalculate?

The second issue I want to consider is Haley's argument that Jesus made a fateful miscalculation as far as the outcome of his trial was concerned, and that this miscalculation provides a glimpse into Jesus' character; the fact that he was "a man with a passion to determine what was to happen in his environment" (1986, 50).

In one sense, Haley seems to want to give Jesus the benefit of the doubt. If, hypothetically, we were in Jesus' position and were examining what we might gain or lose by arranging to be arrested, "our gains and losses would be estimated in terms of the probabilities in a situation where the outcome was uncertain" (1986, 49). This being the case, we would know that we were taking a risk, and that in this case we were risking our very lives. In other words, being the skillful strategist he had proven himself to be, Jesus surely calculated the risks involved and acted on the basis of this calculation. In addition, skillful as he was, Jesus could not have foreseen that the least probable of all the possibilities would in fact occur. "Even a master tactician cannot take into account all the possibilities, including chance occurrences" (50). The factor of "chance occurrences" is well known to military strategists.

On the other hand, Haley is critical of Jesus, for he also claims that "it would fit his character to move prematurely to gain the whole world" (1986, 50). The fault, then, lies not with Jesus' tactical prowess, but in a more deeply rooted personality or character trait: "a man with a passion to determine what was to happen in his environment" (50).

This passion caused him to act precipitously or to seek to force events to bend to his will, rather than to wait patiently for the opportunity or propitious moment to act. His impatience with Peter's objections—which were probably shared by others in Jesus' organization—to his decision to go down to Jerusalem at this time (Matt. 16:21–23) appears to give evidence of this personality trait.

Haley's view that Jesus was a man of passion who might act precipitously, however, requires careful examination. In my judgment, it is not self-evidently true. In order to assess its accuracy, we need to locate this characterological assessment in the context of the final days of Jesus' life. While efforts to reconstruct what happened have not led to a consensus opinion, a consideration of two scholars' attempts to reconstruct what happened after his disturbance in the temple provides a perspective from which to assess Haley's view that Jesus made a fateful miscalculation that was due, in effect, to a personality trait—namely, a tendency to act precipitously—that worked against his tactical acumen.

Crossan's Reconstruction

Crossan believes that Jesus would have been arrested on the spot for his disturbance in the temple, and would have been executed without a trial. In his view, Jesus' symbolic destruction of the temple "simply actualized what he had already said in his teachings, effected in his healings, and realized in his mission of open commensality" (1994, 133). Commensality is Crossan's term for Jesus' use of table fellowship to break down society's vertical hierarchy and lateral separations. But while there was nothing new or surprising in Jesus' action, "the confined and tinderbox atmosphere of the Temple at Passover, especially under Pilate, was not the same as the atmosphere in the rural reaches of Galilee, even under Antipas, and the soldiers moved in immediately to arrest him" (133). Immediate arrest and execution, without the formalities of a trial, would be entirely consistent with the fact that brutal crowd control was Pilate's specialty. That he would release *any* prisoner during the Passover festival is also "against any administrative wisdom" (141). A decent governor could postpone an execution until after the festival, or allow burial of the crucified by his family—but there is no evidence to suggest that Pilate was anything but a ruthless governor who acted first and asked questions later. Thus, the narrative in Mark 15:6–15 about Pilate throwing the matter up to a clamorous crowd is "absolutely unhistorical, a creation most likely of Mark himself" (141). The very idea of Pilate "meekly acquiescing" to a crowd stirred up by the chief priests would itself be utterly contrary to his brutal crowd control, which was his reason for arresting and executing Jesus in the first place.

Assuming that the followers of Jesus dispersed after his arrest and went into hiding, Crossan is also very suspicious of the Gospel accounts of Jesus' trial, death (including what he allegedly said from the cross), and burial. If none of them were there, "How did Jesus' first followers know so much about his death and burial? How did they know those almost hour-by-hour details given in fairly close and remarkable agreement by all four New Testament Gospels and by the Gospel of Peter outside the New Testament?" (1994, 143). What we have in these accounts is not "*history remembered*" but "*prophecy historicized*" (Crossan, 1994, 145, his emphases). Crossan concludes:

> My best historical reconstruction of what actually happened is that Jesus was arrested during the Passover festival and those closest to him fled for their own safety. I do not presume at all any high-level consultations between Caiaphus or Pilate about or with Jesus. They would no doubt have agreed before such a festival that fast and immediate action was to be taken against any disturbance and that some examples by crucifixion might be especially useful at the start. [Furthermore,] I doubt very much if Jewish police and Roman soldiery needed to go too far up the chain of command in handling a Galilean peasant like Jesus. (152)

It is we who have trouble bringing our imagination down low enough "to see the casual brutality with which he was probably taken and executed" (152).

If one accepts this view of what happened, a host of questions follows, such as whether Jesus was aware that his action would provoke his arrest and summary execution without trial—and if so, what would be his motivation for arranging his almost certain death? In *The Historical Jesus*, Crossan says he doubts "that poor Galilean peasants went up and down regularly to the Temple feasts. I think it quite possible that Jesus went to Jerusalem only once and that the spiritual and economic egalitarianism he preached in Galilee exploded in indignation at the Temple as the seat and symbol of all that was nonegalitarian, patronal, and even oppressive on both the religious and the political level" (1991, 360). In *Jesus: A Revolutionary Biography* (1994), he notes, "What would happen to Jesus was probably as predictable as what had happened already to John. Some form of religiopolitical execution could surely have been expected," and his symbolic destruction of the Temple, in the volatile atmosphere of Passover, "would have been quite enough to entail crucifixion by religio-political agreement" (196).

These statements suggest that Jesus knew he was likely to die a violent death, that he had always lived with the possibility of arrest, and that his actions in the Temple may have been prompted by some combination of a longstanding hatred of what the Temple stood for and an unpremeditated emotional reaction when he actually set foot on the Temple grounds. If this is a reasonably accurate summary of Crossan's views, derived from two different sources, it leads to the conclusion that Jesus probably did not miscalculate. Even if he did, the miscalculation would not have been that he thought he could get arrested and then be acquitted, thus winning the power struggle with the establishment, but rather that he had not calculated upon the likelihood that his action in the Temple would lead to his immediate arrest. In this case, the miscalculation would have been due to his having gotten away with similar provocative actions in Galilee without being arrested. Even this miscalculation, however, would not be very likely. As Pilate governed from 26 to 36 C.E., and Josephus recounts episodes in which his soldiers acted brutally at his request well before Jesus' execution, we may assume that Jesus would not have been surprised that his "explosion of indignation" at the Temple would provoke such brutality. If his disciples sought to dissuade him from going to Jerusalem in the first place, and apparently none participated in the action that resulted in his arrest, we may further assume that Jesus knew the risks involved and acted anyway.

While Crossan's reconstruction of the arrest and execution call into question Haley's view that Jesus made a fateful miscalculation, they do not undermine his portrayal of Jesus as a man who was oriented toward power and used it skillfully. In his discussion of Jesus' understanding of the Kingdom of God in *Jesus: A Revolutionary Biography*, Crossan admits there are problems with "the word *kingdom* as a translation of the Greek word *basilea*," but "what we are actually talking about . . . is *power and rule*, a process much more than a place, a way of life much more than a location on earth. . . . The focus of discussion is not on kings but on rulers, not on kingdom but on power, not on place but on process. The Kingdom of God is what the world would be if God were directly and immediately in charge" (1994, 55, my emphasis). If the kingdom of the heavenly Father is about power and process, not place, then Jesus' power tactics exemplified the way of life that Jesus both envisioned and actualized. After all, the Kingdom is about the empowerment of those who, by necessity or choice, are outside or alien to the religiopolitical establishment.

Sanders's Reconstruction

If Crossan believes that there was no trial before the execution of Jesus, there are many biblical scholars who disagree. In *The Historical Figure of Jesus* (1993), E. P. Sanders notes that it was the responsibility of the high priest to maintain good order in Judaea in general and in Jerusalem in particular. Since Caiaphus served longer than any other high priest during periods of direct Roman rule, this is evidence that he was very capable in this regard: "If the high priest did not preserve order, the Roman prefect would intervene militarily, and the situation might get out of hand" (265). But "as long as the Temple guards, acting as the high priest's police, carried out arrests, and as long as the high priest was involved in judging cases (though he could not execute anyone), there was relatively little possibility of a direct clash between Jews and Roman troops" (265).

Sanders cites an episode that occurred about thirty years after Jesus was executed in which another Jesus, the son of Ananias, went to the Temple during the Feast of Booths (Tabernacles) and proclaimed the destruction of Jerusalem and the sanctuary. This action led to his being interrogated and flogged, first by the Jewish authorities, then by the Romans. He answered questions by reiterating his dirge over the city, and was finally released as a maniac. Sanders uses this case to explain why Jesus was executed rather than merely flogged. To him, the offense of Jesus of Nazareth was much worse. He had a following, perhaps not very large, but a following nonetheless. He had taught about the Kingdom for some time. He had employed physical action in the Temple. He was not a madman. For these reasons, he was politically dangerous."Conceivably he could have talked his way out of execution had he promised to take his disciples, return to Galilee, and keep his mouth shut. He seems not to have tried" (1993, 267).

Sanders believes Caiaphus was primarily or exclusively concerned with the possibility that Jesus would incite a riot. He had Jesus arrested, gave him a hearing, and recommended execution to Pilate, who promptly complied. The blasphemy charge against Jesus was a smokescreen for the real issue, which was that "Jesus threatened the Temple and gave himself airs. The high priest had him arrested because of his action against the Temple, and that was the charge against him. The testimony was thrown out of court because the witnesses did not say the same things. The high priest, however, *had decided that Jesus had to die*, and so he was not willing to drop the case" (1993, 271, his emphasis). Whatever Jesus replied in response to the high priest's question as to whether he considered himself the Messiah would not have mattered. "We do not have to decide whether Jesus answered 'yes' or 'maybe.' The high priest had already made up his mind" (271).

Why did Pilate order Jesus' execution? Because the high priest had recommended it and had charged that Jesus thought he was the king of the Jews. It is doubtful that Pilate thought Jesus was a serious threat for he had no army, so he made no effort to track down and execute his followers. But he probably considered him a religious fanatic "whose fanaticism had become so extreme that it posed a threat to law and order" (Sanders, 1993, 273). In all probability, he received Caiaphus' charge, "had Jesus flogged and briefly interrogated, and, when the answers were not completely satisfactory, sent him to the cross without a second thought" (Sanders, 274). That he put the matter to the clamoring crowd is more than doubtful; this story derives from the desire of the early Christians to get along with Rome and to depict Jews as their real opponents. That Pilate probably ordered the execution without a trial is supported by an appeal that his contemporary, Philo, wrote to the emperor Gaius (Caligula). Among other injustices, this appeal cited "the executions without trial constantly repeated, the ceaseless and supremely grievous cruelty" that marked Pilate's rule (274).

This version of the trial supports Haley's view that the most improbable of all the likely outcomes of Jesus' "audacious attack" on the Temple would be Pilate's decision to let the crowd decide. In the end, Haley nonetheless accepted the Gospel account while Sanders does not. But if Sanders is correct, then Haley's assumptions that the Sanhedrin would not violate its own laws (option 1) or, if it did, no Roman governor would execute Jesus without sufficient evidence (option 2) are simply incorrect; in which case option 3 (the crowd clamoring for his release) and option 4 (the crowd calling for his death) are irrelevant. Sanders's view that it didn't matter much what Jesus may have replied to the high priest also casts doubt on Haley's view that, by remaining silent, Jesus made it impossible for the Sanhedrin to convict him. Also, Sanders seems to entertain the possibility, however remote, that Jesus might have avoided execution had he been *more* forthcoming with Pilate, whereas Haley believes that his *refusal* to speak deprived Pilate of cause to execute him.

On the other hand, Sanders' reconstruction of the trial and execution supports Haley's conclusion that Jesus at last found himself in a situation where what happened was beyond his control. But his explanation for this is not that he "miscalculated the desperateness of his opposition," as Haley suggests, but that he knew his only realistic hope would be divine intervention. Thus, in Sanders's view, it is "highly probable that Jesus knew he was a marked man." Conceivably, he may have thought "that God would intervene before he was arrested and executed," but, "in any case he did not flee. He went to the Mount of Olives to pray and to wait—to wait for the reaction of the authorities and possibly the intervention of God" 1993, 264). The garden of Gethsemane prayer attributed to him (Mark 14:32–42; Matt. 26:36–46; Luke 22:40–46), although represented as private, is "perfectly reasonable," for it suggests that he not only prayed to be spared and hoped he would not die, but also resigned himself to the will of his Father (Sanders, 1993, 264). This would be thoroughly consistent with everything that he had taught regarding the absolute commitment of his organization, and members within it, to the heavenly Father.

Sanders also considers it "possible that, when Jesus drank his last cup of wine [at the Passover meal] and predicted that he would drink it again in the kingdom, he thought that the kingdom would arrive immediately" (1993, 274). If so, the cry attributed to him from the cross from Psalm 22:1, "My God, my God, why have you forsaken me" (Mark 15:34), may well have been "his own reminiscence of the psalm, not just a motif inserted by the early Christians" (Sanders, 1993, 274). In this case, he "may have died disappointed" (Sanders, 276). This conclusion, too, supports Haley's view that Jesus had at last found himself in a situation where what happened was beyond his control.

In short, whether Haley's views regarding the trial and execution of Jesus are credible depends, in part, on which biblical scholar is considered to have put forward the most compelling reconstruction of what Jesus did and what happened to him in Jerusalem. While Crossan and Sanders agree that it was the Temple disturbance that precipitated Jesus' arrest and that he intended his actions there as a "symbolic destruction" of the temple, not merely an objection to its business practices, they agree on little else. Still, their reconstructions suggest that, in acting as he did at the Temple grounds, Jesus had knowingly behaved in a manner that precluded his retaining control of the situation from that time forward. He had, quite self-consciously, placed his fate in the hands of his heavenly Father. If so, the saying attributed to him from the cross, "It is finished" (John 19:30), expresses what he may have thought or felt following his "audacious attack" on the Temple. As he had not built an organization of militia fighters, he must have been aware that this attack on the temple was the culminating act of his career as a prophet of Israel. After this action, nothing from then on would be the same.

Both Sanders and Crossan agree that it was not the size of Jesus' following that caused the authorities to consider him a political threat. Rather, it was the fear that he could incite a crowd to riot; but this is to view his threat from a purely sociopolitical perspective. Haley's analysis of Jesus' power tactics suggests a psychological element as well. If one accepts Sanders's view that Jesus was accorded some sort of audience before the high priest and members of his council, this would mean that for the first time in his life, Jesus was face-to-face with the highest religious authorities in Israel. He was no longer dealing with their proxies in Galilee. What happened in this face-to-face encounter is a matter of conjecture, but Haley's view that Jesus was especially skillful in "putting his critics in their places and never using defensive behavior" must have been impressed upon this group of men as well. As its direct targets, they would not have taken kindly to it. What they had that the religious authorities in Galilee did not was the power to recommend his execution to Pilate and thereby wash their hands of a man who threatened their authority.

Following the Synoptic Gospel accounts, Haley believes Jesus remained silent and noncommittal, his strategy being that he would say nothing to incriminate himself. However, it would be more consistent with his general portrait of Jesus to suggest that Jesus' demeanor before the high priest and members of his council was no different from his rhetorical tactics against his opponents and detractors in Galilee. Had Haley not been warned, perhaps by his reading of Schweitzer's *The Psychiatric Study of Jesus*, to avoid the Gospel of John, he might have made this very point. According to John, Jesus did *not* remain silent during the interrogation conducted by the high priest. In John's version, Jesus responded to the high priest's questions about his disciples and teaching: "I have spoken openly to the world; I have always taught in synagogues and in the Temple, where all the Jews come together. I have said nothing in secret. Why do you ask me? Ask those who heard what I said to them; they know what I said" (John 18:20–21). Whereupon one of the police standing nearby struck Jesus on the face, saying, "Is that how you answer the high priest?" to which Jesus responded, "If I have spoken wrongly, testify to the wrong. But if I have spoken rightly, why do you strike me?" (22–23).

Thus, in John's version, Jesus did not alter his usual tactics at all. To be sure, he did not respond directly to the questions put to him, but his "non-response" was not one of silence. Rather, he told the high priest that he should not rely on the testimony of the accused, but on that of eyewitnesses (of whom there were many), as he had acted publicly, not conspired in secrecy. This response, of course, was viewed as one of insolence and a lack of deference toward the high priest. If Sanders speculates on what Jesus *could* have said to "talk his way out of execution," a more intriguing question, in my view, is what he may *actually* have said to talk his way *into* it.

In any event, if Haley had been less impressed by Lorenz's analogy of the wolf whose acceptance of defeat incapacitates his more powerful opponent, together with its parallel in Josephus' account of the mob of protesters, and had instead applied to Jesus' final days in Jerusalem his earlier account of the alcoholic who says to the bartender, "If you want me out of here, throw me out" (1986, 38), he might not have claimed that Jesus miscalculated and did so on account of his alleged tendency to act precipitously. In fact, the story of the alcoholic would have enabled him to claim that Jesus *was* in fact "the one who determined what was to happen" *through to the very end.* This conclusion, which makes the most sense to me on the basis of Haley's own contention that Jesus was a master tactician, casts doubt on Sanders's view that Jesus expected his heavenly Father to intervene at the last minute, and underscores Haley's related observation that it is even possible to determine what is going to happen from beyond the grave, as events have borne out.

In the surrender tactic, one extends one's neck and allows the victor to make the final determination; that is, to dishonor himself by going for the jugular, or to dignify himself by allowing the vanquished to get up and walk away. In the parable of the alcoholic, one refuses to leave the premises when ordered to do so. The alcoholic declares, "I will not go peacefully. If you want me out of here, you will have to throw me out bodily." This is a very different power dynamic, and one that is congruent with the Temple disturbance, Jesus' last symbolic action. If Jesus told his disciples that he was sending them out among wolves, he must also have known that the surrender tactic can only work if there is honor among wolves, or that there exists a plausible threat of retaliation against the wolf who takes unfair advantage of the other wolf's act of surrender. Absent these assumptions, one must be wise as a serpent and harmless as a dove (Matt. 10:16). Because he exhibits both simultaneously, the alcoholic who has become a disruptive nuisance in another man's tavern "determines the outcome of the interchange" (Haley, 1986, 38). I assume that it is unnecessary to point out that, according to various Gospel accounts, Jesus, unlike John the Baptist, was no stranger to the local tavern scene.

Note

1. Note that Haley selects a text that has to do with the hierarchy in all organizations, and that this text assumes a similar hierarchy in the kingdom of heaven.

References

Capps, D. (2003). Beyond Schweitzer and the Psychiatrists: Jesus as Fictive Personality. *HTS Theological Studies 59*, 621–662.

Crossan, J. D. (1991). *The Historical Jesus*. San Francisco: HarperSanFrancisco.

Crossan, J. D. (1994). *Jesus: A Revolutionary Biography*. San Francisco: HarperSanFrancisco.

Erikson, E. H. (1969). *Gandhi's Truth: On the Origins of Militant Nonviolence*. New York: Norton.

Haley, J. (1986). The Power Tactics of Jesus Christ, *The Power Tactics of Jesus Christ and Other Essays* (2nd ed.). Rockville: Triangle, 19–53. (Original work published 1969)

Haley, J. (1989). *Problem-Solving Therapy* (2nd ed.). San Francisco: Jossey-Bass.

Hoffer, E. (1950). *The True Believer*. New York: Harper.

Josephus, F. (1987). *The Works of Josephus*, W. Whiston, trans. Peabody: Henrickson.

Miller, J. W. (1997). *Jesus at Thirty: A Psychological and Historical Portrait*. Minneapolis: Fortress.

Sanders, E. P. (1993). *The Historical Figure of Jesus*. London: Penguin.

Schweitzer, A. (1948). *The Psychiatric Study of Jesus: Exposition and Criticism*, C. R. Joy, trans. Boston: Beacon. (Original work published 1911)

Schweitzer, A. (1961). *The Quest of the Historical Jesus: A Critical Study of Its Progress from Reimarus to Wrede*, W. Montgomery, trans. New York: Macmillan.

CHAPTER 8

ERIK ERIKSON'S PSYCHOLOGICAL PORTRAIT OF JESUS: JESUS AS NUMINOUS PRESENCE

Donald Capps

In 1981, the psychoanalyst Erik H. Erikson expressed the view that central to Jesus' power to attract a following was the convergence of his numinal "presence" and the power of his words to reactivate others. In this chapter, I wish to focus on that work. I note Erikson's emphasis on the familial roots of the religious ideology of Jesus' day, and his view that Jesus transformed this ideology by presenting a worldview founded on childhood experience, representing the Kingdom of God as the affirmation of the radical potentials of childhood. I develop this interpretation by suggesting that Jesus himself replaces the human mother as the object of trust and the very model of reassurance, and I contend that the "numinousness" of his presence was due to the fact that he represented, in person and word, the return of the repressed; in this case, the role and image of the ancient prophet. I conclude that it was the activation of the prophetic paradigm that led to his death in Jerusalem.

Exposition

In "Beyond Schweitzer and the Psychiatrists: Jesus as Fictive Personality" (Capps, 2003), I noted that Albert Schweitzer's stinging critique of the psychiatric studies of Jesus published in the first decade of the twentieth century has cast a very long shadow, as it has discouraged the use of psychological theories and methods in historical Jesus studies. When such studies *have* appeared, they have received little attention, and their status in historical Jesus studies has been extremely marginal. Erikson's article, published when he was eighty years old, has received minimal scholarly attention.

While Erikson lived eleven years after the essay was published, it was his last significant writing. His original plan was to write a book on Jesus, a project he took up after giving up an attempt to write a book on Sören Kierkegaard. According to his biographer, Lawrence Friedman, his decision to abandon the Kierkegaard project was due to his inability to read Danish and lack of background in Danish history and culture. But he also "seemed to have difficulty relating to Kierkegaard's sense of religious commitment as absolutely binding and specific. Erikson liked the idea of religion, without being religious in any profound creedal sense. His disposition was too playful, and his interests were too broad and changing for that sort of commitment" (Friedman, 1999, 448). As he terminated the Kierkegaard project, he began to focus on "the topic of Jesus of Galilee." It may seem odd that Erikson would find it difficult to relate to Kierkegaard's sense of religious commitment but not have the same difficulty with Jesus, who certainly had a sense of religious commitment no less "binding and specific." But he related to something else in Jesus that was less evident in Kierkegaard. This was the "presence" of Jesus, a quality he had also observed in Gandhi. In the first chapter of *Gandhi's Truth*, he had noted that a day or two before he arrived in India to conduct a seminar on his life cycle theory, he swam in the Lake of Galilee and walked at night on the shores, where "even among militant and pragmatic Israelis, one can never forget Him who had the gift to speak to fishermen in a manner remembered through the ages. Now I sensed again what I had known as a youth, namely, the affinity of that Galilean and the skinny Indian leader enshrined in Delhi. *There is a word for what they seem to have had in common: presence—as pervasive a presence as only silence has when you listen*" (Erikson, 1969, 20, my emphasis).

Friedman suggests that his confidence that he could write "a significant book about Jesus himself and his Galilean ministry" stemmed from the fact that he had recently focused on Thomas Jefferson's interest in Jesus for his own Jefferson lectures, *Dimensions of a New Identity*. "Erikson found the Virginian's inquiry [into the life and sayings of Jesus] captivating and fruitful" (Friedman, 1999, 448).

If Erikson was confident that he could write a significant book about Jesus, his son, Kai Erikson, a professor of sociology at Yale University, felt that his father might never complete the book. Having just become editor of the *Yale Review* in 1979, Kai encouraged him to pre-pare an essay on Jesus for the journal, as a finished article would be preferable to an incomplete book. Erikson was receptive to this idea, and he began to review old notes on Jesus and related subjects for the article, feeling as he did so that "he was working over a concern that had interested him since his *Wanderschaft* years, when he made a woodcut of Mary holding the Christ child in her arms" (Friedman, 1999, 449).

His "discovery" of Norman Perrin's *Rediscovering the Teaching of Jesus* was especially helpful to his own investigations. According to Friedman, Erikson "was aware that for centuries biblical scholars had tried to distinguish the actual words of Jesus from those composed by early Christians after the crucifixion. But he had not wanted to get involved in the vast literature on detecting the 'authentic' Jesus. Per-rin's [book] would do instead." He "accepted Perrin's proficiency" in discerning "what of Jesus' early sayings were probably 'authentic.'" He "did not probe for alternative perspectives. With Perrin's book guid-ing him through the sayings, he felt prepared to describe Jesus' essen-tial character at the origin of his Galilean ministry—the 'genuine presence of a singular man,'" as he expressed it in a letter to a friend in 1976 (Friedman, 1999, 449).

As Erikson set to work on the essay, it threatened to become a sort of "magnum opus," one that included a large number of historical fig-ures from Hitler to Luther to Gandhi to Jefferson, "plus an enormous number of ideas and comments on personal relationships. It was as if he was preparing an autobiographical work—a fully staged drama of characters and issues that had impressed him" (Friedman, 1999, 449). Two things are noteworthy about this larger manuscript. One is that it portrays "the essence of Jefferson's humanity in the process of studying, clipping, and pasting Jesus' sayings for a special Bible" (Friedman, 1999, 449–450). Another is that Erikson "discussed the personification or presence of the leader" and "the power of transform-ing language" (Friedman, 1999, 450). Together, these emphases sug-gested that an individual's own "sense of 'I'" may become clarified in the very act of engaging Jesus as "the Other." Thus, his theme was that the "presence" of Jesus could enable one to become "present" to oneself.

A much shortened version of the essay was published in the *Yale Review.* The editing was his son's work, and Erikson referred to it as "Kai's version." Still, "it remained very much Erik's paper and there was no getting around the fact that his writing capacity had substantially diminished. Even with Kai's editing, the final product remained very difficult to follow. It tended to lack clear focus and the phrasing was often quite imprecise" (Friedman, 1999, 451). If Erikson "had been able to maintain a clear, sustained focus on the sense of I, and to avoid diverse other topics only remotely related to his theme, his 'Galilean Sayings' article might have commanded more attention. But the response was minimal, even among theologians, and it was rarely cited." This, however, did not seem to trouble Erikson, "for he regarded it simply as a very preliminary piece," and he "intended to do more work" on it" (Friedman, 1999, 452). He envisioned a relatively short book, as he was aware that his powers of concentration were not what they had once been. But this, together with periodic visual problems, made the writing process very slow and difficult. His wife and friends brought him stacks of books and articles on Jesus to encourage him in his work, but he sat at his writing table, hoping "the thoughts and words would come" (Friedman, 1999, 454). As the months and then years passed, "he wrote fewer and fewer sentences on the notepads in front of him" (Friedman, 1999, 455). As his son Kai had suspected, his *Yale Review* article would be his final published word on the subject of Jesus.

In the following discussion of Erikson's essay on Jesus, I will summarize its contents, occasionally making references to other writings of his that help clarify observations about Jesus that may otherwise seem rather obscure. I will also employ headings that are not in the original essay, to provide markers to designate the path it follows. Since Erikson's own circuitous route in the essay replicates the manner in which Jesus appears to have moved about Galilee, this use of headings is a modest concession to Friedman's complaint that the essay is "very difficult to follow." After this summary of the essay, I will expand on Erikson's interpretation of the "presence" of Jesus in two ways. First, I will explore mother–son dynamics to which he alludes to make the case that Jesus functioned as the "reassuring mother" for his young male disciples. Second, I will augment Erikson's view of Jesus as a "numinous" presence with reference to Rudolf Otto's comments on Jesus in *The Idea of the Holy*, to Freud's view of the uncanny as the return of the repressed, and to Victor Turner's understanding of the role of the root-paradigm in social drama. These references will provide theoretical support for Erikson's intuitions about the numinous presence of Jesus and will offer a plausible explanation for why Jesus set his face toward Jerusalem, knowing that it would probably cost him his life.

The Galilean Focus of Erikson's Essay

Erikson's essay begins with reference to Thomas Jefferson's "very private preoccupation" with the Gospels, specifically his method of marking each passage "line for line" in terms of "whether or not it spoke to him with the true voice of Jesus." Erikson confesses that when he described Jefferson's search for the "authentic" Jesus in his 1973 Jefferson lectures, he "was not aware of (or not aware of the implications of) the fact that there had emerged in more recent times a whole school of theologians who had developed a method called 'form criticism' in order to discern with a certain methodological rigor which of the early sayings of Jesus could reasonably be considered 'authentic'" (Erikson, 1981, 321). In the meantime, he has familiarized himself with their writings. He cites the writings of Martin Dibelius, Rudolf Bultmann, and Joachim Jeremias, then notes that Norman Perrin's *Rediscovering the Teaching of Jesus* persuaded him "to review some of Jesus' sayings in the first, the Galilean, part of his ministry, when this unknown rabbi addressed the strangely 'mixed' populace of his native region." He wondered whether the fact of these sayings' authenticity might "throw some additional light on the singular and ever far-reaching *power of those words*" (Erikson, 1981, 322, my emphasis). Thus, he indicates that the "power" of Jesus' words will be the focus of his essay.

He admits that he finds the term "authentic" somewhat troubling if it is meant to convey "more than the probable historicity of some words," for it *could* seem to suggest that the Gospel writers' variations of these sayings are somehow "inauthentic." This would be unfortunate, for the Gospels "are a creative art form," one characterized by "a certain freedom of improvisation in reporting a sequence of lively and colorful episodes." Also, the Gospels review Jesus' "reported words" in the Galilean setting in light of the events that occurred "in the second part of his ministry—that is, in Judaea, in Jerusalem." Their purpose was obviously to provide "a testamental backbone for growing Christian communities in and way beyond Palestine—communities such as Jesus himself had never witnessed." All of this later development had "an authenticity of its own, in the form of a new tradition of ritualizations" that was "suited to the individual writers' revelatory idiosyncrasies, to the social trends of the day, and to the receptivity and concerns of readers at that historical moment." Such ritualization is sooner or later apt to lead to "some dead ritualizations," but at least in "its beginnings it all has its own historical 'authenticity.'" This point is important to Erikson because in his "own small way," he will be making use of some "psychoanalytic license" in reflecting on a few of Jesus' sayings and in pointing to "an inner logic" in them that makes them seem authentic to him as "a modern person and a psychoanalyst in the Judaeo-Christian orbit" (Erikson, 1981, 322). In other words, he will be doing for himself—and his contemporary reader—what the Gospel writers did for themselves and their readers. This, he wants to claim, is not an "inauthentic" enterprise.

He also makes clear that he will be confining his study to the *Galilean* sayings of Jesus, thus omitting from his review all sayings attributed to Jesus after his fateful decision to go down to Jerusalem. In a personal conversation with Erikson shortly after the publication of the essay, he emphasized to me that his personal background—growing up in a family headed by a ruling elder in the local synagogue—aided his study of the Galilean ministry of Jesus, but it left him rather unqualified to consider the second stage of Jesus' career, the Judean ministry and events that have been so central to Christianity. At the time he made this disclaimer, it occurred to me that this personal background would also have qualified him to discuss the events in Jerusalem that led up to the crucifixion, but perhaps he realized discussion of those events would place him in a difficult personal position.[1]

To make the case that Jesus' Galilean sayings possess an "inner logic" that "a modern person and a psychoanalyst" can recognize as authentic, Erikson felt he first needed to "locate Jesus and the Galilee of his time in the geography and history of Judaism." Following that, he would "coordinate" this historical pursuit with "a more contemporary search," one that concerns "a vital phenomenon that lies on the borderline of psychology and theology." This "phenomenon" is "the sense of 'I' which is the most obvious and most elusive endowment of creatures with consciousness—and language." Noting that this phenomenon has been treated by various psychologists, including Freud, he cites William James' view in *The Principles of Psychology* on the fact that one's "sense of 'I'" is present whenever one engages in thinking. "Whatever I may be thinking of, I am always at the same time more or less aware of *myself*, of my *personal existence*. At the same time it is I who am aware" (Erikson, 1981, 323). Thus, James proposes that "the total self" is "as it were, duplex," having two aspects, "partly known and partly knower." He calls the one "the me" and the other "the I."

Erikson is especially interested in James's concept of "the I," though he objects strongly to James's view that this "I" is essentially the "thinking" aspect of the self, for there are other ways in which we experience our awareness of the part of us that is to be known—the "Me." Moreover, language is a critical feature of the sense of "I," and this means that the "I" is "the ground for the simple assurance that each person is a center of awareness in a universe of communicable experience," thus affording the "I's" who share this universe a "sense of We." For two or more persons to merge their "I's" into a "We," they must share a common worldview—and such a worldview influences "not only the general outlook of all individuals in a given region but especially their readiness for a new revelatory voice" (Erikson, 1981, 323). Jesus was such a voice.

With this brief explanation of how the "I" is to be understood as a "center of awareness in a universe of communicable experience," Erikson returns to "biblical times," and suggests that two questions arise from this. One is its relevance to Moses' report that, when he asked God for his name, he received the response, "*I am that I am.*" The other is its relevance to the fact that Jesus is reported to have introduced his sayings with, "You have heard. . . . But I say unto you." In both statements, the speaker says "I" and means it. Because he does, the one (or ones) spoken to hear and respond. Thus, there is a connection between the "sense of 'I'" and the power of language (Erikson, 1981, 324).

Having established his emphasis on the "sense of 'I'" and the power of language, Erikson takes a step back, surveying the social panorama of Galilee itself. He notes that there were peaceful, sedentary populations in the Greek cities of Galilee and a countryside populated by Jewish landowners, a few of whom were wealthy. But most were "smallholders," some busy with family handicrafts such as carpentry and pottery, and others who employed hirelings or owned slaves. Then there was a haplessly migratory mass, often looking for work, and "movements of pious terrorists, waiting for their time, which always ended with a mass sacrifice of young lives." Then, again, "there were those who felt defeated in all national (and that meant, of course, religious and national) matters who leaned toward all kinds of messianic movements," and these especially were "a natural audience for Jesus' preaching" (Erikson, 1981, 325).

Having briefly set the social context for Jesus' ministry, Erikson next comments on the fact that Jesus was more than a teacher—he was also a healer. In fact, according to Matthew, "the sayings were of less interest to the crowds than were the cures and the miracles" (Erikson, 1981, 326–327). Responding to the preferences of the crowd, "Jesus seemed to feel driven by his compassion to heal as many as possible even where he also seemed to indicate that he regretted the excessive demand on his time for dramatic 'signs' of the Kingdom's arrival." Moreover, the sayings that accompanied his cures make abundantly clear that his "intention to heal his contemporaries" went "way beyond the mere undoing of the diseases or the misfortunes of some." Clearly, his sayings "were addressed to the malaise of faith which was then a national symptom reflecting the political (and in Judaism this was almost identical with the religious) conditions of that time" (Erikson, 1981, 327).

The stories of Jesus' healings against the backdrop of his concern to address this national symptom are reflective of the "episodic art form" of the Gospels that convey Jesus' "extensive capacity to address the wide variety of groups found in Galilee, and yet to be, potentially, in contact with each individual considered" (Erikson, 1981, 327). To underscore this point, Erikson introduces the story of the healing of the hemorrhaging woman (Mark 5:25–34; also Matt. 9:20–22; Luke 8:43–48), noting that it illustrates Jesus' "selective responsiveness to one person reaching out for him in a big crowd" (Erikson, 1981, 327–328). Erikson seems to imply here that the Gospel, as an "episodic art form," is ideally suited to portray Jesus as a person who drew large crowds, yet was deeply present to single individuals who, for one reason or another, stood out and drew Jesus' attention.

Following his identification of Jesus as a healer on the individual scale and a teacher of healing on the national scale, Erikson returns to the fact that his focus is the *Galilean* period of Jesus' ministry. While he had already provided justification for his emphasis on Galilee, which was the fact that Jesus' own "sense of 'I'" was profoundly connected to the Galilean "sense of We," he adds "an additional justification" derived from one of the very last words of the Passion narratives. Mark 14:28 reports that immediately after the last supper, Jesus and his disciples went out to the Mount of Olives, "where he added to all his sad predictions of the disciples' impending betrayal a most touchingly intimate remark; 'But after I am raised up I will go before you into Galilee.'" Erikson recognizes that Jesus' "reported reference to the resurrection may not be authentic; but this statement suggests on his part or among that of the witnesses what may well have been a feeling shared with them by the earthly Jesus, namely, that Galilee was home" (Erikson, 1981, 328).

The "I" and the "Others"

With these preliminary comments, Erikson asserts that he has "circumscribed" his "overall theme." But what, precisely, is this theme that he has circumscribed? "It is the relationship of Jesus' Galilean sayings to what we call the human sense of *I*, in general; and more specifically, what aspects of these sayings may have promised a pervasive healing quality for the historical and religious malaise of Jesus' time" (Erikson, 1981, 328). Accordingly, he embarks on a discussion of two of Jesus' sayings, and begins by noting that the "most direct reference to the human I" in the Bible is "in the form of an inner light, that is, of luminosity of awareness" (Erikson, 1981, 329). It occurs in Matthew 5:15 (with parallels in Mark 4:21 and Luke 11:33): "Nor do men light a lamp and put it under a bushel, but on a stand, and it gives light to all in the house" (RSV); and again in Matthew 6:22 (with a parallel in Luke 11:34–36): "The eye is the lamp of the body. So, if your eye is sound, your whole body will be full of light, but if your eye is not sound, your whole body will be full of darkness. If, then, the light in you is darkness, how great is the darkness" (RSV). In Luke, the analogy ends on a positive note: "If then your whole body is full of light, having no part dark, it will be wholly light, as when a lamp with its rays gives you light" (Luke 11:36).

These sayings are extremely important to Erikson, as they indicate that "our sense of *I* gives our sensory awareness a numinous center" (Erikson, 1981, 329). In other words, they allow Erikson to make word associations between "I" and "eye" and between "numinous" and "luminous." To underscore this association, he cites an essay by Jacques Lusseyran, who lost his eyesight in a childhood accident, who writes: "Barely ten days after the accident that blinded me, I made the basic discovery. . . . I could not see the light of the world anymore. Yet the light was still there. . . . I found it in *myself* and what a miracle!—it was intact." While endorsing Lusseyran's witness to "the inner light," Erikson issues a cautionary note: "This numinosity, however, seems lost when it is too eagerly concentrated on for its own sake, as if one light were asked to illuminate another." To Erikson, the inner numinosity/luminosity of one person is ultimately dependent on the existence or presence of an "other" who mirrors or reflects it. Thus, "writers who take the sense of *I* seriously will first of all ask what is the *I*'s counterplayer." This question prompts Erikson to comment on his own "developmental orientation," which follows the career of the "I" from its earliest to its latest stage of life. Thus, in each developmental stage, the "I" has one or more counterplayers—an "Other" or "Others," and these "Others" reflect a widening radius of social relations, culminating in the eighth or final stage in all "humankind." In the first stage, however, this "Other" is the maternal caretaker, "whom we shall call the Primal Other: and it seems of vital importance that this Other, and, indeed, related Others, in turn experience the new being as a *presence* that heightens *their* sense of *I*." This "interplay of *You* and *I* remains the model for a mutual recognition throughout life," culminating in the "expectation to which St. Paul gave the explicitly religious form of an ultimate meeting now only vaguely sensed beyond 'a glass darkly' (the Ultimate Other, then)" (Erikson, 1981, 330). Thus, as the developmental ground plan unfolds in stages, new counterplayers appear on the scene, and distinctions are made between "we" and "they," or "my kind" and "their kind"—a complex process of identification and repudiation.

The Fatherly Spirit in the Universe

Erikson next asserts that one important feature of this process for an essay on Jesus is "the necessity—especially in any patriarchal and monotheistic system—to transfer some of the earliest forms of a sense of *I* from their maternal origin to strongly paternal and eventually theistic relationships." Another is the fact that, "throughout all these critical stages with all their involvements, there remains for the *I* a certain existential solitariness which, in these pages, we depict seeking love, liberation, salvation" (Erikson, 1981, 331). In effect, Jesus stands at the very crossroads of these two realities—the patriarchal and monotheistic ideology that affords a collective sense of "We," and the need of "the original sense of I" to "gradually face another fundamental counterplayer, namely, *my Self*—almost an Inner Other" (Erikson, 1981, 330).

Erikson addresses the former reality first. After a brief discussion of the relatively greater self-governance of Galilee under the rulership of one of King Herod the Great's sons, as compared with Judaea, where the Roman governor was in greater control and allowed the Jewish people only "one symbol of central locus and inner autonomy, namely, the Temple" (Erikson, 1981, 335), he focuses on monotheism, "the religious heritage in Jesus' upbringing," and on the fact that it took a patriarchal form. The father–son dynamic is clearly central to this religious heritage. This is especially reflected in the fact that being chosen and being chastised for iniquity are two sides of the same coin. "Both messianic promises and apocalyptic threats become confirmations both of being chosen and of having actively, knowingly, chosen judgment as well as salvation." Thus, "man's evolutionary capacity for guilt becomes a pointed part of his sense of existence." Also, because "creation and procreation" become "one actuality," the "experience of the father in monotheism recapitulates the experience of the father in ontogeny" (Erikson, 1981, 337).

In making this link between the Father of monotheism and the human father who plans a vital role in procreation, Erikson assures his reader that he does not mean "to reduce such faith to its infantile roots." If he did, the "literal believer" could turn the tables, responding "that human childhood, besides being an evolutionary phenomenon, may well have been created so as to plant in the child at the proper time the potentiality for a comprehension of the Creator's existence, and a readiness for his revelations." If Erikson is unwilling to go this far, he *is* prepared to say that "the way the father can be experienced in childhood can make it almost impossible *not* to believe deep down in (and indeed to fear as well as to hope for) a fatherly spirit in the universe" (Erikson, 1981, 337). In this sense, the religious heritage in Jesus' own upbringing recognizes and validates the link between creation and procreation, and makes it nearly impossible for a man not to believe in a fatherly spirit in the universe who chastises the son whom he also loves. Conversely, this very heritage endorses the belief that the human procreator has the same right, indeed, the same obligation to chastise his son precisely because he loves him. As Proverbs 3:11–12 (cited in Heb. 11:5–6) expresses it, "My son, do not despise the Lord's discipline or be weary of his reproof, for the Lord reproves him whom he loves, as a father the son in whom he delights."

How are those whom the Father has chosen identified? Circumcision is the appointed sign of the covenant between father and son. The genitals, therefore, become the primary "physical and emotive" locus of the sense of "I" (Erikson, 1981, 338). However, in selecting the sayings in Matthew 5:15 and 6:22 to link Jesus' sayings and the sense of "I," Erikson has prepared the reader for the proposal that the "eye" is the primary physical and emotive locus of the sense of "I," and has therefore laid the groundwork for his view of Jesus as "a new authoritative voice."

The Son of Man

Erikson's emphasis on the father–son theme in the religious ideology of Jesus' day leads naturally into a brief discussion of the "son of man" passages in Daniel and their relevance to Jesus. While Daniel seems to view this "man-like figure" as emerging from a pack of beastly creatures, or as a human being sitting at God's right hand, of greater importance to Erikson is the fact that "son of man" is "an Aramaic way of simply saying I." Thus, while Messianic meanings were ascribed by others to "Jesus' reference to himself as the son of man," Erikson is more concerned with the fact that Jesus was a man who could say "I" and mean it (Erikson, 1981, 339). This contrasts with "a drunken person [who] says 'I' but his eyes belie it, and later he will not remember what he said with drugged conviction" (Erikson, 1968, 218). Erikson's intention is not to strip Jesus of all the titles projected onto him, for these creative projections had their own authenticity; but by the same token, these projections may obscure the fact that, in referring to himself as "Son of Man," Jesus was affirming that he, most assuredly, had a sense of "I," which "is nothing less than the verbal assurance according to which I feel that I am the center of awareness in a universe in which I have a coherent identity, and that I am in possession of my wits and able to say what I see and think" (Erikson, 1968, 220). Another verbal construction—"You have heard it said . . . But I say unto you"—is powerful evidence that Jesus had this "verbal assurance." Thus, to a social class of "nuisances and nobodies" (John Dominic Crossan's colorful phrase, [Crossan, 1994, 54]), Jesus' ability to claim his own sense of "I," to say what he sees and thinks, was astonishing. As Matthew 7:28–29 reports, "Now when Jesus had finished saying these things, the crowds were astounded at his teaching, for he taught them as one having authority, and not as their scribes."

If Jesus used the phrase "Son of Man" self-referentially, he also, in Erikson's view, encouraged his listeners and followers to make a similar claim for themselves. That is, they too may claim the same verbal assurance expressed in, "It has been said . . . but I say. . . ." They need no longer mouth the outworn "truths" passed down to them by previous generations, or think as their oppressors expect them to think. Rather, they are capable of looking around themselves, making accurate assessments of what they see, and reporting what they see to others. In a word, each and every person is a "center of awareness," a living presence.

But on what basis are these self-claims expressed? Is this merely an act of self-assertion? Erikson's view that from the very beginning of life one's "sense of 'I'" is dependent on a counterplayer—an interplay of *You* and *I*—precludes any such self-grandiosity. His portrayal of the deity as the ultimate bestower of this "subjective halo" onto a mortal (1968, 220) is Jesus' answer too.[2] According to Matthew's Gospel, the critical experience for Jesus in this regard was his baptism, when "he saw the Spirit of God descending like a dove and alighting on him. And a voice from heaven said, 'This is my Son, the Beloved, with whom I am well pleased'" (Matt. 3:16–17). This, too, however, marks a shift in the ritualization of the dominant ideology from the covenant of circumcision to the baptismal covenant.

The Mother Goddess of the Hearth

Erikson introduces the third section of his essay with "a few words on the dangers that can befall yearly and daily ritualizations of such an overwhelming belief in a tough, a central, a cosmic power's benevolence"—that is, in a God who chastises his chosen ones and whose chastisements are a sure sign of his love for them. The primary danger is that adherents of this ideology will develop a social phenomenon "which corresponds to compulsivity in the individual: I call it 'ritualism'" (Erikson, 1981, 339). In *Toys and Reasons: Stages in the Ritualization of Experience*, Erikson noted that adaptive ritualizations have a tendency to degenerate into "ritualisms," and he suggested that the ritualism that stands against the truly confirmatory rituals of the adolescent era is "totalism"—that is, "a fanatic and exclusive preoccupation with what seems unquestionably ideal within a tight system of ideas" (Erikson, 1977). Another danger is "elitism," or "a kind of shared narcissism" that occurs in groups that make a point of their exclusivism (Erikson, 1977, 110). Thus, if the religious establishment of Jesus' day offered a ritualism based on elitism, and the Zealots, "movements of pious terrorists," offered a ritualism of totalism, Jesus sought to offer something different. Erikson identifies this third alternative as the "solidarity of conviction" that stands against the ritualisms of "totalism" and "elitism" (Erikson, 1977, 107).

Ritualisms, however, were a particular danger under the sociopolitical conditions of Jesus' time. The Jewish populace was experiencing "the loss of national power and of cultural consistency under the impact of hellenization. Under such conditions, then, creative enrichment through live rituals can give place to a superconscientious preoccupation with ritualistic details dominated by a compulsive scrupulosity apt to deaden the renewal and rejuvenation which is the essence of an inventive ritual life" (Erikson, 1981, 339). Contributing to this preoccupation with ritualistic details was the fact that "much of the creative life of a great nation had in Judaism been totally absorbed by the religious system: consider only the fact that Jehovah's very sanctified presence, and with it all ritual themes, were soon to be forbidden subjects for representative art, and this at a time when the arts of other nations flowered exactly in their images of the divine" (Erikson, 1981, 339–340). Musical performance and poetic as well as fictional literature were restricted to religious subjects. Little wonder,

then, that the ritualization of daily and yearly life "was mainly concerned with the confirmation of the word as contained in the scriptures and a scrupulous search for their correct interpretation" (Erikson, 1981, 340).

Erikson grants that the great yearly holidays celebrated at the
Temple in Jerusalem may have been occasions of "ritual self-transcen-
dence and of national renewal," but the more familial services in the
synagogues spread over the countryside had turned to "textual preoccupation with the wording of the scriptures," and the daily and weekly
prayers were occasions for "demonstrating one's righteousness" and
little more. To be sure, Galilee in Jesus' time was certainly not unique
in this regard, for "all of these concerns with strictness in ritual life
are, of course, a potential found in all institutions that have outlived
the ideological conditions of their origins" (Erikson, 1981, 340). But
Galilee was ripe for a new voice who spoke with authority and whose
very words had the power to bless and make whole.

If the religious system took a decisive turn toward ritualism, Erikson suggests that there was a countervailing factor in the "ritualization of everyday life." This was Jewish family life. He cites Joseph
Klausner's *Jesus of Nazareth*, published in 1922, which discusses
Jewish daily life. Yet not even Klausner "mentions a 'phenomenon' in
Jewish daily life which both confirmed and compensated for the credal
emphasis on a dominating masculinity of Being." This "phenomenon"
is "the *Jewish mother*" (his emphasis), who, "in daily and weekly life, in
Palestine and throughout the Diaspora, continued to play the role of
a most down-to-earth goddess of the hearth" (Erikson, 1981, 340). A
thoroughgoing analysis of her role in this regard would require "an
intimate cultural history" which Erikson is not prepared to undertake. In the context that concerns him in the essay, however, "the
specific nature of motherhood is really mandatory for any balanced
historical account, for the very basis of any sense of *I* originates in the
infant's first interplay with that primal, that maternal *Other*, and
certainly continues to be nourished by persistent contact with her"
(Erikson, 1981, 341).

Erikson makes no further comments about "the specific nature of
motherhood" in the first half of the first century in Galilee. After all,
the central ideology of the times was patriarchal, and the primary relationship within that ideology was that of fathers and sons. He does,
however, comment later on her absence in the parable of the prodigal
son, and then, near the very end of the essay, refers to the role of Mary
in the development of the early church.

The Galilean Sayings and the Early Stages of Life

With the exception of his references to Jesus' sayings about the eye being the light of the body, the first half of Erikson's essay does not address the Galilean sayings themselves. Now, at the midway point in the essay, he begins to focus on the sayings. He indicates his intention to rely on the methods of the form critics (specifically, their emphasis on Mark and the Q source in Matthew and Luke, and on the criterion of dissimilarity, that is, that a saying may be deemed authentic if it is dissimilar to the views of the early Church or ancient Judaism). The sayings that survive the test "are of immense simplicity, especially if seen against the background of the spatial and temporal sweep of the world imagery of the preceding Judaic religiosity *and* of the gospels to follow" (Erikson, 1981, 341–342). While such simplicity "is of their essence," the "specific art form" of the Gospels permits us "at least to imagine these simple sayings as spoken within the context of a most vivid encounter" (Erikson, 1981, 342). While Erikson does not make this connection explicit, the sayings he selects for discussion and the order in which he considers them correspond to the first three stages of his life cycle model: the infancy stage of basic trust versus basic mistrust (with its virtue of *hope*); the early childhood stage of autonomy versus shame and doubt (with its virtue of *will*); and the play stage of initiative versus guilt (with its virtue of *purpose*). These three stages comprise the period from birth to about age five.

To illustrate his point that the sayings are represented by the Gospel writers as having occurred in the context of a vivid interpersonal encounter, Erikson refers to the healing of the hemorrhaging woman (Mark 8: 25–34; also Matt. 9: 20–22; Luke 8: 43–48), and to Jesus' saying to her, "Your faith has healed you." He also cites the King James version—"My daughter, thy faith hath made thee whole"—noting that it especially "underlines the loving as well as holistic character of all healing." In saying this to her, Jesus "acknowledges the woman's aptitude for trust and her determination to reach out to him as an essential counterpart to his capacity to help her" (Erikson, 1981, 342). He cites other examples in which Jesus emphasizes the role of faith in the healing process (Mark 2:1–12, the four friends who brought the paralyzed man to Jesus; and Mark 10:46–52, where Jesus induced the blind beggar to come to *him*). For Erikson, these citations support Norman Perrin's claim that, whether the healing narratives themselves are authentic, "the emphasis upon the faith of the patient, or his friends, in that tradition is authentic" (Erikson, 1981, 343).

Perrin's claim is largely based on the argument that faith is never demanded in either the rabbinic tradition or in Hellenistic stories, thus, the criterion of dissimilarity. Of greater significance to Erikson, however, is the principle of *coherence*, which "connects a number of stories and suggests an authentic element in all of them even if this element could be more definitely specified in only one or the other. Such 'coherence' is, of course, most convincing if it illustrates what Bultmann conservatively called a new 'disposition of mind' " (Erikson, 1981, 343). Thus, Jesus' therapeutic formula—"Your faith has made you whole"—is only one of many sayings, "all cohering in a basic orientation" that emphasizes "the individual's vital core in the immediate present rather than in dependence on traditional promises and threats of a cosmic nature." This "vital core," of course, is "the sense of 'I,'" and Jesus' emphasis on "faith" identifies one of "the most essential dimensions of a sense of *I*"—namely, the ability "to be active," or at least "not to feel inactivated (or peripheral or fragmented)." Therefore, Jesus' "emphasis on the patient's propensity for an active faith" was not only a therapeutic "technique" applied to incapacitated individuals but also "an ethical message" for the bystanders as part of a population that was weakened in its sense of mastery of its collective fate or unsure of a faith that could promise such mastery (Erikson, 1981, 344).

   To explicate this "active faith" further, Erikson returns to Jesus' saying about the eye being the lamp of the body, noting that the "active faith" that Jesus recognized and evoked has "a numinous sense of aliveness" about it. He connects this to Freud's comment that, while our conscious awareness is not always trustworthy, we would "be lost in the obscurity of depth-psychology" without "the illumination thrown by the quality of consciousness." The German word that the translator has rendered "illumination" is "die Leuchte," which is a word that denotes "luminosity." Such "luminosity" may be understood in both of the two senses of Jesus' saying—that is, as "Leuchter" or lamp, and as "Leuchte" or luminous quality, a shining light. Thus, Freud's "das Ich," which is invariably translated "ego," has a much more profound meaning when we consider its reference to the conscious "I" that exists "on the periphery of the ego" (Erikson, 1981, 344–345). Therefore, Freud's comment about the "luminosity" of consciousness is not far "from the psalmist's acknowledgment of a light given by the creator to the apple of the eye" (Erikson, 1981, 345).

   Erikson's fundamental point here is that there is a profound association between the "active faith" that Jesus viewed as the means of being made whole, his saying about the eye being the lamp of the body, and that quality of consciousness that Erikson (and Freud) have termed "the I." When Jesus declared to others that *their* "faith" had made them whole, he was saying, in effect, that they had exhibited the kind of "self-awareness" or "self-consciousness" that derives from a sense of "I" that is attuned to the immediate present rather than being dependent on traditional promises and threats. In other words, Jesus represents the power of the immediate present, and his sayings therefore address the existential solitariness of the I who seeks love, liberation, salvation.

The next saying that Erikson introduces is Mark 7:15: "There is nothing outside a person that by going in can defile, but the things that come out are what defile." According to Mark, Jesus clarified what he meant by this by pointing out that "whatever goes into a person from outside cannot defile, since it enters, not the heart but the stomach, and goes out into the sewer" (Mark 7:18–20). Given his interest in the "coherence" or "inner logic" of the sayings, Erikson links this saying to the one in Matthew 6:23 (and Luke 11:34) that, when your eye is unhealthy, your whole body will be full of darkness. He also relates it to Freud's concept of the id, that "inner cauldron of drives and passions," reflected in the ensuing list of thirteen evils in Mark 7:21–22 and seven evils in Matthew 15:19. These lists, while unlikely to be authentic, nonetheless specify the kinds of behaviors that occur when individuals are lacking in self-governance—true autonomy—because in each case, they are reacting against their impotence or the overcontrol of others.

Thus, this saying relates to the second stage of "autonomy versus shame and doubt," which involves the acquisition of a capacity for "self-control without loss of self-esteem" undergirding a "lasting sense of autonomy and pride." This self-control ensures the survival and expansion of the trust—in self and others—that is crucial to an "active faith" (Erikson, 1959, 68). Without it, one is condemned to a life of impotence and victimization. Thus, for Erikson, autonomy is not achieving separation and freedom from interpersonal entailments, as some of his interpreters have suggested (cf. Gilligan, 1982, 12), but the capacity for self-governance.[3]

Moreover, when Jesus associates the "inner cauldron of drives and passions" (Freud's "id") with the "heart," he points "to an *inner* seat of passionate conflict from which emerges the multiple temptations by which the sense of *I* is ruefully inactivated and which it therefore can experience as an inner chaos." If these drives and passions are to be manageable, subject to self-governance, this can only occur through "that radical awareness which Jesus here demands" (Erikson, 1981, 346). The traditional "ritualisms," those "phobic avoidances" and "compulsive purifications" that were designed for this, are ineffective. The point of this saying, therefore, is that a judicious exercise of will requires the self-awareness that comes from having a "sense of 'I,'" and not from a system of "phobic avoidances" and "compulsive purifications."

Next, Erikson introduces a saying in which Jesus associates his exorcisms with the arrival of the Kingdom of God: "But if it is by the finger of God that I cast out demons, then the kingdom of God has come upon you" (Luke 11:20). Matthew 12:38 speaks of the "spirit" rather than the "finger" of God, but Erikson likes the physicality of the finger "because it continues the theme of touch which was so prominent in the episode with the [hemorrhaging] woman; except that here, of course, it is the finger of God which is operative through Jesus' actions" rather than the activating touch of the woman herself. As for the Kingdom of God itself, Jesus' various sayings about the Kingdom imply "some play with time," which contrasts with "those grand prophetic predictions of the Kingdom as some final act in history such as decisive redemption" (Erikson, 1981, 347). This vagueness about their temporal boundaries raises the question of its spatial location as well. Where is it? He cites Luke 17:21—"Behold, the kingdom of God is in the midst of you" (RSV)—and notes that this can mean "among you" (as the NRSV prefers) as well as "within you" (as the KJV suggests). He also notes the parallel in Thomas 3: "The kingdom is inside of you, and it is outside of you." Then he cites Luke 17:20: "The kingdom of God is not coming with signs to be observed." This may seem to contradict the saying where Jesus refers to his own observable act of healing, but to Erikson, Luther appears to be on the right track in translating this saying to mean that the Kingdom "does not come with extraneous gestures."

These Kingdom sayings, which in Perrin's view have "high claims on authenticity," "make it clear that Jesus speaks of the Kingdom as an experience of inner as well as interpersonal actualization open to every individual who accepts his mediation." Moreover, if the God to whom this Kingdom "belongs" is "a god whose very being is action, such initiative, it seems, is now certified as a property of human existence—if through Jesus' mediation. For to be the voice announcing such an actuality as a potential in the here and now of every individual—that, it seems, is the essence of Jesus' ministry" (Erikson, 1981, 347). The Kingdom, then, is no longer, if it ever was, "a static territory or a predictable time span," but "a dominion in motion, a Coming, a

Way—a fulfillment in the present which centers on anticipation of a future" (Erikson, 1981, 348).

Erikson's use of the word "initiative" to characterize the "very being" of God, and now, through Jesus' mediation, a property of human existence, implicitly links the Kingdom sayings to the third life stage—initiative versus guilt. This stage (the "play age") is one in which the developing child tests temporal and spatial boundaries. The ability "to *move around* more freely," and the development of a "sense of *language*" provides the necessary conditions for an enlargement of the child's *imagination*, and all three together enable the child to "emerge with a sense of *unbroken initiative* as a basis for a high and yet realistic sense of ambition and independence." The child has been able to walk before this, but only "more or less well" and for "short spans of time." Now, in the third stage, walking and running are among the items in the child's "sphere of mastery," because "gravity is felt to be within." It is now possible to forget the fact that one is walking and to concentrate instead on what one can do with it (Erikson, 1959, 75).

At the same time, "in consequence of vastly increased imagination and, as it were, the intoxication of increased locomotor powers," there emerge "secret fantasies of terrifying proportions." From these comes a "deep sense of *guilt*—a strange sense, for it forever seems to imply that the individual has committed crimes and deeds which, after all, were not only not committed but also would have been biologically quite impossible" (Erikson, 1959, 79). Such allusions to secret fantasies "may seem strange to readers who have only seen the sunnier side of childhood and have not recognized the potential powerhouse of destructive drives which can be aroused and temporarily buried at this stage, only to contribute later to the inner arsenal of a destructiveness so ready to be used when opportunity provokes it" (Erikson, 1959, 75). But by using words like "potential," "provoke," and "opportunity," he means to emphasize "that there is little in these inner developments which cannot be harnessed to constructive and peaceful initiative if only we learn to understand the conflicts and anxieties of childhood and the importance of childhood for mankind" (Erikson, 1959, 79).

As Erikson indicates in *Toys and Reasons*, the ritual element for this stage is the "dramatic element," for the play age offers the child a "micro-reality" in which toys can be used "in order to relive, correct, and re-create past experiences, and anticipate future roles and events with the spontaneity and repetitiveness which characterize all creature ritualization" (Erikson, 1977, 99–100). In adulthood, the "specialized institution" for the dramatic element is the *stage*: "Here, above all, human conflict is projected into a circumscribed space-time in such representative form and supreme condensation that players and audience can experience the catharsis of affects, both timeless and universal. Genuine drama, well played, can shake us to the bones: we know it is 'just a play,' but because of the dramatic condensation of time and space, we experience something of an intensified reality, unbearably personal and yet miraculously shared" (Erikson, 1977, 102).[4]

But the "dramatic" extends beyond the specialized institution of the theatre to the "play," as it were, of human history. Here, the "dramatic element" is reflected in "a peculiar and pervasive form of ritualism, namely, that of *impersonation*, of role-playing on the stage of reality and history in dead earnestness and, in fact, in matters of mortal danger to the self and others" (Erikson, 1977, 102). By this impersonation of a "stance," he does not mean "conscious histrionic behavior in the more gifted and amusing sense." Rather, he has in mind those idealized persons "who seem to personify ideal usurpations and utopias and who, in turn, have the power to sanction the initiatives of others" (Erikson, 1977, 103). Jesus, for example. In fact, these brief comments on "impersonation" have particular relevance to Jesus, and specifically to my previous discussions of him as a fictive personality (Capps, 2000, 2003). Because Erikson is concerned with the "public" Jesus, his comments on impersonation, or "role-playing on the stage of reality and history in dead earnestness," have special bearing on his concern to convey the kind of "presence" that Jesus manifested—one that not only represented Jesus himself as having attained "autonomy" (in the sense of *self*-governance), but also enabled others to do the same. Thus, the Kingdom sayings may be viewed as "utopian," not in the sense of a community set apart, but as announcing "an experience of inner as well as interpersonal actualization" as a potential in the here and now of every individual. This is a "utopia" that takes the form of "a dominion in motion," one recognizable not for the territory it controls but for its *initiative*, or the ability to think and act without being urged or coerced.

Erikson also uses the term "actuality" to express this "dominion in motion." This word harks back to a much earlier essay, "Psychological Reality and Historical Actuality," where he discussed Freud's distinction between "reality testing" and "actuality testing." *Reality* "is the world of phenomenal experience, perceived with a minimum of distortion and a maximum of customary validation as agreed upon in a given state of technology and culture," whereas *actuality* "is the world of participation, shared with other participants with a minimum of defensive maneuvering and a maximum of *mutual activation*" (my emphasis). The crucial factor here is "mutual activation," as it points to the fact that "human ego strength" depends "from stage to stage upon a network of mutual influences within which the person activates others even as he is activated, and within which the person is 'inspired with certain properties,' even as he so inspires others" (Erikson, 1964, 165). The absence of such activation is not passivity but *inactivation*, for "passivity can be an active adaptation, while only inactivation results in paralysis" (Erikson, 1964, 165–166). Thus, Jesus' Kingdom sayings are about an *actuality* that occurs within *reality*, one known by the fact that individuals activate others even as they themselves are activated. Recall that Erikson associated faith with the "activation" of another.[5]

The Wonder of Childhood

Having noted Jesus' sayings on the Kingdom, Erikson moves immediately into a consideration of his sayings on children and childhood. This reflects his own belief that Jesus, through his sayings and healings, presented a worldview that was founded on childhood experience. In effect, Jesus was turning on its head the usual view of human development as a progression from immaturity to maturity. This was especially evident in his sayings about children and childhood, sayings that Perrin included among "a special dozen which exhibit the radical and total character of the challenge of Jesus." Perrin cites Mark 10:14–16 as "*the* most memorable and most pregnant" of all of Jesus' sayings: "Let the children come to me; do not stop them; for it is to such as these that the Kingdom of God belongs. Truly I tell you, whoever does not receive the Kingdom of God as a little child will never enter it." Erikson adds that Matthew's version (Matt. 18:3)—"Unless you turn and become like children"—suggests "a turn like a positive 'metanoia'" (Erikson, 1981, 348).

For Erikson, the very suggestion that the Kingdom of God belongs to children "is a total affirmation of the radical potentials of childhood." This saying is all the more astonishing "in light of the fact that we consider ourselves to be the discoverers of childhood, its defenders against all those history-wide negative attitudes which permitted proud and righteous as well as thoughtless adults to treat children as essentially weak or bad and in dire need of being corrected by stringent methods, or as expendable even to the point of being killed." Yet we are also responsible for the "modern sentimentalization of childhood as an utterly innocent condition to be left pampered and unguided." In view of these trends, "Jesus' saying seems simply revolutionary." Still, its greatest importance lies in the fact that Jesus refers here "to an adult condition in which childlikeness has not been destroyed, and in which a potential return to childlike trust has not been forestalled." Thus, Jesus' primary point is not that children are also welcome in the Kingdom of God, but that the adult experiences the Kingdom of God by assuming the disposition and trust of a little child: "What is suggested, then, is a preservation and reenactment of the wonder of childhood: the 'innocent eye' and ear. Consider in this connection the series of sayings commending the 'seeing eyes' and 'hearing ears' which can comprehend the parables tacitly" (Erikson, 1981, 349).

Thus, what Jesus affirms here is the *continuity* of the sense of "I" from one stage of life to another, a continuity wherein "the adult must not feel that the child, or, indeed, his youth is behind him: on the contrary, only the continuation into maturity of true childlikeness guarantees his faith" (Erikson, 1981, 349). Noting that Perrin speaks of the child's "ready trust and instinctive obedience," Erikson indicates that he is ready to endorse the trust aspect, as in his own writings he has held "that the strength of infancy is trust." But as for "instinctive obedience," it must be emphasized that "the imposition of a merely compelling obedience, with disregard of the child's natural tendency to conform, can almost guarantee inner ambivalence leading either to rebellious negation or to that widespread compulsiveness of adjustment which then is apt to find an expression in personal scrupulosity and shared ritualisms—which Jesus preached against as dangerous to faith" (Erikson, 1981, 350).

If Jesus endorses an adult condition in which childlikeness has not been destroyed, and in which a potential return to childlike trust has not been forestalled, it makes sense to look to the behavior of children for insights into the attitudes and behaviors of adults. Thus, Erikson draws attention to Matthew 11:16–17, where Jesus asks: "But to what shall I compare this generation? It is like children sitting in the market places and calling to their playmates, 'We piped to you, and you did not dance; we wailed, and you did not mourn.'" Then, according to Matthew, Jesus related the children's complaint to the people's failure to respond to John, who came neither eating nor drinking because "he has a demon," and to himself, who came eating and drinking because he is "a glutton and drunkard, a friend of tax collectors and sinners." He counters these responses with the declaration that "wisdom is justified by her deeds" (Matt. 11:18–19).

In Erikson's view, Jesus here proclaims John's historical right to emphasize radical asceticism in his part of the story, while Jesus insists on the legitimacy of his own ritual use of a joyous table-fellowship in his. Thus, "he demonstrates the historical relativity of all forms of daily ritualization, emphasizing that no one has a right to compel others to dance to his piping, or, indeed, to make them compulsively mourn—provided, of course, that whatever rituals one does choose reflect one's function in the 'coming'" (Erikson, 1981, 351). Thus, Matthew's association of the children piping to their playmates with the people's reception of John and Jesus underscores Erikson's point that "the imposition of a merely compelling obedience" is dangerous to faith. But Jesus' comparison of the present generation to children calling to their playmates may also be viewed in terms of Erikson's earlier emphasis on "the world of participation, shared with other participants with a minimum of defensive maneuvering and a maximum of mutual activation" (Erikson, 1964, 165). The children who are calling out to their playmates are complaining that they have done their part, that they have piped and they have wailed, but the others have not done theirs. The others have neither danced nor mourned. So nothing happened, and this is worse than passivity, for "passivity can be an active adaptation, while only inactivation results in paralysis" (Erikson, 1964, 165–166). Paralysis was an affliction that Jesus cured, and his capacity to do so was largely dependent on the fact that his initiative and that of the afflicted were mutually activated. In other words, this saying in Matthew 11:16–17 points to the fact that Jesus sees the Kingdom of God—this "dominion in motion"—as a "world of participation, shared with other participants with a minimum of defensive maneuvering and a maximum of mutual activation."

The Healing of the Generational Process

In concluding his discussion of sayings about children, Erikson observes the tenderness toward children that these sayings convey. Especially in light of the patriarchal days in which Jesus lived, "one cannot help noting, on Jesus' part, an unobtrusive integration of maternal and paternal tenderness" (Erikson, 1981, 349). This joining of the maternal and paternal voices into one, singular voice is reflected in his direct appeal to God as "Abba," an Aramaic term "used only by very small children" (Erikson, 1981, 351–352). Erikson thus contends that Luke's version of the address in the Lord's Prayer—"Father"—is more authentic than Matthew's—"Our father who is in heaven"—because Matthew seems to consider the simple, unadorned word "Father" to be insufficient in its "intimate immediacy." Even more important, however, is the fact that "Abba" not only conveys a "radical diminution of a patriarchal threat" but also has "an implication of a maternal 'touch'" (Erikson, 1981, 352).

There is also the question of how Jesus portrays the Father's response to the appeals voiced in the Lord's Prayer. To explore this question, Erikson turns to the stories of the lost sheep (Luke 15:1–7) and the lost son (Luke 15:11–32). After quoting Luke's version of the former in full, he cites the Gospel of Thomas version, which notes that the lost sheep was the largest and that the shepherd spoke directly to the sheep after having "tired himself out" in searching for it: "I love thee more than ninety-nine" (Thom. 107). Erikson comments: "Here we see Thomas making sense out of the parable by appointing the lost sheep the largest of the hundred and therefore a logical object both of the shepherd's search and of his love" (Erikson, 1981, 353). But Erikson's own take on the story is rather different. Noting the danger to which the shepherd exposed the other sheep, he considers Joachim Jeremias's suggestion that the shepherd saw that the other sheep were safely in the fold before setting off in search of the lost one. He suspects that Jeremias may be working too hard to exonerate the shepherd, for Erikson's own "group psychological orientation makes me feel that there is *some* safety in mere numbers for *some* herd instinct." Nevertheless, "it is difficult not to wonder by what right God or Jesus may pay such exclusive attention to one nearly lost creature—unless, of course, it reminds us of ourselves" (Erikson, 1981, 353). In other words, it all depends on whether the hearer identifies with the ninety-nine who haven't gotten lost or with the one who has. And this leads Erikson to the parable of the prodigal son.

After quoting the parable in full, he first focuses on the two sons, noting that the two distinct parts of the parable make us "alternately sympathize" with both. Yet the parable is so evenly constructed that we can end up "realizing that both brothers are at odds within us too." Thus, the parable may be read as a reflection on our own inner tension. But what interests Erikson more is the behavior of the father as reflective of Jesus' understanding of "Abba." The RSV cites the boy's "distance" at the moment his father saw him, while the KJV makes him as yet "a great way off." The latter suggests "that the father had begun to look out for him and that the immediate welcome he arranged had long been planned," even down to its specific details. Erikson suggests that even lengthy parables can be summarized in a brief saying, and that the last dozen words of this one will do: "Your brother was dead, and is alive; he was lost, and is found" (Luke 15:32). This saying attests to the fact that the Kingdom is both "within" and "among you." The "within" applies to the reconciliation of the two warring selves (the internalized brothers), and thus to the inner wholeness, the singleness of vision and action of the "I," no longer burdened by ambivalence and defensive maneuvering. The "among" applies to interpersonal restoration, the latter realized by means of the fact that "the Abba was steadfast in loving both these sons—so different in familial status and personality." So steadfast, in fact, that some readers may be tempted to say that he acted "almost like a mother" (Erikson, 1981, 355).

That the father behaves almost like a mother raises, for Erikson, a critical issue: If the "parabolic theme" is "the healing of the generational process" itself, then we cannot help but ask, "Was there, in this earthly vision of the comparison, no mother, either dead or alive? And if alive, was she not called to say hello, too?" But having raised the question, Erikson backs off, noting that "a parable is not a case history," as though it reveals something about the storyteller's relationship to his own mother (Erikson, 1981, 355). Also, as for any comparison we might want to draw between the father in the parable and God the Father, Erikson cautions that "in all the masculinity dictated by the patriarchal 'system' and the rules of language, the dominating quality of the deity was that of a pervasive spirit, out of bounds for any personal characterization: 'I am that I am'" (Erikson, 1981, 355–356). In other words, while Jesus appears to draw a comparison between God and the human father in the parable, he would not have thought to "reduce" the deity, notwithstanding the fact that he called him "Father," to this or any other personal or familiar characterization. The central theme of the story is that father and son mutually activated one another, thus demonstrating the Kingdom of God as "dominion in motion."

The parable's meaning, then, in its patriarchal and monotheistic setting, "is the father's *parental* care and above all his forgiveness which permits him to take special chances with the lost ones—that is, to take chances with those who took chances—so as to let them find both themselves and him." Thus, the story "reaffirms generational and existential continuity," and this means that the father and the sons "can find themselves and one another only by gaining their own identity in the very fulfillment of their intergenerational tasks within their cultural and economic matrix (is *that* the missing mother?)" (Erikson, 1981, 356). This parenthetical query harks back to Erikson's *Young Man Luther*, in which he suggested that Luther's use of the word "matrix" in reference to the Scriptures was as close as Luther could come to saying that in the Bible he "at last found a mother whom he could acknowledge" (Erikson, 1958, 208; also 264). But as with his caution against limiting the active spirit of the deity to the actions of the father in the parable, Erikson views the cultural and economic "matrix" as subordinate to the parable's concern with the "intergenerational tasks" themselves. These intergenerational matters are what the storyteller himself especially cares about, what he gives heed and attention to, and what worries and troubles him (Erikson, 1981, 356). Thus, we should not get distracted by the fact that the father behaves almost like the mother, or the fact that the mother appears to be missing. Instead, we should focus on the story's account of the healing of the intergenerational process itself, as this is represented in the mutual activation of the bereft father and the lost son.

The story also reveals the storyteller's own peculiar way of caring for and about these intergenerational tasks. Aware that the father had reason and cause to disown his errant son, Jesus, the storyteller, presents a father who longs for his son's return, and when the son does so, the father explains his own actions to his other son in the simplest, matter-of-fact terms, "Your brother was dead, and is alive; he was lost, and is found." Here, "a pervasive peculiarity of Jesus' care" comes through. This is "his essential nonviolence, and this in spite of an occasional militancy which, in fact, is a necessary trait for the nonviolent" (Erikson, 1981, 356). Erikson adds, "As he seems to advocate a maximum of work and a minimum of 'works,' so [Jesus] demands a maximum of strength but a minimum of violence—whether against the self in the form of debilitating guilt or against others as hatefulness" (Erikson, 1981, 356–357).

The Naturalness of Nonviolence

Having drawn this conclusion from his consideration of Jesus' parable of the lost son, Erikson ends his discussion of Jesus' sayings with Matthew 5:39–41: "But if anyone strikes you on the right cheek, turn to him the other also; and if anyone would sue you and take your coat, let him have your cloak as well; and if anyone forces you to go one mile, go with him two miles." Perrin, who "is somewhat perplexed" by these sayings, concludes that they are meant to be "vivid examples" that "exceed normal and natural" human tendencies to "imitate the reality of God." But Erikson says that here he must disagree with the biblical expert on the basis of his study of "the nonviolent tactics" of one of Jesus' modern followers, Mahatma Gandhi. He agrees that nonviolent tactics need to be shocking to shake up the violent opponent's seemingly so normal attitude and "to make him feel that his apparently undebatable and spotless advantage in aggressive initiative is being taken away from him and that he is being forced to overdo his own action absurdly." But this is precisely the point, for it is human violence that "almost never feels all that 'natural,' even to the aggressor himself—neither the violence against children nor that against loved persons nor even that evoked by declared enemies" (Erikson, 1981, 357). When one acts violently against others, he seeks to maintain his self-esteem by turning the violence of his superego (that "self-negating part of the human conscience developed in childhood") against an evil in others that he wants to deny in himself. In short, it is *nonviolence* that is both normal and natural, and it is *violence* that exceeds normal and natural human tendencies.

Erikson concludes, therefore, that were he to have gone beyond "the Galilean Sayings" to explore "The Judean Passion," he would have focused on Jesus' decision to "confront militantly but nonviolently the violence latent in the political and spiritual deals between the Roman and the priestly establishments by which mortally endangered Israel had learned to live." For, in so doing, Jesus went beyond the father in the parable of the lost son in that he "took chances not just with the lost ones but also with those who act out so strenuously the roles they find appropriate for their superior identity." What followed from this decision was "the crucifixion and the reported resurrection of him who thus became Christ and whose course of life was thus creatively mythologized—from the nativity to the ascension" (Erikson, 1981, 358). And, from that point on, the "mother churches of Christianity developed another kind of authenticity, best illustrated by the then emerging victorious symbolisms—such as that of the cross, which seems to combine the form of homo erectus with his arms all-inclusively extended and that of the son of man dying a deliberately human death under the most vulnerable conditions, only to be resurrected as the savior" and that of "the maternal Madonna who gradually occupied such a shining ceremonial center" (Erikson, 1981, 358–359).

Yet, however important these victorious symbolisms may be, Erikson insists that "the Galilean sayings must count as an event central to our Judaeo-Christian heritage—a step in human comprehension and self-awareness which is by no means fully expressed in, or restricted to, its ecclesiastic fate" (Erikson, 1981, 362). Given that Christianity itself "could not escape manufacturing its own kind of compulsive ritualism," we need to be "even more attentive to the study of the origins and eventual evolution of those simplest revelatory formulations. For their very brevity and simplicity of manifest meaning could never be contrived, and could emerge only when their time had come" (Erikson, 1981, 359).

Thus, in the final analysis, what stands out for Erikson is that the sayings relating to children play a central role in these simple revelatory formulations. This suggests a profound affinity between Jesus' "elemental sayings" and Freud's "psychoanalytic procedure" of "opening up the forgotten recesses of childhood" (Erikson, 1981, 361). If Jesus spoke of "an adult condition in which childlikeness has not been destroyed, and in which a potential return to childlike trust has not been forestalled," Freud offered a *procedure* (psychoanalysis) for making such a "condition" possible. This is a difficult and dangerous procedure, for to open up the forgotten recesses of childhood is to bring to light—recall Jesus' image of the internal lamp—what "ought" to have remained hidden. Even if Jesus did not develop a procedure for opening up these forgotten recesses, his authentic sayings indicate that he challenged the compulsive ritualisms that form a defensive shield against their revelation. In so doing, he challenged the punitive superego itself—the inner voice that lords it over the sense of "I."

In one of his earliest essays, "Children's Picture Books," originally published in 1931, Erikson noted that the advantages of "the mechanism of conscience formation" are that "the child catches up in a short time with thousands of years of upbringing" (Erikson, 1987a, 34). But the disadvantages are that "the cruel and deadly hatred that the small infant once aimed at the overpowerful adults is ever internalized in the course of his capitulation, and since the child must despair of any resistance, his hatred is turned against his own flagging inner world. For no mobilized strength remains dormant: It rages inwardly as soon as the mind's eye perceives even an unconscious stirring of drive intensification. It harms us in a thousand possibilities of obvious or concealed self-punishment and self-degradation, illness and inhibition." Erikson refers to this oversevere internalized authority as the "dangerous self-directed sadism of the soul" (Erikson, 1987a, 35). Now, fifty years later, Erikson is saying that Jesus saw this self-directed sadism of the soul in the children—and their adult counterparts—who were piped to and *could* not dance, or witnessed wailing and *could* not mourn. Their soul belonged to an inner agency, a mechanism, that knew them not. In a word, they were demon-possessed—controlled by an inner tyrant—and were desperate for a healer who could exorcise it, with words of both tender and militant caring.[6]

The Mother Figure in Erikson's Essay

Having summarized Erikson's essay, I now want to expand on two issues that the essay introduces but leaves somewhat ambiguous or unresolved. The first concerns the several instances in which he refers to the mother figure and her role within the patriarchal and monotheistic ideology within which Jesus lived and taught. In focusing on this issue in reference to Erikson's essay, I will expand on my argument of the previous chapter that Jesus expected his followers to renounce the father–son relationship. A similar renunciation of the mother–son relationship was, by and large, not required. This does not mean, however, that this relationship was not a problematic one for the men who joined Jesus' movement. If anything, it posed more serious psychological difficulties, as the break with the father was more decisive, a cleaner break. Specifically, I will argue that if, as Erikson suggests, Jesus envisioned the Kingdom as a symbolic return to childhood, this would not only mean the recovery of a childlike trust in "Abba" but also the reawakening of a highly ambivalent infantile relationship to the "down-to-earth goddess of the hearth (Erikson, 1981, 361).

The purpose of this discussion is to show that, even as Jesus reawakened the "wonder of childhood," he also brought attention to the frustrations of childhood. Unlike Freud, Jesus did not have a procedure "to open up the forgotten recesses of childhood"—one that uncovered "a primal source of neurotic suffering" but also "a treasure of human potentialities." But his sayings on childhood recalled a deep sense of mistrust to which his appeal for childlike trust in "Abba" was addressed. Because the mother is the first human source of trust, she is also identified with the first occasions of mistrust. Weaning is typically the event that provides the infant "with some sense of basic loss, leaving the general impression that once upon a time one's unity with a maternal matrix was destroyed (Erikson, 1959, 62). Thus, the "basic trust versus basic mistrust" stage introduces "into the psychic life a sense of division and a dim but universal nostalgia for a lost paradise." The key aspects of "basic mistrust" in early infancy are the "impressions of having been deprived, of having been divided, and of having been abandoned" (Erikson, 1959, 62–63). I will suggest that Jesus addressed these "impressions" by taking upon *himself* the role of the reassuring mother.

In his Galilean sayings essay, Erikson makes three references to the mother figure. The first occurs in the contrast he draws between the yearly ritualization that occurred at the Temple in Jerusalem and the daily ones that occurred primarily in family life, at the center of which was the Jewish Mother, who "both confirmed and compensated for the credal emphasis on a dominating masculinity of Being" (Erikson, 1981, 340). Erikson indicates that this "most down-to-earth goddess of the hearth" deserves as much attention as he has given to the patriarchal and monotheistic ideology within which Jesus lived and taught. Such attention, however, "would call for an intimate cultural history which is grounded in some special chapters of the Old Testament," though not limited to these, for the mother figure also "represents one of the most consistent trends in Jewish history" and "was to be glorified" in Christian mythology "in the counterpart to the Passion, namely, the Nativity" (Erikson, 1981, 340). Thus, the hearth goddess and the Madonna, each in her unique way, gives ritual force to the patriarchal and monotheistic ideology they share in common. But were Erikson to explore this association further, he would need to get into the "specific nature of motherhood," for "the very basis of any sense of *I* originates in the infant's first interplay with that maternal *Other*, and certainly continues to be nourished by persistent contact with her" (Erikson, 1981, 341). This suggests that one would want to know how Jewish mothers (Mary included) related to their children in the first months and years of life. Especially, did children in Jesus' time experience their mothers as evoking and nourishing their sense of "I"?

Erikson's second reference to the mother figure occurs in his discussion of the parable of the lost son. After noting that the father in the parable "was steadfast in loving both these sons—so different in familial status and in personality," he adds: "Almost like a mother, some readers may be tempted to say." The implication that it is more like a mother than a father to be steadfast in one's love for each of one's children leads to a follow-up question. If this parable's theme is "the healing of the generational process," then one cannot help but ask whether there was, "in this earthly vision of the comparison [between God and the earthly parent], no mother, either dead or alive? And if alive, was she not also called to say hello, too?" (Erikson, 1981, 355). Having raised questions about her absence, however, Erikson withdraws with this cautionary note, "But a parable is not a case history or even history," thus implying that we should not read much if anything into the fact that Jesus does not have a role for the mother in the story.

Yet because Erikson contends that the parable is not a case history, or even presumably material evidence for such a case history, he can go on to depersonalize the "missing mother" by suggesting that she may perhaps be "the cultural and economic matrix" within which the father and sons carry out their respective "intergenerational tasks" (Erikson, 1981, 356). This implies that "she" is the context, the harsh reality, within which—or against which—these three men play out their sad but heroic interpersonal drama. Thus, this story is fundamentally about how two individuals—the bereft father and the lost son—create together a new "actuality" ("a world of participation" which has "a minimum of defensive maneuvering and a maximum of mutual activation") against the formidable constraints of a powerful "reality" represented by the "Primal Other." It is as though patriarchalism and monotheism, the dominant ideological worldview, were a secondary defense against a more powerful reality, that of fate as vested in the mother–infant relationship.

Erikson's observation that the mother is "missing," together with his suggestion that she exists in the depersonalized form of "the cultural and economic matrix," may also prompt us to focus on Jesus in his role as *storyteller* and to ask, "Is *Jesus* himself the missing mother?" After all, if he communicates through this story his own peculiar—parental—kind of caring, then what Erikson said of another saying of his applies here as well—namely, that "one cannot help noticing, on Jesus' part, an unobtrusive integration of maternal and paternal tenderness" (Erikson, 1981, 349). If the cultural and economic matrix is the harsh reality against which this story is told, is Jesus the personal "mother" for whom the sons are longing?

If so, the religion that developed in Jesus' name took a very different path, as Erikson's third reference to the mother figure points out. This reference to the mother figure occurs at the end of his essay, where he briefly discusses the mythologization of the story of the historical Jesus. He pointedly uses the phrase "the mother churches of Christianity" to identify what this creative mythologization was all about. Because the mother is the "Primal Other" who first mediated the numinous to the infant, it makes perfect sense that, in these mother churches, "the maternal Madonna . . . gradually occupied such a shining ceremonial center" (Erikson, 1981, 359).

While declaring that the Madonna theme and the theme of the Passion comprise "another kind of authenticity" (Erikson, 1981, 358), Erikson notes that these mythological themes were subject to a ritualization process which "eventually could not escape manufacturing its own kind of compulsive ritualism" (Erikson, 1981, 359)—one that has inhibited the opening up of "the forgotten recesses of childhood" (Erikson, 1981, 361), the task Freud set for himself. Viewed together,

Erikson's statements about the mother figure give the impression that Jesus' vision of the Kingdom of God is not a projection of the human infant-mother relationship, but instead stands against it. In this regard, it is similar to Jesus' perception of the heavenly Father as utterly different from the human father (cf. Chap. 7, this vol.). To defend this impression, we need to consider Erikson's writings on the weaning process.

The Feeding Ritual and the Elusive Mother

Concerning Jesus' sayings about children and childhood, Erikson suggests that Mark 10:14–16 ("Let the children come unto me") is "a total affirmation of the radiant potentials of childhood," and that Matthew 18:3 ("Unless you turn and become like children") refers "to an adult condition in which childlikeness has not been destroyed, and in which a potential return to childlike trust has not been forestalled." In other words, Jesus is alluding to "a preservation and reenactment of the wonder of childhood" (Erikson, 1981, 349). Erikson's observations here imply that in the meantime, this childlike trust was lost. But how?

Erikson has answered this question in other writings by focusing on the issue of weaning, noting that "our clinical work indicates that this point in the individual's early history provides him with some sense of basic loss" (Erikson, 1959, 62). In his essay on the ontogeny of ritualization, Erikson described the "greeting ceremonial" between the mother and infant in the earliest weeks and months of life (Erikson, 1987b, 576–579). The relationship forged in part through this interaction provides the "first and dimmest affirmation" or "sense of *hallowed presence.*" In turn, this "hallowed presence" forms the essential core of the "Numinous" (Erikson, 1987b, 578).

The weaning that occurs somewhat later in the first stage of life is a very different story. The feeding rituals of two Native American societies that Erikson describes in *Childhood and Society* are especially revealing in this regard (Erikson, 1963, 114–186). One is the Dakota Sioux in the southwest corner of South Dakota, the other is the Yuroks along the lower Klamath River in northern California. In his chapter on the Dakota Sioux titled "Hunters Across the Prairie," he describes the practice of nursing the boy babies, especially the oldest, for three years, and then abruptly withholding the breast while thumping him on the head if he engages in vigorous biting. This procedure is designed to create a ferocious and stoical buffalo hunter when he becomes a man. Such "thumping" would often cause the small child to fly into a wild rage, and this would give the mother great pleasure, for "good future hunters, especially, could be recognized by the strength of their infantile fury" (Erikson, 1963, 137).

In his chapter on the Yuroks titled "Fishermen Along a Salmon River," he shows that a very early weaning time around the sixth month is designed to encourage the baby boy to leave the mother and her support as early as possible and learn to live with little. This is reinforced throughout childhood by the provision of only a limited amount of food at mealtime. The goal here is to train her son to be a fisherman who sets his nets for a prey which may come to him if he pretends that he is not too eager. The gods are said to favor fishermen who do not take the salmon for granted or fail to make their petition for a successful catch in an appropriately deferential manner. Erikson believes that this attitude toward the supernatural providers was reinforced "by a residue of infantile nostalgia for the mother from whom he has been disengaged so forcefully" (Erikson, 1963, 176). Thus, even if the religious ideology of these two societies was based on masculine imagery, the emotional connection between a man and his gods had its origins in the mother–son relationship.

There may be parallels between the early feeding rituals of the Dakota Sioux mothers and those of Galilean mothers, for Josephus claims that Galileans "have always been able to make a strong resistance on all occasions of war; for the Galileans are inured to war from their infancy, and have always been very numerous" (Josephus, 1987, 641). This suggests a similar feeding ritual designed to infuriate; and, of course, the "numerousness" of Galileans suggests sibling competition for a mother's attention and love. By the time of Erikson's visits to the Dakota Sioux, however, the men had been long since reduced to "warriors without weapons" (Erikson, 1963, 166), the fate of the Galileans as well. But there may also be parallels between the childrearing practices of the Yurok mothers and of Galilean mothers. After all, some Galilean men were in fact fishermen. The Gospels are replete with stories of Jesus' own disciples' struggles with uncertain catches and reliance on a Provider whose beneficence was not to be taken for granted. Was *this* how it was between the male child and his mother?

Whether the early Galilean feeding ritual would have resembled one of these illustrative examples more than the other is not, however, the central issue. What *is* at issue is the fact that the feeding ritual between the mother and her son is designed to prepare him to become a productive member of his society when he comes of age. The price paid for this eventuality is that the mutuality and affirmation integral to the very earliest encounter between mother and infant as reflected in the greeting ritual is compromised. The mother must engage in a deliberate act of emotional and material withholding if she is to play her appointed role in the patriarchal system. Erikson does not explore the feeding rituals between the Jewish mother and her son, but we can be reasonably certain that it involved some form of emotional restraint or withholding, leading to some "residue of infantile nostalgia for the mother" in the adult male (Erikson, 1963, 126).

Jesus as Reassuring Mother

With this discussion of the feeding ritual as background, we can see how Jesus' evocation of childhood could reawaken long-repressed ambivalent feelings toward the mother. Her "presence" as the one who soothes and protects her infant recedes in the weaning phase of the feeding ritual. Its place is taken by a mother who disrupts the "bliss" of infancy with a jolt of reality, thereby preparing her son for the adult world that he will one day inhabit (the cultural and economic matrix of his time and place). If Jesus invokes a small child's Father ("Abba") in the paternal dimension of his vision of the Kingdom, it is through his own peculiar caring for his disciples that he acts out the role of the reassuring and protective mother. In effect, Jesus himself fills the need for the "missing mother." As Erikson suggests in *Gandhi's Truth*, a leader, especially one who acts within the religious sphere, assumes the role of one who cares deeply and passionately about certain human longings (Erikson, 1969, 395). To paraphrase Erikson's comments about the human father in Jesus' parable of the lost son, such a leader is "almost like a mother."

The same maternal love is also implicit in Erikson's comment regarding the story of the lost sheep that one wonders "by what right God or Jesus may pay such exclusive attention to one nearly lost creature—unless, of course, it reminds us of ourselves" (Erikson, 1981, 353). Perhaps even the version of this story in the Gospel of Thomas conveys a mother's love—for the shepherd, having tired himself out searching for the lost sheep, speaks directly to him: "I love thee more than ninety-nine." This may imply favoritism, a favoritism comparable to the reference in the fourth Gospel to the disciple whom Jesus loved (John 13:23), but in the context—one sheep having strayed from the rest—the shepherd's declaration of love is precisely what we would expect from a reassuring mother. Then there is a saying that Erikson does not discuss, perhaps because his delimitation of his essay to the *Galilean* sayings precluded this. It occurs in Matthew's account of Jesus' lament over Jerusalem: "Jerusalem, Jerusalem, the city that kills the prophets and stones those who are sent to it! How often have I desired to gather your children together as a hen gathers her brood under her wings, and you were not willing!" (Matt. 23:37). Here is an image that places Jesus in the role of the mother of the children of the city where—like other prophets—he will meet his death. Like the mother hen, he would, if only he were permitted to, protect them with his very own life.

As Peggy Rosenthal points out in *The Poet's Jesus: Representatives at the End of a Millennium* (2000), the fourth-century Syriac poet Ephrem found it "perfectly natural" that Jesus "should be imaged as mother": "He is the Living Breast of living breath; / by His life the dead were suckled, and they revived" (Rosenthal, 2000, 7). Unfortunately, the elaboration of this "authentic" self-reference has been eclipsed by the more pervasive theme of "the glorified Madonna of Christianity." Rosenthal also notes that the American poet Walt Whitman "sometimes sounds like the Gospel Jesus, without making a point of the allusion" (Rosenthal, 2000, 39). If so, there are profound similarities between Jesus' relationship to his male disciples as portrayed in various Gospel accounts of their personal interaction and Whitman's account of himself in "The Wound Dresser," a reflection of his experience as a nurse to the wounded and dying on both sides during the Civil War: "The hurt and wounded I pacify with soothing hand, / I sit by the restless all the dark night" (Whitman, 1992, 201).

The Uncanny Presence of Jesus

The second issue I want to address grows out of Erikson's view that there can be no "I" without an "Other." This raises the question of Jesus' own role as "Other" for those who joined his movement. If, as Erikson suggests, the mother is the "Primal Other" and God is the "Ultimate Other," I suggest that Jesus was the "Numinous Other." This proposal is implicit in Erikson's view that "of all institutions that of organized religion has the strongest claim to being in charge of the numinous." If Erikson's concern was to convey the "singular presence" of Jesus in his Galilean sayings essay, there is a certain paradox in this concern, as the "presence" of Jesus was precisely in the fact that he represented or personified the "numinous." Thus, he was most "present" to others in his "numinous" effect upon them, and this "numinous" effect made them all the more conscious of his "difference" from them—a difference so marked that they began to ascribe to him a supernatural identity (the coming Messiah, the Son of God, and so forth). To clarify what it means to say that Jesus was experienced as the "Numinous Other," we may turn to Rudolf Otto's original concept of the numinous and link this to a related essay by Freud.

In *The Idea of the Holy*, Otto identifies the elements of the numinous and distinguishes in this regard between its form and content. Its form is the "mysterium tremendum," while its content is the "fascinans." *Tremendum*, which evokes the sense of trembling, fear, or dread, has several elements, including awefulness, overpoweringness, and energy or urgency. *Mysterium* adds the element of the "wholly other," or "that which is quite beyond the sphere of the usual, the intelligible, and the familiar" (Otto, 1950, 26). The *fascinans* contributes a sense of mystery to the numinous and is expressed in the wonder and rapture associated with the "mysterious beatific experience of deity" (Otto, 1950, 32). It also has the connotation of longing, as well as solemnity, tranquility, and transport. Taken together, these numinous elements are perhaps best described in the English word "the uncanny" (Otto, 1950, 40), which is itself difficult to define but has the connotation of the mysterious and unfamiliar, especially in such a way as to frighten or make uneasy.

Freud's essay, "The 'Uncanny'" (1995), appeared two years after the publication of Otto's *The Idea of the Holy*. It is basically a study of the German word "unheimlich," which is translated "uncanny" in the English version. The key point of the essay is that the German word "heimlich" can mean familiar, friendly, and intimate, but it can also mean mysterious, concealed, secret, and hidden. Thus, Freud suggests that "heimlich is a word the meaning of which develops in the direction of ambivalence, until it finally coincides with its opposite, unheimlich" (Freud, 1995, 127). How do we explain this? Freud believes the answer lies in F. W. Schelling's observation that "everything is unheimlich that ought to have remained secret and hidden but has come to light" (Freud, 1995, 126). In other words, it is "heimlich" because it is familiar and known to the person or persons involved, but is "unheimlich" because the intention was that it would remain secret or hidden but has unexpectedly been revealed or discovered. A good example is a closely guarded family secret that has been inadvertently disclosed. The moment of revelation is experienced as "uncanny" and is likely to have many if not all of the elements of the numinous as described by Otto.

Freud develops two "considerations" from Schelling's basic insight. First, "if psychoanalytic theory is correct in maintaining that every affect belonging to an emotional impulse, whatever its kind, is transformed, if it is repressed, into anxiety, then among instances of frightening things there must be one class in which the frightening element can be shown to be something repressed which *recurs*." This class of frightening things would then constitute the uncanny, and it would not matter whether what is now experienced as uncanny was originally frightening or whether it carried some other affect at the time. What causes the fright is its *reappearance*. Second, "if this is indeed the secret nature of the uncanny," then we can understand why the heimlich shades into its opposite, the unheimlich, for "this uncanny is in reality nothing new or alien, but something which is familiar and old-established in the mind and which has become alienated from it only through the process of repression" (Freud, 1995, 142).

Freud's view that the uncanny is something familiar that was previously repressed but has now been revealed helps explain the numinous presence of Jesus. In my view, Jesus embodied the uncanny. That is, through his person and message, he evoked what had been repressed and had therefore been transformed into one or another form of debilitating anxiety. How did he evoke these repressed experiences? There are several explanations. One is that in his teachings, he alluded to the need for adults to become as children, thus inviting his listeners, as Erikson puts it, to "open up the forgotten recesses of childhood" (Erikson, 1981, 361). Another is that he talked ominously about things that have been hidden coming to light (for example, the story of the man who found a hidden treasure in Matt. 13:44) and lost persons and objects being found (for example, the parable of the lost son in Luke 15:11–32 and the story of the lost coin in Luke 15:8–9). Hidden treasures are the very embodiment of secrecy and concealment, and the experience of discovering one is certainly uncanny. So, too, is the experience of the father who sees his lost son off at a distance and wonders if his eyes are deceiving him. Erikson's view is that the saying that summarizes this story—"Your brother was dead, and is alive, he was lost, and is found"—is precisely right, as this statement captures the uncanniness of this event. As Freud points out, one of the most uncanny experiences is the sensation of the dead having come back to life. We can well imagine that the father in the story of the lost son thought he was seeing a ghost when he first caught sight of his son, and he may have thought the ghost of his son had come back to do him harm, for belief that the dead come back to avenge themselves is one of humanity's oldest fears (Freud, 1995, 143). Thus, the father forestalls any potential violence by treating his son as if he were visiting royalty.

A third way in which Jesus evoked the uncanny is that he himself was viewed as a prophet who had come back from the dead. As Matthew 16:14 indicates, some people thought he was Elijah, others thought he was Jeremiah, while others nominated other ancient prophets. Otto considered scholarly inquiries into "Jesus's consciousness of Himself" to be "fundamentally impossible," if for no other reason than that "the evidence at our disposal is neither sufficient in quantity nor appropriate to such a purpose" (Otto, 1950, 155–156). Thus, he focused instead on the impression that Jesus made on others. As he put it, "The immediate, intuitive 'divination' of which we are speaking would indeed *not* come as a result of . . . statements by the prophet about himself, however complete; they can arouse a belief in his authority, but cannot bring about the peculiar experience of spontaneous insight that here is something holy made manifest" (Otto, 1950, 156). In other words, his contemporaries sensed that they were in the presence of the uncanny; or, put another way, they experienced the uncanny when they were in his presence. He embodied what Freud also calls "the return of the repressed," citing the return of the religion of Moses after the Hebrew people had repressed it for several centuries (Freud, 1939, 160–164).

If Jesus embodied the return of the repressed, then the prevailing view among Christians that he represented an "advance" or "progression" over the religious establishment of his day needs to be reassessed. In this view, opponents are represented as mired in a dead, outmoded tradition, whereas Jesus is represented as the proponent of something excitingly new and threateningly novel (for example, Crossan's "egalitarian" Jesus). Rather, the foregoing analysis suggests that what made Jesus threatening was the fact that he embodied that which had been repressed on both the individual and collective level. Freud considers particularly fascinating those experiences of the uncanny when "something *actually happens* in our lives which seems to confirm the old discarded beliefs." At that moment, "we get a feeling of the uncanny; it is as though we were making a judgment something like this: 'So, after all, it is *true* that one can kill a person by a mere wish!' or, 'So the dead *do* live on and appear on the scene of their former activities!' and so on" (Freud, 1995, 148).

I suggest that through his actions and teachings, Jesus awakened old discarded beliefs, which in turn evoked affects of fear, amazement, awe, and wonder. In psychoanalytic terms, this was because he was implementing Freud's principle that if "every affect belonging to an emotional impulse, whatever its kind, is transformed, if it is repressed, into anxiety, then among instances of frightening things there must be one class in which the frightening element can be shown to be something repressed which *recurs.*" In effect, Jesus attacked the symptom—the anxiety—and in doing so, brought the repressed material to light. This made him a dangerous man to have around.

"He Set His Face to Go to Jerusalem"

In Otto's view, Mark 10:32 is the biblical text that best expresses and confirms Jesus' numinous effect on the people around him. It conveys the spontaneous responses of feeling when the numinous is directly encountered in experience: "They were on the road, going up to Jerusalem, and Jesus was walking ahead of them; they were amazed and those who followed were afraid." For Otto, this statement "renders with supreme simplicity and force the immediate impression of the numinous that issued from the man Jesus, and no artistry of characterization could do it so powerfully as these few masterly and pregnant words" (Otto, 1950, 158). Furthermore, "the intimations of the numinous impression made by Jesus upon those who knew him occur in the Gospel narrative only, as it were, incidentally to the main purpose of the narrator, who is scarcely interested in them, but absorbed rather in the record of the miraculous." This makes these intimations all the more significant, and we can imagine "how numerous similar experiences must have been of which no trace survives in the records, just because there was no miracle to be told of in connection with them and they were simply taken for granted by the narrator as a matter of course" (Otto, 1950, 159).

Luke's account adds to this the sense of the fatefulness of this moment: "When the days drew near for him to be taken up, he set his face to go to Jerusalem." He appeared to be activating the traditional paradigm of the death of the prophet, and the people on the road with him sensed that he was doing so. One meaning of the word "uncanny" is the "preternaturally strange," which has connotations both of something beyond the normal or ordinary and an anticipatory dread.

While Erikson does not discuss the "Judean Passion," it is safe to say that he would have seen this fateful decision to go to Jerusalem as congruent with Jesus' own unique "sense of 'I.'" In *Identity: Youth and Crisis*, Erikson quotes William James' observation that a man's essential character "is discernible in the mental or moral attitude in which, when it came upon him, he felt himself most deeply and intensely active and alive. At such moments there is a voice inside which speaks and says: '*This* is the real me!'" Such experiences, James continues, always include "an element of active tension, of holding my own, as it were, and trusting outward things to perform their part so as to make it a full harmony, but without any *guaranty* that they will." Make it a guaranty, "and the attitude immediately becomes to my consciousness stagnant and stingless," but remove the guaranty, and I feel "a sort of deep enthusiastic bliss, a bitter willingness to do and suffer anything." While this feeling "is a mere mood or emotion to which I can give no form in words," "it authenticates itself to me as the deepest principle of all active and theoretical determination which I possess" (Erikson, 1968, 19).

This, I suggest, is what Luke's few masterly and pregnant words— "He set his face to go to Jerusalem"—convey. They indicate that at this very moment Jesus "felt himself most deeply and intensely active and alive." What the followers Mark describes must have seen and felt was "the element of active tension" in Jesus, his sense of "holding his own," and of "trusting outward things to perform their part." This, then, was that element of the numinous which Otto calls "energy" or "urgency," which is reflected in "vitality, passion, emotional temper, will, force, movement, excitement, activity, impetus" (Otto, 1950, 23). Thus, the "deep enthusiastic bliss, of bitter willingness to do and suffer anything" that Jesus must have felt at that moment authenticated the action as one that was based on "the deepest principle of all active and theoretical determination" that he possessed. This very action was itself exemplary of the *initiative* of the Kingdom, that dominion in motion.

Activating the Root Paradigm

Jesus' followers' sense of the uncanniness of this moment—when Jesus set his face to go to Jerusalem—was due in no small measure to their awareness that he was activating the traditional paradigm of the death of the prophet. As Erikson implies, he seemed to know that he would eventually need to sacrifice "the Galilean style of ministry" in order "to challenge—yes, nonviolently—the 'powers that be' in Jerusalem" (Erikson, 1981, 328). Such awareness was undoubtedly based on the understanding that a prophet who was in dead earnest about his cause had to make his case in Jerusalem.

To support this sense of the inexorability of this sacrifice and challenge, Victor E. Turner's application of the framework of social drama to the confrontation between Thomas Becket, Archbishop of Canterbury, and King Henry II at the Council of Northampton in October 1164 is particularly relevant. Turner employs a "social-dramatist framework" to explain Becket's decision to challenge Henry and, in so doing, to identify himself with "the root-paradigm" of martyrdom

(Turner, 1976, 156). In a similar way, Jesus identified with the "root-paradigm" of the prophet of Israel, who was prepared, if necessary, to die for his understanding of the Jewish faith.

By "root paradigm," Turner means "certain consciously recognized (though not consciously grasped) cultural models in the heads of the main actors." They have reference "not only to the current state of social relationships existing or developing between actors, but also to cultural goals, means, idioms, outlooks, currents of thought, patterns of belief, etc., which enter into those relationships, interpret them and incline them to alliance or divisiveness" (Turner, 1976, 156). They are not "systems of univocal concepts, logically arrayed," or "precision tools of thought." Nor are they "stereotyped guidelines for ethical, esthetic, or conventional action. Indeed, they go beyond the cognitive and even the moral to the existential domain, and in so doing become clothed with allusiveness, implicitness, and metaphor—for in the stress of vital action, firm definitional outlines become blurred by the encounter of emotionally charged wills." Paradigms of this fundamental nature "reach down to the irreducible life-stances of individuals, passing beneath conscious prehension to a fiduciary hold on what they sense to be axiomatic values, matters literally of life or death." They are not routinely invoked or enacted; rather, they "emerge in life-crises, whether of groups or individuals, whether institutionalized or compelled by unforeseen events" (Turner, 1976, 156). But once they emerge, there is an inexorable quality to them—their consequences seeming utterly inescapable.

In Becket's case, the root-paradigm was that of martyrdom, and once he identified himself with it, he achieved "a peace and certitude of mind and consistency of action that never failed him until the bloody climax." Once he enacted it, "Becket became himself a powerful, 'numinous' symbol precisely because, like all dominant or focal symbols, he represented a coincidence of opposites, a semantic structure in tension between opposite poles of meaning. Becket was at once lion and lamb, proud and meek. The energy of his pride gives drama and pathos to his self-chosen role of lamb" (Turner, 1976, 176).

In citing Turner's analysis of the confrontation between Becket and King Henry, I realize that this illustration is rather anachronistic. After all, for Christians, Jesus himself is the progenitor of the root-paradigm of martyrdom. Still, Turner's view that such root-paradigms are deeply "existential," reaching down to "the irreducible life-stances of individuals," applies to Jesus' decision to go to Jerusalem and confront the authorities there, thus activating the root-paradigm with all its attendant consequences of the death of the prophet. In so doing, he became "a powerful, 'numinous' symbol," which, like all dominant or focal symbols, represents a coincidence of opposites, a semantic structure in tension between opposite poles of meaning. Erikson has something like this "coincidence of opposites" in mind when he says that a certain militancy is a necessary trait for the nonviolent (Erikson, 1981, 356). Had Turner himself discussed the "Judean Passion," he might have compared and contrasted the entry scene, portraying Jesus riding on a donkey, with the Temple disturbance scene, where Jesus overturned the money changers' tables and the seats of pigeon sellers.

My concern here, however, is not to enter into an analysis of the "Judean Passion" comparable to Turner's carefully delineated account of events at the Council of Northampton, but only to make the more general case that, when he set his face for Jerusalem, Jesus was aware that he was entrusting himself to "outward things to perform their part . . . but without any *guaranty* that they will." That is to say, he was placing himself at the mercy of a social drama clothed with allusiveness, implicitness, and metaphor, to the stress of vital action in which firm definitional outlines become blurred by the encounter of emotionally charged wills. This social drama approach provides an effective response to the view advanced by the psychiatrists whom Schweitzer criticized so vigorously that Jesus was suffering under a paranoid delusional system. It was not a private delusional system that held Jesus in thrall. Instead, a root-paradigm of prophetic confrontation with the powers-that-be defined his actions. As Turner puts it, such root-paradigms are "consciously recognized (though not consciously grasped) cultural models in the heads of the main actors" (Turner, 1976, 156). What was in Jesus' head, then, was not the promptings of private delusions, but a long repressed but publicly recognizable cultural model—that of the prophet who risks everything in a personal confrontation with the highest powers of the land.

Jesus: The Self-Reconciled One

In emphasizing Jesus as the numinous other, I have focused on the impression he made on others. But in doing so, I have also implied that he was conscious of himself as a prophet, for the root-paradigm that he activated was that of the death of the prophet in Jerusalem. Unlike debates over whether he viewed himself as the coming Messiah, this admittedly is not a very dramatic conclusion. But it is quite congruent with at least one of the major trends in current Jesus research, that of viewing Jesus as a "holy man."

For Geza Vermes, the key to understanding Jesus as a "religious man" is that, "unlike the rabbis and the Essene teachers who insisted on both the letter and the spirit of the Law, Jesus marched in the footsteps of the great prophets of Israel in placing an almost exaggerated accent on the *inward aspects* and *root causes* of the religious action (Vermes, 1993, 195). The "wellsprings" of such religious action were, for him, a "trusting faith"—the reverse of which is "anxiety, careful forethought, precaution, planned provision for the future," and "an untiring effort to follow God as a model," to "walk in his ways," especially as expressed in Luke 6:36: "Be merciful as your Father is merciful" (Vermes, 1993, 196–206). While congruent with Vermes' view that Jesus "marched in the footsteps of the great prophets of Israel," what has been added here is a psychological understanding of this view, based on Freud's views on the uncanny as the unexpected return of that which has undergone repression.

Conclusion

Thus, the experience of "otherness" that Jesus evoked in the people around him had its origins or basis in the lifting of repressions, both personal and collective. It is the unexpected, disruptive return of hidden, lost, or forgotten things—experiences, ideas, associations, and so on—that creates a sense of the uncanny, with its inevitable emotional ambivalences. A particularly relevant formulation of this point is the psychoanalyst Julia Kristeva's discussion of "otherness" in *Strangers to Ourselves* (Kristeva, 1991). In her view, what is experienced as "Other" is in fact one's own unconscious that has become estranged from oneself owing to the processes of repression. Thus, the repressed is the "strange within us." As her book is about the "stranger," or "foreigner," it interests her that there is no mention of foreigners in Freud's essay on the uncanny. Conceivably, this is because a "foreigner" does not arouse the same "terrifying anguish" as fears of being buried alive, of being at the mercy of the powerful dead, of the dread of the evil eye, and of similar illustrations of the uncanny in Freud's essay. Nevertheless, "in the fascinated rejection that the foreigner arouses in us, there is a share of uncanny strangeness in the sense of the depersonalization that Freud discovered in it. . . . The foreigner is within us. And when we flee from or struggle against the foreigner, we are fighting our unconscious." Thus, "Freud does not speak of foreigners: he teaches us how to detect foreignness in ourselves. That is perhaps the only way not to hound it outside of us"—that is, by projecting it onto an "other" (Kristeva, 1991, 191). Thus, the "numinous" effect that Jesus had on others is likely to have been related to the fact that he was on speaking terms with the "foreigner" inside him.

If he was, as Vermes suggests, a "holy man," this is because he had come to terms with the "alien" in himself and was therefore as "whole" as any mortal could hope to be. Thus reconciled with himself, he personified the fundamental insight that we become present to others as we become present to ourselves. "But when he came to himself . . ." (Luke 15:17) expresses the very heart of the matter.

Notes

1. Discussion of the Jerusalem events would have required Erikson to comment on the role of the Jewish leadership in Jesus' execution. As Friedman shows, the fact that Erikson married a Christian woman and had personal affinities for Christian ideas and rituals was a matter of some concern among his Jewish friends and colleagues (Friedman, 1999, 439–440). Concern for their feelings may well have prompted him to limit his study of Jesus to the Galilean period. As the essay itself makes clear, however, Erikson is no less critical of how early Christianity distorted Jesus' message, as reflected in his sayings, than of the priestly establishment that Jesus confronted in Jerusalem.

2. This statement occurs in the "Theoretical Interlude" chapter of *Identity: Youth and Crisis*. In it, he distinguishes between the "I," the Self, and the Ego. He places the "sense of 'I'" in a religious context by suggesting that even as the Ego has its "counterplayer" in the environment and the Self has its "counterplayers" in other Selves, so the "I" has *its* counterplayer in the deity or Eternal Other. Thus, if to have a sense of "I" is to experience oneself as "the center of awareness in a universe of experience," the "counterplayer of the 'I' therefore can be, strictly speaking, only the deity who has lent this halo to a mortal and is Himself endowed with an eternal numinousness certified by all 'I's' who acknowledge this gift. That is why God, when Moses asked Him who should he say called him, answered, 'I AM THAT I AM'" (Erikson, 1968, 220).

3. In *The Theory and Practice of Autonomy*, philosopher Gerald Dworkin argues that "the conception of autonomy that insists upon substantive independence is not one that has a claim to our respect as an ideal. . . . In particular it makes autonomy inconsistent with loyalty, objectivity, commitment, benevolence, and love" (Dworkin, 1988, 21). I contend that Erikson agrees. In fact, autonomy as self-governance is a critical psychological prerequisite for such connections, commitments, and expressions of mutual concern.

4. The title of the chapter of *Childhood and Society* in which Erikson introduces his life cycle model is "The Eight Ages of Man." This is a direct allu-

sion to Shakespeare's *As You Like It* (act 2, scene 7). Most commentators on his life cycle concept use the word "stages" rather than "ages." Because their use of the word "stages" tends to imply a progressive movement, it is well for us to remember that Erikson's original inspiration was Shakespeare's "All the world's a stage, / And all the men and women merely players, / And one man in his time plays many parts, / His acts being seven ages." For Erikson, then, the word "stage" retains its original dramatic meaning. In this sense, he would not object to the use of the word "stage" to characterize his life cycle model. But it is more accurate to view the eight polarities in his life cycle model as changing "scenes" rather than as progressions in the sense of achievements and accomplishments.

5. Erikson introduces this distinction between "reality" and "actuality" again in *Gandhi's Truth* in a way that is also relevant to his essay on Jesus. After listing the many terms and phrases that have been used to describe Gandhi, he notes: "If . . . I should give his unique presence a name that would suit my views, I would call him a *religious actualist*" (Erikson, 1969, 396). His related comment on what the "great leader" accomplishes is very relevant to Jesus: "The great leader creates for himself and for many others new choices and new cares. These he derives from a mighty drivenness, an intense and yet flexible energy, a shocking originality, and a capacity to impose on his time what most concerns him—which he does so convincingly that his time believes this concern to have emanated 'naturally' from ripe necessities" (Erikson, 1969, 395). In choosing the word "actualist," Erikson avoids the more common term, "activist," for, as he notes in his essay on psychological reality and historical actuality, "passivity can be an active adaptation, while only inactivation results in paralysis" (Erikson, 1969, 105–106).

6. It would not be difficult to demonstrate connections between Erikson's first three stages of the life cycle and the types of healings that Jesus performed, with blindness corresponding to stage one, demon possession to stage two, and paralysis to stage three.

References

Capps, D. (2000). *Jesus: A Psychological Biography*. St. Louis: Chalice Press.

Capps, D. (2003). Beyond Schweitzer and the Psychiatrists: Jesus as Fictive Personality. *HTS Theological Studies, 59*, 621–662.

Crossan, J. D. (1994). *Jesus: A Revolutionary Biography*. San Francisco: HarperSanFrancisco.

Dworkin, G. (1988). *The Theory and Practice of Autonomy*. Cambridge: Cambridge University Press.

Erikson, E. H. (1958). *Young Man Luther: A Study in Psychoanalysis and History*. New York: Norton.

Erikson, E. H. (1959). *Identity and the Life Cycle*. New York: Norton.

Erikson, E. H. (1963). *Childhood and Society* (2nd rev. ed.). New York: Norton.

Erikson, E. H. (1964). Psychological Reality and Historical Actuality, *Insight and Responsibility: Lectures on the Ethical Implications of Psychoanalytic Insight.* New York: Norton, 161–215.

Erikson, E. H. (1968). *Identity: Youth and Crisis.* New York: Norton.

Erikson, E. H. (1969). *Gandhi's Truth: On the Origins of Militant Non-Violence.* New York: Norton.

Erikson, E. H. (1974). *Dimensions of a New Identity: The 1973 Jefferson Lectures in the Humanities.* New York: Norton.

Erikson, E. H. (1977). *Toys and Reasons: Stages in the Ritualization of Experience.* New York: Norton.

Erikson, E. H. (1981). The Galilean Sayings and the Sense of "I," *Yale Review,* 70, 321–363.

Erikson, E. H. (1987a). Children's Picture Books, *A Way of Looking at Things: Selected Papers from 1930 to 1980,* S. Schlein, ed. New York: Norton, 31–38.

Erikson, E. H. (1987b). The Ontogeny of Ritualization in Man, *A Way of Looking at Things: Selected Papers from 1930 to 1980,* S. Schlein, ed. New York: Norton, 575–594.

Freud, S. (1939). *Moses and Monotheism,* K. Jones, trans. New York: Random House.

Freud, S. (1995). The "Uncanny," *Psychological Writings and Letters,* S. L. Gilman, ed. New York: Continuum Books, 120–153.

Friedman, L. J. (1999). *Identity's Architect: A Biography of Erik H. Erikson.* New York: Scribners.

Gilligan, C. (1982). *In a Different Voice: Psychological Theory and Women's Development.* Cambridge: Harvard University Press.

Josephus, F. (1987). *The Works of Josephus,* W. Whiston, trans. Peabody: Hendrickson.

Kristeva, J. (1991). *Strangers to Ourselves,* L. S. Roudiez, trans. New York: Columbia University Press.

Otto, R. (1950). *The Idea of the Holy,* J. W. Harvey, trans. London: Oxford University Press.

Rosenthal, P. (2000). *The Poet's Jesus: Representations at the End of a Millennium.* New York: Oxford University Press.

Turner, V. E. (1976). Religious Paradigms and Political Action: "The Murder in the Cathedral" of Thomas Becket, *The Biographical Process: Studies in the History and Psychology of Religion,* F. Reynolds and D. Capps, eds. The Hague: Mouton, 153–186.

Vermes, G. (1993). *The Religion of Jesus the Jew.* Minneapolis: Fortress.

Whitman, W. (1992). *Selected Poems.* New York: Gramercy.

CHAPTER 9

THE ORIGINAL IMPULSE OF JESUS

Walter Wink

The analysis I wish to share in this chapter participates in a growing effort to cast the original truths of Christianity in new molds that have a more lively appeal for people in our day. For my part, I have been searching among the shards of Judaism and Christianity to see if there are perhaps other ways to interpret, and live out, the original impulse of Jesus. I want to reflect both exegetically and theologically on how that impulse, which Jesus inaugurated, can open us to the present possibilities of the past. I do so as one who is deeply committed to what Jesus revealed. I believe that the churches have, to a tragic extent, abandoned elements of that revelation. I do not, however, wish to throw the whole enterprise overboard. The Gospels continue to feed me, as does all of Scripture, even the worst parts, and some churches are impressively faithful. But if Scripture is to speak to those who find its words dust, we will have to radically reconstitute our reading.

Exposition

My supposition is that something has gone terribly wrong in Christian history. The churches have too often failed to continue Jesus' mission. I grant that the church fathers sometimes understood the implications of the Gospel *better* than the earliest Christians, who lacked the perspective of hindsight. But there is a disappointing side as well: anti-Semitism, collaboration with oppressive political regimes, the estab-

lishment of hierarchical power arrangements in the churches, the
squeezing of women from leadership positions, the abandonment of
radical egalitarianism, and the rule of patriarchy in church affairs.
Those of us who are, to varying degrees, disillusioned by the churches
feel that it is not only our right but our sacred obligation to delve
deeply into the church's records to find answers to these legitimate
and urgent questions:

- Before he was worshiped as God incarnate, how did Jesus
  struggle to incarnate God?
- Before he became identified as the source of all healing, how
  did he relate to, and how did he teach his disciples to relate to,
  the healing Source?
- Before forgiveness became a function solely of his cross, how
  did he understand people to have been forgiven?
- Before the Kingdom of God became a compensatory afterlife or
  a future utopia adorned with all the political trappings Jesus
  resolutely rejected, what did he mean by the Kingdom?
- Before he became identified as Messiah, how did he relate to
  the profound meaning in the messianic image?
- Before he himself was made the sole mediator between God
  and humanity, how did Jesus experience and communicate the
  presence of God?

It is, of course, conceivable that the surviving data do not permit us
to distinguish the Jesus of the Gospels from the Gospel of Jesus. However, it is my considered judgment that there is sufficient evidence to
develop an alternative mode of access to Jesus. Specifically, clues and
traces in the Gospels provide flashes of authenticity that seem incon-
trovertibly to go back to Jesus, or to a memory of him equally true.
When we finish our quest, however, we will not have the historical
Jesus "as he really was," for such a feat is impossible. If we are successful, we will have contributed, through historical reflection and interpretation, to a new myth—*the myth of the human Jesus.*

The Original Impulse of Jesus

In the struggle to become human, I find myself returning over and
over to those ancient texts that, for me, still contain the original
impulse of Jesus. That impulse was the spirit that drove Jesus through
the villages of Galilee and ultimately to death in Jerusalem. It was the
inner fire that impelled him to preach the coming of God's reign, the
spirit that caused him to cry out, "I came to cast fire upon the earth,
and how I wish it were already kindled!" (Luke 12:49). Even though

that impulse may lie buried under the detritus of routinized religion, I am convinced that we can recover priceless rubies among the rubble. For nothing else can provide those who are seekers with the interpretive clues that might enable them to revitalize that tradition.

In reading the texts dealing with the Son of Man, then, I will not seek to get *behind* the text (for that implies that some other, superior text lies behind the received text); rather, I wish to penetrate deeply *into* the text so as to provide an alternative means of access to Jesus. I seek a fresh picture of what Christianity might more truly be in our time. So I invite the reader to join me in the prophetic task of listening for what God might be saying to us today, individually and collectively. I will attempt to carry out that task by means of an "extremely verbatim reading," requiring what the great scholar of Jewish mysticism Gershom Scholem called "mystical precision" (Matt, 1993, 201). To that end, I will employ historical critical tools wherever they seem appropriate and any other approaches that can render valid insights. I will hew to the biblical tradition with unrelenting determination, on the promise, as Jewish scholar Daniel Matt puts it, that we will find God in the details. And if that happens, if the words dissolve into the reality and language into experience, we will understand what mystics have always known: that the exegete stands, with Israel, at the Sinai of the soul, where God still speaks.

The End of Objectivism

What stands in the way of new/ancient readings of Scripture is the whole heritage of positivism and objectivism: the belief that we can handle these radioactive texts without ourselves being irradiated. Biblical scholars have been exceedingly slow to grasp the implications of the Heisenberg principle: that the observer is always a part of the field being observed and disturbs that field by the very act of observation. In terms of the interpretive task, this means that there can be no question of an objective view of Jesus "as he really was." "Objective view" is itself an oxymoron; every view is subjective from a particular angle of vision. We always encounter the biblical text with interests. We always have a stake in our reading of it. We always have angles of vision, which can be helpful or harmful in interpreting texts. "Historical writing does not treat reality; it treats the interpreter's relation to it," according to Brian Stock (Stock, 1990, 80–81). "All history," said the poet Wallace Stevens, "is modern history." All meaning, says Lynn Poland, is present meaning (Poland, 1985, 473). "All truly creative scholarship in the humanities is autobiographical," says Wendy

Doniger O'Flaherty (O'Flaherty, 1986, 219–239). And "historical crit-icism is a form of criticism of the present," according to Walter Kasper (Childs, 2000, 85). All that is true, but only partially. For historical criticism still can help us discover an understanding of that past which holds out to us present meaning.

According to Hal Childs, the past is not an object we can observe. It is an idea we have in the present about the past. History is constantly being rewritten from within history. Thus there is no absolute per-spective available outside of history that could provide a final truth of history (Childs, 2000, 227–228). Childs contends that Jesus of Naza-reth, as a real person who once lived but now no longer exists, is unap-proachable by historical-critical methods. Obviously it is possible to continue to reinterpret the documents that reveal his one-time pres-ence in history. But this is a reinterpretation of meaning in the present and not a reconstruction of the past. Following Jung, Childs believes that the question of whether we can ever know what happened in the past is, in the final analysis, undecidable. All we can know is its effect on us today.

While I agree with much of Childs's critique, I believe he goes too far when he declares that the past is unapproachable by historical meth-ods. For historical criticism still can help us recover an understanding of the past that holds out to us present meaning. The text is a brute fact, not a Rorschach inkblot onto which any conceivable interpreta-tion can be read. The great, if limited, value of the historical-critical approach is that it debunks arbitrary notions of what the text might mean. From every hypothesis and reconstruction it demands warrants, or reasonable evidence, within the text. Arguments can sometimes be falsified by historical and literary data. Not just anything goes, but only positions that other scholars can examine and debate. To discern the past in its present meaning, it is absolutely essential that we have as accurate a picture of the past as possible. We do not need "a final truth of history," but only approximate truth, backed up by evidence.

We can find meaning in the present, not *instead of* a reconstruction of the past, but *by means of* a reconstruction of the past. There is not just one horizon, the present, but two—past and present. It is their interplay and dialogue, often tacit and even unconscious, that provide meaning. It is this built-in, self-critical aspect of historical method that prevents pure subjectivity or the attitude that anything goes. So I want two things at once: to overcome the objectivist illusion that disinterested exegesis is possible, and to affirm the present meaning of the past by means of the most rigorous possible exegesis.

The *present* meaning of the historical Jesus has been the unconscious agenda of the Jesus quest these past two centuries. Driving that enormous undertaking was an inchoate desire among Christian scholars to recover something numinous and lost *within themselves* and within contemporary religion. The means used, however, were not capable of rejuvenating the springs of faith. In fact, the historical approach became a kind of Midas touch. The very act of projecting that longing for the numinous back into the first century concealed its present motivation. This meant that the Jesus found in the past, however much a projection of modern religious ideals, could not then be brought forward into the present. To do so would violate those very scientific principles that had been used to recover Jesus in his original setting. Having found him again, in all his compelling modernity, scholars had to abandon him to the past. For no one was aware, until Albert Schweitzer exposed it, that the real driving force behind this scholarly exertion was, in fact, a modern longing to be encountered by the divine. It was that very longing that scholarship pretended to be able to dispense with by its objectivist methodology and detached attitude. Paradoxically, the Jesus they found by scholarly means was located on the far side of an unbridgeable gulf—the past—a gulf that was created by the very method scholars had chosen to recover Jesus as their contemporary.

No legitimate quest for the historical Jesus is possible as long as the real motives behind the quest are denied. Once the false objectivity of historians has been renounced, however, we can acknowledge that most scholars study the past *in order to change its effect on the present.*

The Myth of God Incarnate versus the Myth of the Human Jesus

It is not, however, a choice between the human, non-mythological Jesus versus the divine, mythological Christ. For *both* are archetypal images. The human Jesus of the Quest has *already* entered into the archetype of humanness and seems to have affected people thus, even during Jesus' active ministry. Indeed, the Son of Man was already archetypally charged as early as Ezekiel 1 and Daniel 7.

The quest of the historical Jesus, then, functions in the service of the myth of the human Jesus. It attempts to recover the humanity of Jesus to liberate it from the accretions of dogma that have made Jesus a God-Man. For two centuries scholars have believed that they were simply going behind the Gospel traditions to their earliest forms. But the scandalous lack of historical consensus reveals the true situation:

they were not recovering Jesus as he really was; rather, they were forging the myth of the human Jesus. And this is as true of "unbelievers" as "believers," as true of liberals as conservatives. Ultimately, we find ourselves reading the myth of the human Jesus in the light of our own personal myths.

No wonder there was no scholarly consensus. Every picture of Jesus scholars produced was inevitably invested with that scholar's projections onto Jesus, positive or negative. And since these projections were by definition unconscious and disguised the scholar's own personal needs and interests, we scholars often became dogmatic about our exegetical conclusions where only tentative answers were appropriate. We had to be dogmatic, it seemed; the myth of the human Jesus that we were unwittingly helping to fashion offered us a kind of salvation. Since the driving spirit behind the quest was the hope of discovering our own humanness in God, the very meaning of our lives hung in the balance. And because each scholar brought his or her own set of needs to the quest, there could never be unanimity as to what the historical-critical results would be. Our contributions to the quest, then, are not "the truth" about Jesus but, rather, personal probes of various values into the humanity of Jesus. Each such contribution, however unavoidably subjective, adds to the wild proliferation of flowers and weeds that make up the riotous garden of Jesus studies.

I in no way deplore these efforts to construct a new, liberating Jesus-myth. I believe it is the most important theological enterprise since the Protestant Reformation, urgently to be pursued. The only problem is that so many scholars believed they were producing objective historiography rather than creating a necessary new myth. That myth, to be sure, draws on historical methodologies. But it marshals them in the service of what I hope will become a powerful mythic alternative to the Christ-myth that we have known these past two thousand years. *Historical criticism is essential for Jesus research because the myth of the human Jesus is itself historically constructed.* As Bruce Malina puts it, "While history must be imaginative, it should not be imaginary" (Malina, 2001, 7).

In short, the quest for the *historical* Jesus has all along really been the quest for the *human* Jesus. There is no need for consensus or unanimity as to what constitutes authentic Jesus tradition. The myth of the human Jesus is a wide field with room for many divergent views. Yet it is a field with boundaries. It is still possible to reject, on historical-critical grounds, constructions that are not supported by the text— though there will be no agreement even over the boundaries. Thus, most scholars will reject the idea that Jesus was a mushroom or a psychopath, though some scholars have argued that he was.

It is not the case, then, that we scholars have initiated that quest. Rather, the archetype of the Human Being initiated it as long ago as Ezekiel and, if some scholars are right, even earlier in myths of the Primal Man. And it continues to provide the dynamic impetus that has driven that quest ever since. We are not the drivers but the driven.

The Jesus quest is faced with two major limitations, however: the paucity of the biblical data, and the poverty of our selves. The myth of the human Jesus cannot simply be spun out of the air, because that myth insists on the historicity of the human Jesus. The myth itself demands that we provide warrants for all our assertions and a plausible synthesis of the data. I believe that fallible persons such as we can nevertheless exercise those critical judgments in such a way as to provide information about the human Jesus. It is precisely that wager that leads exegetes to engross themselves in that "extremely verbatim reading" that the mystics talked about. We cannot abandon the historical method because it provides us with one of the most powerful tools we have for constructing the myth of the human Jesus.

Scholars seek to rectify the limitation on our data by turning over every leaf in search of new information about the ancient world. Newly discovered texts, new ways of reading texts, new disciplines applied to the texts, all provide invaluable aid in understanding Jesus' world and his own relation to it. Such research participates in a perpetual feedback loop in which our interpretation of solitary sayings and deeds of Jesus continually modify our overall picture of him, while our overall picture in turn exercises a powerful influence on the way we read the solitary pieces.

It is by now a truism that there is inadequate information to write a biography of Jesus or even to profile his personality. And it is no doubt true that the scholarly reconstructions of the *teaching* of Jesus (for which we have considerably more data) do not carry the religious impact that the mythologized Gospels do. *That is why we must attempt to recover the archetypal meaning of the "son of the man." Only then can we hope to offer an alternative to the perfect, almost inhuman Christ of dogma that has dominated these two millennia of Christian orthodoxy.* I and others similarly inclined are trying to reconstitute Christianity in a more humane direction. For that task, we seek a Jesus who is not the omnipotent God in a man-suit, but someone like us who quested for God at the center of his life and called the world to join him. What we do not know how to do, or even whether it can be done, is to position ourselves in such a way as to experience the Human Being as numinously activating, religiously compelling, and spiritually transformative. If such a thing is possible, new liturgies, music, meditative practices, disciplines, and commitments will spontaneously spring up.

Even if we are able to recover something of the human Jesus, we will still be subject to the second limitation mentioned above: the poverty of our selves. No matter how vast our knowledge of Jesus' period, unless we are also doing something about our spiritual inadequacies, we will be unable to proceed closer to the mystery of Human Being but will simply continue to circle its perimeter, accumulating ever more information without ourselves being changed by the encounter.

No scholar can construct a picture of Jesus beyond the level of spiritual awareness that she or he has attained. No reconstruction outstrips its reconstructor. We cannot explain truths we have not yet understood. We cannot present insights we have not yet grasped. Our picture of Jesus reflects not only Jesus, but the person portraying Jesus, and if we are spiritual infants or adolescents, there are whole realms of human reality that will simply escape us. As Gerald O'Collins remarked, writing about Jesus betrays what we have experienced and done as human beings (O'Collins, 1983, x). Or as a very wise black woman in Texas once said to me, "You caint no more give someone something you ain't got than you can come back from somewhere you ain't been."

The Jesus quest as it manifests today entails a high, but necessary, cost—self-exposure, self-mortification, and personal transformation. Once we step out from behind the screen of historical objectivism into Heisenberg's universe, we become as much the subject of study as Jesus.

After all, "Jesus," "quest," and "Scripture" are not merely artifacts for study or the name given an inquiry. They are great religious impulses and archetypal powers—not just "out there" in the texts to be studied, but already "in here," in the self who is fascinated, repelled, driven, wounded, and possibly healed by these mighty realities.

The Myth of History

The historical-critical method cannot deliver Jesus as he really was. But we should never have demanded that it do so. Its real contribution has been to sift through the Jesus traditions to establish the elements of a reconstruction. We can create the myth of the human Jesus because, as W. Taylor Stevenson has noted, the historical approach is basically a *mythic* way of perceiving the world. The idea of history *is* our modern myth (Stevenson, 1969, 6).

To be sure, the myth of history is falsified when we pass from claiming that reality is historical in nature to insisting that reality can *only* be discerned by use of historical method. Historical investigation cannot, for example, establish whether some people truly love others or are acting from the motives they give for their behavior. Historical study, while indispensable, is incapable of providing the kind of insights that can make the Bible come alive with the power to facilitate transformation—which is the manifest intention behind its writing and preservation in the first place. Every historical image of Jesus that is created serves the myth of the human Jesus, because today we are constituted by the myth of history.[1]

However much scholars differ on details, and however much they quibble over interpretations, what most do agree on is that Jesus really was a human being and that our historical findings can help us recover aspects of his humanity. Because traditional Christianity suppressed his humanness in favor of his divinity, the recovery of Jesus' full humanity is felt as a remedial and even, for some, a sacred task.

That Jesus really lived is, to be sure, required, not by some putative historical science, but by the Christian myth itself. Faith is not dependent on historiography, but it can certainly be helped by it. Historical criticism can fashion possible alternative images of Jesus that can free us from oppressive pictures spawned by churches that are too often themselves oppressive. Critical scholarship can help us recover Jesus' critique of domination. It also permits us to appreciate him without an overlay of dogma that claims absolute truth and negates the value of other approaches to understanding Jesus.

Jesus' Original Impulse

My goal in studying the Gospels is to recover what Jesus unleashed—the original impulse that prompted the spread of his message into new contexts that required new formulations in his spirit. In this essay, I have attempted to develop a perspective on Jesus using the historical critical method, depth psychology, and a critique of domination. I have developed that critique more fully in Chapter 6 of *Engaging the Powers* (Wink, 1992). To summarize that critique briefly, Jesus condemned all forms of domination:

- patriarchy and the oppression of women and children;

- the economic exploitation and the impoverishment of entire classes of people;
- the family as chief instrument for the socialization of children into oppressive roles and values;
- hierarchical power arrangements that disadvantage the weak while benefiting the strong;
- the subversion of the law by the defenders of privilege;
- rules of purity that keep people separated;
- racial superiority and ethnocentrism; and
- the entire sacrificial system with its belief in sacral violence.

Jesus proclaimed the Reign of God (or "God's Domination-Free Order") as not only coming in the future but as already dawning in his healings and exorcisms and his preaching of good news to the poor. He created a new family, based not on bloodlines, but on doing the will of God. He espoused nonviolence as a means for breaking the spiral of violence without creating new forms of violence. He called on people to repent from their collusion in the Domination System and sought to heal them from the various ways they had been dehumanized by it.

In my analysis of texts in this book, I privilege Jesus' critique of domination over all other viewpoints because after a lifetime of study I have found it to be the most radical and comprehensive framework for understanding what he was about. Using a critique of the Domination System as my selective grid enables me to recover emphases lost as the Gospel was domesticated in the early church. Although occasionally Jesus' teachings were further radicalized (as in Stephen's speech in Acts 7 or the extension of the mission to include Gentiles), the more pronounced tendency of the tradition was to accommodate the Gospel in significant ways to structures of domination (for example, the treatment of women in later New Testament writings). This critique of domination does not replace the historical criteria worked out with such care by New Testament scholars. It does provide the primary criterion for discerning what was revelatory in Jesus' life and message.

I should add that I am using "revelatory" not in a theological but in an epistemological sense (Poland, 1985, 468). I regard a "revelation" as any new idea that comes bursting upon the world with sufficient force to bring about positive change in people and history. A revelation is not, as modern thought has insisted, a private, subjective *experience* that happens to individuals. It is a public, historic occasion, an open ledger on the account of actual events. What we call a revelation is a positive mutation in the history of thought or being. Buddha was a revealer, as was Lao-Tzu, Zoroaster, Muhammad, St. Francis, Karl Marx, Sigmund Freud, Mohandas Gandhi, Teilhard de Chardin, Carl Jung, and others—some of far less fame and accomplishment. But it was Jesus who exposed the Domination System with such devastating effect, and it was Jesus who envisioned God as nonviolent and all-inclusive. There were antecedents, of course, but the revelation Jesus brought was so utterly at odds with the world's power arrangements that we are still far from taking its measure today.

I am concerned not so much with whether Jesus actually said something as whether it is true, regardless of who said it. If truth is our goal rather than historicity, then revelation is a far more appropriate category than facticity for weighing the impact of Jesus. If something is revelatory, if it provides insights about becoming more fully human, if it exposes the Domination System for what it is, then we may call it "true." But we should not assume that something is true because Jesus said it; rather, he would have said it because he thought it was true. Some sayings later developed by various churches are no doubt true; it is even conceivable that some things Jesus said are not true, though most of these would have been filtered out in the process of transmitting the tradition (though the church did courageously retain passages that were clearly disconfirmed, such as the second coming, Mark 9:1 par.).

The myth of the human Jesus *requires* that Jesus must have made mistakes, had flaws in his personality, sinned, and otherwise exhibited imperfect (that is, human) behavior. But the issue of historicity, while occasionally crucial, is far less significant than *consistency with the original impulse of Jesus*, whether articulated by him or by his followers later. That impulse was the spirit that drove Jesus through the villages of Galilee and ultimately to risk death in Jerusalem. Working from the vantage point provided by a critique of domination, the criteria of historicity can be employed when needed to isolate texts that illuminate the human Jesus. To be sure, this involves us in a hermeneutical spiral (*not* a circle) in which the fragments are interpreted by that critique, and that critique is modified by the fragments, and on and on. All historical work proceeds thus. Indeed, failure to continue the spiral is to abort the entire enterprise. Consequently, if a critique of domination fails to account for significant elements of the tradition, it would have to be modified or abandoned altogether.

The presence of a perspective does not spell the end of objectivity; we are still required to provide warrants for our claims. Once one abandons the chimera of disinterestedness, however, objectivity is free to become what it should have been all along: just another name for simple honesty and the willingness, like Schweitzer, to be changed by what we discover.

I listen intently to the Book. But I do not acquiesce in it. I rail at it. I make accusations. I censure it for endorsing patriarchalism, violence, anti-Judaism, homophobia, and slavery. It rails back at me, accusing me of greed, presumption, narcissism and cowardice. We wrestle. We roll on the ground, neither of us capitulating, until it wounds my thigh with "new-ancient" words. And the Holy Spirit is right there the whole time, strengthening us *both*.

That wrestling ensures that our pictures of Jesus are not mere repetitions of the prevailing fashion. They can be a groping for plenitude, an attempt to carry on the mission of Jesus, and an effort to transcend the conditioning of the Domination System. And in the end, we may not just be conforming Jesus to ourselves, but in some faint way perhaps conforming ourselves to the truth revealed by Jesus.

My deepest interest in encountering Jesus is not to confirm my own prejudices (though I certainly do that) but to be delivered from a stunted soul, a limited mind, and an unjust social order. No doubt a part of me wants to whittle Jesus down to my size so that I can avoid painful, even costly, change. But another part of me is exhilarated by the possibility of becoming more human. So I listen in order to be transformed. Somehow the Gospel itself has the power to activate in people that "hunger and thirst for justice" that Matthew 5:6 speaks about (whether by Jesus or by someone else of the same mind). There are people who want to be involved in inaugurating God's domination-free order, even if it costs them their lives. *Respondeo etsi mutabor*: I respond though I must change (Rosenstock-Huessy, 1969, 751). And in my better moments, I respond *in order to change*.

Truth is, had Jesus never lived, we could not have invented him.

Notes

This chapter was adapted from Wink, W. (2002). *The Human Being: Jesus and the Enigma of the Son of the Man*. Minneapolis: Fortress, 2–16.

1. As Hal Childs commented to me, "a significant dimension of our ontology today, our core being, is the myth of history. This is why 'history' is so important to us, why it is so important to perceive and portray Jesus historically. We conceive of ourselves as historical be-ings; history is our be-ing. History does not mean 'true facts.' It is a grand narrative with ontological status, which because of its ontological status, feels absolutely real at a

pre-reflective level within us, as our being. I am trying to make this myth more conscious, but because it is still mostly unconscious, or we are mostly unconscious to it, there is ongoing confusion as we try to think about it."

References

Childs, H. (2000). *The Myth of the Historical Jesus and the Evolution of Consciousness.* SBL Dissertation Series 179. Atlanta: Scholars Press.

Malina, B. (2001). *The Social Gospel of Jesus: The Kingdom of God in Mediterranean Perspective.* Minneapolis: Fortress.

Matt, D. C. (1993). New-Ancient Words: The Aura of Secrecy in the Zohar, *Gersom Scholem's Major Trends in Jewish Mysticism 50 Years After,* P. Schafer and J. Dan, eds. Tübingen: Mohr.

O'Collins, G. (1983). *Interpreting Jesus.* London: Chapman.

O'Flaherty, W. D. (1986). The Uses and Misuses of Other Peoples' Myths. *JAAR, 54,* 219–39.

Poland, L. M. (1985). The New Criticism, Neoorthodoxy, and the New Testament. *Journal of Religion, 65,* 468.

Rosenstock-Huessy, E. (1969). Farewell to Descartes, *Out of Revolution.* New York: William Morrow & Co.

Rowbotham, S. (1989). *Toward a Feminist Theory of the State,* C. A. MacKinnon, ed. Cambridge: Harvard University Press.

Stevenson, W. T. (1969). *History as Myth.* New York: Seabury.

Stock, B. (1990). *Listening for the Text: On the Uses of the Past.* Baltimore: Johns Hopkins University Press.

Wink, W. (1992). *Engaging the Powers.* Minneapolis: Fortress.

CHAPTER 10

SOCIAL IDENTITY, STATUS ENVY, AND JESUS AS FATHERLESS CHILD

Andries G. van Aarde

The discomfort historians have with giving a psychohistorical portrayal of Jesus can be attributed to Albert Schweitzer's sharp criticism of psychopathologists' attempts to analyze Jesus (Joy, 1948, 19). Some of these psychological studies were triggered by Schweitzer's own work. He had placed the emphasis on Jesus as a "wild apocalyptic prophet." This, and the reference in Mark 3:21 that Jesus' own family thought him to be insane, led psychologists to question Jesus' sanity and to ask whether he was suffering from hallucinations and paranoia. All of this resulted in Schweitzer writing a doctoral thesis in psychiatry on a psychopathological analysis of Jesus entitled *The Psychiatric Study of Jesus: Exposition and Criticism* (Schweitzer, 1913/1948). He investigated the psychopathological phenomena of hallucination and paranoia and found that Jesus did not suffer from them.

Schweitzer, as a trained theologian and historical scholar, was not only interested in therapeutic matters. From a historical and literary perspective, he had a problem with the unsophisticated use of textual evidence (Schweitzer, 1906/1913, 362–367). Schweitzer was heavily influenced by Martin Kähler (1896/1969, 14). Theologians and exegetes who followed Schweitzer's lead, such as Rudolf Bultmann (1926/1988, 8–10) and Ernst Käsemann (1954/1960, 187–214), labeled the Freudian approach to biblical interpretation "psychological fallacy." Reading psychobiographical constructs of Jesus, Karl Barth said decisively: "I do not know this man" (Jüngel 1990/1995,

87). According to Albert Schweitzer, psychopathologists "busy themselves with . . . Jesus without becoming familiar with the study of the
historical life of Jesus. They are completely uncritical not only in
the choice but also in the use of sources. . . . We know nothing about
the physical appearance of Jesus or about the state of his health"
(Schweitzer, 1913/1948, 44–45, 47). Bultmann was prompted by Albert
Schweitzer's finding that exegetes who draft biographies of Jesus
often project their own ideologies onto their images of Jesus. Such ideologies include the exegetes' own ideas regarding ethical-religious
perfection, goodness, sinlessness, and holiness. These are projected
onto the inner being of the person Jesus (Joy, 1948, 19, 23).

Bultmann's student, Ernst Käsemann, agrees with this. "Bei einem
Leben Jesu kann man schlechterdings nicht auf äußere und innere
Entwicklung verzichten. Von der letzten wissen wir jedoch gar nichts,
von der ersten fast gar nichts außer dem Wege, der von Galiläa nach
Jerusalem, von der Predigt des nahen Gottes in den Haß des offiziellen
Judentums und die Hinrichtung durch die Römer führte" (Käsemann,
1954/1960, 187–214).

It is in this same vein that the work of David Stannard is relevant.
In 1980, Stannard wrote a book with the title *Shrinking History: On
Freud and the Failure of Psychohistory*. He pointed out four problems in
the works of historians who make use of psychoanalytical investigations within the Freudian paradigm: therapy, logic, theory, and culture. Being in accord with most of the aspects of his thesis, I also am
suspicious of some recent psychoanalytic studies of Jesus, such as John
Miller's book, *Jesus at Thirty: A Psychological and Historical Portrait*
(van Aarde, 2002a, 2002c). My historical and literary problems with
Miller's thesis are the following:

1. His uncritical acceptance of the fourth-century patristic tradition
in the work of Epiphanius, Panarion 3.78.10, is problematic. According to this tradition, Joseph died soon after the family visited the Temple in Jerusalem, and the twelve-year-old Jesus shamed the wisdom of
scribes (Bertrand & Ponton, 1955, 141–174; Meier, 1991, 317, 353
note 6). However, historically and critically seen, it is also almost
impossible to argue for the historical authenticity of the Lukan episode of the child Jesus in the Temple. Social scientific critics would
rather explain Luke's narration in light of the way in which youth in
antiquity is described. Josephus (*Ant.* 5.10.4), for example, refers to
the wisdom of Solomon at the age of twelve when he was enthroned,
and also to the wisdom and spiritual maturity of Daniel at age twelve
(De Jonge, 1978, 323). Many inscriptions from antiquity refer to the

wisdom of children that does not match their age (Kleijwegt, 1991, 126-130).

2. His deductionistic inference that Jesus performed duties as a surrogate father (Stein, 1966) is dubious. According to Miller, Jesus had an "emotionally secured" childhood on account of Jesus' "love of the word 'Abba' as a term for addressing God" and Jesus' positive sayings on children, as well as his use of the father–son relationship as image in his parables (Miller, 1997, 39–40).

3. The use of New Testament evidence in Miller's work exhibits a debatable historical and social scientific methodology with regard to the evolution of the Jesus tradition. Yet, remaining reliant on a sound social-psychological model, I am convinced that the fragmentary and scattered biographical data of Jesus' life can be explained in a coherent manner. Without being ethnocentric, one can use insights from social psychology and social anthropology to develop such a construct.

My presupposition is that Jesus probably grew up without a father in his life. I argued for this position in my book *Fatherless in Galilee: Jesus Child of God* (van Aarde, 2001).

The Ideal Type Model

Modern psychiatry and psychology tend to describe the behavior of collectivistic-oriented people, of whom we read in the Bible, in terms of modern individualistic Western categories (Pilch, 1997; Bourguignon, 1979). Viewed from this perspective, Stannard's "problem of logic" pertains to making a conclusion about someone's behavior based on psychoanalysis, while completely lacking empirical observation (Stannard, 1980, 53–82). In the case of Jesus, information in the New Testament and other related literature from antiquity provides the data for an empirical investigation. The fact that we do not have Jesus' words as recorded by himself but only as transmitted by witnesses may easily lead to two fallacies. The first is that it would be impossible to determine the core of the mindset of the historical Jesus. The second fallacy is that it may be deemed undesirable to undertake an historical Jesus investigation because the real Jesus is the Jesus to be found on the surface level of the Bible and not behind the text.

Taking the complexity of the Jesus tradition seriously does not mean that a historian is unable to construct a coherent mosaic of probabilities because of scattered, isolated evidence. In this regard, Max Weber's notion of "ideal type" can be helpful. According to Weber, an ideal type is a theoretical construct in which possible occurrences are brought into a meaningful relationship with one another so that a coherent image may be formed of data from the past (Weber, 1949, 89–112). In other words, as a theoretical construct, an ideal type is a conceptualization that will not necessarily correspond with empirical reality. As a construct displaying a coherent image, the ideal type does influence the conditions of investigations into what could have happened historically.

The purpose of establishing an ideal type is to account for the inter-relationships between discreet historical events in an intelligible manner. Such a coherent construct is not formed by, nor based on, a selection from what is regarded as universally valid. In other words, an ideal type refers to what is common to all relevant cases of similar concrete situations of what could in reality have happened. It is, therefore, no logical-positivist choice based on either inductive or deductive reasoning.

By using the model of an ideal type to develop a construct of Jesus as a fatherless figure who called God his father, I am not claiming that this construct is based on what is common to all fatherless people in the first-century Galilean situation. That would amount to inductive historical reasoning. Neither is it based upon what is common to most types of cases of fatherless people in the Galilean situation. That, again, would amount to deductive historical reasoning.

The ideal type model enables one to concentrate on the most favorable cases. I am particularly interested in the question of why the historical Jesus linked up with John the Baptist and submitted to the baptism for the remission of sins. I am also interested in why, once his road deviated from the Baptist, Jesus, so unconventionally for his time, became involved with the fate of fatherless people, especially women without husbands and children without fathers. The answers to these questions could rely on a construct of an ideal type regarding someone in first-century Herodian Palestine who was "healed" from the stigma of being a fatherless son and started a ministry of healing/forgiving "sinners" (van Aarde, 2000, 1–19). Jesus died because of the subversiveness of this ethos. It all happened against the background of the ideologies of the Second Temple Judean cult and Roman imperialism.

My aim is to provide an explanation of the historical figure of Jesus, trusting God as his father, destroying conventional patriarchal values, and, at the same time, caring for the fatherless, within the macro-sociological framework of family distortion and divine alienation in the time of Herodian Palestine. The ideal type should be historically intelligible and explanatory. It should rely on contemporary canonical and non-canonical texts that have to be interpreted in terms of a chronological stratification of relevant documents. It should also make sense within a social stratification of first-century Herodian Palestine (Fiensy, 1991, 158; Stegemann & Stegemann, 1995, 74).

The question at stake regards why Jesus was baptized—in other words, washed from iniquities to live a proper, ethical lifestyle. My understanding of Jesus' baptism is that it was a ceremonial event through which "sinful sickness" was addressed and healed. The unfortunate relationship with his family and his critique against the patriarchal family provide a clue for understanding the stigmatization that caused the "iniquity" from which he suffered. Jesus' birth record tells us of more than just this stigma of being fatherless and why he had a tense relationship with his family and townsfolk in Nazareth. Textual evidence prompts us to inquire critically whether Joseph fulfilled any role in Jesus' life and, moreover, whether Joseph was an historical figure at all.

The Quest for the Historical Joseph

The historical critical investigation of the first phase of the life of the child Jesus gave the following results: We do not know whether Jesus of Nazareth was conceived while his mother, Mary, was engaged to Joseph. It is unclear whether Joseph was the biological father of Jesus. Mary seems to have been his biological mother. We are uncertain whether Jacob was the father of Joseph and, therefore, whether Jesus was indirectly of Davidic descent. It seems as though Joseph was the name of the man who adopted Jesus as his child. Other than this reference, Joseph did not seem to fulfill any role at all in the life of Jesus (van Aarde, 2001).

Because of early, independent, multiple attestation, it is historically improbable that Mary gave birth to Jesus as a result of having been either raped or seduced by an unknown man. Yet it is also uncertain whether Mary was a virgin at the time of conception. She probably became pregnant when Herod the Great was the king of the Jews. The story of the manger, shepherds, and magi should be regarded as unhistorical. This also applies to the reports that the birth took place in Bethlehem, that children were murdered as a result of Jesus' birth, that Jesus was taken to Egypt by his parents after his birth, that John the Baptist was the cousin of Jesus or of priestly descent, and that Jesus was taken to the Temple as a child where Simeon and Anna saw him.

Apart from the reference to Joseph in the genealogy of Jesus, Joseph is also called a woodworker in the Gospel of Matthew, and Jesus is mentioned as being his son. Mark mentions that Jesus was a woodworker. Luke does not make any reference at all in this regard but does indicate that Jesus is Joseph's son. There are no other references to Joseph in any document originating before 70 C.E. In the New Testament documents originating after 70 C.E., reference is made to Joseph's righteousness, his Davidic ancestry, his dream, the angel's conversation with him, his "holy marriage" to the impure Mary, his trip to Egypt with his family, and his trip to the Temple with Mary and Jesus.

In the documents originating since the second century, we find further mention of Joseph's righteousness and elaboration on the fact that he was a woodworker, that he was very old (eighty-nine years) when he took Mary in as his wife, that he never had sex with her, that his youngest son, James, was still a child when this happened, that he also had other children, and that he died at the age of 111 (Schaberg, 1994a, 708–727).

Historically seen, it is highly problematic to refer to Joseph as the father of Jesus at all. These references do not occur in writings originating before the beginning of the separation of the Pharisaic synagogue and the church after the destruction of Jerusalem in 70 C.E. and the termination of the earliest Jesus movement in Jerusalem. No known father played a role in the life of the historical Jesus.

Seen thus, an altogether different portrait of Jesus emerges. It is a picture of a "sinner," away from his home village, trapped in a strained relationship with relatives, but experiencing a fantasy homecoming in God's Kingdom. It is probably within such circumstances that an "imaginary reality" that the Spirit of God created brought about Jesus' altered consciousness of encountering the care of a heavenly father. He both attested to and lived this reality. Through the stories and letters of associates, Jesus became the icon of God's forgiveness of sin and daily care.

My thesis is that the "ethical example" that the Old Testament Joseph figure fulfilled in Hellenistic-Semitic literature served as a model for the transmitters of the early Christian tradition (Niehoff, 1992). The authors of the Gospels of Matthew, Luke, and John also knew the Joseph tradition. They found themselves, like others during the period from 70 C.E. until 135 C.E., in synogogical controversies about Jesus' "illegitimacy." They counteracted by positioning Jesus as the "son of Joseph, the son of Jacob," of Egypt fame.

Joseph sired children from his gentile Egyptian spouse, Asenath. Asenath's virginity is not mentioned in the Genesis account; however, both the nature of Joseph's marriage to Asenath and her virginity were already widespread literary topics in the first century C.E. For example, Josephus (Jewish Antiquities 2:9), parallel to Joseph and Asenath, refers among others to both their "most distinguished marriage" and Asenath's virginity (Niehoff, 1992, 106). This reference alone rules out the possibility that the author of Joseph and Asenath took this topic from the evidence in the New Testament. What is in all probability the case is that both the tradition in the Gospel material in the New Testament and documents like *Joseph and Asenath* share a common idealization of Joseph's holy marriage. It is furthermore remarkable to notice that "rabbinic Midrash is . . . concerned with Asenath's alien origin and [that] this disturbing fact is accounted for in numerous ways" (Aptovitzer, 1924, 239–306; Niehoff, 1992, 107).

The children from the "holy marriage" between Joseph and Aseneth formed the "house of Makir." Makir was the adopted grandson of Joseph, born in Egypt (Michaud, 1976, 77–135). Manasseh and Ephraim were born to Joseph by Asenath, daughter of Potiphera, priest of Heliopolis (On) in Egypt (Gen. 46:19). As Jacob legitimated Manasseh and Ephraim (Gen. 48:8–12), Joseph did the same to Makir, son of Manasseh who also was born in Egypt (Gen. 50:23b). The Makarites became the forefathers of the Israelites who settled in the northern parts of Israel. The Judeans labeled them "Samaritans."

For the puritan Judeans, the name "Samaritan" was equivalent to being a bastard (the Talmudic tractate Kiddushin 75a; cf. Masseket Kutim 27; Montgomery, 1968, 180–181). Samaritans were people with no right to enter the Temple in Jerusalem because they were not the "true" children of Abraham (Egger, 1986; Coggins, 1975, 53). Joseph and Judah became the symbols of challenge and riposte regarding impurity and purity in cultic life (Malina, 1981/1993, 28–55, especially 33). In John's Gospel (John 8:48), the Judeans labeled Jesus, accused of being illegitimately born, as a "Samaritan" and "demon-possessed."

In Hellenistic-Semitic literature, such as the *Testaments of the Twelve Patriarchs* and *Joseph and Asenath*, the "righteous" Joseph, despite defamation, became the ancestor of children whose sins were forgiven, who were given their daily bread, and who were instructed to forgive others their trespasses, give others their share of God's daily bread, and to request God that they not be tempted to disobey their father's will. The motive of compassion and forgiveness of sin by Joseph the patriarch is the most outstanding theme in *The Testaments of the*

Twelve Patriarchs (Hollander, 1981; Sklar, 1996; Zerbe, 1993; Argyle, 1951–1952, 256–258). The Gospel tradition in the New Testament shares and, in striking ways, makes use of this tradition in its depiction of Jesus (Hollander, 1981, 65, 69–70, 73; Sklar, 1996, 51). In *The Testaments of the Twelve Patriarchs*, powerful parallels exist between Joseph recorded in Matthew and Joseph the patriarch. One example is the reference to the "righteous (= good) person" (Matt. 1:19; Test. Gad 6:3–4, 7) who "has not a dark eye," for "he shows mercy to all people, even though they are sinners"; "on the poor person he has mercy; with the weak he feels sympathy" (Test. Benjamin 4:4d, Test. Zebulon 6:5, 7:3). This deliberate resemblance should not surprise us. In *The Testaments of the Twelve Patriarchs*, next generations are instructed to imitate "our father Joseph." In her work *The Figure of Joseph in Post-Biblical Literature*, Maren Niehoff finds that, "for one reason or another, Joseph seems to represent for each narrator a certain Ideal Type" (Niehoff, 1992, 52).

The same is true with regard to Matthew's Joseph and the Joseph depicted in the romance *Joseph and Asenath*. Whereas *The Testaments of the Twelve Patriarchs* in its present form is dated in the second or third century C.E., it actually goes back probably to the second century B.C.E., while *Joseph and Asenath* is dated in the period between 100 B.C.E. and 115 C.E. (Chesnutt, 1996, 286). The latter is a Hellenistic-Semitic romance that focuses on God's intervention in making Joseph the patriarch (parallel to the Joseph in the Gospel tradition) take Asenath, an "impure" woman, though a virgin, into his house. It is a story of a "holy marriage." Against this background, Greek-speaking Israelites who became Christians retold the life of the Jesus of history. For some of them, Jesus, despite slander, became the icon of God's forgiveness of sin and daily care (Test. Gad 4:1–2), thanks to the God of his father (Gen. 49:25), Joseph, son of Israel.

No Christian writing that originated between the years 30 C.E. and 70 C.E. indicates anything about Joseph's connection with the Jesus of history. Such a conclusion has far-reaching consequences for historical Jesus research. It seems that Joseph did not die early in Jesus' life. Historically seen, we have no evidence for such an assumption except the fourth-century C.E. reference in Epiphanius. The earliest textual evidence reveals that Joseph entered the scene rather belatedly, at a time when Jesus was already crucified.

For Greek-speaking Israelites, Joseph was an ethical paradigm. For Pharisees he was the symbolic adversary of Judah (Test. Gad 2:3–4 for riposte against the "covetousness" of Judah by selling Joseph for "thirty pieces of gold"). For the Judean Pharisees, Joseph was the fore-father of people who either came from the pagan world or mixed with them—those Joseph-people whom the Judeans regarded as bastards because they were a mixture of the children of God and gentiles, peo-ple who should be treated as if they have no parentage (van Aarde, 1998, 315–333).

Who was first—the chicken or the egg? Who claimed first that the fatherless Jesus was the son of Joseph: Pharisees who regarded such a charge as a denotation of illegitimacy, or Greek-speaking Christians among the Israelites who regarded such a claim as a denotation of the intervention of God who turns slander into exaltation? We do not know—but what is important is that these two different perspectives relate to the way in which one looks at Jesus. He was either the ille-gitimate son of Joseph or the legitimated child of God on account of his adoption by Joseph.

An Inflation of Historical Probabilities?

Having constructed Jesus' "whole life" within first-century Herodian Palestine, it seems to me that it is not an inflation of historical proba-bilities to say that the following features of Jesus' life go together (van Aarde, 2003):

- Records show he was born in a context in which there are indications that "opponents" alleged that he was born out of wedlock;
- A father figure was absent in his life;
- He was an unmarried bachelor;
- He had a tense relationship with mother and other siblings;
- He was probably forced from farming to carpentry;
- He was stigmatized as a "sinner," which led him to be associ-ated with a revolutionary baptizer;
- He spiritually experienced an altered state of consciousness in which God was present and acted like a Father;
- He abandoned craftsmanship, if he ever was a woodworker;
- He was "homeless" and led an itinerant lifestyle along the lake-shore;
- His journey seemed never to take him inside the cities Seppho-ris and Tiberias but was restricted to the plains, valleys, and hills of Galilee;
- He assembled a core of close friends;

- He defended fatherless children, patriarchless women, and other outcasts;
- He called them a "family" by resocializing them into God's household by empowering healing as an agent of the Spirit of God;
- He offended village elders by subversive teaching and actions;
- He outraged Pharisees, Herodians, chief priests, and elders in Jerusalem by criticizing the manipulative ploys and misuse of hierarchical power by the Temple authorities;
- He was crucified by the Romans after an outburst of emotion at the outer Temple square;
- He died under uncertain circumstances and his body was not laid down in a family tomb;
- He was believed to be taken up to the bosom of father Abraham to be among the "living dead" as Scriptures foretold;
- He was believed to be God's beloved child who was already with God before creation, and who is now preparing housing that is actually already present for those who still live by his cause.

In other words, what comes before and after "Jesus at thirty," to use John Miller's expression, seems to be his fatherlessness.

Let me repeat: fatherlessness is an ideal-typical construction of the Jesus of history and the Jesus of faith. I cannot prove that this image is the "real" Jesus. However, this ideal type should be historically intelligible and explanatory with regard to the textual evidence and archaeological findings. Vice versa, it should rely on contemporary canonical and non-canonical texts, including archaeological artifacts, which have to be interpreted in terms of a chronological stratification of relevant documents. It would also have to be congruent with the social stratification of first-century Herodian Palestine; and also such that the ideal type of Jesus' social identity as being fatherless can also be explained social-psychologically and cultural-anthropologically. The "status envy hypothesis" and anthropological information about sleeping arrangements provide data for a model in terms of which such a social identity can be justified.

Status Envy and Social Identity

In the peasant society of Jesus' world, the family revolved around the father. The father and mother are the source of the family—not only in the biological sense, but because their interaction with their children creates the structures of society. A peasant economy is geared toward subsistence—the mere maintenance of the family, rather than investment in the future. This is the peasant father's goal, and therefore the socialization process employed in such communities is one that fosters the child's dependence. In the peasant society of the first-century Mediterranean world, everyone had a social map that precisely defined one's position in terms of identity, kinship, and expected behavior (Scott, 1989, 71; depending on Jerome H. Neyrey).

In the 1960s, a cross-cultural study on the father's position in the family as it relates to the process of identification of children was done from the perspective of social psychology at Harvard University. At a symposium during which the evidence of this research was tabled, Roger V. Burton of the National Institute of Mental Health and John W. M. Whiting of Tulane University shared a paper, a shortened revision of which was published in 1961 in the *Merrill-Palmer Quarterly*. This research, supported by cross-cultural material, was related to what is called the "status envy hypothesis." Specifically, the evidence focuses on the effect of father absence in the household. The outcome of the inquiry differs from some other theories of identification in that, in terms of their hypothesis, a relationship that fully satisfies both parties is not conducive to identification. According to the status envy hypothesis, for children to identify fully with others, it is necessary that they openly consume resources, which are, however, denied to the children. In other words, love alone will not produce identification unless the people a child loves withhold from him or her something he or she wants. This is particularly true during the process of socialization. This process involves familiarizing the child with the privileges and disabilities fundamental to the structure of a particular society.

As part of the cultural rules of every society, there is a status system that gives privileged access to resources for some positions in the system and, at the same time, debars other positions from controlling and consuming them. Were these resources inexhaustible and equally and completely available to all, there would be no learning by identification because there would be no such thing as status envy. Such, however, is never the case. No one in a household in any society has unlimited access to every resource. Societal taboos make it practically impossible. It is inevitable that some resources will be withheld, and that someone will want them. It is particularly true in agrarian societies with limited goods and that are patrilocal in nature. In societies with patrilocal residence, a man spends his whole life in or near his place of birth. This results in a core of closely akin blood-related male residents, supplemented by wives drawn from neighboring communities. The women are literally and figuratively outsiders. It is the men who are the locus of power and prestige; "adult males are the ones to be envied" (Burton & Whiting, 1961, 89).

Identification is achieved by the imitation of a status role that is envied (Burton & Whiting 1961, 85). This happens not overtly but in fantasy or play, and the driving force is envy of the person who enjoys the privileged status to which one aspires. In every society, statuses have names or labels. The family, especially the father, was at the center of the first-century Mediterranean world. Beyond the family lay the village, beyond that the city, and further still the limits of the world. This understanding of society served as an analogy for the concept "Kingdom of God" (Scott, 1989, 79; Theissen, 1999). The father's role in the family was not only representative of God, but he was also the one who had to ensure that God was worshipped and obeyed. One had to belong to a family to enjoy God's blessing, and within the family, the father's status was divinely ordained (Hamerton-Kelly, 1979, 27).

A person's identity is his or her position or positions in the status system of a particular society. Three kinds of identity can be distinguished: attributed, subjective, and optative (Burton & Whiting, 1961, 85). Attributed identity consists of the statuses assigned to a person by other members of his or her society. Subjective identity consists of the statuses a person sees himself or herself occupying. And finally, optative identity consists of those statuses a person wishes he or she could occupy but from which he or she is debarred.

The aim of socialization in any society is to produce an adult whose attributed, subjective, and optative identities are isomorphic—"I see myself as others see me, and I am what I want to be." However, such isomorphism necessitates a transition marked by status debarment, which produces status envy and a reaching out from attributed to optative identity. That is, to become an adult who wishes to have a father, a person, according to the status envy hypothesis, would be deprived of the privilege of having a father during infancy. When society then permits him or her to occupy this privileged status, there is agreement on what he or she wants to be, on what society says he or she is, and on what he or she sees himself or herself to be.

Obviously, one's optative identity derives from status envy, and it should always be objective and realistic. According to this theory, a fatherless infant who has been supplied everything by his or her mother would not identify with her as he or she already occupies the privileged status. We can presume that if a man wishes to have a fictive family, he did not occupy a privileged status within his biological family during infancy. And one could continue on this line: If someone is said by members within the community of Israelites to be the son of Abraham and the son of God, these labels could express status envy and optative identity. The first name is an expression of a position within the extended genealogical family of Israel; the latter, the symbolic or fantasized expression of the mentioned position of having or being a father. In normal conditions, both types of labels are expressions of attributed identity. Having a position in the family is an identification of secondary nature, while having a father is a primary identification.

In Cross-Cultural Perspective

Cross-cultural studies yield significant variables bearing on the hypothesis as postulated. Specifically, the social structure of a sample of societies was judged for the degree to which the father and adult males in general occupied privileged statuses as perceived by the infant, and later by the child (Burton & Whiting, 1961, 88–89). One such measure of privileged status and therefore of status envy in childhood is provided by the sleeping arrangements that pertain to a society (Whiting, Kluckhorn, & Anthony, 1958, 359–370). Another measure of privileged status pertains to marriage arrangements.

Sleeping Arrangements

Because it is the place where resources of greatest value to a child are given or withheld, a child's bed is at the center of its world during infancy. Those who share sleeping arrangements with the child become the child's models for primary identification. The key question in this regard is whether the father also sleeps with the mother. A baby sleeping on its own in a separate room is something quite unique. In thirty-six out of sixty-four societies examined, the parents sleep apart during the nursing period so that the infant enjoys its mother's exclusive attention at night. In the remaining twenty-eight societies, the parents sleep together, with the child either sleeping in the bed with them or placed in a crib or cradle within reach of the mother.

It follows that, in terms of the hypothesis postulated, the different situations prevailing would have a profound effect on the child's primary identification. If the parents sleep together, they both bestow and withhold resources, so that the envied status would be either parent. The infant perceives the juxtaposition of privilege to be between itself and an adult. On the other hand, where the parents sleep apart, the mother assumes a vast importance in the child's life. The juxtaposition of privilege is between the child and her. Because she sometimes withholds resources, she is the person who is envied. Therefore, in societies where infants enjoy their mothers' exclusive attention in terms of sleeping arrangements, the optative identity of boys may be expected to be primarily of a cross-sexual nature, while those reared in societies where, because of the sleeping arrangements, both adults withhold resources and therefore are envied, the optative identity of boys is more likely to be directed to adulthood as such.

Residence patterns also provide the conditions for secondary optative identity in the case where sex-determined statuses are relatively unprivileged because of primary cross-sex optative identity. Patrilocal societies would produce a conflict between primary and secondary optative sex identity where you have exclusive mother–child sleeping arrangements. In societies with maximum conflict in sex identity, for example, where a boy initially sleeps exclusively with his mother and where the domestic unit is patrilocal and hence controlled by men, initiation rites at puberty resolve this conflict in identity.

In the above-mentioned sample of sixty-four societies, there are thirteen in which there are "elaborate initiation ceremonies with genital operations" (Burton & Whiting, 1961, 90). All thirteen of these have the exclusive mother–infant sleeping arrangements, which according to the hypothesis, would cause a primary feminine identification. Furthermore, twelve of these thirteen had patrilocal residence, which would produce the maximum conflict in identity and hence the need for an institution such as an initiation rite to help resolve this conflict. Initiation rites serve the psychological function of replacing the primary feminine identity with a firmly established male identity (Burton & Whiting, 1961, 90). This is accomplished by means of hazing, deprivation of sleep, tests of manliness, and painful genital operations, all of which will be rewarded with the high status of manhood if the initiate endures them unflinchingly. By means of the symbolic "death and rebirth" through the initiation rites performed at puberty, a male born in these societies leaves behind the woman-child status into which he was born and is reborn into his optative status and identity as a man. It is also referred to as a "clarification of status." Centering in on the "spoiled identification" of foundlings in the Greco-Roman world in terms of Victor Turner's concept of "liminality," John Corbett refers to this kind of "rebirth"/"resurrection"/"integration into the community" as a "clarification of status" (Corbett, 1983, 312).

Although women fulfilled the primary, gender-specific role of child-bearing, the mother of a household was empowered to ensure that the other female members of the household regularly bore children as well (Matthews & Benjamin, 1993, 25). Her role as manager of the household was not gender specific. The responsibility for ensuring that everyone was fed and that the food would last entailed careful stewardship of the resources the village allocated to her household. It necessitated absolute control over this aspect of household life (Matthews & Benjamin, 1993, 25). The mother was not only the child bearer and manager of the household; she was also the teacher of its women and children. In respect to boys, this role was transferred to the father once the boy became a young man, participating in the communal labor of the village. As storyteller, the mother communicated community traditions to her children. Typical female behavior included taking the last place at table, serving others, forgiving wrongs, having compassion, and attempting to heal wounds (Malina, 1981/1993, 54).

Various studies that focus on the factor of father-absent households in the early life of boys support the postulated hypothesis of status envy. Specifically, some of these studies, done from the perspective of present-day Western society, indicated that "war-born" boys from father-absent households not only behaved like girls in fantasy behavior but also showed very little aggression (Burton & Whiting, 1961, 93). This kind of performance derives from the first, or primary identification, of the boys. Their secondary identification led to behavior, overtly and in fantasy, that produced father-like performance.

Sigmund Freud held that the child's identification with its father originates in the child's desire to be like the father, but that this is later replaced by the drive to replace the father in the mother's affections (Hamerton-Kelly, 1979, 38). Contrary to Freud's contention that the father is at the center of consciousness, Hubertus Tellenbach is of the opinion that the role of the father figure has vanished today from the Western psyche (Tellenbach, 1976, 7–11). In the seventies, Tellenbach was the chairperson of the Department of Clinical Psychopathology at the Psychiatric Clinic in Heidelberg, Germany. From years of studying young schizophrenics, he found that the father played no role whatsoever in their lives. According to Tellenbach, the Oedipal "Phase des Vaterprotestes in der Vorgeschichte so gut wie immer fehlte" (Tellenbach, 1976, 7). He demonstrated that the "disappearance" of the father today is the outcome of a long process, which he traces back in art and literature.

From a macro-sociological perspective, the disappearance of the father might be seen as something that has its roots in the period during which "simple agrarian societies" in the Middle East developed into "advanced agrarian societies" (Lenski, Nolan, & Lenski, 1970/1995, 188–222). Although kinship ties remained of great importance for individuals throughout the agrarian era, these were no longer the "chief integrating force" in advanced agrarian societies (Lenski et al., 1970/1995, 213).

Such profound economic changes, especially with regard to Herodian Palestine, had an inevitable effect on kinship patterns and social relationships. The extended family (the beth-av) was slowly breaking up (Fiensy, 1991, 132). The Hellenistic period inaugurated far-reaching change for many Israelites who had previously lived in extended family units, subsisting through communal labor on isolated farms. They now found themselves most commonly in nuclear families, living and working on large estates (Fiensy, 1991, 121).

It seems that only two options were open to peasants if they needed to adjust to their income when their families disintegrated because their "agro-economic" base was removed (Wolf, 1966, 15): they could either increase their production or reduce their consumption. The former strategy necessitated putting more labor into their piece of land, but this strategy was hardly worthwhile in terms of returns. So they were propelled to try to supplement their income from the land. They could hire themselves out as day laborers doing seasonal agricultural work, work temporarily in the fishing industry, or perhaps become craftsmen (Fiensy, 1991, 95). Neighbors of the courtyard of the village, which became the only viable economic unit, started to function as a social supportive unit. This was true of village life in the ancient Mediterranean world, and as children seldom left the village upon attaining adulthood, neighbors increasingly constituted the socioeconomic basis of relationships (Fiensy, 1991, 135; Harper, 1928, 106). Ties of blood or marriage generally related villagers to each other.

Marriage Arrangements

Marriage arrangements in Judean society were very tightly linked to the way the Temple cult in Jerusalem was organized. The Temple cult also determined the classification of both people and politics. This means that holiness was understood in a highly specific way. "To be holy meant to be separate from everything that would defile holiness" (Borg, 1987–1991, 86–87). When someone was considered a nobody, such a person would have no identity and would experience a tense relationship with villagers, even with close relatives. Status envy would therefore come as no surprise.

Marriage regulations determined by the Temple cult in Jerusalem would have continually reminded a Galilean of Jerusalem. The Torah determined the rules prescribing who could marry whom. The hierarchy making up the pattern of the Temple community was clearly visible in the post-exilic marriage regulations. According to the way in which society was organized, three types of marriage strategies can be distinguished in the world of the Bible: "reconciliatory," "aggressive," and "defensive" (Malina, 1981/1993, 159–161). These three types are broadly related to three successive periods in the life of Israel: that of the patriarchs, the kings, and the post-exilic second Temple period.

Regulations with regard to marriages during the post-exilic Second Temple Period were determined strongly by cultic purity regulations. Marriages were only allowed when they took place within the ambit of one's own group of families, the "family of procreation"—that is, the "house of Israel" (Malina, 1981/1993, 50). Marriages were geared toward the continuation of the "holy seed"—that is, of the physical "children of Abraham" (Malina, 1981/1993, 137–38). These marriage arrangements were embedded in the stratification of people from holy, to less holy, to impure (Jeremias, 1969, 271–73, inferred from m.Kiddushin 4:1; m.Horayoth 3:8; t.Rosh hash-Shenah 4:1; and t.M'gillah 2:7). This hierarchy of holiness determined who could marry whom, and who could enter the Temple:

- Priests
- Levites
- Full-blooded Israelites
- Illegal children of priests
- Converts (proselytes) from heathendom
- Converts from the ranks of those who had previously been slaves but had been set free
- Bastards (born from mixed-marriage unions or through incest)
- The fatherless (those who grew up without a father or a substitute father and therefore were not embedded within the honor structures)
- Foundlings
- Castrated men (eunuchs)
- Men who had been eunuchs from birth

- Those with sexual deformities
- Hermaphrodites (bisexual people)
- Gentiles (non-Israelites)

These fourteen groups can be divided into seven categories; the priests, Levites, and "full-blooded" Israelites formed the first three categories. Illegal (not illegitimate) children of priests were children born of marriages that were inadmissible to priests. A priest was forbidden to marry women who already "belonged to a man," such as widows, divorcees, or women who had been raped. These "illegal children" of priests formed, with both groups of proselytes (converts from heathendom and freed slaves), the fourth category. Bastards, the fatherless, foundlings, and the castrated formed the fifth category. Those born eunuchs, those with deformed genitals, and hermaphrodites—in other words, people who could not marry at all—made up the sixth category. People with another ethnic orientation—those who, in other words, were outside of "God's people as people of the covenant"—formed the seventh category. Any involvement with these people was very strongly discouraged in Israel.

The second to the last category, the sixth, could make no biological contribution to the continuation of "holy seed," the "children of Abraham." "True Israel" actually consisted only of the first three categories. They could, with certain limitations, freely intermarry. People from the fourth category ("illegal children" of priests and proselytes) did belong to Israel and were allowed to marry Levites and "full-blooded" Israelites, but daughters among these "illegal children" and daughters of proselytes were under no circumstances allowed to marry priests. The fifth category was simply deemed "impure"—people outside of the covenant, doomed as far as the Temple in Jerusalem was concerned, not to approach any closer than the Temple square, the so-called court of the gentiles—which is to say that they were obliged to live as if God did not exist; people labeled as not forming part of the children of Abraham and therefore not being children of God (Sanders, 1993, 229). If a man like this wanted to get married, he could do so only with an "impure" woman, among whom the gentiles too were categorized. Otherwise, such a person remained unmarried. In a society in which the honor of a man, in fact his entire social identity, was determined by his status as a member of the family of Abraham and his contribution to the physical continuation of that family, one's status as being unmarried had serious implications, to put it mildly.

Does Jesus Fit the Model?

The image of the historical Jesus as the fatherless carpenter, the unmarried son of Mary who lived in a strained relationship with his village kin in Nazareth, probably because of the stigma of being fatherless and therefore a sinner, fits the ideal type of the fifth category described above. Although innocent as a child who was not supposed to know the nature of sin, the historical Jesus was denied the status of being God's child, doomed not to transmit the status of proper covenant membership and therefore not allowed to enter the congregation of the Lord in the light of the ideology of the Temple cult and its systemic sin.

Yet he was someone who shared the vision of John the Baptist that remission of sin could be granted by God outside the structures of the Temple. Both before and after his baptism and breach with John the Baptist, Jesus was noted for association and friendship with "sinners" and for his trust in God as his father. This attitude is certainly subversive toward the patriarchal values that underlined the marriage strategy of the Second Temple Period. The historical claim may therefore be made that, in terms of the criteria of the period of the Second Temple, Jesus was regarded as being of illegitimate descent in the sense of his being fatherless. On account of their "permanent sin," fatherless men (boys over the age of twenty) were not allowed to enter the Temple (cf. Deut. 23:3) or to marry a "full-blooded" fellow Israelite ([Babylonian] Y'bamot 78b; Fiensy, 1991, 165). Fatherlessness would not lead to a "clarification of status" with regard to the boy's social identity.

In first-century Mediterranean society, child rearing established both the feminine quality of nurture and the male quality of assertion in the behavior of children (Pilch, 1991). In early childhood, the boy learned nurturing values, but these became displaced by the "clarification of status" that marked his passage at puberty from the gentle world of women to the authoritarian world of male values. It is a kind of transformation that develops out of a parenting style in the Near East through which the boy learns from his father (or male-next-of-kin) that, to use the words of James Barr, "Abba isn't Daddy" in the Western sense of the word (Barr, 1988). In an aggressive and hierarchical world of men, a boy learned at puberty, when "clarification of status" takes place, to reject the comfort of childhood and the warmth of feminine values and to embrace instead the rigors of manhood, subjecting himself in unquestioning obedience to the severity of the treatment that his father and other males might inflict upon him.

However, if "clarification of status" is lacking because of fatherlessness, one can anticipate a diffused identity. It is likely that status envy could cause, as Donald Capps suggests with regard to Jesus, the "child . . . as an endangered self" to desire "to be another man's son" (Capps, 1992, 21). In the words of Jane Schaberg, "the paternity is canceled or erased by the theological metaphor of the paternity of God" (Schaberg, 1994b). The resources, which were withheld in Jesus' case, would be those that a father was expected to give his son. Since Jesus called God his father, it seems that the followers of Jesus interpreted his suffering as a filial act of obedient submissiveness to God, his heavenly father.

Because of the assumption that the primary identification of Jesus was never "clarified" by a secondary identification, the fatherless Jesus seemingly behaved in a "mother-like" manner as an adult (Jacobs-Malina, 1993, 2). It can be seen in his sayings and deeds in which he advocated and acted a behavior of taking the last place at table, serving others, forgiving wrongs, having compassion, and healing wounds. Such a "conflict laden" performance caused spontaneous, if not intentional, anti-patriarchal behavior.

Jesus' attributed identity seems to consist in his fatherless status; in his being as the members of his society perceived him. This position, assigned to him because of the purity ideology during the Second Temple Period, would lead to his debarment from being a child of Abraham—that is, a child of God, a nobody who was not permitted to marry a "full-blood Israelite." Jesus' subjective identity seems to consist in the status he saw himself occupying: the protector and defender of the honor of outcasts like abandoned women and children, giving the homeless a fictive home. And, finally, Jesus' optative identity, which consists in that status he wished he could occupy but from which he was debarred, seems to be a child of Abraham, child of God—which could be the reason why the fatherless Jesus called upon God as his father.

Jesus made use of a symbol that, in his culture, signaled a most intimate bond—that of the father–son relationship. A father without a son had no honor or credibility. A son without a father had no honor or identity. However, even in his use of this symbol, Jesus subverted the cultural arrangements of his time. According to these hierarchical arrangements in the culture, the patriarch represented his family before God. No one in the family could experience God's presence without being embedded in the realm of the father. Jesus, however, did not use the metaphor of "father" as the way to God; rather, he used the metaphor of "child." The argument was that the father figure symbolizes in patriarchy the representation and access to the presence of God. Jesus expected that people should become like children to experience God's presence and not to be "fathers" or to find access to God through the father figure. Whosoever is not like a child cannot experience the presence of God. Even more radical than this is that Jesus did not use the child who had been legitimized by the father as symbol. According to Mark 10:13–16, Jesus pointed to street children without parents as a symbol of those who belonged to the realm of God (van Aarde, 2002b).

It seems as though Jesus expressed his own experience by means of this symbol. As a fatherless figure, Jesus saw himself as the protector of fatherless children in Galilee as well as of women who did not "belong" to a man (Mark 10:2–12). These women and children were regarded as outcasts, as they did not fit into the patriarchal system. Jesus himself in many ways acted like a woman. Jesus not only called God "father" but also lived among the outcasts as if they and he were children of God—in other words, as their "fictive" brother. As the cause of Jesus expanded, the metaphor "child of God" became part of Christian language usage, as Christians experienced God's presence in their lives through their embeddedness in the identity of Jesus as child of God.

References

Aptovitzer, V. (1924). Asenath, the Wife of Joseph. *Hebrew Union College Annual, 1*, 239–306.

Argyle, A. W. (1951–1952). The Influence of the Testaments of the Twelve Patriarchs upon the New Testament. *Expository Times, 63*, 256–258.

Barr, J. (1988). Abba Isn't "Daddy." *Journal of Theological Studies, 39*, 28–47.

Bertrand, F. G., & Ponton, G. (1955). Textes patristique sur Saint Joseph. *Cahiers de Josephologie, 3*, 141–174.

Borg, M. J. (1987/1991). *Jesus: A New Vision—Spirit, Culture, and the Life of Discipleship.* San Francisco: HarperSanFrancisco.

Bourguignon, E. (1979). *Psychological Anthropology: An Introduction to Human Nature and Cultural Differences.* New York: Holt, Rinehart, Winston.

Bultmann, R. (1926/1988). *Jesus (Neuausgabe).* Tübingen: Mohr-Siebeck.

Burton, R. V., & Whiting, J. W. M. (1961). The Absent Father and Cross-Sex Identity. *Merrill-Palmer Quarterly, 7*, 85–95.

Capps, D. (1992). The Desire to Be Another Man's Son: The Child Jesus as an Endangered Self, *The Endangered Self,* Monograph Series 2, R. K. Fenn & D. Capps, eds. Princeton: Center for Religion, Self and Society, Princeton Theological Seminary, 21–35.

Chesnutt, R. D. (1996). From Text to Context: The Social Matrix of Joseph and Aseneth, *SBL 1996 Seminar Papers.* Atlanta: Scholars Press.

Coggins, R. J. (1975). *Samaritans and Jews: The Origins of Samaritanism Reconsidered.* Atlanta: John Knox.

Corbett, J. H. (1983). The Foster Child: A Neglected Theme in Early Christian Life and Thought. Traditions in Contact and Change: Selected Proceedings of the 14th Congress of the International Association for the History of Religions, *Canadian Corporation for Studies in Religion,* P. Slater & D. Wiebe, eds. Wilfrid Laurier University Press, 307–321.

De Jonge, J. (1978). Sonship, Wisdom, Infancy: Luke 2:41–51a. *New Testament Studies, 24,* 317–354.

Egger, R. (1986). *Josephus Flavius und die Samaritaner: Eine terminologische Untersuchung zur Identitätsklärung der Samaritaner.* Freiburg (Schweiz): Universitätsverlag. (Novum Testamentum et Orbis Antiquus.)

Fiensy, D. A. (1991). *The Social History of Palestine in the Herodian Period: The Land Is Mine,* Studies in the Bible and Early Christianity, 20. Lewiston: Edwin Mellen.

Hamerton-Kelly, R. (1979). *God the Father: Theology and Patriarchy in the Teaching of Jesus, Overtures to Biblical Theology.* Philadelphia: Fortress.

Harper, M. (1928). Village Administration in the Roman Province of Syria. *Yale Classical Studies, 1,* 105–168.

Hollander, H. W. (1981). *Joseph as an Ethical Model in the Testaments of the Twelve Patriarchs. Studia in Veteris Testamenti Pseudepigrapha.* Leiden: Brill.

Jacobs-Malina, D. (1993). *Beyond Patriarchy: The Images of Family in Jesus.* New York: Paulist.

Jeremias, J. (1969). *Jerusalem in the Time of Jesus: An Investigation into Economic and Social Conditions during the New Testament Period.* Philadelphia: Fortress.

Joy, C. R. (1948). Introduction: Schweitzer's Conception of Jesus, *The Psychiatric Study of Jesus: Exposition and Criticism,* A. Schweitzer, translated and with an introduction by C. R. Joy and a foreword by W. Overholser. Boston: Beacon.

Jüngel, E. (1990/1995). The Dogmatic Significance of the Question of the Historical Jesus, *Theological Essays* (vol. 2), J. B. Webster, ed., A. Neufeldt-Fast & J. B. Webster, trans. Edinburgh: T. & T. Clark, 82–119.

Kähler, M. (1896/1969). *Der Sogenannte Historische Jesus und der Geschichtliche, Biblische Christus, Neu Herausgegeben von E. Wolf* (vol. 2), *Systematische Theologie* (4th ed.). München: Kaiser Verlag.

Käsemann, E. (1954/1960). Das Problem des Historischen Jesus, *Exegetische Versuche und Besinnungen* (vol. 1). Göttingen: Vandenhoeck, 187–214. Originally published in *Zeitschrift für Theologie und Kirche, 51,* 125–153.

Kleijwegt M. (1991). *Ancient Youth: The Ambiguity of Youth and the Absence of Adolescence in Greco-Roman Society.* Amsterdam: Gieben.

Lenski, G., Nolan, P., & Lenski, J. (1970/1995). *Human Societies: An Introduction to Macrosociology* (7th ed.). New York: McGraw-Hill.

Malina, B. J. (1981/1993). *The New Testament World: Insights from Cultural Anthropology* (rev. ed.). Louisville: Westminster.

Matthews, V. C., & Benjamin, D. C. (1993). *Social World of Ancient Israel, 1250–587 BCE*. Peabody: Hendrickson.

Meier, J. P. (1991). *A Marginal Jew: Rethinking the Historical Jesus*, vol. 1: *The Roots of the Problem and the Person*. New York: Doubleday.

Michaud, R. (1976). *L'histoire de Joseph, le Makirite (Genese 37-50)*. Paris: Éditions du Cerf.

Miller, J. W. (1997). *Jesus at Thirty: A Psychological and Historical Portrait*. Minneapolis: Fortress.

Montgomery, J. A. (1968). *The Samaritans: The Earliest Jewish Sect. Their History, Theology and Literature*. New York: KTAV.

Niehoff, M. (1992). *The Figure of Joseph in Post-Biblical Jewish Literature, Arbeiten zur Geschichte des Antiken Judentums und des Urchristentums 16*. Leiden: Brill.

Pilch, J. J. (1992). Beat His Ribs While He Is Young (Sir 30:12): Cultural Insights on the Suffering of Jesus. Unpublished paper presented at the Context Group Meeting in March, Portland, OR.

Pilch, J. J. (1997). Psychological and Psychoanalytical Approaches to Interpreting the Bible in Social-Scientific Context. *Biblical Theology Bulletin*, 27(3), 112–116.

Sanders, E. P. (1993). *The Historical Figure of Jesus*. New York: Allen Lane Penguin.

Schaberg, J. (1994a). The Infancy of Mary of Nazareth (Proto-James and Pseudo-Matthew), *Searching the Scriptures*, vol. 2: *A Feminist Commentary*, E. Schüssler-Fiorenza, ed. New York: Crossroad, 708–727.

Schaberg, J. (1994b, October). The Canceled Father: Historicity and the NT Infancy Narratives. Paper presented at the Westar Institute's Jesus Seminar, Santa Rosa.

Schweitzer, A. (1906–1913). *Geschichte der Leben-Jesu-Forschung, Zweite, neu bearbeitete und vermehrte Auflage des Werkes Von Reimarus zu Wrede*. Tübingen: Mohr-Siebeck.

Schweitzer, A. (1913/1948). *The Psychiatric Study of Jesus: Exposition and Criticism*, C. R. Joy, trans. Boston: Beacon.

Scott, B. B. (1989). *Hear Then the Parable: A Commentary on the Parables of Jesus*. Minneapolis: Fortress.

Sklar, H. W. (1996). The Fighter of Horizons: The Story of Joseph as a Model for Social and Spiritual Reconciliation. Unpublished master's thesis, Graduate Theological Union, Berkeley.

Stannard, D. E. (1980). *Shrinking History: On Freud and the Failure of Psychohistory*. New York: Oxford University Press.

Stegemann, E. W., & Stegemann, W. (1995). *Urchristliche Sozialgeschichte: Die Anfänge im Judentum und die Christusgemeinden in der mediterranen Welt.* Stuttgart: Kohlhammer.

Stein, R. H. (1966). *Jesus the Messiah: A Survey of the Life of Christ.* Downers Grove: InterVarsity.

Tellenbach, H. (1976). *Das Vaterbild im Mythos und Geschichte: Ägypten, Griechenland, Altes Testament, Neues Testament.* Stuttgart: Kohlhammer.

Theissen, G. (1999, June). Die politische Dimension der Verkündigung Jesu. Paper presented at the International Symposium, Jesus in neuen Kontexten: Sozialwissenschaftlichen Perspektiven der Jesusforschung, Evangelische Akademie Tutzing, 25–27.

van Aarde, A. G. (1998). Matthew 27:45-53 and the Turning of the Tide in Israel's History. *Biblical Theology Bulletin, 28*(1), 16–26.

van Aarde, A. G. (2000). Understanding Jesus' Healings. *Scriptura, 18,* 1–19.

van Aarde, A. G. (2001). *Fatherless in Galilee: Jesus as Child of God.* Harrisburg: Trinity Press International.

van Aarde, A. G. (2002a). Jesus as Fatherless Child, *The Social Setting of Jesus and the Gospels,* B. J. Malina, W. Stegemann, & G. Theissen, eds. Minneapolis: Augsburg, 65–84.

van Aarde, A. G. (2002b). Jesus and Joseph in Matthew's Gospel and Other Texts. *Neotestamentica, 35,* 1–21.

van Aarde, A. G. (2002c). Jesus als vaterloses Kind: Eine kulturübergreifende und sozialpsychologisches Perspektive, *Jesus in neuen Kontexten,* W. Stegemann, B. J. Malina, & G. Theissen, eds. Stuttgart: Kohlhammer, 98–111.

van Aarde, A. G. (2003). Does Historical Jesus Research Have a Future? *Verbum et Ecclesia, 24*(2), 553–556.

Weber, M. (1949). *Max Weber on the Methodology of the Social Sciences,* E. A. Shils & H. A. Finch, trans. & eds. Glencoe: Free Press.

Whiting, J. W. M., Kluckhorn, R., & Anthony, A. (1958). The Function of Male Initiation Ceremonies at Puberty, *Readings in Social Psychology,* E. E. Maccoby, T. M. Newcomb, & E. L. Hartley, eds. New York: Holt, 359–370.

Wolf, E. R. (1966). *Peasants.* Englewood Cliffs: Prentice Hall.

Zerbe, G. M. (1993). *Non-Retaliation in Early Jewish and New Testament Texts.* Sheffield: JSOT Press.

CHAPTER 11

A Way Forward in the Scientific Investigation of Gospel Traditions: Cognitive-Critical Analysis

Paul N. Anderson, J. Harold Ellens, and James W. Fowler

While biblical scholarship has been quite open to integrating multiple disciplines into exegetical and hermeneutical studies, only recently have psychological studies been welcomed to the table.[1] There are good reasons, however, for this reluctance. Too easily have psychological approaches to the Bible been used to produce results more conducive to the interpreter's interests, therefore depriving the Bible of its voice and co-opting its authority. Likewise, "psychologizing the text" has rightly become a charge to be avoided, in favor of more chaste and measured exegetical approaches.[2] A further vulnerability of psychological approaches to the Bible, or to any other text, is the specious character of the methodologies used. Where some schools of psychology have greater and lesser degrees of credibility—within the field and otherwise—these reputations and their subjective appraisals have given way to more "objective" approaches to interpretation. For these and other reasons, the last century or more of biblical scholarship has prized the historical-critical method above all others, displacing nearly all psychological approaches to biblical interpretation and anything bearing a close resemblance.

However, the problem with objectivistic approaches to the study of the Bible is that it was written by *subjects*—human beings—seeking to engage hearers and readers personally.[3] Communication, expression, and the preservation of memory are subjective ventures, not objective ones, so one's approach to interpretation must be adequate for the task at hand. While reading one's situation and needs into the text might distort the text's most basic meanings, it is also true that texts can legitimately have more than one valid meaning. In fact, the most powerful of texts are considered classics because of the rich and prolific variety of meanings they continue to convey. For this reason, the best tools available for getting at the meanings of texts should be employed, and the best of psychological approaches to interpretation includes *cognitive criticism—analyzing the ways biblical writers came to think about issues in relation to their perceptions and experiences.* Aside from the hermeneutical value of employing such tools, the interest of the present investigation is to consider the impact cognitive-critical analysis might have upon the scientific investigation of Gospel traditions. In that sense, cognitive criticism is adopted as a primarily historical-critical tool rather than a hermeneutical one, although that venture could also be profitably explored.

Such a contribution is needed because of the *limitations* of the ways historical-critical analyses have been conducted until now. First, historical-critical methodologies have been afflicted by an *overly objectivistic approach to historiography.* Too easily, modernistic understandings of what "history" consists of have dominated our approaches to Gospel traditions, resulting in the privileging of empiricism and facticity over other more fitting measures of truth.[4] The result has been the setting up of mechanistic grids for determining historicity and the default rejection of anything not measuring up to contrived standards. In this regard, developing disciplinary approaches to assessing subjective factors in historiographic analysis will allow a more nuanced approach to Gospel-tradition analysis, with the result that valuable insights might be contributed to understandings of the material's character and origin.

A second limitation of historical-critical methodologies is that they *fail to account for human factors* in originative and developing Gospel-tradition histories. All four Gospels make clear allusions to the disciples not understanding things Jesus said and did but that with time they developed fuller understandings. This implies a dialogue between earlier perceptions and later understandings, affected by emerging experiences and new perceptions. Without some attention given to discovery and evolving understandings, earlier traditional material gets misunderstood by critics and thus labeled wrongly. A cognitive-critical analysis, however, would allow for movement in understanding, and it would factor in the correlations between theological content and human experience.

A third limitation of historical-critical methodologies is the way that historical-critical methodologies set up categories of naturalism versus supranaturalism[5] and exclude everything that does not measure up to the former standard. Understandings of the miraculous in the modern era are not necessarily the same as such during the first century of the Common Era, and taking into account factors of human perception broaden the possibilities for our understandings of realism. For instance, more adequate knowledge regarding how something may have come to be experienced or perceived as "wondrous" in the ancient Mediterranean world is extremely helpful for deeming reports within or without modern canons of historicity. Without cognitive-critical tools for interpretation, reports of traditional perceptions and developments lose their resilience and suffer at the hand of overly brittle measures of historicity proper.

A fourth limitation of historical-critical methodology involves the *inadequacies of assuming that Gospel traditions were disembodied sets of ideas* floating from one region to another, without factoring in the human element in their development and conveyance. Even if contemporary religious ideas played roles in the formation of traditional content, questions of why particular typologies were embraced and how they were assimilated by particular human beings are weighty considerations in the investigation. It could also be a fact that particular renderings of Jesus within distinctive Gospel traditions may have been related to the gifts and ministries of those particular Christian leaders; therefore, ways the human sources of Gospel traditions ideated and came to conceive of their understandings are important considerations for getting Gospel traditional analysis right.

A fifth limitation of historical-critical methodologies is that *redaction analysis and source-critical inferences often fail to account for more nuanced ways one tradition may have influenced another*. As scholars are now exploring oral developments of Gospel traditions and interfluential[6] relations between them, cognitive approaches to how these interactions may have worked may indeed provide helpful ways forward. Understanding how the collectors, crafters, and purveyors of Gospel material may have done their work, based upon their own understandings of things, adds to the realism of how Gospel traditions may have emerged. Cognitive criticism thus affords greater nuance to investigations of Gospel interrelations and the lack thereof.

In the *selecting* of cognitive-critical tools to be used for exegetical analysis, several criteria should be employed. First, the best and most useful models should be selected over alternative ones. Methodologies that have earned the respect of cognitive theorists and are based on convincing research and nuanced use stand the greatest chance of being serviceable over the long run. Second, tools need to be selected that are appropriate to the task for which they are being used. The character of the epistemological inquiry should determine the selection of the tools, and cognitive-critical means should be employed along with other useful tools in an interdisciplinary fashion. Third, tools need to be used in ways that facilitate getting at the truth of a Gospel narrative rather than promoting the agenda and interests of the interpreter. In that sense, the same measures of neutrality and disinterest relevant to the use of other methodologies apply here. Fourth, the results of the uses of tools should be repeatable by other theorists, and they should be comprehensible to those wishing to ascertain their validity. Finally, tools should be selected that offer the fullest interpretive value; yet this will only be ascertained after the results of the analysis are presented and reflected upon.

The particular tools I have used to get at the epistemological origins of John's dialectical presentation of material include the crisis-transformational model of James Loder and the faith-developmental model of James Fowler.[7] Their works were applied to Johannine and Markan Gospel traditions along the lines of two theological interests: ascertaining perceptions of Jesus' humanity and divinity, and interpreting the miracles of Jesus. In the first theme, perceptions and experiences gave rise to reflection as to what sort of a being Jesus was; the second interest addressed individuated reflections as to why miracles happened and why they did not. The development of both of these themes can be inferred in Markan and Johannine traditions, and they may even have been in dialogue with each other along the way. Insights from these analyses, then, relate to gaining a fuller understanding of the experiential/reflective processes early Christians must have gone through in telling the stories of Jesus, and they also cast light on how these things relate to readers and hearers in later generations. In that sense, Gospel writers and traditions were more like ourselves than we might have thought.

About This Study

The present study includes four sections. Following this introduction is a review of my book, *The Christology of the Fourth Gospel* (Anderson, 1996), by J. Harold Ellens. In this excellent review, Professor Ellens comments upon the book and its place within the history of interpretation. His insights into its place within emerging psychological approaches to the Bible are especially significant, but he also knows the scholarly literature about John well enough to comment valuably on the book's impact within Johannine studies and biblical theology at large. His words are greatly appreciated, and his insights are, as usual, keen and insightful.

The third section is an abridged version of my "reception report" on the same book presented at the 1998 Orlando AAR/SBL meetings. The original version gathered the highlights of over thirty-five reviews, including international ones, and it sought to make sense of what aspects of the book appear to make contributions among reviewers, what aspects are more controversial, and what sorts of ways the book might further cognitive-critical approaches to studying Gospel traditions. The abridged version in this chapter addresses comments and critiques that refer to the latter concern, focusing on the reviewers who commented upon the uses of Fowler (1981) and Loder (1981), as well as related cognitive-critical contributions.

The fourth section is a response to the third, also presented at Orlando, which allows James Fowler to comment evaluatively on how well *The Christology of the Fourth Gospel* employs his and Loder's models in conducting Gospel tradition-history investigations. As well as engaging the present monograph and essay, Professor Fowler was asked to comment on ways his faith-development work might be applied to other sorts of biblical studies, including prospects for the future. It is in the service of that larger venture that these three sections and the introduction are contributed to the present collection. Indeed, the greatest measure of whether cognitive-critical approaches to biblical texts are serviceable to exegetical studies is the degree to which they catch on. That being the case, the success of the present venture will only be able to be ascertained from the reflective perspective of the future.

In some ways, psychological approaches to biblical interpretation are today where sociological approaches were two and three decades ago—just getting going, and still in the nascent stages of their development. However, as particular approaches to biblical interests call for the use of cognitive-critical methodologies, new vistas will be opened and new opportunities may emerge for getting closer to the central meanings of biblical texts. Not all approaches will be of equal value. Some will be limited by the adequacy of the method, and some will be limited by the extended use of a worthy tool. Nonetheless, the measured and reflective employment of a worthy cognitive-critical tool not only opens up our insights into original meanings of classic

biblical texts; it helps us consider what those texts might mean for
later readers as well. If the present studies contribute toward that venture, they will have served a valuable purpose indeed—but only the
reader will be able to decide if that is so.

A Review by Ellens of Anderson's Work on John's Christology: A Case Study in the Cognitive-Critical Analysis of Gospel Traditions

New Testament studies have been considered a field of research that
is an inch wide and a mile deep, and this is especially true of Gospel
studies. While saying something new about a Gospel text is not
impossible, and while saying something worthy is only slightly less
uncommon, the great challenge is to contribute both within the same
analysis. Such is the case for this interdisciplinary treatment of John's
notoriously intriguing Christology, as Paul N. Anderson has added
cognitive-critical analysis to the mix of literary, historical, and theological exegetical approaches (Anderson, 1996). In so doing, not only
are the primary issues of Johannine studies critically engaged, but the
epistemological origins of John's Christological tensions are meaningfully elucidated. This is what makes this work important for biblical
studies and Christian theology in general, as well as for the exploration of new and effective methodologies in particular. The present
review, therefore, endeavors to assess the value of this creative monograph as a case study for cognitive-critical approaches to the scientific
analysis of Gospel traditions.

This superb volume of New Testament exegetical study is a revision and expansion of Professor Anderson's doctoral dissertation, suc-
cessfully submitted and defended at the University of Glasgow in
1988. At the time of this review, its author was serving as visiting
associate professor of New Testament at Yale Divinity School, on a
leave of absence from George Fox University in Oregon. D. Moody
Smith asserts in the opening sentence of his laudatory foreword that
this book "is at once one of the most concentrated and intensive exegetical studies and one of the most wide-ranging and suggestive
essays on Johannine Christology that I have seen" (Anderson, 1996,
iii). Professor Anderson states that John's portrayal of Jesus is one of
the most fascinating and provocative in the New Testament. It presents him as both human and divine, and this tension has been a prolific source of debate and disagreement within Christianity and
beyond. The purpose of this work is to explore the origins and char-

acter of the Christological tensions of the Fourth Gospel by means of seeking a deeper understanding of the dialectical process of thought by which the evangelist has come to embrace such a distinctively unitive *and* disunitive Christology. To illustrate this tension, Anderson cites the entertaining quote from Conybeare in his review of Loisy's *Le quartrieme evangile*, to the effect that if Athanasius had not the Fourth Gospel, Arius would never have been refuted; adding that if Arius had not the Fourth Gospel, he *would never have needed refuting* (Anderson, 1996, 1f.).

Anderson's book is an example of consummate scholarship, thoroughness, and attention to detail, both in its formal structure and in its exhaustive exegetical contents. Its ten chapters are structured within three major parts, each of which is augmented by an articulate introduction and a concise summary of findings and conclusions. The book also includes eight appendices and five bibliographies. It is in his seventh chapter that Anderson's contribution to the cognitive analysis of Gospel traditions stands out most impressively (Anderson, 1996, 137–166). Here the dialectical character of John 6 and the rest of the Fourth Gospel are analyzed by means of building upon Bultmann's and Barrett's descriptions of dialectical thinking, bolstered by the work of cognitive theorists James Fowler and James Loder. This chapter covers such scholarly issues as the linguistic and redactional characteristics of the text, Jesus' ironic response to the miracle-seeking crowd, John's view of sacraments with parallels to what Ignatius called the "medicine of immortality," and the dialectical means by which the evangelist not only reflects upon the ministry of Jesus, but also the literary means by which he engages his audience in an imaginary dialogue with his narrative subject: Jesus. The conclusion, "On 'Seamless Robes' . . . and 'Left-Over Fragments,'" draws the findings of the book together into a synthesized whole, and four epistemological origins of John's Christological tensions are sketched in the final section. These consist of an agency Christology, the dialectical thinking of the evangelist, the dialectical situation of the evangelist, and literary devices employed to engage the reader in the subject of the Johannine narrative—Jesus (Anderson, 1996, 252–265).

It is not possible in a review, even an extended one, to present the full argumentation of a book of such detailed analysis as this volume presents; however, at least offering the following sweeping summary and some selected illustrative excerpts of method and argument illumining the author's work is required. In 1858 David Strauss described John's Gospel as a seamless robe woven neatly together from top to bottom, an indivisible literary unity. Wellhausen, Bultmann, and others opposed this unitive appraisal in favor of emphasizing John's disunitive features. In doing so, they sought to account for the origins of John's material, especially addressing questions of John's Christological tensions. Why, for example, does the Gospel present us with both *very high and quite low* Christological material? Why was the evangelist so clearly ambivalent about who Jesus was, and what was the significance of those convictions he maintained? What did the Gospel's author really intend to say about Jesus' relationship to God as Father? Was it a relationship of equality, or subordination? Anderson sharpens these questions by putting the inquiry this way: Is the Christological unity and disunity of the Fourth Gospel attributable to tensions *external* to the evangelist's thinking, or *internal* and inherent to it? This is why he was compelled to address literary, historical, and theological issues together. The results of one investigation affect the others, and this will always be so.

Anderson concludes that the simple oppositioning of diachronic and synchronic approaches has not been very helpful, but that a third option that takes into consideration the dynamics of rhetoric and cognition may be more useful: namely, a combined "synchronicity of authorship and diachronicity of audience. This moves the poles of the tensions to the 'dialogue' between the evangelist and the rhetorical targets of his evolving context. A high correlation exists between recent commentators' understanding of John's Christological unity and disunity and the theory of composition adopted by each scholar. This fact suggests that, as progress is made in understanding more about John's Christological unity and disunity, one's insight into composition issues will be enhanced, and *vice versa*" (Anderson, 1996, 253). The crowd, the Jews, the disciples, Jesus, and Peter provide a literary and hermeneutical guide to various watershed turns in the Johannine literature and community.

Bultmann has asked the right questions, but neither his approaches nor his answers adequately demonstrate stylistic or linguistic disunity at a sufficient level to infer more than one literary source. Moreover, the kind of disparate narrative and interpretive comments we find in the text do not clearly demonstrate an editor's adding of disparate material other than that which might have been added later, but probably still originating with the Johannine evangelist. Furthermore, the "contextual difficulties identified by Bultmann are not as problematic as he argues. They do, however, play a central role in his disordering and reordering the discourse material in John 6, so as to bolster the credibility of his theory of composition. More realistically, they betray the evangelist's use of irony, serving to dislocate—and then to relocate—the reader's thinking along the lines of the ethos of the Johannine Jesus" (Anderson, 1996, 254).

Bultmann's treatment of the eucharistic reference in John 6 shifts the focus from John's Christology and urges that the combination of the references to flesh and blood, manna, and nourishment in Christ makes the text seem more disparate than it actually is. In fact it is a literary, stylistic, and theological unity when one realizes the ironic, psychodynamic, and rhetorical devices at play in both the words of the crowd and of Christ. Anderson cites Fowler's structuralist model of personality theory and faith development, as well as Loder's study of the dynamic formation of transforming encounters to explain, in keeping with the Gospel text, what it must have been like for a first-century follower of Jesus to "encounter in him theophanically the transforming presence of the love of God" (Anderson, 1996, 255). For example, the human sources of the traditions underlying Mark and John understood the same events in Jesus' life in remarkably different ways. Without connecting them necessarily with particular personalities, Anderson nonetheless follows the lead of Papias, the second-century writer, in referring to them as "Petrine" and "Johannine" perspectives. Comparing the two with regard to the story of the feeding of the 5,000 demonstrates that there is a series of different levels of perception evident in the Johannine narrative, indicating that the author was moving along a continuum of reflective maturation that ended with the perception of the centrality of being nourished by Jesus as the Bread of Life.

Similarly, with regard to the crowd's interpretation of the sea crossing and Jesus' reaction to it, the author of John's Gospel goes through more steps of developing awareness and interpretation than does the author of Mark's Gospel. These are psychological, cognitive, and rhetorical issues of style and stimulus. "These and a matrix of other perceptual differences may account for much of the interpretive divergence between the 'bi-optic Gospels,' Mark and John. In other words, at least two of Jesus' followers understood his mission and ministry in significantly different ways, and some of these differences extended well into the sub-apostolic era" (Anderson, 1996, 255). The first author, writing in the late 60s C.E., with less time of reflection, digestion, and church tradition development under his belt, has a human Jesus—that is, a lower Christology. The second author, writing in the late first-century C.E., with more decades of psycho-theological reflection, cognitive processing, and a much longer period of the church's confessional and theological unfolding behind him, has a higher Christology of an exalted Christ in tension with a human Jesus: the man from Nazareth who is the Christ of God. This Jesus moves smoothly back and forth in John 6 from God's agent to human discussant. Countering and complementing the view of Peder Borgen, "the section reflects a homily, perhaps given as a Christianized form of midrash, ... and the 'text' with which it begins is not an Old Testament passage (about manna in the wilderness), but the narration of events in the ministry of Jesus. . . . Thus, the invitation to choose the life-producing Bread over other kinds of 'bread' is the exhortative fulcrum of John 6" (Anderson, 1996, 257). Thus, Anderson accounts for the unity and disunity in the Gospel, and the tensions it produces are

attributable to the following factors: a) . . . the dialectical process of theological reflection in keeping with contemporary examples. Two of these include the tension between a present and future eschatology, and the apparent tension between determinism and free will in John. . . . b) What has appeared to be subordinationism versus egalitarianism between the Father and the Son in John is actually a reflection of the *evangelist's agency christology*. The Son is to be equated with the Father precisely because he represents the Father identically. . . . c) The evangelist's ambivalence toward Jesus' signs is an indication of his *reflective dialogue with his tradition*, in which he continues to find new meanings in the significance of Jesus' words and works. . . . d) The tension between the flesh and glory in the evangelist's christology is the result of an *encounter theology*, and the theophany on the lake is a prototypical example of such an encounter. It may even have been formative. Analogous to Paul's experience on the road to Damascus, the memory of this event remained transcendent from the earliest stages of the tradition to its later written rendition, and its slant is fundamentally different from the pre-Markan account. . . . e) A final explanation for some of John's unity and disunity involves the *dialogical means by which the evangelist seeks to engage the reader in an imaginary conversation with Jesus*. By means of local and extended irony, misunderstanding dialogues, discourses which employ rich metaphors christocentrically, and by portraying the stories of other people who encounter Jesus in the narrative, the evangelist woos, cajoles, humours and shocks the reader. In doing so, he seeks to create a *crisis*—a temporary sense of disturbance and dislocation—as this is the *first and prerequisite* step in any experience of knowing. The evangelist adapts to the specific needs of his sector of Christianity, but never does he stray far from his christocentric understanding of God's love, which is always and continually initiating a saving/revealing dialogue between God and humanity. . . . Thus, truth, in the christological sense, must be understood in subjective, personal terms, as well as objective ones. (Anderson, 1996, 260–264)

From this most cursory of all possible treatments of this watershed volume in Johannine and Christological studies, it is clear that Paul N. Anderson has given profound attention to the key issues at stake in his field of work. He has thoroughly digested, in a fair and balanced manner, the immense work of the scholars who have crafted the long and erudite history of the perplexing questions here addressed. He is exhaustive in his treatment of and frequent extended, often multipage, references to the works of Rudolph Bultmann (130 citations), C. K. Barrett (40), Peder Borgen (45), Raymond E. Brown (45), Robert Fortna (35), Robert Kysar (25), Barnabas Lindars (30), D. Moody Smith (30), and the like. Though Anderson has not extensively addressed such issues as Jesus' use of terms such as Prophet, Son of God, Messiah, and Son of Man (the particular current interest of this reviewer), the psychological, rhetorical/oratorical, dialogical/dialectical, theological, and particularly Christological implications of this surprisingly generative volume of careful and detailed textual analysis are of immense value in the study of each of these knotty questions.

Perhaps the greatest value and interest of this book lies in the fact that, while it is of the most exquisitely intense form of scholarly investigation, it remains a most delightfully readable volume which will be of as great an interest and accessibility to the informed lay person as to the most superior and esoteric scholar—and, in my judgment, it is equally necessary to both. Sell your bed and buy a copy of the attractively packaged and decently priced second printing by Trinity Press International (1997). Do it right away! You cannot afford to miss or forget it—there will be a large hole in the fabric of your worldview! This is a definitive volume in the field, which will require the attention of every serious scholar from now on and of every honest inquirer into this arena of truth.

Human Sources of Gospel Traditions—A Report by Anderson on the Reception of *The Christology of the Fourth Gospel* and Implications for Further Study

It is indeed a high privilege to receive such a learned and thoughtful review of one's work as the one provided above by J. Harold Ellens. Not only does he put his finger time and again on the really pressing issues addressed in my book, but he also does so with lucidity and insight. Especially significant is his picking up on the relations

between composition theories, historical issues, and theological interpretation. These interests are intertwined in John, and that is why one
must deal with one of these features to get at the other two—and vice
versa. Especially helpful is the way Professor Ellens has featured the
various epistemological origins of John's Christological tensions. This
is the central conclusion of the book, and he comments helpfully on
the importance of each (Anderson, 1996, 252–265). Thinking of John's
theological tensions in these ways will help, I believe, in understanding its rich material, and this especially applies to the dialectical thinking process of the evangelist. These issues will be unpacked further, as
the following reception report engages the critiques of my work in
ways I hope will facilitate truth-seeking (and truth-finding) inquiry
itself.

John's Christology presents the interpreter with one of the most
fascinating labyrinths of issues and conundrums one can imagine. It
has the highest presentation of Jesus' divinity in the New Testament,
and it presents the clearest picture of Jesus' humanity and subordination to the Father. It contains futuristic and realized perspectives on
eschatology, and its view of miracles is both elevated and existential-
ized. Indeed, 1,900 years of debate have followed in its wake, and the
classic theological discussions of the Christian era have sought to
make sense of its distinctive witness to Jesus as the Christ, often with
opposing sides of debates *both* citing the Gospel of John. What the
church fathers explained by means of metaphysical constructs, modern scholars have addressed by means of diachronic explanations of
composition, among others.

While one approach alone cannot do justice to John's rich set of unitive and disunitive features, the present work seeks to account for the
epistemological origins of these and other tensions by means of applying literary, historical, and theological analyses. As well as these
approaches, the present work also applies sociological and cognitive
studies in interdisciplinary ways, seeking to make the best use of the
best tools available for addressing particular issues at hand. As Wayne
Rollins pointed out several years ago, these ventures not only work
with different disciplines, but they seek to cast light on the history of
Gospel traditions themselves.

This abridged essay, then, presents a few examples of the discussion
of the character, assets, and limitations of applying cognitive-critical
tools to Gospel-tradition analysis in reviews within the scholarly
community, then suggests ways to conduct further study. The most
impressive thing about the reviews and comments so far is that nearly

all of them comment on the dialectical character of the Fourth Evangelist as being key, and nearly in unison declare the cognitive-critical approach to the Johannine tradition to be the most provocative-yet-promising aspect of this study. Time will tell if such is the case.

A Critical Assessment of Johannine Tradition Analysis

Gospel traditions were not disembodied sets of ideas floating around detached from human thought and experience in the first Christian century. No. Gospel traditions were formed, transmitted, and preserved in the memories, convictions, and aspirations of living human beings seeking to connect the momentous past with subsequent contexts and needs. They drew upon Jewish and Hellenistic theological and mythic constructs, but at the same time were creative agents of synthesizing work, connecting recollections and narrations of kairotic events with subsequent situations in the light of emerging experience. In that sense, the human sources of Gospel traditions were themselves practical theologians—asking questions of meaning and seeking to understand the implications of a God, who, in Pauline terms (2 Cor. 5:19), was "in Christ reconciling the world" to Godself.

While this book uses cognitive and other methodologies in assessing the epistemological origins of John's Christological tensions, it is not simply a psychological approach to a biblical interest. It is a historical/critical investigation into the character, origin, and formation of Gospel traditions. Nor does it "psychologize the text" without having considered other approaches. It engages leading historical, literary, and theological issues pertinent to the topic, attempting to make the best use of the most appropriate methodologies for the particular problems facing critical analyses of the text. Some of these require linguistic analyses of language, and some require scientific analyses of ways humans experience, perceive, and reflect upon significant events. Such require the use of cognitive analyses precisely because assumptions of how the human sources of Gospel traditions "must have" or "cannot have" functioned are already operative within interpretive analyses, but often without any basis in psychological research. In that sense, this study challenges uncritical assumptions regarding cognitive factors already at work among biblical scholars, which have not been effectively analyzed in keeping with any sort of research-based model. They simply stand as unquestioned pillars upholding elaborate interpretive structures, which may indeed be recognized as being in great danger of collapse in the face of their foundations' rigorous scrutiny.

For this and other reasons, my work begins with examining the soundness of prevalent approaches to John's Christological unity and disunity employing literary, historical, and theological means of analysis. *The Christology of the Fourth Gospel* thus aspires to the same enterprise of scientific analysis as have the studies of Bultmann and others, seeking to infer the epistemological origins of John's Christological tensions. Any sound theory, however, must possess theoretical validity *and* evidential veracity. Both of these aspects are thus measured as scholarly views on a number of issues are tested analytically. Methods found to be sound are retained and built upon, while those found lacking become the starting place for new questions and ventures.

An all-too-easy fallacy of text analysts is to project their methods onto their subjects, disregarding social, psychological and experiential realities. The problem is not that they are scientific analyses versus other sorts but that constructs rooted primarily in linguistic analysis, without the benefit of sociological and psychological considerations, bear so little resemblance to actual life represented in ancient texts. The present work thus advocates a shift in scientific tradition analysis from a text-dominated enterprise to one that also includes human experience in the formative processes studied.

Three *traditionsgeschichtlich* (history of traditions) assumptions in particular are challenged by this work: first, that because John's treatments of Jesus' signs are filled with tension, the evangelist must have used an alien source with which he disagrees. Bultmann and others reason that he has taken over an alien signs source, with which he feels ambivalent, replacing wonder-attestation endings with his own existentializing valuations. Theoretically, this solution sounds plausible, although it goes against the opinion of the redactor, whoever that might have been. And, as Daniel Merkur has pointed out, diachronic literary solutions to content-oriented problems are always more intrusive and therefore less likely, unless compelling evidence requires such a move. Where the diachronic solution especially falls flat, however, is in terms of the evidence. Given the feeble veracity of these leading *traditionsgeschichtlich* views, validity analysis must be applied. Indeed, it may be possible that the only way to explain theological tension between John's inclusion of signs and their existentialization is to infer a corrective use of an alien signs source—despite the lack of convincing evidence. If this is the case, the critical scholar needs to know. On the other hand, if one might have thought dialectically about the value of signs—even within one's own tradition— such a model needs also to be assessed in terms of its plausibility and validity. *James Fowler's faith-development work thus supplies a fitting approach to such an analysis regarding the emergence and formation of the Johannine tradition.*

A second *traditionsgeschichtlich* opinion accompanies the first, assuming that because John's tradition is so different from the Synoptic presentations, and because John's material has the most elevated presentation of Jesus, John's tradition cannot be regarded as having any connection to the historical ministry of Jesus and must be relegated to a late-and-only-late spiritualization of Jesus and his ministry. If this is so, we need to acknowledge it and move on. However, veracity here is weak also. *The use of James Loder's transformation analysis here applies in seeking to account for the distinctive origin of the Johannine tradition.*

A third issue, then, relates to historical-critical views as to what may and may not have been possible. Ironically, in an attempt to rescue the Gospels from their embarrassing miracles, even more wondrous schemes have been devised to account for how the material came together, if indeed it had no basis in actual events. Bultmann's approach, for instance, assumes it is more believable to infer three independent sources underlying John, which after being gathered by the evangelist became disordered and were then reordered (wrongly) by the redactor, who added further dissonant content. This gives Bultmann "permission" to reorder the material in ways that conveniently confirm his earlier source designations and explain John's Christological tensions accordingly. This is the sort of work referred to by Mikhail Bakhtin in his critique of modernistic literary-critical methodologies: "Underlying the linguistic thinking that leads to the construction of language as a system of normatively identical forms is the practical and theoretical aim of studying dead foreign languages that have been preserved in written texts" (1983, 42).

It cannot be too strongly emphasized *that this philological aim has largely determined the character of all European linguistic thought.* It grew up and matured over the corpses of written languages. Nearly all the main categories, nearly all the basic approaches and skills, were evolved while trying to breathe life into these dead corpses.

A great divide exists, though, between real problems and imagined problems based on modernistic categories foisted upon ancient literature. In this sense, most of our historical-critical and literary-critical paradigms have been constructed without the benefit of considering the best scientific research as to how humans come to ideate, emote, and reflect upon the foibles of human experience. Cognitive criticism attempts to get back into the living realities represented by classic texts. Where literary-critical assumptions are sound, though, one is happy to build upon them. Where they fall short, either in terms of theoretical validity or empirical veracity, they must be improved upon. This is what both my book and this further discussion attempt to do.

A Report on the Reception of
The Christology of the Fourth Gospel

By the end of 1999, the book had been reviewed by forty-two reviewers, and due to the European first printing, at least half of the reviews are in journals outside the United States. All of them were positive, and some even furthered discussions by their engagement. A few review summaries and input relevant to the cognitive-critical analytic aspect and the application of the work of Fowler and Loder are cited below. They are drawn from the published reviews and engagements along with several informal comments, with an eye to their implications for future research.[8]

Positive responses to the book expressed appreciation for a wide range of features, including its exegetical method, its analysis of key Johannine themes, its analysis of the apostolic origins of the Johannine tradition, Johannine Christology, its treatment of ecclesiology, its theory on the evolution of sacraments, its discussion of Johannine/Synoptic relations, the literary analysis of John's text, and technical features such as footnotes, appendices, summaries, tables, and bibliography.[9] Negative responses were largely confined to questions about the history of the Johannine situation and wondering whether "Petrine" and "Johannine" trajectories could be inferred within the Gospel traditions.[10] One of the most significant comments, in my view, is that of Robert Kysar, who used his *Review of Biblical Literature* review to declare his change of opinion regarding John's use of sources.[11] The single most positive aspect of nearly all the reviews, however, involved numerous comments on the *significant interdisciplinary contribution it makes, especially in the application of cognitive studies by Fowler and Loder to the critical analysis of Gospel traditions.* Several commented on this being the most likely to be a controversial aspect of the book, but that it also could be the most provocative and stimulating.[12]

Some reviews expressed a bit of caution about building on the constructs of those whose works are built on those of Piaget and Kohlberg. In response, it is important to note that Loder and Fowler's works are both substantive enough in their own rights to be considered on the bases of their own merits. In particular, Fowler's original

program is constructed on an empirical base of 359 extensive interviews, and as he included women in his survey, his work is not subject
to the same criticisms as Kohlberg's. I recently interviewed Robert
Sternberg, a leading psychologist at Yale University, about the work,
and his impression is that Piaget and Kohlberg were making a come-
back. While deconstructing the giants in any field becomes the rage at
any given time, his feeling is that, despite particular weaknesses of
their theories, the likes of Piaget and Kohlberg seem *less* likely to slip
off the docket than they did a decade ago. Conversely, the works of
several of their critics, not rooted in empirical research, have largely
run their courses. For these and other reasons, worries about the
works of leading faith-development theorists becoming all too quickly
supplanted by alternative approaches may be disregarded.

One review judges, but does not elaborate on the basis for the judgment, that the use of psychological approaches is less than helpful.
After an otherwise positive review, Francisco Contreras Molina
(1997, 375) declares, "Se trata, pues, de un libro sugerente, conoce bien
el mundo joánico, está muy actualizado, pone al corriente de la más
reciente bibliografía exegética. Como salvedad indicamos que tal ves
peca de un exceso de interpretación psicológica con detrimento de la
interpretación teológica del evangelio." (One is treated, then, to a suggestive book which knows well the Johannine world, is very developed, and puts into play the most recent exegetical bibliography. As a
reservation we indicate that sometimes it sins from an excess of psychological interpretation to the detriment of the theological interpretation of the Gospel.) No basis is offered for the latter judgment,
though, nor is there any statement of how theological interpretations
should suffer at the hand of psychology-related exegetical *pecados*, or
even *pecadillos*, at least in this particular case. Assuming that theol-
ogization *did not* involve psychological or cognitive processing is not
adequate either historically or theologically. While the concern for
temperance is understood, the superficial questioning of the enterprise is unconvincing. More discerning is Alan Kolp's pre-publication
review:

> In what is a creative—but, I am sure, will be a controversial—move,
> Paul [Anderson] introduces the world of faith development into Johan-
> nine scholarship. He looks at people such as James Fowler and James
> Loder to gain a critical sense of the way faith is born in people's hearts.
> The Johannine gospel is explored to chart how people's hearts develop
> into the depth of life eternal! Many will see this focus as a digression to
> Paul's scholarly main thrust; however, it could be key! (Kolp, 1995, 55)

Prospects for Further Research

Kolp's prediction indeed comes true in the following discussion of several works, including one of the most engaged and sustained reviews by Michael Daise of Princeton. While Daise feels the nuanced uses of Fowler and Loder are effective, he raises questions relating to the use of cognitive studies within historical-critical investigations. First, he wonders whether the same sort of cognitive dialectic would have existed between an author and alien sources, as well as reflecting an inward dialogue (Daise, 1996). I believe this could have been the case, but the fact of insufficient diachronic evidence pushes one toward a more unitive Johannine tradition, with tensions inherent to it.[13] Second, he questions whether cognitive-critical methodologies can be used effectively to determine origins and developments of Gospel material, as evidence could equally be argued in more than one direction. Nonetheless, Daise rightly points to one of the most provocative results of this investigation: namely, that the exploration of John's material as reflecting first-order cognition rather than second-order patterns of thought suggests the primitivity of John's material, rather than its lateness.[14] Daise thus offers the following observation on the future of an approach that employs new methodologies from other disciplines: "The value of Anderson's work lies not so much in establishing a new paradigm of Johannine christological development as in offering new (interdisciplinary) criteria by which historical data about that development may be assessed. If others follow his lead, the literary, rhetorical, and sociological methodologies which have recently enhanced Johannine studies will be further enriched by techniques and models drawn from psychological research."

Addressing things from a different standpoint, James Loder, in *The Logic of the Spirit*, asserted that my treatment of the sea-crossing Theophany does not go far enough (Loder, 1998, 247, 333). In holding that a transformative encounter with the Divine actually changes physical realities internal and external to one's world, Loder says: "My point with Anderson's carefully worked out exegetical study is that the theophany was not merely making things better; it actually altered the physical reality at stake. This is a paradigm for how the spiritual presence of Christ works in the formation and transformation of the believer and his world." Again, while one might argue that such may indeed have been the case, the scope of the present analysis is more modest. It sought to confine itself to the cognitive factors at work in how one experiences and perceives such realities.[15] It should be stated, though, that perceived realities *are* realities too; they need not be moved from subjective categories to objectifying ones to be regarded as important or genuine. While there are many directions interdisciplinary cognitive-critical works could take, addressing the following questions could indeed be profitable and serviceable.

To what degree were the sources of Mark, and to a lesser degree, Q, L, and M, also affected by cognitive factors in the origin and formation of their traditions? Indeed, our approaches have appropriately employed *religionsgeschichtlich* (history of religions) methods, but why were particular motifs, schemas, and mythologies chosen to convey the story of Jesus? As well as sociological and contextual factors, such interests may also have involved psychological ones, and analyses into the relations between Christological models chosen and experiential and psychological factors could be profitable. Especially telling could be the relation between the distinctive ministries of early Christian leaders and the ways they crafted and presented distinctively the ministry of Jesus. This is part of the approach I take in exploring the formation of the Petrine and Johannine traditions, which may have been in dialogue with each other for over a half a century—even continuing beyond the lives of particular leaders, who then come to play typological roles after their deaths.[16]

In what other areas might the works of Fowler and Loder be employed in the analysis of other Johannine issues? For instance, if the *Ego Eimi* motif from its inception bore with it theophanic associations within the evangelist's reflection, to what degree might it have served as a rubric within which to organize the Johannine presentation of Jesus' discourse ministry? Or, to what degree does the problem of the delay of the *Parousia* affect the evangelist's understanding of eschatology, leading to an unanticipated appreciation of the work of the spiritually present Christ in the community of faith and a clarification of what Jesus did and did not say regarding the *Parousia?* These and other classic theological themes could benefit from the fitting application of cognitive-critical analyses.

Are there other cognitive models that might be drawn into the analysis of Gospel traditions besides those of Fowler and Loder? These are two models that assist a disciplined analysis of Gospel traditions, but others also abound with their own merits and appropriateness for particular application. Robert Sternberg, a leading psychologist at Yale University, and my colleagues at George Fox University Graduate School of Clinical Psychology have made a few suggestions, but I would be delighted to learn of other models that others feel have merit for such application. Cognitive dissonance theory, wisdom analyses, and other studies in cognitive dialectics are a few approaches that offer exciting ways forward. I appreciate also James Fowler's comments below as to some of the profitable ways cognitive-critical biblical analysis might be employed beyond Gospel-tradition studies. With Fowler, I would value seeing what a Pauline scholar does with cognitive-critical analyses of Romans 7, and perhaps Philippians 4. These sorts of approaches would indeed be valuable, and I would be very supportive of their exploration.

Finally, while he has reservations about the historical plausibility of my reconstructions of Johannine tradition and community history, and while he questions the applicability of modern analyses of cognition and faith development for a first-century writer, John Riches best captures the gist of what I was trying to address with the whole project. Whether it relates to the evangelist's "guessing points or naming stars," he picks up on an important contribution of the book— a reinterpretation of what it means for John to be considered the "spiritual Gospel." Perhaps John's dynamic tensions do not suggest removed distance from the transforming career of Jesus, but radical proximity to it. Says Riches,

> I have always been fascinated by the breaks and gaps in the text of the Fourth Gospel as well as by the sense of development and forward movement in the Gospel as a whole, at least up to the Farewell Discourses. . . . Paul Anderson's wonderfully researched study of John's Christology focuses these questions around a discussion of John 6 and directly confronts the most significant challenge to a view of the chapter's unity, that of R. Bultmann. What he proposes is a reading of the evangelist's thought which recognizes its dialectical character . . . and sees this as a central characteristic of the evangelist's thought: theological reflection on the mystery of the incarnation which requires a disciplined wrestling with opposed modes of thought none of which can ever exhaust the reality of what is being contemplated. (Riches, 1999)

What C. K. Barrett rightly put his finger upon in identifying the "dialectical thinking" of the Fourth Evangelist, the works of Fowler and Loder illuminate when applied in cognitive-critical ways (Barrett, 1972). Ironically, this is precisely the sort of cognitive operation Bultmann believed was required of dialectical theologians today, although he refused to allow a first-century thinker to operate on such levels of cognitive operation (Bultmann, 1969). His *traditionsgeschichtlich* mistake, thus, was to invest in the science of "breathing life into the corpses of ancient texts" rather than the science of engaging the *human vessels underlying Gospel traditions* from whom these texts emerged. Whether cognitive-critical tools will facilitate further exploring human realities underlying the origins, developments, and meanings of classic texts, only time will tell. When used in conjunction with other methodologies and with a fair amount of modesty, however, who knows? They might yet open interpretive doors that have hitherto remained closed.

A Response by Fowler to the Use of Psychological Theory in Paul Anderson's *The Christology of the Fourth Gospel*: Its Unity and Disunity in the Light of John 6

I write with excitement about Paul Anderson's original and rewarding study of John 6. It uses a variety of methods common to New Testament scholars. In addition, it adds a method of analysis that draws on developmental and transformational psychologies. As one of the two researchers and authors from whom Anderson draws his psychological points of analysis and interpretation, I am honored to have this opportunity to respond to his 1996 book, *The Christology of the Fourth Gospel.*

John's Gospel as a Religious Classic

John's Gospel (like all Gospels) is a religious "classic." I use the term in the sense of Hans George Gadamer and David Tracy: A classic is an expression of the human spirit that gathers into a fitting unity something that is fundamental, recurring, and universal in our experience. It brings into nuanced focus some nexus or knot that perennially perplexes or gifts our species. Or it captures, in form and media that prove illuminative, some breakthrough of sublime transcendence that again and again both forms and washes clear the gates of our perception. A classic stands the test of time. It brings to expression something that is fundamentally true about the human condition but does so in a way that respects the essential complexity, the stubborn persistence, and the honest opacity of its subject matter (Gadamer, 1975; Tracy, 1981). Classics capture what Paul Ricoeur has called a "surplus of meaning" (Ricoeur, 1967). They exhaust our capacities of interpretation before we have exhausted their meanings. There is a penumbra of mystery around the heart of any true classic. It gives rise to conflicts of interpretation and discloses surprising depths as we inquire into its multiple layers of meaning.

A *religious* classic, in Tracy's usage, is a special instance of the larger idea of the classic. A religious classic, also an expression of the human spirit, has the special quality that it conserves and makes powerfully accessible moments that may be called "disclosure-concealment events." A religious tradition is constituted by a series of mutually interpreting, unified, and tensional events of disclosure of the Whole by the power of the Whole. These moments of disclosure are also moments of concealment. God's self-disclosure never exhausts God's being. Likewise, our apprehensions and expressions of disclosure events are never adequate fully to appropriate what they offer. Again there is a surplus of meaning, and an essential opacity, giving rise to conflicts of interpretation.

The Process of Creating a Classic Text versus Being Capable of Comprehending a Classic Text

In bringing faith development theory and its descriptions of the conjunctive stage of faith into the discussion of biblical hermeneutics, we have to distinguish between the processes of creating a classical text and the process by which a postmodern reader becomes capable of appreciating classical texts in their fullness. It is one thing to say that readers who would fully grasp and honor the "honest opacity" of a classic's text must have found the limits of the individuative-reflective stage's dichotomizing rationality and be ready for transition. It is another to suggest that the original articulators or writers of a classic text must also have made a similar cognitive and spiritual passage.

Let us view for just a moment the epistemological sequence of adult developmental stages in faith development theory.[17] We start with the *synthetic-conventional* stage. This stage depends upon the emergence of formal operational thinking—the capacity for "thinking about our thinking," and the ability to use abstract concepts to capture and convey narrative and other meanings. It involves mutual interpersonal perspective-taking, where one begins to construct others' perspective upon the self and to make an effort to understand their reactions and interpretations of our behavior. Religiously, it involves the ability to appreciate symbols as rich representations of clusters of meaning. The synthetic-conventional stage locates authority external to the self, or in internalized versions of established authority. It does not yet have a well-developed capacity for third-person perspective-taking, in which the self sees itself and those with whom it has relations from an independent angle. It therefore lacks the ability to analyze and achieve some measure of objectivity regarding the meanings at stake in the interchanges between self and others. Religious communities principally composed of persons best described by synthetic-conventional faith tend to form around authoritative leadership and to rely upon their authorizing interpretations of religious traditions.

The *individuative-reflective* stage grows out of two decisive cognitive and emotional steps. These steps may come in sequence or simultaneously. First, developing the capacities for third-person perspective-taking, the person becomes capable of constructing an inquiring and evaluative approach to interactions with significant others. The relationship itself (whether with a person or a group) becomes an object of inquiry and evaluations. Ethically, this means being able to reason about relations—just and unjust, fair and unfair—with a new kind of "objectivity." Second, the symbols and narratives of a religious tradition, and one's relation to (or through) them, can be objectified and critically analyzed. With the exercise of these new capacities, the locus of authority shifts from external to internal. This is the step Kant referred to in his essay "What Is Enlightenment" when he cried out *"Sapere Aude"*—trust the capacities of your own thinking or knowing. This stage thinks in dichotomous terms: either/or. It funds demythologizing strategies, converting parabolic and narrative materials into conceptually mediated insights. The individuative-reflective stage, with its new analytical capacities and its confidence in conscious analysis, has less capacity for, and attentiveness to, the not-conscious sources of insight and distortions in personal or group knowing. It tends to disvalue symbol, myth, ritual, and non-cognitive sources of faith-knowing. This stage looks for intellectual formulations regarding faith and living that have the qualities of ideological clarity, apparent comprehensiveness, and affirmation of the possibilities of individual mastery and control.

The *conjunctive* stage can arise from one or more sources. Central among these may be fatigue of the ego and the conscious self from the processes of trying to manage a complex world without ways to comprehend factors that elude the cognitive structures with which they operate. For many men (and some women) the transition to the conjunctive stage begins with an "ego leak"—an experience of failure, of fatigue or of ennui, that signals that a persistent blindsiding is going on. Vaguely, one realizes that the meaning-making ego requires richer resources and ways of making sense of the self's connection to larger and deeper powers and resources. For women, it may come with the growing confidence that the spiritual limits of inherited institutionalized traditions are not adequate to sustain the affective and moral lives they are evolving. Conjunctive faith requires coming to terms with the unconscious dimensions of behavior and meaning-making. It

involves the embrace of paradox and polarities: It means acknowledging that we are both old and young, masculine and feminine, weak and
strong, conscious and unconscious, good and evil. Paul bespeaks this
awareness in Romans 7 where he says, "The good I would do, I do not
do; the evil I would not do, I do. Who will deliver me from this body
of death?"

It may be that the faith stage theory captures something timeless as
regards the ways human beings, as persons and groups, go about the
making of meaning. I hope this is the case. But as this account suggests, faith stage theory also takes its particular course in part because
of the historical and cultural movements we think of as *pre-modern*,
modern, and now, *postmodern*. I have taken this brief excursus to call us
to suitable caution about utilizing a twentieth-century theory to illumine first- and second-century texts.

There is the danger with this kind of anachronism that we might
assume that the writer of John's Gospel must have been a conjunctive-
stage individual to assemble or write the Johannine text. This is a possibility that may or may not have been so. I find another explanation
more likely—and more confirming of the Christ event as a genuine
locus of revelation. In the response of first-century persons and communities to the acts and teachings and to the death and resurrection of
Christ, transformations occurred and new patterns of consciousness
and radical faith were evoked. New practices took form, giving rise to
communal efforts to bring to expression the radical and unexplainable
news that had occurred among them. In that effort—a group effort—
gradually there arose formulations, in teaching and writings, and in
sacraments and practices, of the revelatory paradoxes of the incarnation. These gave structure and content to the memories and hopes, the
proclamations and teachings of the communities of faith.

The Gospel of John became a classic because its narrative and
images brought to expression the elements of faith, of cosmology, of
liturgical celebration, and of theological struggle the early Christian
communities faced. It has demonstrated durable power perennially to
awaken and form new levels, depths, and configurations of understanding and faith in hearers and readers. A classic rises from a structuring and struggling to conserve and communicate new gestalts of
transforming apprehension.

The contemporary adult reader of John's Gospel may approach it
from the variety of structuring stages of faith that we have examined.
As Paul Anderson suggests, this leads to differential and to less or
more adequate interpretations of that text. In his careful and construc-

tive criticisms of Bultmann's demythologizing and existential analysis of John's Gospel, Anderson—rightly, I think—sees Bultmann's exegetical and theological reading of John as shaped by the cognitive and emotional features of the individuative-reflective stage. This funds Anderson's judgment that the dichotomous logic of post-enlightenment scientific reason and the existentialist response to it flattens the Gospel's dialectical power. The text is genuinely revelatory and constitutes a classic because of those features that the first-century narrators and writer(s) minted and assembled. In hitherto unprecedented ways, they brought to word gestalts of meaning too big, too consequential, and too weighty to be captured, either in the available symbol systems or in their era's commonly used structuring forms of cognition. In a practical sense, this cognitive and spiritual stretch helps constitute at least part of what we mean when we speak of revelation and of the divine inspiration of scripture.

Anderson suggests that "John's" Gospel brings the narrative of God's self-giving in Jesus as the Christ to expression through a conjunctive stage structuring. This, he claims, involves the holding together of affirmations that may seem to be contradictory. The text holds together what Nicholas of Cusa referred to as *coincidentia oppositorum*—the convergence and mutual embrace of opposites. Anderson is saying that, in the polarities that John holds together in these paradoxical affirmations, new creation occurs.

Illustrating his own dialectical mindset, Anderson has held the Fowler and Loder uses of psychology (development and transformation) in one frame. This is proper. But often Loder and his followers deny that this can or should be done. Important anthropological issues in theology—issues of sin and its manifestations in cognition and action—are part of this debate. Loder believes that transforming moments involve the relinquishing of self-confident, self-referencing rationality and its replacement with a post-critical faith and epistemology of brokenness and grace. I agree with this, but don't want to limit the transformations in faith-knowing and faith-living to one kind or locus of transformation. It is also worthwhile to note that, strictly speaking, neither Loder nor I is a psychologist. Both of us have training in theology, ethics, and the social sciences. We are readers and researchers in psychology, but I believe it is true to say of Loder, as it is of me, that our use of psychology is ultimately in the service of theological anthropology—theology's account of the dynamics of human being and becoming.

Anderson's Contributions

By his use of faith development and transformational perspectives, Anderson has genuinely illuminated the dialectical and transformational dynamics of John's Gospel. He has given us a new appreciation of paradoxical and dialectical images in John that require to be held together rather than dichotomized or systematic. He has helped us recognize that truth takes form in the meaning space created *between* the apparently tensional dualities that the Gospel of John holds together.

Anderson's thesis and use of faith development theory has significant implications for the churches' use of John's Gospel. The narratives and themes of John 6 have long been loci of difficulty for those who would define orthodox Christian belief. The larger book has also been a source of division regarding the question of who may be "saved." Such passages as John 3:16 and John 14:6: "I am the way and the truth and the life. No one comes to the Father except through me," have been used as strong leverage for evangelical efforts to bring people to acceptance of Christ. At the same time, this use of the Gospel has been a stumbling block for those who hold that interpreting the text that way actually diminishes and distorts the remarkable truth claims that come to expression in John's Christology.

I would like to see Anderson's approach carried over into the interpretation of Pauline theology as well. It seems to me that Paul cries out for interpretation via conjunctive epistemology. Holding together the witness of Jews and Christians (Rom. 9–11), affirming the duality and tension at the heart of human beings and in himself (Rom. 7), and affirming both that there is a transforming relationship with Jesus Christ ("If anyone is in Christ, that person is a new creation") and a gradual process of maturation in faith ("When I was a child, I spoke like a child") suggest that Paul Anderson could faithfully spend a scholarly lifetime continuing his fruitful work.

Notes

1. See Wayne Rollins's epoch-making monograph outlining the history of psychological approaches to the Bible (1999). Rollins shows how psychological studies have been used and misused in biblical studies throughout the modern era and compellingly demonstrates the role of the Bible in the founding and development of disciplinary psychology.

2. This is one of the reasons Albert Schweitzer so vigorously opposed the use of psychological approaches to interpretation (1913/1948). In the disser-

tation of one of Schweitzer's four doctorates (the medical one), he launches out polemically against those who employ psychology inappropriately in sketching imagined portrayals of Jesus having more of a lodging in the mind of the interpreter than in the historicity of reported events.

3. Walter Wink's book *The Bible in Human Transformation: Toward a New Paradigm for Biblical Study* (1973) wrought an impressive change in biblical interpretation. No longer were interpreters able to justify staying a "safe distance" from the text, when all other humanistic and scientific ventures advocate intimate engagement with one's subject.

4. See Parker Palmer's approach to the character of truth; it is not limited to objective categories but includes subjective ones as well (1983). Further, in our quests for truth, it is not only we who seek the truth, but we are also sought by truth, until we (in Pauline terms) come to know fully, even as we are fully known. In that sense, the quest for truth engages the life of spirituality (and psychology) rather than being against it. This connection is borne out in nearly every facet of scientific discovery, as well.

5. As a contrast to supernaturalism, the workings of the divine in the settings of humans, supranaturalism is even less elevated. Historical-critical scholars have tended to oppose the historicity of anything even hinting at the wondrous-producing "explanations" often more wondrous than the amazement-evoking realities being addressed. Considering how ancient witnesses, or their purveyors, came to perceive something as wondrous provides a realistic alternative to rejecting all appeals to wonder in the name of modernistic historiography.

6. During oral stages of Gospel traditional history, if there was contact between two traditions, resulting influences may have traveled in both directions, not just one. One example is the early Markan and Johannine traditions, which appear to have enjoyed an interfluential set of contacts during the oral stages of their traditional developments. Put otherwise, as preachers heard each other tell stories, they may have influenced each other in the ways their stories were told. For John and Mark, as independent traditions, one mistake is to assume that one must have influenced the other only (see Anderson, 1996).

7. J. Harold Ellens refers to them as structuralist and psychodynamic models of human development, accordingly. James Fowler refers to his and Loder's work as being that of religious anthropologists rather than psychological theorists proper. The reason I refer to their approaches as cognitive-critical is that both of them deal with cognition—the means by which persons perceive, experience, and reflect upon matters of personal importance.

8. Letters and notes have come in from Ernst Käsemann, John Riches, Raymond Brown, C. K. Barrett, Craig Koester, Jeff Staley, and Lloyd John Ogilvie, among others. These letters and reviews are available in an archival file at the Yale Divinity School Library.

9. Perhaps the most extensive engagement of the work so far is found in David DeSilva's new introduction to the New Testament (2004, 392–474). In his chapter on John, he integrates well my theories of John's origins with engaging interpretive discussions. In particular, he works creatively with my treatment of the presentation of Peter and the Beloved Disciple in John, complete with its ecclesiological implications.

10. Informally, several European scholars have objected to my reference to Peter's being presented as "returning the Keys of the Kingdom to Jesus" in his declaring Jesus (alone) to possess the words of eternal life in John 6. Granted, one is overstating the case slightly for effect, but seven similar-yet-different parallels between Peter's receiving the Keys in Matthew 16:17–19 and presentations in the Gospel of John are not insignificant. In response to Graham Stanton's excellent point (1999) that Matthean ecclesiology was also "familial" and "egalitarian," I was able to clarify my view. Whether John's corrective to rising institutionalism in the late first-century church was aimed at a Matthean "text" or not, the primary target was probably the likes of Diotrephes (3 John 9–10), who may have been advancing his own positional leadership based upon a view of Petrine (either Matthean or Ignatian) authority (Anderson, 1999a).

11. Kysar's change of mind (1999) is especially significant, as he has been a leading advocate of source-critical (diachronic) analyses of John's composition. An emerging set of theories as to the origins of John's material has therefore been developed in other essays, addressing John's relation to the Synoptics (Anderson, 2001, 2002), the history of the Johannine situation (Anderson, 1997), and the dialectical character of the Father–Son relationship in John (Anderson, 1999b), evoking engagement in other settings.

12. According to James McGrath (1997), "Anderson's approach enables him to make helpful, fresh insights into John's Gospel. In one footnote (pp. 154f. n. 21) he cites psychological research into elderly eyewitnesses in order to see whether John ben Zebedee should be as easily excluded from the list of possible authors as is often the case. While he is clearly familiar with psychological literature, sociological and literary factors are also kept in view. . . . Anderson's book is an absolute must. My own regret is that it reached me *after* I wrote my article on John 6!"

13. This is a case where my claims are somewhat misunderstood. While I do not claim John could not have been based in a derivative way on Mark or on sources (this cannot be demonstrated), my research simply demonstrates the evidence for such views is pervasively insufficient, requiring an alternative approach. Likewise, while the human thinkers underlying "Petrine" and "Johannine" traditions need not be connected with particular personalities (a misunderstanding of several reviewers—see Anderson, 1996, 155, notes 21 and 22), they still cohere into unitive trajectories *whoever* their originative sources might have been.

14. According to Daise (1996), "The most intriguing implication Ander-

son draws from his dialectical theory is that the Fourth Gospel's Christology was formulated, not by second or third generation Christians half a century after Jesus' death (as is conventionally understood), but by one of Jesus' followers during Jesus' own lifetime." In conjunction with this point, several reviewers also commented on the importance of Appendix VIII (Anderson, 1996, 274–277), which uncovers an overlooked first-century clue to Johannine authorship.

15. See the further exploration of cognitive factors in apprehending the sea-crossing Theophany in Anderson (1995); included also in this collection.

16. Explorations of ecclesiological developments between Johannine and Matthean traditions, for instance, are explored futher in Anderson (1997, 2002). Likewise, treatments of John and Mark as "the Bi-Optic Gospels" are developed further in Anderson (2001, 2002).

17. The classic text is *Stages of Faith: The Psychology of Development and the Quest for Meaning* (Fowler, 1981). For discussions that relate the faith stages to pre-modern, modern, and postmodern forms of cognition, consciousness, and faith, see Fowler (1996).

References

Anderson, P. N. (1995). The Cognitive Origins of John's Christological Unity and Disunity. *Horizons in Biblical Theology*, *17*, 1–24.

Anderson, P. N. (1996). *The Christology of the Fourth Gospel: Its Unity and Disunity in the Light of John 6. Wissenschaftlich Untersuchungen zum Neuen Testament* II 78. Tübingen: J. C. B. Mohr (Paul Siebeck); American printing, Valley Forge: Trinity Press International (1997).

Anderson, P. N. (1997). The *Sitz im Leben* of the Johannine Bread of Life Discourse and Its Evolving Context, *Critical Readings of John 6*, A. Culpepper, ed., Biblical Interpretation Supplemental Series 22. Brill: Leiden, 1–59.

Anderson, P. N. (1999a). A Response (to the Reviews of R. Kysar, S. Schneiders, A. Culpepper, G. Stanton, & A. Padgett). *Review of Biblical Literature*, *1*, 62–72.

Anderson, P. N. (1999b). The Having-Sent-Me Father—Aspects of Agency, Irony, and Encounter in the Johannine Father-Son Relationship. *Semeia*, *85*, 33–57.

Anderson, P. N. (2001). John and Mark—the Bi-optic Gospels, *Jesus in Johannine Tradition*, R. Fortna & T. Thatcher, eds. Philadelphia: Westminster/John Knox Press, 175–188.

Anderson, P. N. (2002). Interfluential, Formative, and Dialectical—A Theory of John's Relation to the Synoptics, *Für und wider die Priorität des Johannesevangeliums*, P. Hofrichter, ed., Theologische Texte und Studien 9. Hildesheim, Zürich, & New York: Georg Olms Verlag, 19–58.

Bakhtin, M. (1983). The Latest Trends in Linguistic Thought in the West (also attributed to V. Voloshinov), *Bakhtin School Papers*, A. Shukrnan, ed. Oxford: RPT Publications, 31–50.

Barrett, C. K. (1972). The Dialectical Theology of St. John, *New Testament Essays*. London: SPCK Press, 49–69

Bultmann, R. (1969) The Significance of "Dialectical Theology" for the Scientific Study of the New Testament. *Faith and Understanding* (vol. 1), R. Funk, ed., L. P. Smith, trans. London: SCM, 145–164.

Bultmann, R. (1971). *The Gospel of John*, G. R. Beasley-Murray, R. N. W. Hoare, & J. K. Riches, eds. Philadelphia: Fortress.

Daise, M. (1996). Review of *The Christology of the Fourth Gospel* by Paul N. Anderson. *Koinonia, 8,* 100–106.

DeSilva, D. A. (2004). *An Introduction to the New Testament: Contexts, Methods & Ministry Formation.* Downers Grove: InterVarsity.

Fowler, J. W. (1981). *Stages of Faith: The Psychology of Human Development and the Quest for Meaning.* San Francisco: Harper & Row.

Fowler, J. W. (1984). *Becoming Adult, Becoming Christian: Adult Development and the Christian Faith.* San Francisco: Harper & Row.

Fowler, J. W. (1996). *Faithful Change: The Personal and Public Challenges of Postmodern Life.* Nashville: Abingdon.

Gadamer, H. G. (1975). *Truth and Method.* New York: Seabury.

Kolp, A. (1995). Review of *The Christology of the Fourth Gospel* by Paul Anderson. *Quaker Religious Thought, 27*(4), 53–55.

Kysar, R. (1999). *Review of Biblical Literature,* 38ff.

Loder, J. (1981). *The Transforming Moment: Understanding Convictional Experiences.* San Francisco: Harper & Row.

Loder, J. (1998). *The Logic of the Spirit: Human Development in Theological Perspective.* San Francisco: Jossey-Bass.

McGrath, J. (1997). Review of *The Christology of the Fourth Gospel* by Paul N. Anderson. *Theological Gathering, 3.*

Molina, F. C. (1997). Review of *Christology of the Fourth Gospel* by Paul N. Anderson. *Achivo Teologico Grandino, 60,* 375.

Palmer, P. (1983). *To Know as We Are Known: A Spirituality of Education.* San Francisco: Harper & Row.

Riches, J. (1999). Archive, Yale Divinity School Library; including the original paper presented at Orlando and an Appendix with evaluative statements and individual responses.

Ricoeur, P. (1967). *The Symbolism of Evil.* New York: Harper & Row.

Rollins, W. G. (1999). *Soul and Psyche: The Bible in Psychological Perspective.* Minneapolis: Augsburg Fortress.

Schweitzer, A. (1913/1948). *The Psychiatric Study of Jesus: An Exposition and Criticism.* Boston: Beacon.

Stanton, G. (1999). *Review of Biblical Literature.*

Tracy, D. (1981). *The Analogical Imagination.* New York: Crossroad.

Wink, W. (1973). *The Bible in Human Transformation: Toward a New Paradigm for Biblical Study.* Philadelphia: Fortress.

CHAPTER 12

THE MYTH OF HISTORY AND THE EVOLUTION OF CONSCIOUSNESS: A JESUS SCHOLAR IN PSYCHOLOGICAL PERSPECTIVE

Hal Childs

> One who looks outside,
> dreams;
> One who looks inside,
> awakes.
>
> —C. G. Jung[1]

Jesus said, "Let one who seeks not stop seeking until one finds. When one finds, one will be troubled. When one is troubled, one will marvel and will rule over all."

—*The Gospel of Thomas: The Hidden Sayings of Jesus* (Meyer, 1992, 23)

The word "seeking" in *The Gospel of Thomas* quotation implies a vague trouble or doubt. Something is not quite right, or else why the "seeking?" I had been involved in the quest for the historical Jesus for about two decades when a vague disquiet began to intrude on my assumptions about the historical Jesus and the methods used to approach him. Perhaps the "quest" itself is such a "seeking," a response to an inner troubling and doubt. When we observe the origins of the quest for the historical Jesus during the eighteenth and nineteenth centuries, we see a serious dissatisfaction with the theological Christ on the part of the early questors (Schweitzer, 1906/1968, 4–5). My own disquiet led me on an intensive period of research to probe the philosophical and psychological foundations of the quest for the historical Jesus, which resulted in a doctoral dissertation (Childs, 1998, 2000). The results were highly unexpected. The overall process, spanning many years, was as much a personal journey of transformation as it was an intellectual exploration, if not more so. For me, the themes in the above quotation from *The Gospel of Thomas* express the dynamics of such a journey. With this essay I present an overview of that journey, which continues to be profoundly challenging, by following the themes of the *Thomas* quotation.

Exposition

Seeking Leads to Intimations of Trouble

During my research, I had a startling and disorienting insight into the work of John Dominic Crossan. I was exploring the work of many historical Jesus scholars,[2] including Crossan's *The Historical Jesus: The Life of a Mediterranean Jewish Peasant.* Published in 1991, this 500-page book is a tour de force in the field of historical Jesus scholarship. It is a substantial and creative historical exploration of the life and times of Jesus. Approximately 200 pages are devoted to detailing the carefully structured historical method used to get at the man, Jesus, and his historical context. Only then does Crossan spend another 200 pages writing about Jesus himself. The historical edifice of this book was, and is, impressive and convincing.

However, my belief in the convincing nature of Crossan's achievement was rattled by an unexpected shift in perspective. For some reason I cannot pin down, the aftermath of a conversation with a New Testament colleague revealed some cracks in the impressive and convincing facade of Crossan's massive work. I had the uncanny realization that looking at Crossan's history of Jesus was like looking at the movie set of an old Western town. The fronts of the buildings look authentic enough, but if you look behind them, what you see is a scaffolding of two-by-fours holding up the fronts of false buildings.

What shifted here was not simply that other facts could replace Crossan's facts; rather, what I found called into question was the nature of *fact* itself and the arbitrary nature of the structure of historical narrative. These cracks opened into deeper, more serious concerns. I want to affirm that I am not applying this image of false building fronts literally to the work of Crossan or any other Jesus historian. Their work is not a "false front" propped up by mere scaffolding. I believe Crossan's historical Jesus work is substantial, creative, and important. What this view of the "false front buildings" suddenly did was to relativize what Crossan had created with his historical narrative and the historical *knowledge* with which he built his narrative. The tacit truth claims of the historical narrative were revealed as relative; the seeming solidity of history was shaken.

Two other problems emerged during my research that intensified my sense of trouble and doubt. First was the growing awareness that the quest for the historical Jesus was producing an unruly proliferation of multiple images of the historical Jesus, and the second was the idea of history as myth, or the myth of history.

Too Many Jesuses

The 1980s and 1990s saw a wonderful resurgence of historical Jesus studies, so much so that it was called "a Renaissance in Jesus studies" (Borg, 1994, 3–17). Also impressive about this phase of historical Jesus research was the addition, to traditional exegetical and historical methods, of other research fields such as sociology, economics, cultural anthropology, and psychology.[3] Added to this was a more richly textured awareness of multiple and vital Judaisms in first-century Palestine, in contrast to a traditional tendency to view the Judaism around Jesus as monolithic and in decline (Harrington, 1987). However, this prodigal outpouring of interest and research had a dark side. The quest for the historical Jesus seemed to be foundering under its own weight.

Failure of Method

Crossan himself stated that historical Jesus research is "something of a bad joke" and that there are a "number of competent and even eminent scholars producing pictures of Jesus at wide variance with one another" (Crossan, 1988a, 3). Others also noticed this troubling multiplicity, so that "the vast variety of interpretations of the historical Jesus that the current quest has proposed is *bewildering*" (Koester, 1994, 544, emphasis added). William Telford, referring to a reviewer's comment that "dozens, perhaps hundreds of different Jesuses can be constructed" *using the same texts and scholarly apparatus*, suggests that perhaps this is "the problem and challenge of Jesus Studies today" (Telford, 1994, 46–47, emphasis added). This problem of the "same texts" and the same "scholarly apparatus" (research methods) producing widely divergent images of Jesus leads some scholars to use words such as "hopeless" and "embarrassment" about the situation. Dennis Polkow draws attention to "a hopeless diversity of historical Jesus pictures in modern scholarship" (Polkow, 1987, 356). Crossan is acutely aware of this problem and calls it an "academic embarrassment." He goes on to say that "the problem of multiple and discordant conclusions forces us back to questions of theory and method" (Crossan, 1991, xxviii). Polkow also viewed the problem of multiple Jesus images as a problem of method, and proposed the need for a standardized and unified method in historical Jesus studies. However, Irvin Batdorf, in a review of eleven historical Jesus scholars, found no necessary correlation between method and image of Jesus. He simply concludes that it is the personal interpretive perspective of the scholar that determines the resulting picture of Jesus, in spite of the method used (Batdorf, 1984, 187–215). The bane of academia, subjectivity, is here intruding itself into the sacrosanct realm of critical method.

The Scholar's Psychological Conflict

The fact that this diversity of historical Jesus images leads scholars to feel hopeless and embarrassed points to the crux of the problem, an unconscious psychological conflict. It is this disturbing and darker conflict at the heart of Jesus research that leads to the question, "Why can't historical method narrow the field and focus in on the one true and original historical Jesus, as opposed to what is really happening, the prodigious and seemingly mercurial dispersion of images?" This fact of historical Jesus research, the increase of Jesus images rather than the limiting of Jesus images, raises troubling questions about history, historical research, the historian, and the role of subjectivity throughout.[4]

One response to the deluge is to strengthen and improve historical method and attempt to gain control over unruly subjectivity and personal bias. But will this really improve things? The betrayal of the promise of history as a rational science is not a failure of method but an opportunity to make the conflicts conscious and take a deeper look at what we expect of historical method. The unrelenting proliferation of multiple images of the historical Jesus pushes us to go deeper into the assumptions that guide our understanding of history, historical knowledge, and history writing. The expectation that historical method should protect us from the subjectivity and personal bias of the writer of history is untenable. This leads us into the myth of history and the connection between history and psychology. But before we explore the myth of history, I will examine what I believe is a psychological dichotomy between method and meaning in the work of Crossan.

Seeking and Finding Trouble with Crossan

This overview of the quest for the historical Jesus raises questions about the efficacy of historical critical method in relation to Jesus. But what happens if we take a focused look at one historical Jesus scholar?[5] The fact that Crossan became the focus of this study was both accidental and fortuitous. I never intended to put Crossan's work under such scrutiny, but my unexpected insight that aroused doubt about the edifice of *The Historical Jesus* pushed me to go deeper into his work. The good fortune is that Crossan's work on the historical Jesus spans several decades and is an excellent sample of rigorous method and creative interpretation. But it is precisely within this division between rigorous method and creative interpretation that the problem resides. This is not only a methodological and philosophical problem but a psychological problem as well. Though it is not a psychological problem that is amenable to a Freudian analysis, it is a problem that is amenable to both a Jungian understanding and solution. But why is this division between method and interpretation a problem?

Unconscious Worldview and Expectations

First, it is a problem because, as shown above, the biblical critics themselves have identified it as such. For Crossan, this problem is a "bad joke" and an "embarrassment." It is truly a stumbling block for scholarship if research method (historical criticism, etc.) has no real controlling influence over interpretation (image of Jesus). Second, if Jesus scholars are "bewildered," "helpless," and "embarrassed" in relation to their own collective work, then there must be core assumptions influencing their work that remain profoundly unconscious. It is this conflict between expected result and actual result that points to an unconscious dynamic within the scholar. However, this unconscious dynamic is not really personal as it has little to do with one's childhood upbringing and relationship with one's parents. It is a collective and cultural unconscious dynamic that has its historical origin in the rise of the Enlightenment in eighteenth-century Western Europe.

The optimistic hope of the Enlightenment was that the illumination of reason would be able to control all of human life. This belief gave rise to a point of view known by the shorthand term "positivism." I have described it this way:

> Briefly, positivism can be characterized as maintaining a particular theory of knowledge (epistemology) and a particular theory of reality, i.e., being, (ontology). Its theory of knowledge asserts that a researcher, using rational principles and methods, can determine objective and value-neutral facts without bias or interpretation, and can employ the facts without influencing them. This theory of objective knowledge rests on the ontological assumption that the researcher and the object of

> research are discrete and separate entities (the Cartesian subject-object
> split). And one basic assumption of historical positivism is that the his-
> torian can accurately report what actually happened in the past. (Childs,
> 2000, 9–10)

This notion of positivism—that reality (the concern of ontology) can
be carved up into discrete and neat packets of observers and things
observed, subjects and objects—has come under critical scrutiny, and
there are very few, if any, contemporary historical Jesus scholars who
would accept its tenets. Through new developments in philosophy,
psychology, ecology, and modern physics, many now believe that all
of reality is fundamentally (i.e., ontologically) a unified whole. The
observer and observed are always inextricably intertwined and exert
a mutual and unavoidable influence on each other. Nevertheless, my
point is that our *conscious* awareness about the limits of positivism, also
known as the Cartesian worldview, has not penetrated into the unconscious. The unconscious assumptions and hopes of positivism still
haunt the historical Jesus scholar's dream of controlling personal bias
in historical Jesus research. I believe this is an impossible and untenable goal in the light of a contemporary psychological and unifying
worldview that is completely at odds with our Enlightenment and
Cartesian legacy. What is at stake is the foundational view of reality.
The achievements of the Enlightenment and rational thought are
highly desirable. My aim is not to subvert rational thought but to shift
its foundation and alter its self-understanding.

Inner Conflict Unresolved

The division between method (historical research) and interpretation (image of Jesus) is a problem when a scholar tacitly assumes that
it is possible to separate method and interpretation, and then is
shocked when the results of research show that method and interpretation cannot be separated. Every method of research is already, even
before it delivers any facts, an interpretation that shapes and influences the facts it purportedly discovers. Rather than discover facts, a
method of research creates them. We will see more of this circularity
when we examine history writing and the hermeneutic circle below.
But the problem of dichotomizing method and interpretation is also
a psychological conflict. If it is enough of an inner conflict, it will
trouble, and thus engender reflection and consciousness. Conscious
thought can lead us to change what is no longer working. However,
such a conflict can also exist within us unconsciously; it can remain a
silent dissonance that has not yet risen to awareness. As such, it does

not trouble us, and we feel no need to change anything—"if it ain't broke, don't fix it." It is also true that such a conflict can nibble at our awareness but perhaps not be strong enough to threaten our preferred way of doing things, so we can avoid it, gloss over it, or attempt to fix it by doing more and better of the same. This reaction has been a general response of Jesus scholars in their attempts to improve research methods. While this response can have some beneficial effects, it is not unlike remodeling a building that really needs a new foundation. This is how I see Crossan's work on the historical Jesus. His work spans three decades and illustrates the problem of trying to separate method and interpretation.

Finding More Trouble

The process of "finding" entails getting closer to, and becoming more conscious of, the conflict that troubles. When I read Crossan's very creative work on the historical Jesus, I find a clear distinction between the research methods utilized to determine the "words" of the historical Jesus and the interpretive methods brought to those words. This distinction is so perfectly normal within conventional scholarly approaches to the historical Jesus that at first nothing seems amiss. However, I found myself becoming increasingly troubled by this perfectly normal Jesus researcher's methodology, and a closer look at Crossan's approach helped clarify my dis-ease.

With his book *In Parables: The Challenge of the Historical Jesus*, Crossan brings together a literary and structuralist interpretation to what he believes to be the original "words" of the historical Jesus. Here, the original words of Jesus are the parables, and they are retrieved from the Gospel documents with historical critical methods. Crossan understands that we do not have the actual words of Jesus in the Gospel (and other extra-canonical) documents as these texts already are interpretations of what Jesus said. But Crossan does believe that there are layers of interpretation and reinterpretation in the Jesus textual traditions, and that it is possible to work back through these layers and reconstruct what he calls the "parabolic complex." The parabolic complex is claimed to be a structural unity that preserves and conveys the original meaning of Jesus (Crossan, 1973, xiii–xvi).

Two Historical Methods Prove Ambiguous

The method used to achieve this original meaning is called "transmissional analysis" by Crossan. This technique is a widely used scholarly method also known as "tradition-critical" or "history-of-traditions analysis" (Crossan, 1985, 7). This method is central and crucial to Crossan's aims. It attempts to write the history of the transmission of a text through its varied forms back to its earliest form. Another crucial step is to apply the criterion of dissimilarity to the earliest form. The criterion of dissimilarity seeks to show a clear distinction between the earliest form of a saying of Jesus and prevailing Jewish and Christian contexts. If the saying can be shown to derive from neither Jewish or Christian settings, then it is assumed it is from Jesus. There are serious problems with these seemingly rigorous critical methods, captured in the realization that the reconstruction of Jesus' parabolic complex is *Crossan's* reconstruction of Jesus' parabolic complex. The scholar's personal interest is always involved and plays an influential role in every judgment at each step of this critical process.

It is true that critical methods, by the fact that they are "critical," imply that a certain distance is provided between the object and the observer and that this distance enables some measure of objective and rational thought about the object, in this case the texts related to Jesus. Distance and reason are thought to place a check on the subjective involvement and personal interpretive bias of the scholar. What is forgotten is that critical distance and reason do not eliminate the subjective involvement of the scholar. Instead, what has happened is that critical methods have blinded us to the very real presence of subjective judgment at every stage of the critical process.

In the two examples cited here, one must note first that transmissional analysis requires subjective decisions and personal judgments about the so-called different forms of a saying and their chronological relationship.[6] Second, the criterion of dissimilarity is completely dependent on the scholar's reconstruction of the Jewish and Christian contexts that are supposed to be distinct from the saying of Jesus. In other words, the Jewish and Christian settings shown to contrast with the sayings of Jesus do not exist as objective entities independently of the scholar. They are as much historical reconstructions as are the recovered sayings of Jesus. It should be immediately apparent that the image of the historical Jesus and the image of the historical Jewish and Christian contexts exist together in an interpretive circle that is complex and difficult to sort out. Nevertheless, Crossan, in this book (*In Parables*), believes he has established the definitive parabolic complex of the historical Jesus and thus exhibits a historical positivism regarding the facts about Jesus.

Choose Your Reality

The paradox between Crossan's historical method and his interpretive approach is more sharply drawn when we see what he means by "in parables." For Crossan the phrase "in parables" refers to an experience one must have directly, which cannot be grasped cognitively. Like a joke, you either "get it" or you don't. The joke can be explained, but that is not the same experience. So Crossan views Jesus as using parables to transmit a direct experience of an alternative reality that is more full of possibility because it is God-infused. Crossan believes that "in parables" expresses the true nature of reality itself, and he refers to several contemporary poets and thinkers to illustrate this point:

> "Only the imagination is real!" (William Carlos Williams). "So, say that final belief/Must be in a fiction" (Wallace Stevens). "Truth is knowing that we know we lie" (W. H. Auden). Crossan then cites Roland Barthes, who declares that historical positivism's claim on the facts is dead, historical narrative is dying, and history has more to do with intelligibility than with chronology. Following Barthes is a citation from Werner Heisenberg: ". . . method and object can no longer be separated." (Childs, 2000, 41; citing Crossan, 1973, xiv–xv)

So what does all this mean? Imagination, fiction, lying! The facts are dead, and chronology is meaningless, and most of all, method and object are inextricably fused? This view of "reality" is a shocking juxtaposition to the claim that we can retrieve the historical facts about Jesus using a historical critical method. Again, we are left with the realization that we do not have *the* reconstruction of the original parabolic complex of the historical Jesus, but *Crossan's reconstruction*. It might even be more accurate to call it Crossan's creative reinterpretation, more akin to a new Gospel than asserting a reliable historical archeology.[7] This would be more in keeping with the worldview of "in parables." Instead, Crossan reserves a creative worldview for interpretation and a historical positivist worldview to establish the facts. Even if this is not his conscious intent, it is the resulting impression.

Hidden Subjectivity

Crossan's *The Historical Jesus* begins by explicitly addressing scholarly subjectivity in the quest for the historical Jesus. Here, he states that the lack of coherence in the scholarly world regarding the figure of Jesus is cause for embarrassment. He is acutely aware of the problem when he says, "It is impossible to avoid the suspicion that historical Jesus research is a very safe place to do theology and call it history, and do autobiography and call it biography." Therefore, so as not to "add to the impression of acute scholarly subjectivity in historical Jesus research," he goes on to "raise most seriously the problem of methodology and then follow most stringently whatever theoretical method was chosen" (Crossan, 1991, xxviii). Without embarking on a detailed demonstration of his method here, suffice it to say that the method shows a remarkable commitment to positivist assumptions and goals (Childs, 2000, 29–40). The beauty of Crossan's thorough depiction of his method in this book is that, on the surface, nothing is hidden about how and why he gets his historical Jesus "facts."

What is hidden, however, is revealed with his own words when, after describing his methodological structure and process, he says, "It is clear, I hope, that my methodology does not claim a spurious objectivity, because almost every step demands a scholarly judgment and an informed decision. I am concerned, not with an unattainable objectivity, but with an attainable honesty" (Crossan, 1991, xxxiv). While I believe this is true about Crossan's intent, some of his own language in this regard is interesting. When Crossan refers to the decisions he must make personally about his method and his material, he uses the words "judgment," "scholarly judgment," or "informed decision." When he refers to the personal decisions other scholars must make, he uses the phrase "acute scholarly subjectivity" (Crossan, 1991, xxviii). Why is Crossan making "judgments" but other scholars are caught up in "subjectivity?" What Crossan does not say, and should say, is that every step of his methodology is infused with personal and cultural, conscious and unconscious, interpretive preferences or bias (Childs, 2000, 38).

We Are All in This Together

Crossan does state that he does not claim an unattainable objectivity, yet at the same time the elaborate and impressive structures of his method embody their own hidden rhetoric. This tacit rhetoric has a convincing power that unintentionally panders to the unconscious desire for positivist facts within all of us. I am as much a child of the Enlightenment and historical positivism as Crossan. While in my earlier work I referred to Crossan as a "closet positivist" (Childs, 2000, 256), I must accept this sobriquet for myself as well. It is not quite an accurate epithet, for to be in a "closet" usually means we are intentionally hiding from the world what we truly know ourselves to be. But it can also mean to hide from ourselves something we know but would rather not fully accept and confront.

My psychological assessment of Crossan, and any historical Jesus scholar for that matter, is that he is not knowingly trying to conceal positivist intent in his historical Jesus research. The examination of Crossan's historical Jesus work leads me to believe the situation is more akin to his left hand not knowing what his right hand is doing. I can only come to this conclusion because in his work two methods that rely on mutually exclusive worldviews (a rational Cartesian subject-object split versus a hermeneutic subject-object unity) lie side by side without overt conflict. This says to me that an incipient conflict remains mostly unconscious, and, thus, left hand (creative interpretation) and right hand (rational positivism) work are split off from each other. In summary, I come to the following conclusion about Crossan's work in general:

> Throughout his work Crossan fails to address the unwarranted assumptions that guide the historical critical quest for the historical Jesus and yet, he does acknowledge in part the inescapable hermeneutic relationship between the historian and history. This however leads to his ontologically split approach to Jesus. On the one hand, his literary approaches to the Jesus traditions are creative, playful and inventive, while on the other hand, his playful and hermeneutic sensibilities have not had any impact on his Jesus-historiography—he continues to write about Jesus as if he were writing about the actual Jesus. (Childs, 2000, 57)

This "finding" in the work of Crossan leads me to more "trouble" as I probe more deeply into the psyche of the writing of history (historiography) in general. There are several historians who, stepping back and taking a critical stance toward their own craft, have come to a clear understanding of the problem of history writing itself. This also shows that the "trouble" I find with Crossan splitting his historical and interpretive methods is not personal to him but collective and shared by us all.[8]

The Trouble in History

The word "history" is itself ambiguous. It points to something that is real, and it also points to something that is written down. History is the word we use to refer to the past, the actuality of life lived before our lives now—people who really lived, and events that really happened. History is also the word to designate the written record of the past, the story of times gone by. The text about people and events of the past is not what actually happened but someone's memory of what happened, even if he or she was an eyewitness. The difficulty is that we equate the *hard* reality of the real, the actual lived life of the past, with what is really a *softer* reality of the written story of the past. But while I will emphasize the mutability of the historical narrative, I am not questioning the reality of the actual past. It is just that our access to the past is only through writings (and other artifacts) of the past and our interpretations thereof.

The past itself is not an object we can observe in the present. Time and life are ephemeral. Unfortunately, history itself is not the concrete reality we would like it to be and have been led to believe it is through positivist ideals about historical reporting. Paradoxically, however, the being of history can only be the being of the historical narrative, because history has no being other than the memory of the present that has passed. But because history is also associated with "facts," we tend to think of it in terms of things—something objective that we can touch, measure, and handle. The unconscious effect of historical positivism lends history this sense of a fixed reality. What we so easily forget is that the word "history" is a name we give to time, and time has little to do with fixed things. Time, we might say, is a process of the unfolding of being, and we can give various names to it. As Peter Munz makes clear with the title of his book, *The Shapes of Time*, the idea of "history" is only one possible way to interpret time—to put one mask, among others, on the face of time (Munz, 1977, 38).

History as Interpretive Relation

Positivist notions in the field of history share the same dichotomy between fact and interpretation, as we found in Crossan's work. This dichotomy, however, is a falsification of reality: "Sir George Clark once described history as a hard core of fact surrounded by a pulp of disputable interpretations. E. H. Carr, wittily and with greater perspicacity stood the statement on its head. 'History', he wrote in *What is History?*, 'is a hard core of interpretation surrounded by a pulp of disputable facts'" (Munz, 1977, 248).

The so-called facts of history cannot exist independently of interpretation. "Historical facts are not established from pure data—they are postulated to explain characteristics of the data. Thus the sharp division between fact and interpretation upon which the classical view insisted and which the revisionists have accepted, does not exist" (Gossman, 1978, 27, citing Murray Murphey).

The positivist historian believes that facts can exist as objective entities, independently of the historian, and does not realize the subjective nature of historical "fact" (Stevenson, 1969, 14). Historical events are subjective events, because they are always related to a subject: the obvious subject who lived in the past, but also the subject of the present historian. There can be no historical event without a subjective relation, as noted in the following:

> They are not as subjective as a text of pure fiction created for an occasion, but have more in common with such a narrative than with the event-structure of the external world. Let us not be deceived by the skepticism of much historical writing, that arid criticism of documents that pretends to take the reader behind their rhetorical facades and into a world of sober facts. *Historical writing does not treat reality; it treats the interpreter's relation to it.* For an event does not stand alone as an isolated object of thought, except by abstraction. It can only be understood as one element in a narrative that is stated or implied. (Stock, 1990, 80–81, emphasis added)

History as Circle and Fiction

History, in a significant way, is quite circular. We in the present are a product of the past, and we in the present are the ones writing about the past. In this sense, the present does not discover the past but creates the past as a literary artifact in the present. History is always written in the present from the vantage point of the present. It is the structure of the narrative of history, the structure of story (which is also the structure of myth), that gives history its meaning and intelligibility. The structure of story—that is, plot—is to some extent an arbitrary construct we use to interpret the formless nature of time. Time and life do not have beginnings, middles, and ends, but this is just what the structure of narrative is—and this structure gives the story of history its intelligibility. The historian decides when the story will begin and end. The historian knows how the story will turn out. These are all things the active participants in the past did not know—could not know, at the time of their living—but over which the historian in the present has complete control. This control is what gives history writing its power to conquer experience, to subject experience to its narrative.

Critical thinkers about history writing have also compared the historical narrative to the novel. Paul Veyne asserts, "History is not a science, and has little to expect from sciences; it does not explain, and has no method. Better still, history, about which much has been said for two centuries, does not exist." For Veyne, "historians tell of true events in which man is the actor; history is a true novel." And like the novel, "history sorts, simplifies, organizes, fits a century into a page" (Veyne, 1984, x, 4). By "true," Veyne means that history is an account of events that have happened, but by no means does the historian grasp events "directly and fully." History is "always grasped incompletely and laterally, through documents" that are themselves not events; history is written from "traces, impressions." In this light, he states that "history is mutilated knowledge" (Veyne, 1984, 13).

Unconscious Positivism

In spite of the growing awareness that history is a construct and not the immediate representation of reality, an interesting dichotomy continues to exist in the writing of history:

> Many modern historians . . . have repudiated the goals and premises of historical realism, and certain aspects of the rhetoric of the old historical realism have in fact disappeared from modern historical texts. But there seems to have been no radical reform of the *historian's mode of writing* comparable with the changes that have affected literary writing and fiction in the last half-century. *Historical texts continue to recount calmly events and situations located in the past as though the "age of suspicion" had never dawned.* (Gossman, 1978, 36, emphasis added)

This state of affairs affirms my own suspicion about a conflict between conscious awareness and unconscious functioning in the writing of historical Jesus scholars. The facts about the historical Jesus are reported with a similar calmness, while the deeply problematic and actual nature of history and history writing apparently remains completely beyond the sphere of awareness.

Foreshadowing and Memory

There are other important areas that contribute to the subjectivity of history that I can only mention here. In literary criticism, the notions of "foreshadowing" and "sideshadowing" highlight the difference between the predictability of outcome in history writing and the thick and unpredictable nature of actual reality (Bernstein, 1994). Foreshadowing is a literary technique based on foreknowledge, and while it is usually associated with fiction, it makes its appearance in history writing. Sideshadowing is a concept introduced by Bernstein to indicate "a present dense with multiple, and mutually exclusive, possibilities for what is to come" (Bernstein, 1994, 1). It emphasizes the random and haphazard nature of reality, and the impossibility of knowing ahead of time any specific outcome. The density and overwhelming number of actual events reminds us that the "totality of what happened is so large and broad that it cannot be surveyed, and the mere subdivision of that totality into definable and specific events distinct from one another is part of the historian's activity" (Munz, 1977, 233). This inevitable and arbitrary process of selection reminds us that history and memory are related.

History is the daughter of memory. Our understanding of memory today is more sophisticated because of psychophysical studies of the brain. This neurological and cognitive research demonstrates the subjective and contextual nature of memory and reveals its plasticity. We now know that memory is a complex of factors that adapt and change over time (Schacter, 1995, 1996). "The idea that storage and retrieval of explicit memories involves binding together different kinds of information from diverse cortical sites provides a biological basis for the notion that retrieval of a memory is a complex construction involving many different sources of information—not a simple playback of a stored image" (Schacter, 1995, 19).

The Myth of History

Hayden White is a historian whose ideas about the literary nature of history are indispensable for grasping the imaginative, subjective, and interpretive essence of history writing. As he puts it: "We experience the 'fictionalization' of history as an 'explanation' for the same reason that we experience great fiction as an illumination of a world that we inhabit along with the author. In both we recognize the forms by which consciousness both constitutes and colonizes the world it seeks to inhabit comfortably" (White, 1978, 61).

In his willingness to explore the close similarities between fiction and history, White opens the door to an understanding of history as myth. In my usage, the word *myth* does not mean false, untrue, or superstition. Myth is first a story or a narrative that speaks of matters of the heart, of the soul, of being itself. Myth is the language of the unconscious. While the colloquial usage of the word myth is pejorative and dismissive, we know from Joseph Campbell, C. G. Jung, and others that myth speaks to deep truths about the human condition and to another, greater reality (often personified as gods and goddesses, both bad and good) with which the human condition participates. We can see that myth, read rightly, is not a primitive and mistaken attempt to explain reality but rather a phenomenology showing us the aliveness and meaning of being. History is our modern myth.[9]

However, if myth is a problematic, multivalent word, why not say "the narrative of history" instead of the "myth of history"? I chose the phrase, "the myth of history," intentionally precisely because both of these words, "myth" and "history," carry deeply entrenched and antithetical associations: myth is false, history is true; myth is subjective, history is objective. In other words, both "myth" and "history" are loaded with unconscious assumptions, and I hope the dissonance that occurs by putting them together will generate consciousness about truer and deeper meaning. What is really at stake is overcoming the hardened opposition between myth and history. This popular and simplistic antagonism is still a problem at the heart of the quest for the historical Jesus. It is our modern legacy from the Enlightenment and the rise of reason, science, and historical consciousness. In part, it is through the examination of history and historiography that I hope to contribute to softening the opposition between myth and history and seek the meaning of the myth of history.

History Slips Away, but Not Quite

Once I understood the limitations of history, it seemed that historical critical method had less to do with discovering facts than with creating new stories. Historical criticism questions our received knowledge here in the present (Krentz, 1975, 45) and offers new plots for the same data (in our case, the Jesus texts). When I assert that we have no facts, only interpretations, I mean that our interpretations function as facts within communities of consensus. I am not proposing an extreme relativism in which any point of view is equal to every other point of view; that all truths are equal. What I am trying to do is shift the foundation on which we establish our "facts," our interpretations, and see the subjective dimension and creativity that is always present. This does not eliminate our search for truth, but it does eliminate the unrealistic positivism that creeps into our desire for absolute truth. If we are honest about our "facts" as interpretations, we can openly include other areas of value in creating our "facts," such as psychology, ethics, and aesthetics. We must admit that facts are never value-neutral and make the values in our "facts" (i.e., interpretations) explicit.

Conviction and Identity

Depth-psychology can offer us a phenomenology of consciousness and maturity that can deepen self-understanding of our commitments to particular truth-claims, stories, historical facts, and images of Jesus. What is it that gives any explanatory hypothesis—any story—its convincing power? It is not an abstract, objective logic, for even logic is a "story" one must have faith in for it to be gripping. We all know that convictions are not easily swayed by facts. Something much deeper is at work at a level of being outside of surface consciousness. This level of being is a core and unconscious dimension of our being and identity, often with a "religious" quality to it—just as one can have a religious fervor for the positivist ideal of objectivity. Whenever we have a conviction about something, such as my own theory about Crossan's positivism and the myth of history, we can know that something of the unconscious is at work. To know that the unconscious is involved is not to dismiss the conviction with an *argumentum ad hominem*, nor to level the superficial psychological charge of "that's just your projection." The awareness of the presence of the unconscious as a vital and creative partner in knowing and interpreting is a powerful key for increasing self-understanding and world-understanding.

What has happened to me at this point is that my conviction about the solidity and dependability of history has been eroded by my research into historiography. At first this is terribly troubling, leaving me disoriented, with no ground to stand on. It is as if I am suspended over an abyss. There is no easy way out, and there is no going back to an earlier naïveté. The first intimation of trouble in the problems of the quest for the historical Jesus has now become full-blown and unavoidable Trouble—history as I knew it has evaporated! Yet what also emerges is a sense of liberation, for the source of the original trouble has been found. The earlier trouble, engendered by the problems in the quest for the historical Jesus, is now fully conscious and so partially resolved by a more honest and realistic view of history and the writing of history. This realization presses for the fashioning of a new understanding of the relationship between history, the unconscious, and consciousness, and of the role of depth-psychology in the quest for the historical Jesus. I sense that the Trouble I've seen could now lead to something less troubling.

From Trouble to Marvel

Just as Emma Jung is reported to have said, "There are egos and there are egos, and the problem is to find the right one,"[10] so here, there are psychologies and there are psychologies, and this project requires the right one. And the "right one" here is not a psychology in the grip of Enlightenment rationality, not another social science among others, an ego psychology that cannot see beyond its personal nose. It must be a depth-psychology of the unconscious that goes beyond Freud's materialistic and rationalistic reductions, does justice to the empirical facts of experience, and reaches for a phenomenology of the spirit, of the infinite, of mystery, of being.

The analytical psychology of C. G. Jung, read together with Martin

Heidegger's hermeneutic phenomenology of being, suits this purpose very well. For Heidegger, this means a phenomenology that observes and describes being beyond the personal. Heidegger wants to make explicit those structures of being that make our being possible. The word *hermeneutic,* meaning interpretation, indicates that Heidegger knows phenomenology cannot be abstractly objective but is always interpretive. The very structure of being, it turns out in Heidegger's analysis, is itself always hermeneutic. We are always involved in a hermeneutic circle. This concept overlaps with Jung's notion of the collective unconscious. All our interpretations must always rest upon an a priori unconscious understanding.

We approach *being* through the verb *to be* in all its forms. Therefore, from the perspective of Jung's depth-psychology and Heidegger's phenomenology, we *are* the psyche, we *are* our experience, we *are* being, we *are* life. Psyche and life are not something additional we *have* or can possess, they are states of being that we *are.* At its simplest this is to say that psyche, as understood by Jung, is not *some-thing* inside of us (as it is for Freud), but that psyche is lived life itself. As Jung liked to say, the psyche is not in us, we are in the psyche. By reading Jung and Heidegger together, we have an understanding of life (psyche and being) that gives us a new window, really a new door, through which to approach the problem of the historical Jesus. I believe this doorway, framed by psyche and phenomenology, gives us a new way to understand the quest for the historical Jesus.

Reinterpreting Heidegger

It is true that Heidegger would hate to have his phenomenology read in relation to psychology because he made great efforts to avoid the personalizing tendency and intra-psychic nature of psychology. Heidegger rejected psychology as a way to approach being. Jung, in his turn, rejected Heidegger, because Jung was committed to empirical evidence and refuted pure philosophizing. The irony is that Heidegger's phenomenology of being has the same empirical foundation as Jung's psychology, because both are focused on developing a description of existence that is based on the observation of experience. Both are looking for a description of the basis of human experience that goes beyond the individual person. In my view, both succeeded, which is why reading them together expands our understanding of their respective work, in spite of their own thoughts about each other's discipline.

Within the history of New Testament interpretation, it is important to note Rudolf Bultmann's (1884–1976) influence on how Heidegger is generally understood by New Testament scholars. Bultmann sought to reinterpret the basic message of the Gospels by demythologizing the ancient kerygma (the proclamation by the Gospel texts of Jesus as the Christ). He brought a Heideggerian existential interpretation to what he saw as the mythological and antiquarian language of the Gospels. Unfortunately for New Testament historical critical studies, Bultmann's existential interpretation of Heidegger has obscured the profound hermeneutic and historicist significance of Heidegger for ontology in general and the ontological foundations of historical studies in particular (Childs, 2000, 23).[11]

Collective Subjectivity

It is our natural tendency to think about the unconscious in personalistic and individualistic terms and to view subjectivity as the inner province of the singular person. Jung's view of the psyche includes a collective unconscious that we can think of as a collective subjectivity within which we all live. The collective unconscious is not some kind of cosmic or super mind, which is another thing or entity. It is our potential and disposition for typical human ways of being (Childs, 2000, 117; Clarke, 1992, 117). Jung's phenomenology of the psyche and the collective unconscious and Heidegger's analysis of being reveal common foundational (i.e., universal) structures of subjectivity.[12]

The "Religious" Nature of Deep Subjectivity

For Jung, the deepest level and center of our collective subjectivity is what he called the self. This is not to be confused with the personal self, the ego, the individual "I." Though not normally capitalized, I prefer to capitalize Jung's concept of the Self to make this distinction within the unity of the psyche more explicit. The Self is never known directly but is experienced via religious and mythological images such as the Christ in Christianity, or the Buddha in Buddhism. With regard to the quest for the historical Jesus, it is the presence of the Christ image as a projection of the Self that is most important.

Differentiating Consciousness

In the Christian tradition, the figure of the historical Jesus and the Christ image are always fused. However, while the quest for the historical Jesus distinguishes between the Jesus of history and the Christ of faith, from a depth-psychological point of view, the Self is always unconsciously in the background in relation to the figure of Jesus.

This is in keeping with both Jung's and Heidegger's understanding of being. The Self as a primordial structure of being is always *a priori* to individual ego consciousness. The ego always emerges out of the collective unconscious, which always precedes it and remains its fundamental ground, through a process of successive differentiations. These differentiations of consciousness can occur throughout the life cycle and can also be understood as the evolution of consciousness, individuation, or progressive incarnation.

The development of historical consciousness and the move to bring critical historical thinking to the figure of Jesus Christ is a step in differentiating the original fusion of Jesus and Christ. This is why I view the quest for the historical Jesus as a stage in the cultural and historical evolution of consciousness, and as a process of individuation. However, this development in culture and history has been mostly collective and unconscious. I believe that the quest for the historical Jesus cannot succeed in its traditional aim of recovering the original Jesus of Nazareth. Yet, and more importantly, I do believe that the quest for the historical Jesus "is the misplaced, externalization of the process of individuation—the quest for the historical self as the conscious realization of one's own God-given archetypal individuality. In other words, within Jung's frame of reference, I suggest that the quest for the historical Jesus is an unconscious projection of the individuation process, and as such, that there is a moral imperative from the self (i.e., God) for the project to be *consciously* so conceived" (Childs, 2000, 98).

Archetypal Be-ing

From Jung's point of view, the Christ as a symbol of the Self is a potential within every individual. As an archetype, the Self is not an entity or a thing, but a way of being that is a possibility for any person. Archetypes, in Jung's thought, are not nouns, but verbs. They symbolize unconscious ways of relating to others and the world. Archetypes are not images but shared dynamics of being that structure our experience (Brooke, 1991, 146–147). For example, the mother–child relationship is structured archetypally and at first quite unconsciously, but it has infinite variations within cultures and homes. Just so, the person–God relationship is structured archetypally and unconsciously by the Self and has infinite variations. The degree to which the mother and growing child become conscious of their relationship has a profound effect on its health and benefit to each. A mother–child relationship that does not change over thirty to forty-plus years is a destructive and sad situation. So, too, the person–God relationship needs to grow in consciousness, or else the "God" potential (the Self) within the individual remains truncated and undeveloped. Let me say that such a process is not individualistic by any means and has profound implications for community and world.

Evolution of Consciousness

The historical and psychological are the incarnational myths of our time. We take for granted that history and psychology provide accurate and true access to reality. If we take the idea of incarnation and understand it psychologically, it could mean to manifest meaning in the particulars of our daily living. History and psychology are modern myths of meaning with the explanatory power to convince us of their truth. Although not every historical or psychological narrative speaks the same truth to everyone, there are multiple myths and narratives, and they often conflict. When we understand the role of the unconscious in different myths and their conflicts, we see the opportunity for revelation, insight, and more consciousness rather than only pitfalls and obstacles.

Conclusion

I see a new role for the quest for the historical Jesus within the context of an evolution of consciousness. "The quest for the historical Jesus is best understood and undertaken, not as a quest for the historic Jesus, nor a quest for a historical understanding of a plausible Jesus, but as the evolving differentiation of consciousness in relation to the projection of the Self" (Childs, 2000, 165). Jung understands individuation as self-realization, and self-realization involves the integration of unconscious contents. For Jung, unconscious contents always include a life-world and the reality of "God" (also known as the collective unconscious) that transcends the individual identity. Self-realization as the differentiation of consciousness is the integration of aspects of the Self, and this is a modern form of incarnation.

To differentiate consciousness is to die to an unconscious identification with a particular story about how to be, such as how to be a father, or any other role. This achieves a new relative freedom of self in relation to the former story. Jesus is the model in the Christian West for being human, and for the God–person relationship. Multiple and different images of the historical Jesus open up new stories about how to be human and how to be in relation to God. Every achievement of consciousness, no matter how small, realizes (i.e., incarnates) the mythic process of crucifixion and resurrection. To become conscious is to experience death and resurrection in daily life.

The idea of the myth of the historical Jesus frees me from the confusion and trouble of the Cartesian and positivist aims to recover the one, true historical Jesus. When the formerly assumed solidity of history dissolved into the myth of history, I suffered a form of vertigo. I was adrift and disoriented. The dissolution of the historical Jesus produced, and continues to produce, anxiety and bereavement. Yet, there is an even more secure gain as a new foundation is revealed; one that is profoundly inside me, and not only outside me. And while this new foundation is an ever-changing process that transcends me personally, it also connects me to all of history with new meaning—I (we) participate in the evolution of consciousness. So, in the end, I come through seeking, finding, and troubled, to a provisional form of "marvel" and "rule over all."

> The *myth of the historical Jesus* also suggests that we will, and can only, have *many* stories about the historical Jesus, many different kinds of *Gospels.* To continue to strive for the "one true Gospel," or the "one true historical Jesus," actually cuts us off from the reflections at the bottom of the deep well that are not obstacle, but gift, and potential revelations of self, world and God. (Childs, 2000, 261)

To "rule over all" is not a form of control or domination. Taking place as it does in the context of wonder and marvel, it is a new myth of meaning, a new hermeneutic key, that frees us to live fully with the unfolding of being. The myth of history and the myth of the historical Jesus make us co-creators with "God" by bringing our life-world into increasing consciousness and deeper meaning.

Notes

1. Source for Jung's work unknown.

2. Among the works consulted, see Borg (1984, 1987, 1994); Breech (1983, 1989); Charlesworth (1988); Chilton and Evans (1994); Crossan (1973, 1976, 1991); Downing (1987); Fiorenza (1983); Harvey (1982); Horsley (1987); Johnson (1996); Mack (1988); Meier (1991); Meyer (1979); Riches (1982); Sanders (1985); Scott (1981); Theissen (1987); Vermes (1973, 1993); Witherington (1994, 1995).

3. My research included many psychological treatments of Jesus and Christ spanning most of the twentieth century. These include: Berguer (1923); Cramer (1959); Dolto and Severin (1979); Dourley (1981); Edinger (1987); Garvie (1907); Hall (1917); Hitchcock (1907); Hobbs (1962);

Howes (1984); Hurt (1982); Kunkel (1952); Leavy (1988); Leslie (1965); McGann (1985); Miller (1981); Rizzuto (1979); Rollins (1983); Sanford (1970); Schweitzer (1948); Stein (1985); Ulanov (1975); Wolff (1987); Wuellner and Leslie (1984).

4. We are not the first generation to notice this problem. See Schweitzer, who said, "There is no historical task which so reveals a man's true self as the writing of a Life of Jesus" (Schweitzer, 1906/1968, 4). George Tyrrell's dismissive comment, also at the turn of the century, that the Christ image of Adolf Von Harnack is simply his own reflection at the bottom of a deep well, has become an accepted symbol of subjectivity as a stumbling block in contemporary historical Jesus studies (Tyrrell, 1909, 44).

5. Here I present the results of research that can be followed in detail in Chapter 2, "John Dominic Crossan's Historical Method" in Childs (2000), 21–57.

6. I have shown elsewhere how the structure of Crossan's method of transmissional analysis is very like Freud's now repudiated method of dream interpretation (Childs, 2000, 44–49). I suggest that transmissional analysis is not an epistemological process (the recovery of knowledge and facts from the past), but a hermeneutic process (a creative interpretation in the present).

7. Another book of Crossan's that cannot be examined here but is also imbued with the dichotomy between traditional Cartesian ontology (the view of reality that rationally splits subject and object) and a hermeneutic ontology (a creative and interpretive view of reality that unites subject and object) is his *Raid on the Articulate: Comic Eschatology in Jesus and Borges* (Crossan, 1976). This is a powerful literary comparison between the language of Jesus and the language of Jorge Luis Borges, but its foundation rests on a split view of reality. Crossan does not acknowledge that the "language of Jesus" is *Crossan's Language of Jesus*. See the extensive analysis in Childs (2000, 51–55).

8. Crossan has refuted my claims about his unconscious positivism in his review of my book. First as a presentation at the November 2000 meeting of the Psychology and Biblical Studies Section of the Society of Biblical Literature in Nashville, Tennessee, titled "Historic and Historical Knowledge: A Response to Hal Childs," and later published as Crossen (2003, 469–475). See this special issue of *Pastoral Psychology* for six other reviews of my book and my response.

9. For an earlier exploration of the idea of the myth of history, see Stevenson (1969). Although somewhat dated by the theological concerns of the 1960s, this little and unfortunately forgotten book contains a wealth of insightful thought that will not be out of date for a long time.

10. Verbal communication to the author by Elizabeth Boyden Howes.

11. For this project, Division I of Heidegger's *Being and Time* (1962) is most important. My approach to Heidegger is guided by Charles Guignon's *Heidegger and the Problem of Knowledge* (1983). With this work, Guignon

shifts the emphasis away from reading Heidegger as a mainstream existentialist "by raising to prominence the historicist and hermeneutic dimensions
of *Being and Time.*" Guignon's work highlights Heidegger's profound ontological and hermeneutic critique of Cartesian metaphysics and epistemology.

12. I have detailed this rich overlapping in the thought of Jung and
Heidegger in Chapter 4, "Jung's Phenomenological Psychology and the
Christ," in Childs (2000), 97–149.

References

Batdorf, I. W. (1984). Interpreting Jesus since Bultmann: Selected Paradigms and Their Hermeneutic Matrix. *Society of Biblical Literature Seminar
Papers, 23,* 187–215.

Berguer, G. (1923). *Some Aspects of the Life of Jesus from the Psychological and
Psycho-analytic Point of View,* E. S. Brooks & V. W. Brooks, trans. New
York: Harcourt, Brace.

Bernstein, M. A. (1994). *Foregone Conclusions: Against Apocalyptic History.*
Berkeley: University of California Press.

Borg, M. J. (1984). *Conflict, Holiness and Politics in the Teachings of Jesus.*
Lewiston: Edwin Mellen.

Borg, M. J. (1987). *Jesus: A New Vision.* San Francisco: Harper & Row.

Borg, M. J. (1994). *Jesus in Contemporary Scholarship.* Valley Forge: Trinity
Press International.

Breech, J. (1983). *The Silence of Jesus: The Authentic Voice of the Historical Man.*
Philadelphia: Fortress.

Breech, J. (1989). *Jesus and Postmodernism.* Minneapolis: Fortress.

Brooke, R. (1991). *Jung and Phenomenology.* London: Routledge.

Charlesworth, J. H. (1988). *Jesus within Judaism.* New York: Doubleday.

Childs, H. (1998). *The Myth of the Historical Jesus and the Evolution of Consciousness: A Critique and Proposed Transformation of the Epistemology of John
Dominic Crossan's Quest for the Historical Jesus from the Perspective of a Phenomenological Reading of C. G. Jung's Analytical Psychology.* Unpublished
PhD dissertation, Graduate Theological Union, Berkeley.

Childs, H. (2000). *The Myth of the Historical Jesus and the Evolution of Consciousness.* Atlanta: Society of Biblical Literature Dissertation Series.

Chilton, B., & Evans, C. A., eds. (1994). *Studying the Historical Jesus: Evaluations of the State of Current Research.* Leiden: E. J. Brill.

Clarke, J. J. (1992). *In Search of Jung: Historical and Philosophical Enquiries.*
London: Routledge.

Cramer, R. (1959). *The Psychology of Jesus and Mental Health.* Los Angeles:
Cowman.

Crossan, J. D. (1973). *In Parables: The Challenge of the Historical Jesus.* New
York: Harper & Row.

Crossan, J. D. (1976). *Raid on the Articulate: Comic Eschatology in Jesus and Borges.* New York: Harper & Row.

Crossan, J. D. (1985). *Four Other Gospels: Shadows on the Contours of Canon.* Minneapolis: Winston.

Crossan, J. D. (1988a). *The Cross That Spoke: The Origins of the Passion Narrative.* San Francisco: Harper & Row.

Crossan, J. D. (1988b). Materials and Methods in Historical Jesus Research. *Forum, 4,* 3–24.

Crossan, J. D. (1991). *The Historical Jesus: The Life of a Mediterranean Jewish Peasant.* San Francisco: HarperSanFrancisco.

Crossan, J. D. (1995). *Who Killed Jesus? Exposing the Roots of Anti-Semitism in the Gospel Story of the Death of Jesus.* San Francisco: HarperSanFrancisco.

Crossen, J. D. (2003). Historical Knowledge: A Response to Hal Childs. *Pastoral Psychology, 51*(6), 469–475.

Dolto, F., & Severin, G. (1979). *The Jesus of Psychoanalysis: A Freudian Interpretation of the Gospel,* H. R. Lane, trans. Garden City: Doubleday.

Dourley, J. P. (1981). *The Psyche as Sacrament: A Comparative Study of C. G. Jung and Paul Tillich.* Toronto: Inner City.

Downing, F. G. (1987). *Jesus and the Threat of Freedom.* London: SCM.

Edinger, E. (1987). *The Christian Archetype: A Jungian Commentary on the Life of Christ.* Toronto: Inner City.

Fiorenza, E. S. (1983). *In Memory of Her: A Feminist Reconstruction of Christian Origins.* New York: Crossroad.

Freud, S. (1927). *The Future of an Illusion.* New York: Vantage.

Garvie, A. E. (1907). *Studies in the Inner Life of Jesus.* New York: George H. Doran.

Gossman, L. (1978). History and Literature: Reproduction or Signification, *The Writing of History: Literary Form and Historical Understanding,* R. H. Canary & H. Kozicki, eds. Madison: University of Wisconsin Press, 3–39.

Guignon, C. B. (1983). *Heidegger and the Problem of Knowledge.* Indianapolis: Hackett.

Hall, G. S. (1917). *Jesus, the Christ, in the Light of Psychology.* Garden City: Doubleday.

Harrington, D. J. (1987). The Jewishness of Jesus: Facing Some Problems. *Catholic Biblical Quarterly, 49*(1), 1–13.

Harrisville, R. A., & Sundberg, W. (1995). *The Bible in Modern Culture: Theology and Historical-Critical Method from Spinoza to Käsemann.* Grand Rapids: Eerdmans.

Harvey, A. E. (1982). *Jesus and the Constraints of History.* Philadelphia: Westminster.

Heidegger, M. (1962). *Being and Time,* J. Macquarrie & E. Robinson, trans. New York: Harper & Row.

Hitchcock, A. W. (1907). *The Psychology of Jesus: A Study of the Development of His Self-consciousness.* Boston: Pilgrim.

Hobbs, E. C. (1962). *Self-Understanding vs. Self-Consciousness*. Berkeley: Pacific Coast Theological Group.

Hoeller, K., ed. (1988). *Heidegger and Psychology*, a special issue from the *Review of Existential Psychology & Psychiatry*.

Horsley, R. (1987). *Jesus and the Spiral of Violence*. San Francisco: Harper & Row.

Howes, E. B. (1984). *Jesus' Answer to God*. San Francisco: Guild for Psychological Studies Publishing House.

Hurt, K. F. (1982, Spring/Summer). The Quest of the Psychological Jesus (Jungian Reading of Mark). *Unitarian Universalist Christian, 37*(1–2), 21–31.

Jarrett, J. L. (1992). Jung and Hermeneutics. *Harvest: Journal for Jungian Studies, 38*, 66–83.

Johnson, L. T. (1996). *The Real Jesus: The Misguided Quest for the Historical Jesus and the Truth of the Traditional Gospels*. San Francisco: HarperSanFrancisco.

Jung, C. G. (1931/1953–1978). Archaic Man, *The Collected Works of C. G. Jung* (vol. 10), H. Read, M. Fordham, & G. Adler, eds., R. F. C. Hull, trans. Princeton: Princeton University Press, 50–73.

Jung, C. G. (1940/1953–1978). Psychology and Religion, *The Collected Works of C. G. Jung* (vol. 11), H. Read, M. Fordham, & G. Adler, eds., R. F. C. Hull, trans. Princeton: Princeton University Press, 3–105.

Jung, C. G. (1948/1953–1978). A Psychological Approach to the Dogma of the Trinity, *The Collected Works of C. G. Jung* (vol. 11), H. Read, M. Fordham, & G. Adler, eds., R. F. C. Hull, trans. Princeton: Princeton University Press, 107–200.

Jung, C. G. (1951/1953–1978). Aion: Researches into the Phenomenology of the Self, *The Collected Works of C. G. Jung* (vol. 9), H. Read, M. Fordham, & G. Adler, eds., R. F. C. Hull, trans. Princeton: Princeton University Press, ii.

Jung, C. G. (1952/1953–1978). Answer to Job, *The Collected Works of C. G. Jung* (vol. 11), H. Read, M. Fordham, & G. Adler, eds., R. F. C. Hull, trans. Princeton: Princeton University Press, 355–470.

Jung, C. G. (1953–1978). *The Collected Works of C. G. Jung* (20 vols.), H. Read, M. Fordham & G. Adler, eds., R. F. C. Hull, trans. Princeton: Princeton University Press.

Jung, C. G. (1954/1953–1978). Transformation Symbolism in the Mass, *The Collected Works of C. G. Jung* (vol. 11), H. Read, M. Fordham, & G. Adler, eds., R. F. C. Hull, trans. Princeton: Princeton University Press, 201–296.

Jung, C. G. (1961). *Memories, Dreams, Reflections*, A. Jaffé, recorder & ed., R. Winston & C. Winston, trans. New York: Vintage.

Koester, H. (1994). The Historical Jesus and the Historical Situation of the Quest: An Epilogue, *Studying the Historical Jesus: Evaluations of the State of Current Research*, B. Chilton & C. Evans, eds. Leiden: Brill, 535–545.

Krentz, E. (1975). *The Historical-Critical Method*. Philadelphia: Fortress.

Kunkel, F. (1952). *Creation Continues: A Psychological Interpretation of the First Gospel*. New York: Scribners.

Leavy, S. (1988). *In the Image of God: A Psychoanalyst's View*. New Haven: Yale University Press.

Leslie, R. C. (1965). *Jesus and Logotherapy: The Ministry of Jesus as Interpreted Through the Psychotherapy of Viktor Frankl*. Nashville: Abingdon.

Mack, B. (1988). *A Myth of Innocence: Mark and Christian Origins*. Philadelphia: Fortress.

McGann, D. (1985). *The Journeying Self: The Gospel of Mark Through a Jungian Perspective*. New York: Paulist.

Meier, J. P. (1991). *A Marginal Jew: Rethinking the Historical Jesus* (vol. 1). New York: Doubleday.

Meyer, B. F. (1979). *The Aims of Jesus*. London: SCM Press.

Meyer, M., trans. (1992). *The Gospel of Thomas: The Hidden Sayings of Jesus*. New York: HarperSanFrancisco.

Miller, D. (1981). *Christs: Meditations on Archetypal Images in Christian Theology*. New York: Seabury.

Munz, P. (1977). *The Shapes of Time: A New Look at the Philosophy of History*. Middletown: Wesleyan University Press.

Polkow, D. (1987). Method and Criteria for Historical Jesus Research. *Society of Biblical Literature 1987 Seminar Papers, 26*, 336–356.

Richardson, W. J. (1988). The Place of the Unconscious in Heidegger, *Heidegger and Psychology*, K. Hoeller, ed., a special issue from the *Review of Existential Psychology and Psychiatry*, 176–198.

Riches, J. (1982). *Jesus and the Transformation of Judaism*. New York: Seabury.

Rizzuto, A. (1979). *The Birth of the Living God: A Psychoanalytic Study*. Chicago: University of Chicago Press.

Rollins, W. G. (1983). *Jung and the Bible*. Atlanta: John Knox.

Sanders, E. P. (1985). *Jesus and Judaism*. Philadelphia: Fortress.

Sanford, J. A. (1970). *The Kingdom Within: A Study of the Inner Meaning of Jesus' Sayings*. New York: Lippincott.

Schacter, D., ed. (1995). *Memory Distortion: How Minds, Brains, and Societies Reconstruct the Past*. Cambridge: Harvard University Press.

Schacter, D. (1996). *Searching for Memory: The Brain, the Mind, and the Past*. New York: BasicBooks.

Schweitzer, A. (1906/1968). *The Quest of the Historical Jesus: A Critical Study of Its Progress from Reimarus to Wrede*. New York: Macmillan.

Schweitzer, A. (1948). *The Psychiatric Study of Jesus*, C. R. Joy, trans. Boston: Beacon.

Scott, B. B. (1981). *Jesus, Symbol-Maker for the Kingdom*. Philadelphia: Fortress.

Stein, M. (1985). *Jung's Treatment of Christianity: The Psychotherapy of a Religious Tradition*. Wilmette: Chiron.

Stevenson, W. T. (1969). *History as Myth: The Import for Contemporary Theology*. New York: Seabury.

Stock, B. (1990). *Listening for the Text: On the Uses of the Past.* Baltimore: Johns Hopkins University Press.

Telford, W. R. (1994). Major Trends and Interpretive Issues in the Study of Jesus, *Studying the Historical Jesus: Evaluations of the State of Current Research,* B. Chilton & C. A. Evans, eds. Leiden: E. J. Brill, 33–74.

Theissen, G. (1987). *The Shadow of the Galilean: The Quest of the Historical Jesus in Narrative Form.* Philadelphia: Fortress.

Tyrrell, G. (1909). *Christianity at the Cross-Roads.* London: Longmans, Green.

Ulanov, A. B., & Ulanov, B. (1975). Jesus as Figure and Person, Symbol and Sacrament, *Religion and the Unconscious.* Philadelphia: Westminster, 97–117.

Vermes, G. (1973). *Jesus the Jew: A Historian's Reading of the Gospels.* Philadelphia: Fortress.

Vermes, G. (1993). *The Religion of Jesus the Jew.* Minneapolis: Fortress.

Veyne, P. (1984). *Writing History: Essay on Epistemology.* Middletown: Wesleyan University Press.

White, H. (1978). The Historical Text as Literary Artifact, *The Writing of History: Literary Form and Historical Understanding,* R. H. Canary & H. Kozicki, eds. Madison: University of Wisconsin Press, 41–62.

White, H. (1987). *The Content of the Form: Narrative Discourse and Historical Representation.* Baltimore: Johns Hopkins University Press.

Witherington III, B. (1994). *Jesus the Sage: The Pilgrimage of Wisdom.* Minneapolis: Fortress.

Witherington III, B. (1995). *The Jesus Quest: The Third Search for the Jew of Nazareth.* Downers Grove: InterVarsity.

Wolff, H. (1987). *Jesus the Therapist.* Oak Park: Meyer-Stone.

Wuellner, W. H., & Leslie, R. G. (1984). *The Surprising Gospel.* Nashville: Abingdon.

CHAPTER 13

JESUS AND TRANSFORMATION

Paul N. Anderson

Transformational leadership differs greatly from transactional leadership. Transactional leadership conditions others to think in terms of penalties and rewards, thus motivating actions and reactions according to the interests of the individual. It is self-oriented, conditioning others along the lines of desired outcomes, but, as the motivating factors are external, adherence to those values and behaviors is tied to their reinforcement. When the systems of reward diminish, so do corollary commitments. In that sense, transactional leadership is situational and reward specific.

Transformational leadership, on the other hand, works to move the insight and motivation of the individual to higher planes of understanding and reasoning. It inculcates values whence behaviors come, but it is not focused on outcomes alone. The motivational aspects of transformational leadership relate not to rewarding the self but to helping the individual ideate and valuate beyond oneself to considerations of others, the needs of the community, and finally the appeal of transcendent truth. Jesus embodied *transformational* leadership, sometimes even against transactional leadership and in furthering his mission. He often provoked his audiences to higher planes of perception by the use of cognitive dissonance.

Exposition

Envisioning Jesus as a transformational leader of this sort may challenge our understandings of Jesus in ways that feel alien. One conception at stake is that of a Jesus who came to bring a new set of transactions, a supercessionist view of Christianity. Instead of Jewish forms and religious practices, one might envision the Jesus movement as instituting a new religious system by which adherents receive gifts from God if they "do it right" and "believe rightly" from a Christian standpoint. Salvation, one might assume, depends upon using the right language or performing the correct ritual action to receive the divine gift of grace. Or one might construe the New Covenant as a new set of transactions in the age of the Spirit in which performing the right expressions of worship effects the receipt of charismatic gifts of the Spirit. We might even construe a conditional covenant wherein faithfulness to God's principles brings about prosperity, health, success, and psychological well-being; but all of these perspectives fail to take seriously the *transformative* aspects of Jesus' deeds and mission.

Another misconception envisions Jesus as bringing a radically new approach to religious and social life—a radical reformer, introducing new and innovative teachings. This would be partially true, but every instance in which Jesus brought a "new" teaching can be found already explicated in Hebrew Scripture and tradition. In that sense, the innovations of Jesus should be understood as conservative attempts to preserve and elevate the spiritual core of Jewish law rather than doing away with it. When you consider *how* Jesus taught, as well as *what* Jesus taught, you see a prophetic invitation backward and forward to the center of God's commands rather than focusing on their boundary edges. Again, in transactional approaches to divine commands, keeping the law is effected by interpreting general principles in terms of particular stipulations, thereby achieving faithfulness by following prescribed actions. Jesus, however, went back to the core values of the law—the supreme love of God and love of neighbor—seeking to recover the core as the basis for understanding and deed. In these ways, Jesus *was* an innovator, but one who sought to conserve the heart of the divine covenant rather than effecting a break with it. Likewise, he *was* a radical, but the radicality of Jesus should not be seen as revolutionism proper; rather, it sought to make the root and center of the ways of God[1] primary rather than their boundary edges.

A third conception of Jesus such an investigation might challenge is that of a soft and mild Jesus, seeking to do no harm and helping people be nicer to others. One can understand how Jesus gets perceived in these ways; he called for the love of enemies as well as the love of God and neighbor. He took pity on the outcasts and healed the sick. He embraced children and exorcised the tormented. He advocated modified compliance with Rome, as long as one's loyalty to God was firm. He used parables and familiar images to make the Kingdom of God come alive for his audiences, and he calmed people's fears by inviting them to trust in God's provision earnestly. In these and other ways, we see Jesus as a comforter of the disturbed, helping people deal more effectively with their givens and situations. And yet, he worked in provocative ways as well. His mission also involved the disturbance of the comfortable, helping people catch glimpses of how to live responsively to God's workings in the world. The transformative aspects of Jesus' ministry extended beyond maintaining harmony, and these incisive actions should also be taken seriously in considering how he furthered his mission.

All of these images of Jesus fit, to a degree, but Jesus was also more—and less—than these conceptions might suggest. Jesus as a transformer of individual and societal perceptions not only called for attitude and cognitive change, he also provoked such movement by introducing *crises of category* in the thought of his audiences. Perceptual and attitudinal change always involves a crisis by which ways of dealing with one's reality no longer work, leading that person to explore new approaches and paradigms. Indeed, it is acknowledged in most theoretical schools of learning, development, and cognition that moving from one plane of understanding to another is most often precipitated by a crisis wherein one's tools for problem solving and operation are revealed to be inadequate to the more complex and exception-laden challenges at hand. Effective teachers will also introduce a crisis wherein subjects are forced to explore new, more advanced levels of thinking and operating.[2]

Much of Jesus' ministry shows evidence of such an interest. We may think that he came to meet people's needs and help them deal more effectively with the world within and the world without; but that's not all he came to do. He also came to provoke, to cajole, to create crises by which people would find it impossible to continue living on the same planes of thought, perception, and action to which they had grown accustomed. In particular, Jesus sought to transform perceptions of what God expects of humanity with relation to the Divine Being and with relation to one another. Considering his actions from

the perspective of cognitive dissonance theory helps bring Jesus'
transformative mission into clearer focus.

Cognitive Dissonance Theory

When Leon Festinger's book on cognitive dissonance theory was
published nearly a half century ago, it immediately caught the imagination of psychologists and cognitive theorists alike. Rather than
assume that humans were motivated primarily by physiological drives
or the will to power, Festinger argued that humans possess an innate
drive toward congruity and consonance. Where contradictions are
perceived between one's self-conceptions and one's behaviors, or perhaps between two competing self-perceptions, one is driven to reconcile the discrepancies and move toward a more consonant self-concep-
tion. This theory is constructed on several planks in its platform.
First, *"the reality which impinges upon a person will exert pressures in the
direction of bringing the appropriate cognitive elements into correspondence
with that reality"* (Festinger, 1957, 11). Put otherwise, the drive to
establish and maintain cognitive consonance is real, and humans will
work to either rectify self-perceptions or to modify their behaviors to
reduce dissonance.[3] Dissonance may arise from logical inconsistency,
because of cultural mores, because one specific opinion is included in a
more general opinion, and because of past experience (Festinger,
1957, 14). Awareness of incongruities and inconsistencies, therefore,
causes the subject to seek to rectify the dissonance and move toward
greater consonance and authenticity.

A second assertion is that *"if two elements are dissonant with one
another, the magnitude of the dissonance will be a function of the importance
of the elements"* (Festinger, 1957, 16). This being the case, relatively
minor incongruities matter little. They cause little anxiety and do not
threaten one's conception of self. On the other hand, if the importance
of the issue is high, either in the thought of the individual or the contextual group, one will experience accordingly great motivation to
reconcile the dissonance. This leads to a third assertion, namely, that
*"the total amount of dissonance . . . will depend on the proportion of the rel-
evant elements that are in question with the one in question"* (Festinger,
1957, 17). Thus, the number of issues involved is a factor of the dissonance magnitude in addition to their importance. A fourth inference,
factors in *"the proportion of relevant elements"* involved (Festinger, 1957,
18), leads Festinger to calculate a fifth factor—namely, that *"the maximum dissonance that can possibly exist between any two elements is equal to
the total resistance to change of the least resistant element"* (Festinger, 1957,

28). The reason is that adjustment in one direction or another will tend to reduce the level of experienced dissonance. Therefore, when the forces of dissonance extend beyond forces of resistance, adjustment will eventually transpire.

A sixth plank in Festinger's platform relates to the motivational aspects that are factors of cognitive dissonance: "*The presence of dissonance gives rise to pressures to reduce or eliminate the dissonance. The strength of the pressures to reduce the dissonance is a function of the magnitude of the dissonance*" (Festinger, 1957, 18). Based on this point, it can be assumed that the alleviation of dissonance affects human decision-making. Therefore, dissonance can be reduced by any of three options: the elements among the dissonant relationships may be changed, new cognitive elements and understandings may be added, and the importance of the elements themselves may be reduced. Post-decisional dissonance is also a reality, but it decreases the more that the positive and negative rewards are considered after the fact. On the other hand, favorable attitudinal change can be observed to be higher when the subject must rationalize an action with less extrinsic reward. Another observation is that action causes its own sort of reflective appraisal, sometimes evoking cognitive change in retrospect.

Attitude change happens as a result of dealing with cognitive dissonance in several ways. First, attitude sometimes follows action. Where people take up a new set of actions, changes in attitude often follow as a means of reducing the dissonance between one's new behavior and one's interest. If the behavior continues, attitude will tend to adapt to the new behavior in ways that affirm it. Second, where the extrinsic reward might be low, subjects often tend to compensate and attribute to the action a greater sense of meaning, lest dissonance over meaningless action threaten consonance. Contrary to reward-and-punishment motivation, cognitive dissonance theory shows that people actually come to value a behavior more highly if the ownership is forced to come from within instead of without. A third aspect of attitudinal change involves changing one's opinion about former investments if it is seen that they are inconsistent with other values. By showing the apparent contradictions between values, understandings are forced to function on higher levels as the present set of tools and operations are no longer equal to the challenges at hand. These are some of the ways that cognitive dissonance evokes changes in attitude and perception—themselves aspects of transformative cognition.[4]

Applying this theory to Jesus' mission, many of his actions cannot be best understood as intended to meet people's needs or to explain the way of the Kingdom by means of illustrative object lessons. Many of his actions seem more provocative than comforting. Nor does he simply try to motivate people to do more, or do things better. Many of Jesus' deeds appear to have been aimed at heightening the cognitive dissonance of his audiences, seeking to transform their ways of thinking about things, especially regarding the transcendent character of God and what God expects of humanity. This method of operation can be inferred by considering Jesus' dissonance-producing deeds.

Jesus' Dissonance-Producing Deeds

In distinguishing the Jesus of history from the Jesus of the faithful, scholars have devised several criteria for determining historicity.[5] The first criterion is that of *dissimilarity*. Simply put, aspects of Jesus' ministry least similar to emerging developments in early Christianity are less likely to have been concocted, and by default are more likely to be considered historical. Second, the criterion of *multiple attestation* infers that an event or saying appearing in more than one Gospel setting, especially if appearing in slightly different ways so as to avert suspicions of derivation in one direction or another, may be considered more authentic. A third criterion is *coherence*: the view that a presentation cohering with what we think Jesus was like, rather than idiosyncratic ones, stands a greater chance of being authentic. A fourth criterion is that of *naturalism versus supernaturalism*, which distinguishes the realism of history from the more embellished features of hero stories and theological interests. When all of these criteria are employed, several basic features of Jesus' ministry stand out as most likely to be considered authentic. These include his relation to John the Baptist, his cleansing of the Temple, his dining with sinners, his breaking the Sabbath, and his declaration of the love of God.[6] Considering each of these actions and themes in the light of cognitive dissonance theory heightens particular aspects of Jesus' transformative intentionality.

Before considering these deeds of Jesus, however, something of the religious and social backdrop of first-century Palestine is in order. Jesus' ministry began during the tenth decade of the Roman occupation, and Jewish groups and institutions had to find ways of adjusting to the occupation.[7] *Sadducees*, managers of the Temple system and its priesthood, found it convenient to exchange compliance with Rome on a variety of issues for Roman support. They emphasized the importance of ritual purity, requiring the exchange of Roman money for Jewish money before purchasing an acceptable animal for the appropriate sacrifice. The *Essenes*, in turn, rejected the Jerusalem aristocracy as collaborating with Rome and set up alternative communities in the wilderness and in villages to fulfill their understandings of God's righteousness. The Qumran community had strict regulations for entering and participating in the community and viewed its membership as the "children of light" versus their adversaries and those whom they called "children of darkness." The *Pharisees* advocated faithfulness to God by emphasizing complete observance of the Torah. They were active in every major Jewish community, and they were known for setting up a hedge around the Law, ensuring its observance by stipulating what faithfulness required.

A variety of resistance movements emerged, including those led by what Josephus calls *"prophets,"* those who were called *"zealots,"* and those known as *Sicarii* dagger men. The commonality between these individuals and groups is that they believed in the forcible overthrow of the Romans, in keeping with the Maccabean uprising and the prophetic heroes of old.[8] By contrast, *apocalyptists* believed God's intervention would come from the heavens and that God's enemies would be dealt with from on high. In the meantime, they called for perseverance and faithfulness to God's ways, as opposed to assimilation.

While there was a great deal of variety between these first-century C.E. movements and a fair amount of interchange between them, they also shared a variety of commonalities. First, they believed in a covenantal relationship between Israel and God, in which the Jewish nation was called to faithfulness in particular ways. The Law was meant to be kept, and religious measures were set to specify the legal, cultic, and societal standards to be achieved. In addition, ritual means of purification were established as means of redeeming the individual from shortcomings or infractions, and systems were quite clear in terms of what was required.[9] A second feature of these systems is that people were regarded as pure or impure depending on the degree to which they were able to adhere to expected standards. The adherents were considered "righteous," while non-adherents were labeled "sinners."[10] This led to a third feature, which involved the marginalization of those who did not measure up in particular ways. Avoiding such social alienation also provided an impressive motivation for pursuing religious observance and attaining religious purity.[11] It was in such a setting that the ministry of Jesus should be envisioned.

Ironically, connectedness to the love of God and experiencing the love of others in community were casualties of such systems. Psychologically, even one's conception of self was forced into the categories of either merited esteem or self-denigration. The Decalogue, however, was from the beginning a gift of grace. The first four commandments of Moses are intended to restore the vertical relationship between God and humanity; the last six commandments are intended to restore the horizontal relationship between persons. In that sense, Jesus refused to answer the lawyer's question as to which was the greatest of the commandments. To single out one would have been to neglect the other nine; the question involved a no-win proposition. Rather, Jesus responded by getting to the core of the Law: the love of God and the love of neighbor (Mark 12:28–31).[12] By citing these two summaries of the Law, Jesus shows familiarity beyond the Exodus rendering. He also knew the interpretations following the Decalogue in Deuteronomy and Leviticus, apparently affording a broader understanding than a legalistic appraisal would afford. In addition to expounding the love of God and neighbor directly in his teachings, Jesus also enacted it through his works. Five of the most likely historical features of Jesus' ministry here deserve consideration, and each of these can be seen to be furthering the mission of Jesus by means of precipitating cognitive dissonance.

The first feature of Jesus' ministry commanding notice is *his association with John the Baptist.* One thing common to all four Gospels is the inauguration of Jesus' ministry in conjunction with the ministry of John the Baptist. Clearly, his public ministry's beginning is marked by his baptism by John, and Jesus' notoriety builds upon John's. The mistake, however, is to build an understanding of Jesus' mission based on a partial or misguided notion of what John was doing. Two leading misconceptions include the identification of John as a militaristic prophet desiring to overthrow the Romans by means of a resistance movement, and the interpretation of John's baptism as a new religious requirement superceding one set of religious requirements with another. Neither of these appraisals fit. Even in Josephus' listing of first-century Galilean prophets, he refers to John as a far more authentic prophet than militaristic leaders such as Theudas, the Samaritan, and the Egyptian.[13] And in Jesus' commands to put away the sword and to love one's enemies, he is presented in ways greatly contrastive to contemporary prophetic leaders. On the second point, not only does Jesus' own ministry diminish the plausibility of such a view, but it fails to understand the main point of John's baptismal testimony. In the light of cognitive dissonance theory, what John, and therefore Jesus, was doing becomes clearer.

Rather than seeing John as instituting a new ritual to which Jesus submitted, it is better to view John's immersion of people in the Jordan and elsewhere as a declaration of the prolific availability of divine grace and the life of the Spirit. John's ministry should be viewed as a *contrast* to confining access to the grace of God to ritual means of purification, either in Jerusalem, Qumran, or other cultic settings. When contrasted to the Jewish ritual purification baths, required to make one "clean" before entering the Temple area or other worship areas, the actions become clearer. At the Essene Gate entrance to Jerusalem, and in Qumran, pools for ritual purification show two sets of stairways—one descending, another ascending. In the Qumran pool, there are four stairways leading out of the water, and in both cases a rail divides the "impure" descenders from the "pure" ascenders. Impurity is transferred by touch, so one would not want to be made impure by touching another who had not yet been purified. Other features also figured in here. For one thing, getting clean was an important practical matter. In a dusty and unsanitary setting, getting cleaned up before entering settings of worship would have been a worthy practice on several levels. For another, running (living) water was required for the purification to be effective. This is also understandable, as the less stagnant the water source, the more effective its cleansing would be. It might also be argued that the Jewish *mikva'ot* cleansing pools (also found in many homes) were designed to bring the luxury of a "river bath" into the city. Rainwater was stored during some months of the year, and it was used later for cleansing purposes, fulfilling the washing requirements of the Torah and also serving practical purposes. Ritual purity, however, also became one of the benefits of particular sorts of bathings and cleansings, and it functioned to mark insiders and outsiders in cultic ways.

The effect of John's baptizing crowds of people would have jarred the thinking and experience of Jewish populations in several ways. First, it would have made cleansing available to the many instead of constricting it to the few. Trips to religious centers were no longer required to attain purity before God, if that is an association the action would have carried. Second, it would have called people to repentance, away from their compliance with Rome, rather than the sort of compromise evident in the Jewish leadership and their accommodation to Roman ways and expectations. Calling people to repentance would have had ethical and social implications aimed at renewing the religious identity of Israel. A third association would have connected the free-flowing water of the Jordan with the free-flowing work of the Holy Spirit, and this meaning is clearly picked up in the ministry of Jesus. In fact, every time the baptisms of Jesus and John are mentioned in the Bible, it is done in a contrastive and intensifying way: John baptized with water, but Jesus baptized with fire and the Holy Spirit. In that sense, water immersion prefigures spiritual filling characteristic of the Jesus movement in Acts.

By inviting the multitudes to repentance, by challenging leaders regarding their complicity with Rome, by tying ethical repentance to purification, and by declaring the prolific availability of the grace of God, John's baptismal ministry created cognitive dissonance for the individual construing the receipt of grace only through ritual means of purification. By baptizing in the wilderness, John was declaring boldly that purification and the "remission of sins" were tied to ethical living and authenticity rather than with the symbolization of such in cultic expressions. Viewing Jesus as continuing the ministry of John in his own ministry, then, clarifies other aspects of his work. While the Fourth Gospel poses an awkward set of statements on Jesus and baptism (Jesus baptized with his disciples near the place where John was baptizing [John 3:22], although it is emphasized in the next chapter [John 4:2] that it was Jesus' disciples that baptized, but he did not), it is likely that Jesus' ministry continued in the trajectory of John's. In that sense, he continued to expand access to God's love and grace by his actions and teachings.

A second feature of Jesus' ministry deserving consideration is his *cleansing of the Temple*. While the Synoptics present this event as happening at the end of Jesus' ministry (as it well may have),[14] John presents it at the beginning. Especially if the Jerusalem leaders were indeed offended enough to want Jesus put to death upon his next visit to Jerusalem (after the otherwise commendable healing of the paralytic in John 5), this event must have created a huge disturbance. And it does not appear to have been an accident. Wrong is the view that Jesus fell into a fit of rage and lost control over his composure, flailing away at people and animals alike. The text says nothing of violence against humans, or even that animals were beaten—only that Jesus made a whip of cords and drove them all out—people, sheep, and oxen alike (John 2:15). A second misconception is clarified in considering Mark's text. In Mark alone, Jesus arrived the day before and looked around; because it was late, though, he departed and returned the next day (Mark 11:11). This suggests a calculated move rather than a fit of rage. So what were aspects of the calculation, and what did Jesus seek to accomplish in his demonstration the following day?

In terms of cognitive dissonance, he challenged the religious establishment and its practices in the name of God and God's purposes for the Temple. God's desire was to make the Temple a "place of prayer" for the nations, but the money changers and animal vendors had made it into a "den of robbers." By ejecting from the Temple those who had rejected others—except they follow prescribed norms of right sacrificial offerings—Jesus figuratively "turned the tables" on those who operated the Temple systems of exchange. As a prophetic demonstration, Jesus created dissonance in the thinking of any who might have witnessed the event. He brought judgment on those who were operating an otherwise sacred system, claiming to reject that system in the name of the one purportedly authorizing, and even requiring, its service—God. In that sense, Jesus sought to bring an end to systems functioning to accord ritual purity to those who could afford it while denying access to divine grace to the *am ha-a'retz*—the poor of the land, who would never be able to afford the price of ritual purity. By symbolically purging an institutional system of cultic purification, Jesus placed himself on the side of those unable to afford such a commodity as well as those who, for whatever reason, were dehumanized as outsiders for cultic reasons. This would also have challenged the self-perceptions of those managing such systems. The strong judgment by Jesus must have produced dissonance in their thought, possibly leading to transformed understandings of what God requires and what God does not.

A third example of Jesus' ministry in which cognitive dissonance featured prominently is the *healing of the infirm on the Sabbath*. Jesus' healing of the sick is one of the most noted aspects of his ministry, but one feature about this work often escapes notice—namely, that he performed several of his healings on the Sabbath.[15] This note carries over into all four Gospels, and it is a feature of Jesus' ministry that is unlikely to have been concocted. What also escapes notice is the fact that the religious authorities were often portrayed as having been upset at his healing on the Sabbath. This was because it was a practice deemed as being against the Sabbath regulation not to work on the Sabbath. Unlike other healers and doctors who might have made money as a result of their medical services, Jesus instructed his followers to minister without accepting money from others, nor did he accept remuneration himself.

In Jesus' first healing on the Sabbath in the Synoptics, the man with the withered hand, the healing is performed in the Synagogue. When the Pharisees challenge him about his legal violations of Sabbath laws, Jesus responds by asking whether it is lawful to do good or harm, to save life or to kill, on the Sabbath (Mark 3:4). After he healed the man, the Pharisees are reported as immediately holding counsel with the Herodians as to how they might destroy Jesus (Mark 3:6). He obviously had threatened their authority in challenging their sensibilities as to what God required. The second set of Sabbath healings in the Synoptics is mentioned only in general. After Jesus preached in the Synagogue at Nazareth, he experienced rejection, as a prophet is "not without honor" except in his hometown.[16] Only Mark mentions the performance of healings, but Luke adds special significance to the ministry. Luke connects Jesus' inaugural message with the year of Jubilee (Isa. 61), when the debts of all would be forgiven and healing and deliverance would be restored to all; then he "explains" the fact that not all who needed to be were healed—only some—harking back to the days of Elijah. Mark describes the response of the crowd in stark terms: because of their lack of belief, even Jesus could do no miracles (except lay his hands on a few sick people and heal them). Luke adds a third and fourth Sabbath healing—the healing of the crippled woman in one of the Synagogues (Luke 13:10–17) and the healing of the man with dropsy on the way to the home of a Pharisaic leader (Luke 14:1–6). In both of these, the wisdom of leading an ox or a donkey to water, or setting an ox (or son) free if it falls *into a well*, is given as legitimation for breaking Sabbath codes.

The Gospel of John presents both of Jesus' most detailed healings as having happened on the Sabbath, leading to extended discussions among the Jewish leaders. The healing of the paralytic in John 5 raises questions of Jesus' authority (John 5:9–18), and when the discussion continues upon his next visit to Jerusalem (John. 7:22f.), the authorities are presented as still being troubled over his healing on the Sabbath. Likewise, the healing of the blind man in John 9 occurs on the Sabbath, and once again, consternation is expressed over it (John 9:14–16). In these passages, Jesus' authority is questioned, which leads Jesus to further controversy as he claims to be acting on behalf of the one who sent him—God. What becomes apparent when considering the six instances where Jesus performs healings on the Sabbath is that he seems to be doing so as a matter of working deconstructively as well as constructively. He desires wholeness for those he heals, but he also apparently chooses to perform healings on the Sabbath as a means of creating a crisis of dissonance in the thought of bystanders. Rather than seeing Sabbath observance as a matter of meeting legalistic requirements, it is invoked as a facilitator of redemption and wholeness. In healing on the Sabbath, Jesus provoked a cognitive crisis within the thought of those who perceived otherwise. By creating a dilemma between two "goods" involved with keeping Sabbath regulations and celebrating the healing of the infirm, Jesus challenged the legalistic clout of the former with the existential authority of the latter. From the resultant dissonance, the central value of the Sabbath demands reconsideration.

A fourth sort of dissonance-producing action of Jesus was *his dining with "sinners" and tax collectors*. This action might not appear to modern readers as particularly shocking, but table fellowship in ancient Judaism had far more significance than just the pleasure of eating together. Within the Jewish practice of the communion offering, sharing food together was understood as a sacramental event reconciling neighbors and family members to each other in the presence of God. Even enemies were reconciled in the sharing of bread together (Ps. 23:5; 41:9). In Jesus' first event of sharing table fellowship (Mark 2:13–17), Jesus is presented as calling Levi the tax collector (son of Alphaeus), which apparently drew criticism from scribes and Pharisees. They asked Jesus' disciples why he dined with "tax collectors and sinners." Upon hearing about their challenge, Jesus responded that it was not the well who needed a physician, but the ill. Jesus "came to call not the righteous, but the sinners" (Luke 5:32b adds "unto repentance"). Both Matthew and Luke contain an extended set of Jesus sayings about John (probably from the Q tradition, Matt. 11:7–19; Luke 7:24–35), including statements about his ministry in the wilderness, his prophetic-messenger ministry (based on Mal. 3:1), the Kingdom's suffering of violence (by the rejection once more of "Elijah"), and a final statement linking Jesus and John the Baptist. While John's coming without eating and drinking was interpreted as having a demon, when Jesus came both eating and drinking, he was accused of being a "glutton and a drunkard" and "a friend of tax collectors and sinners."[17] In cognitive dissonance theory, their resistance to change is presented as having been at a high level of magnitude.

Beyond these presentations of Jesus' sharing fellowship with tax collectors and sinners, Luke describes another incident in which these sorts of unacceptable people were drawing near to Jesus, evoking the consternation of the scribes and Pharisees regarding Jesus' dining with such (Luke 15:1–3). It is at this point that the Lukan Jesus tells the three parables of lostness and redemption involving the lost sheep (Luke 15:4–7), the lost coin (Luke 15:8–10), and the lost son (Luke 15:11–32). In these passages, Luke, in contrast to Mark, emphasizes the redemption of the lost and the sinners and their repentance as a factor in the happy ending. This theme in Luke is then typified by two other distinctive passages. A parable is first told about a Pharisee and a tax collector who went up to the Temple to pray. The Pharisee thanked God for his righteousness and privilege, whereas the tax collector, not even lifting his eyes to heaven, beat on his breast and called out for mercy as a sinner. In Jesus' teaching, it is the *latter*, the humble, who went away justified, not the self-exalted (Luke 18:9–14). A few verses later, the Lukan Jesus' dining with Zachaeus leads climactically not only to his repentance but also his penance—he gave half his goods to the poor and repaid what he had stolen fourfold (Luke 19:1–10). In these ways, the Lukan Jesus not only receives sinners and tax collectors but leads them full circle unto repentance.[18]

More striking and dissonance-producing, however, is the Markan Jesus (and probably closer to the historical Jesus), whose dining with "sinners"—*even before they repent*—makes a powerful statement. It declares the forgiveness and acceptance of God, available in the present, to be received in faith by any who will be open to it. Repentance may follow as a fitting response to the gracious love of God, but it is not presented here as a precondition. That is the *shock* of it. This dissonance-producing message of unmerited acceptance is explicitly manifested by Jesus' declaration that people's sins were forgiven. Back to the healing of the paralytic in Mark 2:1–12, Jesus declares the man's sins were forgiven. Therefore, not only were the Jewish leaders offended at his healing on the Sabbath, but they were also exercised over his claiming the authority to forgive people's sins. They found it blasphemous (Mark 2:6–7; Matt. 9:3; Luke 5:21), for only God has the authority to forgive sins.[19] Jesus was probably not unaware of such understandings, which is all the more reason why his receipt of "tax collectors and sinners," even before they repented, and, likewise, his declaration of forgiveness to the infirm should be interpreted as dissonance-producing actions. Extending unmerited favor in the name of God challenges all systems of deservedness—an aspect of conventionality that cannot be transcended except by revelation. This is why Jesus had to come.

A fifth dissonance-producing action of Jesus is *his references to God as his loving Father.* Among the Gospels, only in Mark 14:36 does Jesus refer to God in the diminutive sense, *Abba*, and this intimate reference to the Deity has great theological significance. The human–divine relationship revealed by Jesus restores humanity to the intimacy of God's love, and it invites humanity to approach God in an I–Thou structure of relationship rather than an I–It relationship. While the occasion of Jesus' prayer was in the Garden of Gethsemane, with only

Peter, James, and John present, the meaning of the reference possessed great capacity to influence people's thinking. One can understand why the Apostle Paul picked it up and used it in Romans 8:15 and Galatians 4:6. Believers are given the "Spirit of Adoption" by which we, too, cry out "Abba-Father," enjoined to the Deity by the bonds of love. Joachim Jeremias has even argued that this was the first reference to the Deity in intimate, diminutive terms in the history of world religions, and though an overstated claim, the innovative character of its mention by Jesus still stands.

The Father–Son relationship is nowhere as intertwined in any of the Gospels as it is in the Gospel of John. Here the Son is equal to the Father, while also subordinate to the Father. Jesus and the Father are one, but the Son can do nothing except as instructed by the Father. When Jesus was challenged as to his authority, he claimed to speak solely on the Father's behalf and stated that to see him is to behold the Father who sent him. Needless to say, these claims were provocative, indeed. One can understand why Jewish authorities would have been troubled by anyone making such claims—whether they originated with the historical Jesus or whether they were part of the emerging Christology of Johannine Christianity, reflecting its worship experience and evangelistic outreach to Jewish family and friends. The origin of Jesus' claiming to have been sent by God was probably the *Shaliach* (sending) motif of Deuteronomy 18:15-22, where the authentic prophet says nothing on his own but only what God has instructed him to say.[20] On that basis, his work must be obeyed as the word of God, and his authenticity is certified by his predictive words having come true. An inauthentic prophet, or one who speaks simply on his own behalf, needs not be heeded, and blasphemy is punishable by death (Lev. 24:10–23). In his references to the intimacy of God's love and his divine commission, Jesus not only taught about the love of God at the heart of the Torah, he personalized it. It may even be said that this is how he taught his followers to pray, "*Our Father in heaven, hallowed be thy name*" (Matt. 6:10; Luke 11:2; see also Mark 11:25f.), with the same sense of intimacy. We forget, though, how much of a shock such utterances must have been to his audiences; yet, such is the way of transformative leadership. New perspectives emerge as the limitations of former ones are challenged by dissonance.

In various aspects of Jesus' ministry, he employed considerable numbers of dissonant relationships, as well as their magnitudes, in furthering his transformative mission. Therefore, the same sort of analysis can be performed on other aspects of Jesus' ministry in addition to the five mentioned above. His healing (and touching!) of lepers must have raised eyebrows; his cursing the fig tree (the symbol of Israel's prosperity) must have shocked his followers; his engaging demoniacs and setting them free from their inward turmoil must have evoked consternation; his welcoming of children, women, and Samaritans into his inner circle would have been counter-conventional; his transforming of the Passover meal and interpretations of familiar Scriptures would have been regarded as creative innovations; and especially his teachings on the way of the Kingdom, reversing the value of the first and the last, would have been striking indeed. In fact, one of the remarkable things about the parables of Jesus is that the first major parable in Mark (the sower, the seeds, and the soils, Mark 4:1–29) implies that the parables are given not as elucidators of the Kingdom but as vehicles of judgment by which insiders are distinguished from outsiders. Luke and Matthew soften this theme, but Mark's Jesus uses parable to create dissonance so that transformative understanding might take place.

Transformative Incongruity and Resultant Congruity

In these and other ways, the transformative ministry of Jesus is thrown into sharp relief by considering aspects of cognitive dissonance at work in the actions and teachings of Jesus. Time and again, Jesus is presented as driving a wedge between conventional understandings of the ways things work, in relation to religious life and otherwise, and, by causing a crisis of category, Jesus prepares the way for new understandings to emerge. Many of these themes may also be interpreted in sociological perspective, but cognitive dissonance theory allows the focus to remain on how such actions would have affected the individual—with relation to the societal setting and otherwise. A particular value of applying cognitive dissonance theory to Gospel narratives is that it not only helps one understand more clearly what the Jesus of history may have been doing but it also allows present-day interpreters to apply it in the settings within which they find themselves. Consider the impact of imposed incongruity and of movement toward transformative congruity in the above examples, with implications for today.

With John's wilderness baptisms and Jesus' relation to his ministry, a new day in spirituality was being announced. Rather than constricting purification and spiritual renewal to cultic rites done in proper ways, John's provocative actions signified the prolific availability of God's ever-present grace and empowerment. Repentance and remission of sins were therefore no longer tied to ritual means of purification; instead they were tied to turning from compromise and injustice and receiving the gift of God's grace by faith. The Jesus movement built upon this call for renewal, and baptism came also to signify spiritual immersion in the transforming power of the Holy Spirit. In that sense, the baptism of Jesus was held to be one of fire and the Holy Spirit, and John's immersion of believers in the free-flowing waters of the Jordan prefigured the immersion of believers in the free-flowing presence of the Holy Spirit. A considerable mistake for Christian interpreters, however, would be to construe Christian baptism as a supercessionist rite replacing Jewish ones as the divine requirement. The connection of the ministries of Jesus and John points, rather, in the direction that all who respond to God's grace and presence fully in faith receive them fully with power. Perception and experience are thus transformed, as one looks to the substance of which outward forms are but a shadow (Heb. 9-10).

In Jesus' cleansing the Temple and dining with "sinners," he can be understood to have been challenging the purity laws of Judaism by which some were accorded the grace of God and others were not. Two directions of interpretation have been applied to this understanding, and both have valid points to make. First, in extending table fellowship to "sinners and tax collectors," Jesus was declaring (with divine agency) their reconciliation with him and, therefore, to God—even before they repented. This statement of radical inclusivity functioned to draw people into the love of God as enacted by Jesus, and it may even have led to repentance as a response of gratitude to the gift of grace. In this sense, Jesus demonstrates the same unmerited favor he also announces from God. The other way people have interpreted these actions is to see them as drawing in the poor of the land, the *am ha-a'retz*. Unable to afford the appropriate sacrificial animal, including the exchange of currency at a loss, vast segments of society had become relegated to the status of "sinners" as a result of the Temple system. Jesus' overturning the money-changers' tables and driving out the animals was a way of saying that the reception of God's grace is not conditioned upon the attainment of ritual purity by means of proper cultic practice. Jesus was therefore drawing in the poor of the land and all others who had become alienated by the boundary-marking functions of the Temple system as an institution. In so doing, he was driving a dissonance-producing wedge between human understandings of divine requirements and the perdurant will of God that all should be reunited in human–divine relationship. And in doing so in the name of God, he was correcting conventional views of God's requirement for humanity.

By breaking Sabbath codes, Jesus was also seeking to drive a wedge between conventional understandings of God's requirements and the original intention of the Sabbath from the divine perspective. Jesus, in performing commendable healings, wondrous deeds furthering the very wholeness the Sabbath was intended to facilitate, exposed the dissonance between regulated observance of the Law and the center of its redemptive function. Healings and feedings provided the occasion for such an endeavor, but many were not healed who probably needed to be. In that sense, many of Jesus' healings were making a point as to the authentic nature of Sabbath observance, and his breaking the letter of the Law in pointing to its center functioned to make these distinctions apparent.

Ultimately, communicating the love of God to humanity was the central concern of Jesus and his mission. In addition to enacting prophetic challenges to conventional interpretations of the divine will, Jesus pointed time and again to the love and grace of God, inviting humanity to respond to it in faith. He also modeled an intimate relationship with God, calling God "*Abba*" (parallel to the diminutive "daddy" in English). While Matthew and Luke did not pick up on that significant statement in Mark, they did include the prayer Jesus taught his disciples, inviting them to pray to God as the collective Father of all who would seek his favor.

Aspects of attitude change, a feature of cognitive dissonance theory, may also be inferred when considering John's dialectical material. For one thing, as Jesus' subjects were often given little extrinsic incentive to embrace his teaching or ways, they may have come to value the changes he was calling for as a means of dealing with the resultant dissonance. For another, Jesus sometimes walked people into a new reality, affecting their behavior, expecting a change in attitude as a result. The Temple cleansing, dining with "sinners," and teaching his disciples a new pattern of praying exemplify this approach to attitude change. Transformed thinking sometimes emerges as a result of reflecting upon one's reformed actions. A third approach to attitude change involved reflection upon former understandings and later ones. While Jesus did not come to abolish the Law, he did claim to "fulfill" it by getting at its center rather than its boundary measures. In both the magnitude of importance and in the number of expressions, Jesus sought to transform the thinking of his audiences by introducing crises making it impossible to address the new experience with their current set of cognitive tools. In dealing with cognitive dissonance, Jesus effectively brought about transformed perspective in the thinking of his audiences, which involved a central aspect in the furtherance of his mission.

Conclusion

In these and other ways, the larger set of provocative actions taken by Jesus created dissonance within the thinking of first-century Jewish groups, forcing people to stretch beyond their present means of approaching the human–divine relationship. By creating cognitive dissonance, individuals would have been motivated to explore other ways to pursue a right relationship with God and one another. By using cognitive dissonance, Jesus can be seen to have furthered his mission in conveying the accessibility of God's presence and love in ways that did not merely present his audiences with an alternative form of transaction, a varied form of conventional religion similar to the Judaism of his day; rather, he demonstrated transformative leadership. In lifting people's understandings to new ways of seeing things, in pointing people to the center of Hebrew Scripture and tradition, and in enacting God's inclusive love, Jesus ushered in a new age—an age of divine grace to be received by the human response of faith to the divine initiative, restoring later generations to the original vision of the Jewish faith. By so doing, he employed cognitive dissonance as a means of facilitating transitions in the thinking and actions of his audiences with missional intentionality. He did not simply exchange one mode of transactional operation for another; he demonstrated transformative leadership by raising the vision and perspective of his audiences to new levels they otherwise would not have reached.

Notes

1. The origin of the word "radical" is *radix*, which in Latin means "root." The radicality of Jesus should be conceived as his seeking to restore the root and core of Jewish teachings rather than departing from them, or rather than being satisfied with a legal approach to core values. By aiming at the core rather than one of its stipulations, one is more likely to approximate the center of the value. Likewise, measuring insiders and outsiders according to their placement along erected boundaries creates artificial divides between insiders and outsiders, at times rewarding (depending on how the line is drawn) distance from the center over proximity to it. Worse, however, is the dehumanizing effect of according insider/outsider valuations to persons on

the basis of legalistic and arbitrary measures. These are the sorts of issues Jesus came to rectify.

2. See, for instance, the works of James Loder and James Fowler. Loder argues that it is a crisis experience—a shock—that forms the basis for any knowing event, wherein one's mind searches for a stance of interpretation regarding the event. Fowler's six stages of faith development observe, as did Kohlberg's, that one will operate on a particular level of reasoning until it is no longer adequate. Inadequacy is introduced by the crisis of facing a situation wherein one's current modes of analysis and operation are insufficient. Thus, cognitive crisis and the resulting dissonance marks the occasion for developmental transition and cognitive growth (Loder, 1981; Fowler, 1981).

3. In somewhat different terminology, Carl Rogers describes the incongruity between one's perceived and experienced realities as being a leading factor in one's level of inward anxiety. The role of the therapist, then, helps one achieve a greater sense of congruity. In that sense, truth is liberating and restoring of inward well-being (Rogers, 1951).

4. More can be considered regarding discussions of cognitive dissonance theory, including attitude change, in the books by Robert A. Wicklund and Jack W. Brehm (1976), and Jean-Leon Beauvois and Robert-Vincent Joule (1996).

5. A further discussion of criteria for determining historicity, including the strength and weaknesses of the leading criteria, may be seen in Anderson (2000). Engagements with Professors Borg, Powell, and Kinkel may be considered in Anderson (2002a); especially significant is the discussion of how these criteria are used and represented.

6. In addition to being discussed briefly in the *QRT* essay (Anderson, 2000, 24-29), these aspects of Jesus' ministry are among those most frequently presented in "red" and "pink" type (definitely authentic and probably authentic) by the Jesus Seminar (Funk & the Jesus Seminar, 1998).

7. More of these movements and ways they maintained their group standards of identity and concern can be considered in John Riches's text on the world of Jesus in first-century Judaism (1990, 68–86). According to Riches, "setting priorities for members' behavior and devising ways of reinforcing such behavior, were other, related ways of enabling the group to withstand the erosion of its values and norms" (Riches, 1990, 68).

8. More about these movements can be seen in Richard Horsley's book, which analyzes Jesus' ministry with the Roman occupation as the backdrop (Horsley, 2003).

9. On these matters John Riches's presentation of Jesus and his attempts to *transform Judaism* (1980) is impressive. He draws in the works of religious anthropologist Mary Douglas and distinguishes between literal meanings of myths and their symbolic functions as inculcators of values. In considering factors involved in religion and change, Riches shows how Jesus employed

language in surprising and unexpected ways to transform people's understandings of God's ways and expectations for humanity (Riches, 1980, 20–43). Riches and Millar take these ideas further in showing how the conjoining of unlikely associations affects perceptual change within the cognitive process (Riches & Millar, 1985).

10. Professor Sanders' discussion of whether the "sinners" to which Jesus reached out redemptively involved genuinely sinful people, or whether they were simply regarded as sinful, over-identifies the poor of the land as the specific group referred to in the Gospels (Sanders, 1985, 174–211). Indeed, it probably did include the poor, and while it probably did include genuinely treacherous persons such as tax collectors and others, the pejorative label of "sinner" also would have included any who did not live up to the letter of the Law and any who had not achieved ritual purity through prescribed means.

11. Riches's chapter (1980, 112–144) on Jesus and purity laws outlines effectively a variety of ways Jesus challenged such laws, pointing instead to the love of God that transcended them all (145–167).

12. The first four of the Ten Commandments addressed the human–divine relationship in Exodus 20:1–11: monotheism, forbidding of graven images, forbidding of taking God's name in vain, and Sabbath observance. These Jesus summarized by quoting the *Shema*: affirming the oneness of God and the priority of loving God with all of one's heart, strength and might (Deut. 6:4f.). The last six Commandments in Exodus 20:12–17 involve honoring parents and the forbidding of murder, adultery, stealing, bearing false witness, and covetousness. These Jesus summarized in citing Leviticus 19:18—commanding persons to love one's neighbor as oneself.

13. See the fuller comparison–contrast between Jesus and first-century prophets in "Jesus and Peace" (Anderson, 1994). Jesus appears to have distanced himself from such nationalistic movements, reflected in the Messianic Secret in Mark, and even in his fleeing the crowd's popularistic designs on his future in John 6:14f. Especially in his teachings around the command to love one's enemies (Matt. 5:38–48), Jesus provides his followers creative and transformative means of dealing with the Roman presence beyond the fight/flight dichotomies. Walter Wink's outlining of Jesus' "third way" in this instance marks a turning point in biblical interpretation.

14. Note the four presentations of the Temple cleansing in Matthew 21:12f.; Mark 11:15-17; Luke 19:45f.; John 2:13-17. In the following passages in all four Gospels, discussions of Jesus' authority follow (Matt. 21:23-7; Mark 11:27-33; Luke 20:1–8; John 2:18–22), and in the Synoptics Jesus volleys back their question regarding his authority to an inquiry regarding the ministry of John the Baptist—was his ministry from heaven, or from men? Because of their fear of challenging John's prophetic (and popular) authority, which was clearly tied to that of Jesus, they refused to give an answer. In John, Jesus promises a sign, but it will be the sign of the resurrection—rais-

ing up "this temple" after three days, evoking yet another misunderstanding from the unbelieving crowd.

15. The healing on the Sabbath in Matthew 12:9–14, Mark 3:1–6, and Luke 6:6–11 follows the confrontation of Jesus and his disciples for plucking grain on the Sabbath in Matthew 12:1–8, Mark 2:23–28, and Luke 6:1–5. The explanation after the Pharisees' confrontation over the plucking of grain argued back to David's example in feeding his soldiers during the days of Abithar. Then Jesus makes the point that the Sabbath was made for humanity; humanity was not made for the Sabbath.

16. The passages here include Matthew 13:53–58, Mark 6:1–6, and Luke 4:16–30. Luke's rendering has two extended additions to this passage in which Jesus is presented as declaring his liberating mission: first (Luke 4:16–22), he has come to proclaim release to the captives, recovery of sight to the blind, to set at liberty the oppressed, and to proclaim the year of the Lord's favor (Isa. 61:1–2). Second (Luke 4:25–30), Luke describes times during the ministry of Elijah when not all people were healed, only some, and this caused some to want to kill him in Nazareth.

17. Also found in the Matthean tradition is the cliché-ridden association of tax collectors and harlots, who will receive entry into the Kingdom before the dilatory son who did not carry through with his promise to labor in the father's vineyard (Matt. 21:28–32).

18. The adulterous woman passage in John 8:1–11 is not found in the earliest manuscripts of John, but some early manuscripts locate it within Luke. Whether or not the Lukan tradition was its first textual "home," the narrative does show a characteristically Lukan ending. While Jesus does not condemn the woman (and he also challenges others who also bore guilt not to cast the "first stone"), he also calls her to repentance: "Go and sin no more." Here, the conventionality and accountability aspects of Jesus' ministry to "sinners" are emphasized by later Gospel traditions, perhaps as a balance to his dissonance-producing unmerited acceptance. In that sense, cognitive dissonance can be seen to be operative not only among the Jewish audiences of Jesus during his historical ministry, but it was also apparently operative within the emerging traditions of the church. The Lukan traditions added accountability to such a "dangerous" gift of grace.

19. Luke adds the content that the woman's anointing of Jesus was a factor of her gratitude for his ministering to her, despite her sinfulness (Luke 7:36–50). Having located the event in the home of a Pharisee (rather than the home of Simon the leper, or even the home of Mary and Martha, both described as being in Bethany), Luke presents Jesus as again declaring forgiveness. This is also reported as having offended those present, and the event takes a turn toward redemption and the disconcerting (to some) forgiveness of sins. It should be said that Luke also probably had access to the Johannine rendering (John 12:1–8), which is why he moved the anointing to the *feet* of Jesus rather than his *head*, as in Mark and Matthew. It might also

be conjectured that his familiarity with the Johannine oral tradition (explaining such an unlikely move) might have involved the hearing of the name "Mary," associating the sister of Lazarus with another Mary of possibly more questionable repute. This might account for Luke's conjectural additions and his connecting the event with Pharisaic objection to Jesus' unfettered forgivingness. See Anderson (2002b).

20. See Anderson (1999) for a full treatment of the Father's sending of the Son in John, including implications for understanding Jesus' sense of his own mission rooted in Deuteronomy 18.

References

Anderson, P. N. (1994). Jesus and Peace, *The Church's Peace Witness*, M. Miller & B. Nelson Gingerich, eds. Grand Rapids: Eerdmans, 105–130.

Anderson, P. N. (1999). The Having-Sent-Me Father-Suspects of Agency, Irony, and Encounter in the Johannine Father-Son Relationship. *Semeia*, *85*, 33–57.

Anderson, P. N. (2000). On Jesus: Quests for Historicity, and the History of Recent Quests. *Quaker Religious Thought, 94*, 5–39.

Anderson, P. N. (2002a). A Response to Professors Borg, Powell and Kinkel. *Quaker Religious Thought, 98*, 43–51.

Anderson, P. N. (2002b). Interfluential, Formative, and Dialectical, a Theory of John's Relation to the Synoptics, *Für und wider die Priorität des Johannesevangeliums, Theologische Texte und Studien* (vol. 9), P. Hofrichter, ed. Hildesheim. Zürich and New York: Georg Olms Verlag, 19–58.

Beauvois, J., & Joule, R. V. (1996). *A Radical Dissonance Theory*. London/Bristol: Taylor & Francis.

Festinger, L. (1957). *A Theory of Cognitive Dissonance*. Stanford: Stanford University Press.

Fowler, J. W. (1981). *Stages of Faith: The Psychology of Human Development and the Quest for Meaning*. San Francisco: Harper & Row.

Funk, R. W., & the Jesus Seminar. (1998). *The Acts of Jesus: The Search for the Authentic Deeds of Jesus*. New York: HarperSanFrancisco.

Horsley, R. A. (2003). *Jesus and Empire: The Kingdom of God and the New World Disorder*. Minneapolis: Fortress.

Loder, J. (1981). *The Transforming Moment: Understanding Convictional Experiences*. San Francisco: Harper & Row.

Riches, J. K. (1980). *Jesus and the Transformation of Judaism*. London: Darton, Longman and Todd.

Riches, J. K., & Millar, A. (1985). Conceptual Change in the Synoptic Tradition, *Alternative Approaches to New Testament Study*, A. E. Harvey, ed. London: SPCK, 37–60.

Riches, J. K. (1990). *The World of Jesus: First-Century Judaism in Crisis*. Cambridge: Cambridge University Press.

Rogers, C. (1951). *Client-Centered Therapy: Its Current Practice, Implications, and Theory*. Boston: Houghton Mifflin.

Sanders, E. P. (1985). *Jesus and Judaism*. Philadelphia: Fortress.

Wicklund, R. A., & Brehm, J. W. (1976). *Perspectives on Cognitive Dissonance*. Hillsdale: Lawrence Erlbaum Associates.

CHAPTER 14

THE BIBLE AND THE ALCHEMY OF LANGUAGE IN PSYCHOLOGICAL PERSPECTIVE

Schuyler Brown

The world was disappearing into shadow, and all that was left was cupped within the soft light of the church. The church itself was wrapped around by all the leaves and lanes of Worcestershire, and Worcestershire was wrapped around by all of England. Into this sheltering bowl there dropped the *Nunc Dimittis,* so serene and simple that it reached out beyond the grey stone walls, beyond the dusky churchyard where a blackbird sang; it reached out all the way to my mother in the distant north and told me how far from her I was.

Lord, now lettest Thou thy servant depart in peace—I could get so far, and then a deep emotion, a compound both of happiness and sorrow, welled up in me and stopped my voice. It was more than simple grief at being parted from my mother, though that was part of it; it was sorrow, sorrow so poignant that it was close to joy, for the beauty, the exact rightness, of this passing moment.

—A. Quayle (1990)

True religious language enchants and informs, addressing its rhythmic and symbolic speech to regions of the mind which are inaccessible to argument, and evoking moments of awe and love which no exhortation can obtain. It has meaning at many levels, and welds together all those who use it, overriding their personal moods, and subduing them to its grave loveliness.

—E. Underhill (1937, 113)

It lives on the ear like a music that can never be forgotten, which the convert hardly knows how he can forego. Its felicities often seem to be

almost things rather than mere words. . . . In the length and breadth of
the land there is not a Protestant, with one spark of religiousness about
him, whose spiritual biography is not the Saxon Bible.
                                —Frederick Faber (as quoted in Neill, 1977, 135n)

1978, the year I came to England to teach at Heythrop College (University of London), was also the year I discovered Jung, or perhaps I should say, the year that Jung found me. Among the many debts that I owe to him, one of the most important has been the retrieval of the truth of the Bible: not the truth of ancient fact or inerrant doctrine, but truth in the etymological sense of the Greek word *aletheia*, "no longer hidden." Thanks to Jung, the Bible's numinous radiance is once again "a lamp to my feet and a light to my path" (Ps. 119:105), which fill my world with meaning and purpose.

For Jung, the numinosity of the biblical text lies in its archetypal imagery. What binds the Old and New Testaments together, despite all differences in doctrine and historical context, is the common store of imagery that runs through both volumes, though sometimes with typological shifts. It is the biblical images (whether individual metaphors or extended narratives) that illumine our experience in the world and provide a catalyst for spiritual transformation, resisting all reductionistic conceptualizations of the imagination. "We sin against the imagination whenever we ask an image for its meaning, requiring that images be translated into concepts" (Hillman, 1977, 8).

The Bible has the power to move us, to stir our emotions in ways we scarcely understand. The reader who experiences the transformative reality mediated by the Scriptural text cannot help being touched emotionally. Indeed, it is not uncommon for the reading or hearing of Scripture to result in tears or uncontrollable sobbing. This emotional response wells up spontaneously within the reader or hearer from a deep level of the psyche. It is a response to something not of our own making; we are not acting, but being acted upon. Something in the text has elicited feelings of enlargement, union, or emancipation that may have no specific intellectual content (James, 1902/1975, 410). This experience comes about not through discursive reasoning but through an intuitive sense that penetrates the darkness where God is (Exod. 20:21).

The emotional impact of Scripture may lead to dramatic visible results, such as the return to Jerusalem of the Emmaus disciples after they heard the risen Lord interpret the Scriptures (Luke 24:13–35). The Bible has served as the catalyst for the *sudden* conversion of St. Augustine, St. Anthony, and John Wesley—whose heart, like the hearts of the Emmaus disciples, was warmed by hearing the Scripture expounded. The *devotional* reading of the Bible leads to the *gradual* transformation of the life of the reader, refracting his or her interests, questions, and concerns into a divine word of consolation and instruction.

The Bible brings those who have such experiences face to face with the creative sources of their existence and reveals to them the deepest meanings of their lives. When Scripture is called a "delight" (Ps. 1:2) and "sweeter than honey and drippings of the honeycomb" (Ps. 19:10), surely more is suggested than the mere communication of ideas.

> Who can tell the pleasure
> Who recount the treasure
> By thy Word imparted
> To the simple-hearted?
> (Baker, n.d., 452)

Only the image has the power to produce psychological symptoms of deep emotion, of "feeling shivers along the spine, weeping in sympathy, or being transported in awe" (Culler, 1982, 39).

For Jung, biblical imagery was primarily visual, the images generated in our minds through reading the sacred text: the burning bush, the Virgin Mother, the cross, the coming of the Son of Man. By considering the Bible as a *"verbal* icon," I hope to extend Jung's retrieval of the power of the image and its crucial role in a society dominated by conceptual thinking. Let us explore together the transformative power of the *acoustic* images the Bible contains.

The importance attributed to sound in Eastern religion should make us attentive to the phonetic dimension of biblical language. Mantras are words that have power, even though they have no definable meaning (Coward & Goa, 1991). In the Hindu tradition, spiritual awareness is mediated by the sound rhythms, intonations, pitch, and modulations of the ancient Vedic hymns, quite apart from their verbal meaning (Smith, 1993, 132). In fact, many Brahmans in the nineteenth century recited the hymns by heart, without any understanding of what they meant (Smith, 1993, 302). Although the disjunction of sound and meaning is not part of the Christian experience, the Eastern example should make us open to the power of acoustic images in mediating to us the mystery of God.

The importance of sound in reading the Bible is obvious once we consider the primacy of the spoken word in Christian tradition. "Gospel" meant oral proclamation, or *kerygma*, before it came to designate a written text, and the word still retains this older meaning today.

The Form Critics tell us that the sayings of Jesus (prefaced by the introductory formula, "Amen, amen, I *say* to you") went through a generation of oral transmission before the first written Gospel was composed.

Christianity's attachment to the spoken word may have something to do with Jesus' relationship to the prophetic tradition, in which divine revelation is prefaced with the introductory formula, "Thus *says* the Lord. . . ." Although all language is ambiguous, spoken language—through personal contact and contextualization—has a directness lacking in the endless "deferral" of writing. When Paul writes, "Scripture *says* . . ." (Romans 4:3), he is expressing a desire to retrieve the spoken word of revelation through a text, which, strictly speaking, does not say anything.

The Christian church, like many other religions (Coward, 1988; Graham, 1988), has privileged the oral performance of Scripture. Right down to the present day, Scripture has always been read *aloud* during worship, and in this reading, sound is obviously crucial. When Scripture ceases to be memorized and recited, its vitality in the life of the individual tends to decrease.

Christianity began at a time when oral culture was only just giving way to written culture (Achtemeier, 1990, 3–27). Writing was often an aid to oral performance rather than an independent form of communication, and silent reading was virtually unknown (Achtemeier, 1990, 15–17).[1] Even today, when silent reading has become the norm, it is usually accompanied by involuntary vocalization.

Shortly before Jung's death in 1961, there was a significant shift in the understanding of text and language and, consequently, of truth. The two dominant paradigms for biblical interpretation, the theological and the historical, both understand "truth" to consist of a single, stable meaning that the text imposes on the literary work, assisting the fragility and imprecision of memory. In the classical understanding, text is the indelible trace of meaning intended by the author, which protects it against forgetfulness and the vagaries of the spoken word. The linguistic sign, made up of the signifier and the signified, is a closed unity that conveys an original, univocal, definitive meaning and prevents it from going astray. The task of interpretation is to establish, with semantic exactitude, the original meaning that the material text enshrines. The one true meaning of the text is authoritatively determined by the unchanging rules for how a text is to be read.

Around 1960, a new understanding of text begins to emerge. Language is viewed less as the vehicle of a fixed ideational content and

more in its own right, in the subtlety and infinite variety of its transformations. The discoveries of psychoanalysis played a key role in
this development. As long as the ego could be viewed, with Descartes, as a unified thinking subject, the text could be considered a
form of communication; a message transmitted by one thinking subject (the author or sender) to another thinking subject (the reader or
receiver). But once psychoanalysis revealed the ego to be part of the
multiplicity of fragmentary personalities called complexes, this com-
munications model became inadequate for understanding text. When
the multiplicity of the psyche gazes into the text, it finds there a corresponding multiplicity.

When text is no longer constrained to function as the conveyer of
one univocal, definitive meaning, it retrieves the active energy of the
spoken word. Heidegger has said that "language speaks" (Heidegger,
1971, 190). Similarly, according to the French linguist Roland Barthes, "the text works" (Barthes, 1973, 1015–1016)—deconstructing
the language of communication and representation, and reconstruct-
ing another language in which the interplay of words is freed from the
limitations of authorial intention. The meaning of words is the meaning they *can* have in the interpersonal linguistic system from which they
emerge (Culler, 1976, 113). The text is a fragment of language placed in
a context in which a variety of possible meanings can intersect and
interact. There is always language before the text and around the text.

Barthes sees a connection between the work of the text and the
work of the dream (Culler, 1976, 113). There, too, word-play and
sound-play have an important role, especially for James Hillman and
his followers. In the modern theory of text, as in a dream, the subject
is no longer the master of acoustic and visual images but rather is the
one through whom these images carry out their ceaseless interplay.

We are in the dream, and the dream is in us. The text dwells in us,
as we dwell in the text. The duality between text and interpretation is
overcome: "there is not a subject and an object. . . . 'The eye by which
I see God is the same eye by which God sees me'" (Barthes, 1975, 16).
We are "lost" in the web of words. As my opening quotation illustrates, the convergence of text and reader (or hearer) reveals a mar-
velous reciprocity. Just as the text sheds light on our present experience, so does that experience reveal new meaning in the text.

When Jung speaks of "the supremacy of the word" as "the distinguishing mark of the Christian epoch" and "the congenital voice of our
age" (Jung, 1953–1978, 10:286), he is assuming the classic understanding of text and of the word as bearer of the concept. As a psychol-

ogist, Jung knew quite well that "the spirit does not dwell in concepts" (Jung, 1977, 167), and he would have agreed with the conviction of James Joyce in writing *Finnegans Wake* that the night world cannot be expressed in the language of day (Ellmann, 1983, 716–717).

But although the classic understanding of text was still in force in Jung's day, Jung anticipates its overthrow by his interest in word association. The understanding of text as communication rests upon the syntactical axis of language, which binds words together and limits meaning through the constraints of grammar and syntax. The syntactical axis is the axis of prose.

The paradigmatic axis joins words together not by grammatical rules but by association—the subject of Jung's experiment. It has been called the axis of poetry, and it corresponds to harmony in music. Communicative language is used in our dealings with the outside world; associative language is expressive—it touches our hearts and souls. Its purpose is aesthetic rather than informational. For the religious imagination, association is more powerful than grammar.

Affective responses, referred to in the spiritual tradition as "consolation" or "desolation," would seem to be the effect of powerful, sometimes disconcerting images that have been woven into the text and that speak directly to the unconscious (Appleyard, 1994, 37). A sudden change of mood for which the reader can assign no obvious cause (Loyola, 1964, 133) suggests a psychological influence emanating from the text, a hidden quality that can no more be defined or explained than the quality of a person's speaking voice.

Expressive language does not share information but has import in itself. In expressive language, conceptuality is not abolished but transcended by engaging an underlying deep structure that imaginably connects disparate concepts. The introverted, expressive function of biblical language is critical for any emotional, transformative reaction. If God is known, paradoxically, in "a cloud of unknowing," then it will be the expressive function of the Bible's language to point toward the ineffable mystery and to dispose the reader to encounter it.

Linguistic association can be based on either meaning or sound. In Jung's association experiment, he discovered that the more the subject's attention was reduced, the more the associations were phonetic (sound-based) rather than semantic (meaning-based). With increasing unconsciousness the associations are "more and more influenced by sound, till finally only a sound is associated" (Jung, 1953–1978, 2:171).

The linguistic system appears to order meanings through acoustic images of similar sound. The correlation between diminished consciousness and susceptibility to phonetic factors suggests that the emotional impact of biblical language has to do not only with visual imagery but also with acoustic images. If, as Jacques Lacan has suggested, "the unconscious is structured like a language" (Lacan, 1968, 32), then we can understand why the sound of the English Bible has played such an important role in our religious history.

Freud had already noted how a particular dream made use of the similarity between the words "violet" and "violate" to express "in the language of flowers" the dreamer's thoughts on the "violence" of defloration. Freud called this an instance of the "verbal bridges" crossed by the paths leading to the "unconscious" (Freud, 1972, 410). The unconscious tends to construct images according to phonetic considerations.

But unlike Freud, who considered this similarity in phonetic patterns to be chance or arbitrary, Paul Kugler has shown that the phonetic pattern of significantly related words reveals an invariance that transcends language difference. The quality of an individual sound may have no symbolic significance, but the invariant relationship *between* sounds points to an archetypal dimension of language. At the unconscious level, the quality of word associations shifts from the semantic to the phonetic. The ability of language to communicate ideas is not its only function. The phonetic links that bind together the linguistic system of the unconscious enable language to "speak" directly to the soul. The unconscious web of linguistic associations interacts with emotionally charged patterns of meaning called complexes (Kugler, 1982).

Through the unconscious assimilation of a linguistic system, which begins in earliest childhood, "man is separated from the material world (external objects of reference) and initiated into a shared archetypal system of meaning-relations" (Kugler, 1982, 117). Language, as an archetypal reality, stands at the intersection of the psychic and physical worlds and, like the ancient alchemist, seeks to mediate between the two. The Bible as "a transitional object" (Winnicott) is both inside and outside the reader, like the matter used in the alchemical experiments upon which, in Jung's understanding, unconscious contents were projected.

Due to liturgical change, this issue of religious language has become critical during the past forty years. Its importance is underscored by the studious avoidance it has received from those in positions of authority. Lewis Garnsworhy, the late Archbishop of Toronto, used to say that he did not consider the preservation of Tudor English to be part of his mission. R. C. D. Jasper, the long-serving chairman of the English Liturgical Commission, waits until the thirteenth chapter of his book (Jasper, 1989) before raising the question of language, then expresses his frustration with linguistic issues by remarking, "For too long writers had been content to imitate Cranmer." Even the Prayer Book Society seems to value Cranmer's work mainly as a barricade against doctrinal liberalism and to shy away from the language issue.[2]

Nonetheless, according to Cranmer's most recent biographer, "The widest aftermath of Cranmer's life and work is to be found in the realm of language and of cultural identity. Every Western European language has certain key texts of literature, and for English-speakers one of that handful of texts is *The Book of Common Prayer*. Whatever its content, the Prayer Book's language was created by an individual with a natural ear for formal prose: for sound and sentence construction. For this reason, Cranmer deserves the gratitude not merely of the Church of England, but of all English speakers throughout the world" (MacCulloch, 1996, 630–631).[3]

The sixteenth century was the greatest period in English literary history, when language was certainly not considered to be simply a means of communication. The English Bible was officially promulgated during the same reign, which saw an attack on painted and sculpted images (Duffy, 1992). This latter is an expression of the "intensification of rational consciousness" to which the Protestant Reformation, in Jung's view, gave a major impetus (Jung, 1953–1978, 11:199). But the iconoclasm of the English Reformation was not complete. In place of the *visual* imagery of the medieval church ("the people's Bible") were substituted the "*verbal* icons" of the English Bible and its liturgical transposition, *The Book of Common Prayer*.

The consternation that greeted the replacement of the Prayer Book with modern rites has had less to do with the repudiation of Reformation doctrine than with "the suppression of a language. People have been rendered speechless. They have lost their speech, their way of talking of God and to God" (Martin, 1993, 24–25).

Modern liturgists have striven for simplicity and clarity in the creation of new texts. These characteristics are essential in the language of communication, but they may be inappropriate in religious language, whose purpose is not communication. We do not pray to God to tell God what God already knows. There is a clarity of statement that suits material objects but that simply does not apply to spiritual things. The failure to grasp this critical issue is reflected in the remark of Professor Dennis Nineham: "The question which should be uppermost in people's minds is to find the best instrument for purveying the meaning of God's Word, not whether the language was as beautiful or as dignified as it could be. People do not go to church primarily for an aesthetic fillip" (Spur, 1995, 190–191).

When language is treated simply as a means to convey meaning, and beauty is dismissed as an "aesthetic fillip," the expressive potential of language is ignored and its power to help us *feel* towards God" (in T. S. Eliot's evocative phrase) is lost (Eliot, 1957, 25). For religious language to function expressively, aesthetic and especially phonetic considerations are crucial. Where such considerations are ignored or dismissed, it is no wonder that, in one "view from the pew," "the new liturgy doesn't seem so holy anymore" (Collins, 1983, 7).

As the opening quotation from Father Frederick Faber suggests, true religious language is akin to music. Beneath the rhetorical surface structure of the text lies the deep structure of an archetypal world out of which the text has arisen and that it is still capable of reflecting. One could compare the contrast Richard Wagner's music makes between the vocal line and the orchestra: "There [in the orchestra] the primal urge of creation and nature are represented. What the orchestra expresses can never be clearly articulated, because it renders primal feeling itself. No wonder that when we are first exposed to Wagner our attention goes to the orchestra. It puts us in touch with the very depths of our unconscious feelings" (Stanley-Porter, 1987, 39).

The power of biblical language is the power of suggestion (Lerède, 1980), that most mysterious dimension of psychology that mystified Freud because he was unable to find any rational explanation for it. Suggestion has gotten a bad name through its unscrupulous use in the mass media and by totalitarian regimes, and it has been trivialized by its association with hypnosis. But suggestion has also been viewed, like Jung's transcendent function, as the link between consciousness and the unconscious, and as an essential factor in human growth and creativity.

The history of biblical interpretation has been dominated by doctrinal and historical approaches, both of which are based on the communicative function of language. Those studying the Bible from these perspectives regard Scripture as "hypostatized content, invariable and discoverable" (Moore, 1989, 66). Ever since the Enlightenment, these two approaches have exposed the Bible to negative criticism, such as in recent times—Bultmann's demythologization and the Jesus Seminar. Such criticism may be justified, and even necessary, as a counterweight to biblical fundamentalism. However, it has blocked the Bible's capacity to serve as a vehicle for personal transformation. As Jung has observed, "the more critical reason dominates, the more impoverished life becomes" (Jung, 1977, 333). Fortunately, there is an alternative to reading the Bible as a history book or a manual of doctrine. When the Bible is viewed not as content but as catalyst, it can bring the reader into contact with something beyond his or her control, something that touches us and shakes us to the core, regardless of whether we understand it (Whitmont, 1978, 83).

Archetypal exegesis listens for resonances that reading or hearing the text produces in the psyche ("heart speaks to heart"); the Bible serves as a prism between the numinous world behind the text and the reader. When we tune out the Bible's rhetoric and attend instead to its imagery—both visual and auditory—the sacred text regains its function in the "cure of souls." Through the mysterious transfer of archetypal energy, the way is opened for human growth and transformation.

Notes

This essay first appeared under the title, "The Bible and the Alchemy of Language" in *The Guild of Pastoral Psychology* (Guild Lecture No. 279; June 2002). It appears here with permission of the publisher.

1. This was true even of solitary readers. St. Jerome complains in one of his letters that he is unable to read, because he has a sore throat!

2. I have tried unsuccessfully to persuade the Prayer Book Society of Canada, Toronto Branch, to publish Sarah Thomson's important article "The Prayer Book Example: Why Words Matter."

3. See Barthes (1975, 39): "Bliss can erupt, across the centuries, out of certain texts that were nonetheless written to the glory of the dreariest, of the most sinister philosophy."

References

Achtemeier, P. (1990). Omne Verbum Sonat: The New Testament and Its Environment in Late Western Antiquity. *Journal of Biblical Literature, 109,* 3–27.

Appleyard, J. A. (1994). *Becoming a Reader.* New York: Cambridge University Press.

Baker, Sir H. W. (n.d.). *The Book of Common Praise* (Rev. ed.). Toronto: Oxford University Press.

Barthes, R. (1973). *Encyclopaedia Universalis* (vol. 15). Paris, 1015–1016.

Barthes, R. (1975). *The Pleasure of the Text.* New York: Hill and Want.

Collins, P. W. (1983). *More Than Meets the Eye: Ritual and Parish Liturgy.* New York: Paulist Press.

Coward, H. (1988). *Sacred Word and Sacred Text.* Maryknoll: Orbis Books.

Coward, H., & Goa, D. (1991). *Mantra.* Chambersburg: Anima Books.

Culler, J. (1976). *Saussure.* Glasgow: Fontana.

Culler, J. (1982). *On Deconstruction.* Ithaca: Cornell University Press.

Duffy, E. (1992). *The Stripping of the Altars.* New Haven: Yale University Press.

Eliot, T. S. (1957). The Social Function of Poetry, *Poetry and Poets.* London: Faber and Faber.

Ellmann, R. (1983). *James Joyce.* New York: Oxford University Press.

Freud, S. (1972). *Interpretation of Dreams.* New York: Avon Books.

Graham, W. (1988). *Beyond the Written Word.* New York: Cambridge University Press.

Heidegger, M. (1971). *Language, Poetry, Language, Thought.* New York: Harper & Row.

Hillman, J. (1977). *Re-Visioning Psychology.* New York: Harper & Row.

James, W. (1902/1975). *The Varieties of Religious Experience.* London: Fontana.

Jasper, R. C. D. (1989). *The Development of Anglican Liturgy, 1662–1980.* London: SPCK.

Jung, C. G. (1953–1978). *The Collected Works of C. G. Jung.* Princeton: Princeton University Press.

Jung, C. G. (1977). *Memories, Dreams, Reflections.* Glasgow: Fount.

Kugler, P. (1982). *The Alchemy of Discourse.* Toronto: Associated University Presses.

Lacan, J. (1968). *The Language of the Self.* Baltimore: Johns Hopkins University Press.

Lerède, J. (1980). *Les troupeaux de l'Aurore: Mythes, suggestion créatrice et eveil surconscient.* Québec: Editions de Mortagne.

Loyola, I. (1964). *The Spiritual Exercises of Ignatius Loyola.* Garden City: Doubleday.

MacCulloch, D. (1996). *Thomas Cranmer.* New Haven: Yale University Press.

Martin, D. (1993). *Model and Inspiration: The Prayer Book Tradition Today.* London: SPCK.

Moore, S. (1989). *Literary Criticism and the Gospels.* New Haven: Yale University Press.

Neill, S. (1977). *Anglicanism.* New York: Oxford University Press.

Quayle, A. (1990). *A Time to Speak.* London: Barrie & Jenkins.

Smith, W. C. (1993). *What Is Scripture? A Comparative Approach.* Minneapolis: Augsburg Fortress.

Spur, B. (1995). *The Word in the Desert: Anglican and Roman Catholic Reactions to Liturgical Reform.* Cambridge: Lutterworth Press.

Stanley-Porter, D. (1987, September/October). The Fascination with "Tristan und Isolde." *Canadian Opera Company Magazine.*

Underhill, E. (1937). *Worship.* London: Nisbet.

Whitmont, E. C. (1978). *The Symbolic Quest.* Princeton: Princeton University Press.

GLOSSARY

Active imagination: A Jungian technique of exploring levels of meaning in a dream image by expressing that image in new forms, for example, poetry, art, dance, or clay. Jung had observed that "often the hands know how to solve a riddle with which the intellect has wrestled in vain" (Jung, 1953–1978, 8:86).

Amplification: A Jungian technique of dream interpretation that consists of introducing parallels to dream images from folklore, mythology, the history of religions, and personal history, toward the end of finding associations that will assist in the conscious clarification of the dream images.

Analytic psychology: The phrase Jung chose for his psychological approach in distinction from the term *psychoanalysis* used by Freud and *individual psychology* used by Adler.

Anima/animus: Latin for "soul," "person," "life," or "mind." Jung adopted these terms to refer to the unconscious archetypal depiction of the opposite gender. *Anima* refers to the image of the feminine in the masculine psyche; *animus* is the image of the masculine in the feminine psyche. Because these images are unconscious, they can be projected on members of the opposite sex, producing "love at first sight."

Archetype/archetypal image: Jungian psychology speaks of a pattern-making tendency of the collective psyche to portray mainstay human experiences, conditions, and life crises with a glossary of typical images that recur recognizably in slightly different garb in the literature and lore of cultures around the world, past and present. Although this patterning tendency is unconscious, and therefore cannot be directly observed, it can be seen at work in the "archetypal images" it produces in its "stories." These include trans-culturally recurrent figures such as the primordial garden, the divine child, the trickster, the golden age, the wise old man, the suffering servant, the patriarch, the virgin mother, the stages of history, and so on.

Behaviorism: A school of psychology, associated for decades with B. F. Skinner, that holds that the only proper subjects for psychological inquiry are the facts of human and animal behavior and animals and their conditioning. Behaviorism regarded the mind, the psyche, and the soul as inaccessible to psychological inquiry.

Biblical criticism: The art of the scholarly study of biblical texts that emerged in its modern form in the mid-nineteenth century. Until the 1960s, the enterprise involved the diachronic examination of Scripture from the standpoint of the historical, archaeological, literary, and theological critic. Since the 1960s, synchronic forms of biblical criticism have developed that include, among others, rhetorical, feminist, canonical, ideological, social scientific, and psychological criticism.

Canon: Within the field of biblical studies, the word *canon* refers to the collection of writings officially approved by a religious body. For Judaism the canon consists of the Hebrew Scriptures (Old Testament), and for Christianity the Old and New Testaments.

Cognitive dissonance: The discomfort that comes with the tension that can emerge out of a discrepancy between the realities of one's world and one's expectations, or between what we know and what we do. The condition can lead to paralysis of action, or it can serve as moti-vator to take steps to reduce the inconsistency.

Cognitive psychology: The fundamental assumption of cognitive psy-chology is that fears, complexes, and generally negative emotions can be traced to faulty ideas, distorted perceptions, and destructive attitudes or cognitions. The therapeutic goal of cognitive psychol-ogy is to change cognition and to examine the way in which the cli-ent construes reality.

Collective unconscious: In Jung's psychology the collective unconscious (or *objective unconscious*), in distinction from the personal uncon-scious, represents the deepest and broadest level of the unconscious, an inherited function common to the human race. It is the origin of the primordial archetypal images that are the common heritage of humankind.

Complex: Jung coined this term to refer to a psychologically significant entity on which an individual has focused a near-addictive amount of energy and feeling.

Cura animarum: A medieval ecclesiastical phrase meaning "the care or cure of souls" that has been used to define the mission of the church. It is also regarded in some therapeutic circles as the goal of psychology.

Defense mechanism: Also called *ego-defense mechanisms*, these are strategies, often unconscious and neurotic, for defending the self from unpleasant persons or situations. They include the strategies of displacement, denial, repression, suppression, compulsive behavior, transference, sublimation, projection, and reaction formation. In modern psychoanalytic theory they differ from the conscious "coping mechanisms" that a mature person employs to meet threatening circumstances (Hunter, 1990, 269 [E. M. Pattison]).

Demythologization: The term was introduced by New Testament scholar Rudolf Bultmann in the 1950s as a tactic for getting behind the literal meaning of biblical myths to their originating intent and existential relevance.

Displacement: A defense mechanism of redirecting one's defensive or belligerent feelings from the person who "deserves" them to a less threatening person who does not, like the man who barks at his wife at home rather than at the offending boss at work.

Dissociation: The psychological description of an unconscious defense mechanism of the splitting off from consciousness of certain uncomfortable, threatening, or disturbing realities in one's life, resulting in the possibility of memory loss, depression, or even multiple personality.

Exegesis: Derived from a Greek word that means "to lead out," it is used by scholars and literary critics to refer to the scholarly process of "leading out" the meaning of a text, focusing on the meaning of the words in their original historic context and within the framework of the world in which they were written. Exegesis is often described as the art of discerning "what the text said."

Feminist criticism: A school of biblical scholarship that studies Scripture with an eye to the role, valuation, and treatment of women. Three branches have developed: one that focuses on what is perceived as the incorrigibly androcentric and patriarchal character of the Bible; a second that focuses on those voices in the Bible that oppose human oppression, including the oppression of women; a third that seeks to bring to light the significant role of women in biblical culture, despite a perceived male-dominated tendency to dismiss it as unimportant.

Form criticism: A branch of biblical criticism originating in the 1920s aimed originally at studying the "forms" in which the oral traditions behind the Gospels were preserved and transmitted (for example, miracle stories, parables, sayings). In time, it was conceived more broadly as the study of the form or genre of biblical writings and their constituent parts, mindful of the different kinds of meanings and "truths" each conveys and the different functions each is designed to serve (for example, myth, legend, fable, law, psalm prophetic utterance, epistle, gospel, and apocalypse).

Hellenistic Judaism: The vast population of Jews living in the Mediterranean world between the second century B.C.E. and the second century A.D. who spoke Greek, produced the Greek translation of the Hebrew Bible, and developed a literature that incorporated Greek philosophical learning. A good example is Philo Judaeus of Alexandria.

Hermeneutics: Derived from a Greek root that means "interpretation," the term is used currently to refer to the study of the meaning transacted in the exchange between a text and a reader. It is often described as the art of determining "what the text says," with emphasis on the meaning(s) it can convey or catalyze for a present-day reader and on the meaning that the reader brings to the text.

Hermeneutics of suspicion: A phrase introduced by Paul Ricoeur that endorsed the need to read alerted to the ulterior motives, special interests, and ideologies that might be operative in the text being read.

Heuristic: Derived from the Greek root "to find," it refers to an idea or method that is employed toward the end of finding or teasing out further discoveries.

Humanistic psychology: A movement within psychology in the second half of the twentieth century that provided an option to psychoanalytic and behaviorist psychologies in its emphasis on human subjectivity, human potential, and strategies for self-improvement.

Ideological criticism: A branch of biblical studies that seeks to uncover ideologies (for example, racial, ethnic, class, social, political, gender-oriented) implicit in particular biblical authors, biblical texts, and biblical readers and interpretations.

Individuation: A Jungian term for the goal of the life process of becoming the "individual" one uniquely is, through a lifelong process of integrating the psychic components in one's life, and bringing the unconscious to fuller consciousness.

Logia: Greek for "sayings." A technical phrase in New Testament studies referring to the "sayings" of Jesus preserved in oral and literary tradition.

Myth: A foundational story within a culture that provides an interpretation of "how things are." Distinct from fables, which aim at providing moral examples, and legends, which enhance national figures of the past, the myth provides a "storied" introduction to a culture's understanding of physical, metaphysical, cultural, social, familial, personal, and cosmic realities and their meaning.

Neurosis/neurotic: A clinically imprecise term for emotional, behavioral, or cognitive disturbance that is distressing but not totally incapacitating for an individual. With respect to the cause of neurosis, Freud observed that behind a neurosis there is often concealed all the natural and necessary suffering the patient has been unwilling to bear. Karen Horney defined *neurotic anxiety* as a pathological, dysfunction-generating state in which anxiety is disproportionate to reality.

Pathogenic: Producing illness, disease, or dysfunction, physical or psychological.

Persona: A term popularized in Jungian psychology to refer to the face or "mask" one selects consciously or unconsciously as part of the task of adapting to and presenting oneself to the world. Jung commented, "one could say, with a little exaggeration, that the persona is that which in reality one is not, but which oneself as well as others think one is" (Jung, 1963, 397).

Personal unconscious: A Jungian phrase for that part of the unconscious that derives from personal experience of the individual, as opposed to a collective unconscious common to the species.

Post-traumatic stress disorder: "An anxiety disorder characterized by a pattern of symptoms attributable to the experience of a traumatic event. The symptoms of PTSD include (1) re-experiencing the traumatic event, (2) emotional numbing, and (3) any of a variety of autonomic, cognitive or behavioral symptoms" (Hunter, 1990, 931 [N. C. Brown]).

Projection: "A defense mechanism in which one unconsciously attributes one's own unacceptable feelings, desire, thoughts, and impulses to another person. This removes the responsibility for unacceptable qualities or feelings from oneself, thus protecting the ego. An example is a husband who is barely able to control his anger toward his spouse and subsequently becomes suspicious that *she* is angry" (Hunter, 1990, 960 [J. Estelle]).

Psyche: A term used in classical and biblical Greek to refer to the vital force, life, breath, true self, or soul; ultimately adopted in psychoanalytic tradition to refer to the totality of the psychic processes, conscious and unconscious, including affect, perception, cognition, conation, intuition, imagination, rationality, and spirituality, among others.

Psychodynamics: A term that means literally the "power of the psyche," referring to any "psychological theory or therapeutic method that explains and approaches psychological processes in terms of motives and drives" (Hunter, 1990, 989 [M. A. Woltersdorf]). It is also used currently to refer to the dynamic interactive psychic factors at work in human relations, whether in real time or as portrayed and expressed in art and literature.

Psychological biblical criticism: A branch of biblical studies that applies psychological and psychoanalytic insight to the study of the Bible, its origins, its content, its interpretation, and the history of its effects.

Psychologizing: The practice of explaining the essence or origin of events, persons, or entities (for example, art, religion, politics) in exclusively psychological terms.

Q: A code word in New Testament studies to refer to a collection of traditional sayings of Jesus that appear in the Gospels of Matthew and Luke but not in Mark or John. The collection includes the Lord's Prayer and the Sermon on the Mount, among many other "logia" or "sayings" of Jesus. The letter *Q* is an abbreviation of the German word *Quelle* for "source." It is believed that Matthew's sources include the Gospel of Mark, Q, and Matthew's own special material (or M). Luke's sources include the Gospel of Mark, Q, and Luke's own special material (or L).

Reader-response criticism: A branch of literary and biblical criticism that focuses on reading as an act of "construction" and on the role of the reader's values, responses, and attitudes in the process.

Redaction criticism: A branch of biblical studies that examines the effect of biblical authors on their texts, with respect to the principles of organization, selection of materials, interpretive cues, written and oral sources, vocabulary, and points of view they have enlisted or employed in creating and shaping their texts.

Repression: One of several defense mechanisms that consists of excluding unwanted memories, thoughts, or concerns from conscious awareness; living in denial.

Rhetorical criticism: A branch of literary and biblical criticism that focuses on the rhetorical or "persuasive" character, design, and function of a text or text unit within the original rhetorical context of its writing. Rhetoric has been defined as "that quality of discourse by which a speaker or writer seeks to accomplish his purposes." Accordingly rhetorical critics examine the rhetorical literary units, the rhetorical situation or problem, devices of style, and the writer's objective in context (Coggins & Houlden, 1990, 599–600 [J. I. H. McDonald]).

Self: Jungian psychology uses this term to refer to the archetype of the individuated person. This view of self, usually achieved in the second half of life, displaces the personal ego as the center of one's conscious life.

Self psychology: Psychologies that place the self at the center of personality and make the growth or actualization of the self the primary goal of life in general and of psychotherapy and counseling in particular (Hunter, 1990, 1137 [P. C. Vitz]). Representative "self psychologists" include Alfred Adler, Erich Fromm, Carl Rogers, Abraham Maslow, Rollo May, and Heinz Kohut. Kohut's psychology offers a positive perspective on narcissism (Wulff, 1991, 353).

Sitz im Leben: A phrase originating in German biblical scholarship to refer to the "life-setting" (lit., "seat in life") of a biblical text or event. Thus one might speak of the *Sitz im Leben* of John's Gospel, that is, the historical and cultural circumstances of the author of the Gospel and his community at the time the Gospel was being written.

Social scientific criticism: In its broadest sense, social scientific criticism "applies methods and theories to biblical texts in an attempt to reconstruct the social worlds behind these texts . . . while simultaneously illuminating the lives of the people living in these worlds" (Hayes, 1999, 2:478 [N. Steinberg]).

Superego: The part of the psyche in Freudian psychology that represents the introjection of societal, religious, and/or familial values,

obligations, and obsessions that exercise unconscious inner authority in an individual's thoughts, values, and decisions.

Textual criticism: One of the earliest of biblical critical disciplines, dat-
ing to the sixteenth century. It began with the recognition that we
do not have the original Hebrew or Greek "autograph" text of any
biblical book but only centuries of handwritten copies. Furthermore, although the copies largely agree with one another, close
inspection reveals that no copy agrees with any other copy in every
detail. The task of textual criticism is to devise scholarly techniques
for deciding which of the variant readings are corruptions and
which are most likely the original.

Unconscious: "That part of the mind or psyche containing information
that has never been conscious, or that was once conscious but is no
longer" (Hunter, 1990, 1290 [H. Coward]). Jung defined the contents of the unconscious as including "everything of which I know,
but of which I am not at the moment thinking, everything of which
I was once conscious but have now forgotten; everything perceived
by my senses, but not noted by my conscious mind; everything
which, involuntarily and without paying attention to it, I feel, think,
remember, want, and do; all the future things that are taking shape
in me and will sometime come to consciousness" (Jung, 1963, 401).

References

Coggins, R. J., & Houlden, J. L. (1990). *A Dictionary of Biblical Interpretation.*
Philadelphia: Trinity Press International.

Hayes, J. H., ed. (1999). *Dictionary of Biblical Interpretation.* Nashville:
Abingdon.

Hunter, R., ed. (1990). *Dictionary of Pastoral Care and Counseling.* Nashville:
Abingdon.

Jung, C. G. (1953–1978). *The Collected Works of C. G. Jung.* Princeton: Princeton University Press.

Jung, C. G. (1963). *Memories, Dreams, Reflections.* New York: Vintage Books.

Wulff, D. (1991). *Psychology of Religion: Classic and Contemporary Views.* New
York: John Wiley.

INDEX

About the Contributors

PAUL N. ANDERSON is professor of biblical and Quaker studies and chair of the Department of Religious Studies at George Fox University, where he has served since 1989, other than a year as a visiting professor at Yale Divinity School (1998–1999). He is author of *The Christology of the Fourth Gospel: Its Unity and Disunity in the Light of John 6* (1996) and *Navigating the Living Waters of the Gospel of John: On Wading with Children and Swimming with Elephants* (2000). In addition, he has written many essays on biblical and Quaker themes and is editor of *Quaker Religious Thought*. He serves on the steering committee of the Psychology and Biblical Studies Section of the Society of Biblical Literature and teaches the New Testament Interpretation course in the PsyD program of George Fox University. His PhD in New Testament is from Glasgow University (1989), his MDiv is from the Earlham School of Religion (1981), and his BA in psychology and BA in Christian ministries are from Malone College (1978).

ANTHONY BASH serves as honorary fellow in theology and director of Studies in New Testament in the Department of Humanities on the faculty of the University of Hull, England. His fields of specialization include New Testament studies, biblical studies, and the use of social sciences in biblical studies. He has recently written one of the first articles to be published in the *Journal for the Study in the New Testament* on the application of psychological models to biblical interpretation, "The Interpretation of 2 Corinthians 10–13" (2001).

LYN M. BECHTEL received her PhD in biblical studies from Drew University prior to her appointment as visiting associate professor of Hebrew Bible at Drew Theological School and associate professor of Hebrew Bible at Moravian Theological Seminary. Her areas of specialization include the books of Genesis and Job, psychoanalytic theory and the Hebrew Bible, feminist interpretation of the Hebrew Bible, and the biblical experience of shame and shaming. Her publications include "Shame as a Sanction of Social Control in Biblical Israel: Judicial, Political, and Social Shaming" (*Journal of the Study of the Old Testament*, 1991) and "Genesis 2.4b–3.24: A Myth about Human Maturation" (*Journal for the Study of Old Testament*, 1995).

KAMILA BLESSING is an Episcopal priest of twenty years' standing and an "intentional interim" specializing in the health and healing of congregations. She has graduate training in family systems therapy, a PhD in information systems (studying the "people systems" in organizations and their communication) from the University of Pittsburgh, and a PhD in New Testament from Duke University. Her research in New Testament includes the applications of systems theories to Bible interpretation as well as the role of narrative in the maintenance of religious identity groups. Her publications include "Murray Bowen's Family Systems Theory as Bible Hermeneutic using the Family of the Prodigal, Luke 15:11–32" (*Journal of Psychology and Christianity*, 2000) and "The 'Confusion Technique' of Milton Erickson as Hermeneutic for Biblical Parables" (*Journal of Psychology and Christianity*, 2002).

SCHUYLER BROWN received his BA in classical languages from Harvard University in 1952, and as a member of the Jesuit order in the 1950s and 1960s, Brown received licentiates in philosophy (1957), theology (1964), and biblical studies (1969). He received his DrTheol from the University of Münster (Westphalia) in 1969. His academic appointments have included teaching positions at Woodstock College, General Theological Seminary in New York City, the University of London, and as professor of New Testament at the University of Toronto (St. Michael's College). He has served as a lecturer at the Jung Institute in Zurich and in the Training Program of the Ontario Association of Jungian Analysts. His wife, Margaret Eileen Meredith, is a graduate of the Jung Institute in Zurich and a practicing Jungian analyst in Toronto. Brown's publications include *The Origins of Christianity: A Historical Introduction to the New Testament* (1984; rev. ed., 1993) and *Text and Psyche: Experiencing Scripture Today* (1998, 2002).

MARTIN J. BUSS, professor of religion at Emory University, received a BD and a ThM from Princeton Theological Seminary in 1954 and 1955 and a PhD from Yale University in 1958. He has taught in the Department of Religion at Emory University from 1959 until the present, with a specialization in Hebrew Bible. He has examined this literature from a number of perspectives: anthropological, sociological, psychological, and philosophical. His first essay dealing with a psychological approach to the Hebrew Bible was "Self-Theory and Theology" (*Journal of Religion*, 1965).

DONALD CAPPS, psychologist of religion, is William Hart Felmeth Professor of Pastoral Theology at Princeton Theological Seminary. In 1989 he was awarded an honorary doctorate from the University of Uppsala, Sweden, in recognition of the importance of his publications. He served as president of the Society for the Scientific Study of Religion from 1990 to 1992. Among his many significant books are *Men, Religion, and Melancholia: James, Otto, Jung and Erikson and Freud* (1997); *The Freudians on Religion: A Reader* (2001); *Social Phobia: Alleviating Anxiety in an Age of Self-Promotion* (1999); and *Jesus: A Psychological Biography* (2000). He also authored *The Child's Song: The Religious Abuse of Children* (1995).

JAMES H. CHARLESWORTH is the George L. Collord Professor of New Testament Language and Literature as well as editor and director of the Princeton Theological Seminary Dead Sea Scrolls Project at Princeton University. He received his PhD from Duke University and has advanced degrees or study at Edinburgh, the École Biblique de Jerusalem, the Hebrew University, the University of Tübingen, and elsewhere. Charlesworth is editor of the *Old Testament Pseudepigrapha* and *The Dead Sea Scrolls* (the Princeton critical edition and translation). He has written or edited more than sixty-five books and completed the first in-depth study of serpent symbolism in antiquity and the Bible. He introduced the term "Jesus research" into the study of the historical Jesus.

HAL CHILDS is psychotherapist and clinical director at the California Counseling Institute, San Francisco. He holds the degrees of MDiv, MA, and PhD. He is closely affiliated with the work of the Guild for Psychological Studies in San Francisco. His field of specialization is New Testament interpretation and depth psychology, as is amply demonstrated in his trail-blazing doctoral dissertation, now published as *The Myth of the Historical Jesus and the Evolution of Consciousness* (2000).

DERECK DASCHKE received his MA and PhD in Divinity from the University of Chicago Divinity School and is presently assistant professor of philosophy and religion at Truman State University, Kirksville, Missouri. His fields of interest include religion and culture, psychology and religion, religion and health, new religious movements, and apocalypticism and millennialism. His publications include "Mourning the End of Time: Apocalypses as Texts of Cultural Loss" in *Millennialism from the Hebrew Bible to the Present*, edited by Leonard J. Greenspoon and Ronald A. Simpkins (2002) and "Desolate among Them: Loss, Fantasy, and Recovery in the Book of Ezekiel" (*American Imago*, 1999).

CHARLES T. DAVIS III studied at Emory University with Dr. Norman Perrin, graduating with BD and PhD degrees after special study at the University of Heidelberg. Although specializing in New Testament studies, he has also published articles and book reviews in the fields of American religion, computers and the humanities, philosophy, and Buddhist studies. He is the author of *Speaking of Jesus* and currently serves as professor of philosophy and religion at Appalachian State University in Boone, North Carolina, where he teaches biblical literature, Islam, and seminars on symbols and healing.

J. HAROLD ELLENS is a research scholar at the University of Michigan, Department of Near Eastern Studies. He is a retired Presbyterian theologian and ordained minister, a retired U.S. Army colonel, and a retired professor of philosophy, theology, and psychology. He has authored, coauthored, or edited 104 books and 165 professional journal articles. He served fifteen years as executive director of the Christian Association for Psychological Studies and as founding editor and editor in chief of the *Journal of Psychology and Christianity*. He holds a PhD from Wayne State University in the psychology of human communication, a PhD from the University of Michigan in biblical and Near Eastern studies, and master's degrees from Calvin Theological Seminary, Princeton Theological Seminary, and the University of Michigan. His publications include *God's Grace and Human Health* (1982) *Jesus as Son of Man, the Literary Character: A Progression of Images* (2003), *The Destructive Power of Religion, Violence in Judaism, Christianity, and Islam* (2004), and *Psychotheology: Key Issues* (1987) as well as chapters in *Moral Obligation and the Military*, *Baker Encyclopedia of Psychology*, and *Abingdon Dictionary of Pastoral Care*.

JAMES W. FOWLER is Professor of Theology and Human Development at Emory University in Atlanta and lecturer at Candler School of Theology. He was formerly on the faculty of Harvard University. He is currently the director of the Center for Faith Development and one of its primary research project directors. His prolific publications list includes such notable works as *Stages of Faith*; *Life-Maps*; *To See the Kingdom: The Theological Vision of H. Richard Niebuhr*; and *Becoming Adult, Becoming Christian, Adult Development and Christian Faith*. Professor Fowler is one of the great developmental theorists and researchers of the late twentieth and early twenty-first century.

DAVID G. GARBER JR., a PhD candidate at Emory University, is currently completing his dissertation, titled "Trauma, Memory, and Survival in Ezekiel 1–24." After receiving a BA in religious studies from Baylor University, he completed master of divinity and master of theology degrees from Princeton Theological Seminary. For the past two years, he has served as an adjunct professor at the McAfee School of Theology of Mercer University, Macon, Georgia, teaching courses in Hebrew Bible and biblical languages.

ITHAMAR GRUENWALD has served on the faculty of Tel Aviv University since 1967 in the Department of Jewish Philosophy and Program in Religious Studies. He has also been affiliated on a visiting basis as fellow with the Institute for Advanced Studies, Hebrew University; guest professor at the Revell Graduate School, Yeshiva University, New York; Martin Buber Guest Professor at the J. W. Goethe Universität, Frankfurt; and fellow at the Institute for Advanced Studies in Religion, University of Chicago. He has participated as chair and member of various committees of the Council for Higher Education in Israel. His publications include *Apocalyptic and Merkavah Mysticism* (1980), *From Apocalypticism to Gnosticism* (1988), and *Rituals and Ritual Theory in Ancient Israel* (2003).

DAVID JOBLING recently retired as professor of Hebrew Scriptures at St. Andrews College, Saskatoon, Canada, a post he had held since 1978. A native of England, he received his MA from Cambridge University and his PhD from Union Theological Seminary, New York City. He is the author of *The Sense of Biblical Narrative* (2 volumes) and of *1 Samuel* (Berit Olam series). As a member of the Bible and Culture Collective he coauthored *The Postmodern Bible* and coedited *The Postmodern Bible Reader*. He is a former general editor of the journal *Semeia* and a past president of the Canadian Society of Biblical Studies.

D. ANDREW KILLE received his PhD from the Graduate Theological Union in Berkeley in psychological biblical criticism. He is the author of *Psychological Biblical Criticism: Genesis 3 as a Test Case* (2001). As a former pastor, he teaches psychology and spirituality in the San Francisco Bay Area and is principal consultant for Revdak Consulting. He has served as co-chair of the Psychology and Biblical Studies Section of the Society of Biblical Literature and on the steering committee of the Person, Culture, and Religion Group of the American Academy of Religion.

ANDRÉ LACOCQUE is emeritus professor of Hebrew Scriptures at the Chicago Theological Seminary and emeritus director of its doctoral Center for Jewish–Christian Studies. He received his PhD and ThD from the University of Strasburg and honorary degrees from the University of Chicago and the University of Brussels. He is a longstanding member of the American Academy of Religion and the Chicago Society of Biblical Research, and he served as president of the Middle West Region of the Society of Biblical Literature (1973–1975). His publications include *Jonah, a Psycho-Religious Approach to the Prophet* (with Pierre-E. Lacocque, 1990) and *Thinking Biblically* (with Paul Ricoeur, 1998), which has been translated into Spanish, French, Portuguese, Italian, Polish, Hungarian, and Rumanian, with additional translations in progress in Greek and Korean. In 2001, colleagues published a Festschrift in his honor: *The Honeycomb of the Word: Interpreting the Primary Testament with André LaCocque*, edited by W. Dow Edgerton.

BERNHARD LANG received the degree of DTheol from the University of Tübingen and the DHabil from the University of Freiburg. He serves on the Faculty of Arts and Humanities at the University of Paderborn, Germany. He also holds the position of honorary professor of religious studies at the University of St. Andrews, U.K. His fields of specialization include biblical studies, the cultural history of the biblical world, history of Christian spirituality, and the anthropology and theory of religion. His major publications include *Drewermann, interprète la Bible* (1994); *Heaven: A History* (2nd ed., 2001, with many translations); *Sacred Games: A History of Christian Worship* (1997); and *The Hebrew God: Portrait of an Ancient Deity* (2002).

JILL L. McNISH received her JD from Rutgers University, and MDiv and a PhD in psychology and religion from Union Theological Seminary, New York City. Her field of specialization is the interface between psychology, theology, and spirituality. She is currently working in the Blanton-Peale Institute Pastoral Studies Program, New York City, and is engaged in interim ministry with the Episcopal Diocese of Newark. She is author of *Transforming Shame: A Pastoral Response* (2004) and "Uses of Theories of Depth Psychology in Ordained Ministry and the Institutional Church"(*Journal of Pastoral Care*, 2002).

PETRI MERENLAHTI received his PhD from the University of Helsinki and is currently working as research fellow in its Department of Biblical Studies. His field of specialization is narrative criticism of the New Testament and Gospels, with special interest in the Gospel of Mark. He has been a regular participant in the national programs of the Psychology and Biblical Studies Section of the Society of Biblical Literature. His publications include *Poetics for the Gospels? Rethinking Narrative Criticism* (2002).

DAN MERKUR received his PhD from the University of Stockholm and is currently in private practice as a psychoanalytic psychotherapist. He is affiliated with the Department for the Study of Religion, University of Toronto, and enrolled as a candidate at the Toronto Institute for Contemporary Psychoanalysis. His field of specialization is comparative religions. His publications include "'And He Trusted in Yahweh': The Transformation of Abram in Gen 12–13 and 15" (*Journal of Psychology of Religion*, 1995–1996) and *Mystical Moments and Unitive Thinking* (1999).

DAVID L. MILLER holds a BD degree from Bethany Theological Seminary (1960) and a PhD from Drew University (1963). Until 1999 he was the Watson-Ledden Professor of Religion at Syracuse University (New York), and until 2003 he served as a core faculty person at Pacifica Graduate Institute in Santa Barbara. He specializes in the fields of religion and literature, and psychology and mythology, and is the author of four books—*Christs: Archetypal Images in Christian Theology* (1981); *Three Faces of God* (1987); *Hells and Holy Ghosts: A Theopoetics of Christian Belief* (1989); and *Gods and Games: Toward a Theology of Play* (1970)—as well as the editor of the book *Jung and the Interpretation of the Bible* (1995).

JOHN MILLER holds a ThD from the University of Basel and is professor emeritus of religious studies at Conrad Grebel College, University of Waterloo, Ontario. He was cofounder and co-chair of the Historical Jesus Section in the Society of Biblical Literature. He also served as director of Psychiatric Rehabilitation Services at Chicago State Hospital. His writings include *The Origins of the Bible: Rethinking Canon History* (1994); *Biblical Faith and Fathering* (1989); and *Jesus at Thirty: A Psychological and Historical Portrait* (1997).

DIETER MITTERNACHT holds the MDiv, MTheol, MPhil, and DTheol degrees and is currently researcher and lecturer at Lund University in Sweden. He also serves as visiting lecturer at the Swedish Agricultural University and as fellow of the Swedish Council of Research with the research project Social Cognition and Strategies of Persuasion in Pauline Letters. His fields of specialization include Pauline studies, texts and communication (rhetoric and epistolography in antiquity), early Christian identity, and sociopsychological approaches to exegesis. He is also a specialist on the ancient synagogue, participating as a fellow of the research project The Ancient Synagogue: Birthplace for Two World Religions. His publications include "By Works of The Law No One Shall Be Justified" (1988) and *Forum für Sprachlose: Eine kommunikationspsychologische und epistolär-rhetorische Untersuchung des Galaterbriefs* (1999). He has coedited *The Synagogue of Ancient Ostia and the Jews of Rome: Interdisciplinary Studies* (2001).

WILLIAM MORROW received his PhD from the University of Toronto; currently he is associate professor of Hebrew and Hebrew Scriptures at Queen's Theological College and the Department of Religious Studies, Queen's University, Kingston, Ontario. He is the author of *Scribing the Center: Organization and Redaction in Deuteronomy 14:1–17:1* (1995) and various articles related to the composition of biblical law. His publications in the area of psychological biblical criticism include "Toxic Religion and the Daughters of Job" (*Studies in Religion*, 1998).

ROBERT H. NEUWOEHNER earned his doctorate through the University of Denver and Iliff School of Theology joint PhD program in religious and theological studies, where he concentrated his research on the feminine symbolism in the Gospel of John. He has presented papers at national and regional meetings of the American Academy of Religion and the Society of Biblical Literature, and he recently published a psychosymbolic interpretation of John 20:14–18 in the Jungian journal *Psychological Perspectives*. Drawing on thirty years of work with Jungian theory, he has begun developing and offering seminars and workshops to provide "education for the second half of life."

MICHAEL WILLETT NEWHEART is associate professor of New Testament language and literature at Howard University School of Divinity, where he has taught since 1991. He holds a PhD from Southern Baptist Theological Seminary and is the author of *Wisdom Christology in the Fourth Gospel* (1992) and *Word and Soul: A Psychological, Literary, and Cultural Reading of the Fourth Gospel* (2001) as well as numerous articles on the psychological and literary interpretation of the New Testament.

ILONA N. RASHKOW is professor of Judaic studies, women's studies, and comparative literature at the State University of New York, Stony Brook. She has also been the visiting chair in Judaic studies at the University of Alabama. Among her publications are *Upon the Dark Places: Sexism and Anti-Semitism in English Renaissance Bible Translation* (1990); *The Phallacy of Genesis* (1993); and *Taboo or Not Taboo: Human Sexuality and the Hebrew Bible* (2000). Her areas of interest include psychoanalytic literary theory as applied to the Hebrew Bible and, more generally, as applied to Judaic studies, religious studies, feminist literary criticism, and women's studies.

WAYNE G. ROLLINS is professor emeritus of biblical studies at Assumption College, Worcester, Massachusetts, and adjunct professor of Scripture at Hartford Seminary, Hartford, Connecticut. He has also taught at Princeton University and Wellesley College and served as visiting professor at Mount Holyoke College, Yale College, College of the Holy Cross, and Colgate Rochester Divinity School. His writings include *The Gospels: Portraits of Christ* (1964); *Jung and the Bible* (1983); *Soul and Psyche: The Bible in Psychological Perspective* (1999); and numerous articles on psychology and biblical studies. He received his BD from Yale Divinity School and his PhD in New Testament studies from Yale University. He served as president of the New England section of the American Academy of Religion (1984–1985) and is the founder and past chair (1990–2000) of the Society of Biblical Literature Section on Psychology and Biblical Studies.

JOHN SCHMITT is associate professor in the Department of Theology at Marquette University. His special interests lie in the field of monastic and interfaith studies. His publications include, as coauthor,

The Prophets II, volume 7 of *The Storyteller's Companion to the Bible* (1995); "Samaria in the Books of the Eighth Century Prophets" in *The Pitcher Is Broken: Memorial Essays for Goesta W. Ahlstroem*, edited by Steven W. Holloway and Lowell K. Handy (1996); and "The City as Woman in Isaiah 1–39" in *Writing and Reading the Scroll of Isaiah: Studies in an Interpretive Tradition* (1997).

KARI SYREENI received his doctor of theology from the University of Helsinki, Finland, and is professor of New Testament studies at the University of Uppsala, Sweden. His special research interests include the Gospels, New Testament hermeneutics, psychological exegesis, and the Bible and modern literature. His publications include *The Making of the Sermon on the Mount: A Procedural Analysis on Matthew's Redactional Activity. Part I: Methodology and Compositional Analysis* (1987); "Separation and Identity: Aspects of the Symbolic World of Matt. 6:1–18" (*New Testament Studies*, 1994); Metaphorical Appropriation: (Post-) Modern Biblical Hermeneutic and the Theory of Metaphor" (*Literature and Theology*, 1995); and a forthcoming work, *In Memory of Jesus: Grief Work in the Gospels.*

RALPH L. UNDERWOOD, BD, MTh, MA, PhD, is emeritus professor of pastoral care at Austin Presbyterian Theological Seminary, Austin, Texas. He has been a member of the faculty there since 1978. He retired at the end of 2001. Before teaching at Austin Seminary he was director of the Wholistic Health Center in Woodridge, Illinois. His terminal degree is from the University of Chicago Divinity School in religion and psychological studies. A United Methodist minister, he was ordained in 1961. In addition to his article cited in the note of his chapter, his relevant publications are *Pastoral Care and the Means of Grace* (1993) and "Scripture: The Substance of Pastoral Care" (*Quarterly Review*, 1991).

ANDRIES G. VAN AARDE, DD, PhD, is on the faculty of theology and professor of New Testament at the University of Pretoria, South Africa. He is a member of the Context Group and the Jesus Seminar and co-chair of the Matthew Seminar of the International Society of New Testament Studies. His publications include *Fatherless in Galilee: Jesus as Child of God* (2001); "Jesus as Fatherless Child" in *The Social Setting of Jesus and the Gospels*, edited by W. Stegemann, B. J. Malina, and G. Theissen (2002); "Jesus and Perseus in Graeco-Roman Literature" (*Acta Patristica et Byzantina*, 2000); and "Jesus' Father: The Quest for the Historical Joseph" (*HTS Theological Studies*, 1998).

WALTER WINK is professor of biblical interpretation at Auburn Theological Seminary in New York City. Previously he was a parish minister and taught at Union Theological Seminary in New York City. In 1989 and 1990, he was a peace fellow at the United States Institute of Peace. His most recent book is *The Human Being: The Enigma of the Son of the Man* (2001). He is author of *The Powers*; and a trilogy, *Naming the Powers: The Language of Power in the New Testament* (1984), *Unmasking the Powers: The Invisible Forces That Determine Human Existence* (1986), and *Engaging the Powers: Discernment and Resistance in a World of Domination* (1992). *Engaging the Powers* received three Religious Book of the Year awards for 1993, from Pax Christi, the Academy of Parish Clergy, and the Midwestern Independent Publishers Association. His other works include *Jesus and Nonviolence* (2003); *The Powers That Be* (1998); and *When the Powers Fall: Reconciliation in the Healing of Nations* (1998). He has published more than 250 journal articles.

About the Series Editor and Advisers

J. HAROLD ELLENS is a Research Scholar at the University of Michigan, Department of Near Eastern Studies. He is a retired Presbyterian theologian and ordained minister, a retired U.S. Army Colonel, and a retired Professor of Philosophy, Theology and Psychology. He has authored, coauthored, and/or edited 104 books and 165 professional journal articles. He served fifteen years as Executive Director of the Christian Association for Psychological Studies, and as Founding Editor and Editor-in-Chief of the *Journal of Psychology and Christianity*. He holds a PhD from Wayne State University in the Psychology of Human Communication, a PhD from the University of Michigan in Biblical and Near Eastern Studies, and master's degrees from Calvin Theological Seminary, Princeton Theological Seminary, and the University of Michigan. He was born in Michigan, grew up in a Dutch-German immigrant community, and determined at age seven to enter the Christian Ministry as a means to help his people with the great amount of suffering he perceived all around him. His life's work has focused on the interface of psychology and religion.

ARCHBISHOP DESMOND TUTU is best known for his contribution to the cause of racial justice in South Africa, a contribution for which he was recognized with the Nobel Peace Prize in 1984. Archbishop Tutu has been an ordained priest since 1960. Among his many accomplishments are being named the first black General Secretary of the South African Council of Churches and serving as Archbishop of Cape Town. Once a high school teacher in South Africa, he has also taught theology in college and holds honorary degrees from universities including Harvard, Oxford, Columbia, and Kent State. He has been awarded the Order for Meritorious Service presented by President Nelson Mandela, the Archbishop of Canterbury's Award for outstanding service to the Anglican community, the Family of Man Gold Medal Award, and the Martin Luther King Jr. Non-Violent Peace Award. The publications Archbishop Tutu authored, coauthored, or made contributions to include *No Future Without Forgiveness* (2000), *Crying in the Wilderness* (1986), and *Rainbow People of God: The Making of a Peaceful Revolution* (1996).

LEROY H. ADEN is Professor Emeritus of Pastoral Theology at the Lutheran Theological Seminary in Philadelphia, Pennsylvania. He taught full-time at the seminary from 1967 to 1994 and part-time from 1994 to 2001. He served as Visiting Lecturer at Princeton Theological Seminary, Princeton, New Jersey, on a regular basis. In 2002 he coauthored *Preaching God's Compassion: Comforting Those Who Suffer* with Robert G. Hughes. Previously, he edited four books in a Psychology and Christianity series with J. Harold Ellens and David G. Benner. He served on the Board of Directors of the Christian Association for Psychological Studies for six years.

DONALD CAPPS, Psychologist of Religion, is William Hart Felmeth Professor of Pastoral Theology at Princeton Theological Seminary. In 1989 he was awarded an honorary doctorate from the University of Uppsala, Sweden, in recognition of the importance of his publications. He served as president of the Society for the Scientific Study of Religion from 1990 to 1992. Among his many significant books are *Men, Religion and Melancholia: James, Otto, Jung and Erikson and Freud*; and *The Freudians on Religion: A Reader*; and *Social Phobia: Alleviating Anxiety in an Age of Self-Promotion*; and *Jesus: A Psychological Biography*. He also authored *The Child's Song: The Religious Abuse of Children*.

ZENON LOTUFO JR. is a Presbyterian minister (Independent Presbyterian Church of Brazil), a philosopher, and a psychotherapist, specialized in Transactional Analysis. He has lectured both to undergraduate and graduate courses in universities in São Paulo, Brazil. He coordinates the course of specialization in Pastoral Psychology of the Christian Psychologists and Psychiatrists Association. He is the author of the books *Relações Humanas* [Human Relations]; *Disfunções no Comportamento Organizacional* [Dysfunctions in Organizational Behavior]; and coauthor of *O Potencial Humano* [Human Potential]. He has also authored numerous journal articles.

DIRK ODENDAAL is South African; he was born in what is now called the Province of the Eastern Cape. He spent much of his youth in the Transkei in the town of Umtata, where his parents were teachers at a seminary. He trained as a minister at the Stellenbosch Seminary for the Dutch Reformed Church and was ordained in 1983 in the Dutch Reformed Church in Southern Africa. He transferred to East London in 1988 to minister to members of the Uniting Reformed Church in Southern Africa in one of the huge suburbs for Xhosa speaking people. He received his doctorate (DLitt) in 1992 at the University of Port Elizabeth in Semitic Languages. At present, he is enrolled in a master's course in Counseling Psychology at Rhodes University.

WAYNE G. ROLLINS is Adjunct Professor of Scripture at the Hartford Seminary and Professor Emeritus of Theology at Assumption College, Worcester, Massachusetts, where he served as Director of the Ecumenical Institute and Graduate Program of Religious Studies. He has also taught on the faculties of Princeton University and Wellesley College, with visiting lectureships at Yale College, The College of the Holy Cross, Mt. Holyoke, and Colgate–Rochester Divinity School. An ordained minister in the United Church of Christ, he received the BD, MA, and PhD degrees from Yale University, with post-graduate study at Cambridge University (U.K.), Harvard University, and the Graduate Theological Union in Berkeley, California. His writings include numerous articles and three books: *The Gospels: Portraits of Christ; Jung and the Bible*; and, most recently, *Soul and Psyche: The Bible in Psychological Perspective*. He is the founding chair of the Psychology and Biblical Studies Section of the Society of Biblical Literature, an international organization of biblical scholars.